Non-Democratic Politics

D1669507

Non-Democratic Politics

Authoritarianism, Dictatorship, and Democratization

Xavier Márquez

© Xavier Márquez 2017

All rights reserved. No reproduction, copy or transmission of this publication may be made without written permission.

No portion of this publication may be reproduced, copied or transmitted save with written permission or in accordance with the provisions of the Copyright, Designs and Patents Act 1988, or under the terms of any licence permitting limited copying issued by the Copyright Licensing Agency, Saffron House, 6–10 Kirby Street, London EC1N 8TS.

Any person who does any unauthorized act in relation to this publication may be liable to criminal prosecution and civil claims for damages.

The author has asserted his right to be identified as the author of this work in accordance with the Copyright, Designs and Patents Act 1988.

First published 2017 by
PALGRAVE

Palgrave in the UK is an imprint of Macmillan Publishers Limited, registered in England, company number 785998, of 4 Crinan Street, London, N1 9XW.

Palgrave® and Macmillan® are registered trademarks in the United States, the United Kingdom, Europe and other countries.

ISBN 978-0-333-48631-8 hardback
ISBN 978-1-137-48630-1   ISBN 978-1-137-48632-5 (eBook)
DOI 10.1007/978-1-137-48632-5

A catalogue record for this book is available from the British Library.

A catalog record for this book is available from the Library of Congress.

To Nancy and Sophia

Contents

List of Illustrative Material

Figures

Tables

Boxes

Acknowledgments

This book has taken a long time to write, and I accumulated many debts in the process. My first debt is to the students in my 'dictatorships and revolutions' course over the past nine years, who helped me to learn much about the topic of non-democratic government, and forced me to make this material accessible. But I would never have written it without the intervention of my first editor at Palgrave, Steven Kennedy, who first offered me the chance to submit a proposal and urged me on at various points. After Steven retired, Lloyd Langman ably led me to the finish line. Jay Ulfelder, Jeremiah John, and several anonymous reviewers offered substantive and sharp comments on the manuscript; their feedback made it much better, while the errors that remain are all mine. I also felt encouraged by the readers of my blog, *Abandoned Footnotes*, where I first discussed some of the ideas that appear here. A six-month sabbatical in Spain helped me acquire in-depth knowledge of the Franco era, and provided much food for thought; I thank Victoria University of Wellington for the opportunity. My parents, in Venezuela, were constantly in my thoughts as the country of my birth seemed to fall deeper into authoritarianism as I wrote. My attempt to understand the politics of non-democracy is indebted to that background. Finally, I could not have written this book without the support and encouragement of my wife Nancy and our daughter Sophia.

Chapter 1

Introduction: Democracy, Non-democracy, and the Varieties of Political Competition

This is a book about 'non-democracy'. Non-democratic politics takes many forms, and goes by many names. 'Dictatorship', 'tyranny', 'authoritarianism', 'autocracy', 'totalitarianism', and 'despotism' are only some of the many terms scholars and ordinary people use to distinguish non-democratic states from democracies. In order to make sense of this variety, we first need to know what characteristics typically distinguish democratic from non-democratic states.

Democracy is itself a contested concept, capable of taking on many meanings today (Coppedge et al., 2011). What the 'rule of the people' requires of our societies and institutions is controversial. Fortunately for our purposes in this book, however, we do not need perfect agreement on what democracy is, or on what it should be, before we can speak about non-democratic politics. As the economist Joseph Schumpeter (1950) observed in the first half of the twentieth century, the key distinction between states that can be called 'democratic' (even if grudgingly) and states that should *not* be so called (whatever else they might be called) has to do less with abstract notions such as popular sovereignty and the common good than with the forms of political competition for state power prevalent within them.

In particular, the countries we today call 'democratic' display a specific pattern of political competition for control of states (Schmitter and Karl, 1991). Roughly speaking, in democracies multiple organized groups compete for the support of large publics (in theory, all adults) in electoral contests in order to gain control of key offices of the state (for example, the presidency, a majority of seats in the legislature). One important feature of this form of political competition is that formal 'barriers to entry' (Mulligan and Tsui, 2006; Mulligan, Gil, and Sala-i-Martin, 2004) into the competition for power are relatively low: incumbents (the current group or groups controlling the state) have limited abilities to prevent groups with different views about the proper uses of state power from forming, organizing, appealing to the electorate, or assuming office if they win an election, much less physically harming the membership of these groups. In the pithy formulation of political scientist Adam Przeworski (1991, p. 10), democracies are political systems in which 'parties lose elections', precisely because they *cannot* systematically prevent their opponents from winning them.

The definition of non-democracy follows directly from this: non-democracies today are political systems in which groups in control of the state ('incumbents') do *not* lose elections in the normal course of events, sometimes simply because political competition is carried out without the use of elections. There are many reasons why incumbents may *not* lose elections, and hence, as we shall see, there are many varieties of non-democracy. Incumbents may have the power to prevent opposition groups from forming (by banning them or imprisoning their members), from appealing to the electorate (by monopolizing the media or censoring opposition views), or from taking office if they win an election (by counting votes improperly, or refusing to yield office in case of an opposition win). They may also have the power to shape the norms of political competition so as to make elections either useless as a means of attaining power (as in single-party regimes where elections do not serve as a mechanism for the electorate to select among different parties) or to do without them completely (as in hereditary monarchies). In short, incumbents may use force, fraud, or legitimate but non-electoral means so that they remain in power 'by means other than competitive elections' (Gandhi, 2008, p. 7) – even if they originally *gained* power by such means.

Not all incumbents in non-democratic regimes will murder their political opponents, prevent protest activity, or ban opposition groups outright in their attempts to hold on to power. Some non-democratic regimes use such subtle means to ensure that they do not lose elections that they look almost democratic, while others are far more brutal. As we shall see in this book, the international environment, the availability of material resources, the degree of organization of opposition groups, and even the ruler's conscience all matter for the specific forms that non-democratic rule takes. But, however else they may differ, in all non-democratic political systems rulers and ruling elites systematically impose costs (sometimes quite substantial costs) on other groups in order to prevent them from achieving control or even influence over the direction of state policy.

These consciously imposed costs are different from the costs that the structure of political competition imposes on all groups attempting to control the state in a democracy. For example, in all modern democracies there are many costs involved in catching the attention of the public and persuading the masses of the merits of a political programme. Thus groups whose views are unpopular or not well known will necessarily be disadvantaged, even if incumbents do nothing to prevent them from competing for power. Minor parties in the United States find it difficult to appeal to the electorate, but this is mostly because the costs of persuading the public are large within the American institutional setting, and not due to legal disabilities or repressive activities by Republicans or Democrats. Indeed, in (well-functioning) democratic systems, the vast majority of barriers to competing for state power are what we might call 'structural' rather than intentionally imposed by incumbents; even groups openly advocating for the overthrow of democracy are often capable of organizing and attempting to appeal to the electorate without great fear of repression.

Nevertheless, since the costs that incumbents impose on challengers are often a matter of interpretation and degree, it is sometimes difficult to draw clear lines between democratic and non-democratic systems. Elections in Venezuela over the past 15 years, for example, have often been assailed by opposition parties as being unfair due to the government's ability to use state resources for electoral purposes, while the government has brushed off these criticisms by pointing to the genuine popularity of the late president Hugo Chávez and his Bolivarian revolution, the fact that elections have been pronounced free of fraud by international organizations, and the many avenues for political action available to the opposition. (We shall have occasion to revisit Venezuelan politics several times in this book; see also the Venezuela case study included among the online resources for a more detailed discussion.) Political action never takes place in a perfectly even playing field, and political actors are constantly trying to gain advantages over their challengers. As Daniel Arap Moi, a former president of Kenya, once noted, 'politics is not like football, deserving a level playing field. Here, you try that, and you will be roasted' (quoted in Levitsky and Way, 2010, p. 5).

Moreover, as we shall see in Chapter 2, contemporary non-democratic rule has tended to take on the trappings of democracy without the substance, making judgments that some states are 'authoritarian' or 'dictatorships' even more controversial today than in the past. Due to very wide-ranging ideological and geopolitical changes over the last two centuries, most non-democratic rulers today do not dissolve parliament, shoot their opponents, and declare themselves 'presidents for life'; indeed, the vast majority of them argue for their democratic credentials. Yet we can still make rough judgments about how much incumbent advantage is 'too much' for a state to be considered democratic. In particular, throughout this book, we shall make extensive use of a variety of measures created by political scientists to distinguish between democracy and non-democracy on the basis of whether or not political competition proceeds on the basis of free and fair competitive elections (for example Magaloni, Chu, and Min, 2013; Svolik, 2012; Geddes, Wright, and Frantz, 2014; Boix, Miller, and Rosato, 2012; Pemstein, Meserve, and Melton, 2010).

The Importance of Electoral Competition

When we say that the key distinction between democracy and non-democracy hinges on the kind of (electoral) political competition they allow, we are *not* saying that this is all that matters to democracy, or even that the ideal of democracy necessarily *requires* electoral methods of leadership selection. (This is sometimes called the 'electoralist' fallacy.) Ancient Greeks, for example, thought elections were characteristic of 'oligarchic' regimes (where the wealthy ruled), for reasons having to do with the *structural* barriers to entry into political competition they presuppose (when offices are open to election, the poor have difficulty competing for such positions). In their view, sortition (selection by lottery), not election, was more appropriate to the ideals of citizen equality implicit in the notion of *demokratia* ('the power of the *demos*') and *isonomia* ('citizen equality before the law') as they understood it (see Guerrero (2014) for a modern version of this argument). And today, many people think that various forms of participative or direct democracy are viable alternatives to the representative system. Indeed, in some countries, such as Switzerland, much politics happens through referenda, though in such cases we still find parties, and these parties can lose – that is, they cannot systematically prevent their opponents from appealing to the voters and having their preferences enacted as policy if they count on the support of the requisite majorities.

More generally, electoral competition by itself need not enable popular sovereignty, government 'for the people, by the people, and of the people', liberty and equality, or any of the other ideals associated with the notion of democracy (Dahl, 1989). In any case, the democratic ideal has many dimensions, and thus a proper conception of democracy should be multidimensional and not merely electoral (Coppedge et al., 2011). But in modern states sufficient electoral competition is a *minimal* requisite for democracy, and its lack is thus a useful dividing line between 'democratic' and 'non-democratic' politics. And we are less interested here in conceptualizing and measuring democracy and its degrees than in tracing the differences between the forms political competition takes in typical modern-day systems where parties lose elections ('democracies') and the forms it takes in other, non-democratic, regimes where parties do not lose elections, sometimes because elections do not exist.

By labelling some regimes 'democracies' and others 'non-democracies' on the basis of whether there are free and fair elections with multiple parties in them, we are thus not suggesting that democracies are always 'better' than non-democracies. It is true that the idea that electoral forms of accountability should force the groups who control the state to track the interests of the majority of the population is a major argument for democracy; indeed, it is a key argument for saying that the people are somehow sovereign in modern democratic states, despite their lack of direct influence on policy or of control over major decisions. In theory, politicians that depend on popular majorities for their continued control of the state should act in ways that benefit these majorities more often than politicians that do not depend on popular majorities. But the truth of this argument depends ultimately on empirical considerations, not on pure logic. And it is possible that political leaders or groups that are not so constrained may (under some conditions) produce outcomes that better serve the welfare of large majorities. We will consider the possibility that alternative, non-democratic forms of political competition may produce better outcomes than standard democratic institutions in Chapter 9.

Political Regimes and State Capacity

The democracy–non-democracy dichotomy is also not always the most important distinction for thinking about the outcomes of state policies or the quality of government. These may vary systematically for reasons having less to do with the forms of political competition for control of states (democratic or non-democratic) and more to do with the *capacity* of the state itself to govern. Modern states are peculiar organizations; as Max Weber argued in the early twentieth century, they monopolize or attempt to monopolize the ability to use normatively regulated ('legitimate') force within a territory (Weber, 1978, sec. I.i). These organizations use this monopoly to extract resources from sometimes unwilling populations ('taxes') and use these to, among other things, impose binding rules on these same populations ('laws and regulations'), wage war against competing states or dissatisfied groups within the territory, stage rituals and other public spectacles, or even simply use these resources for the private consumption of state elites ('corruption'). Control of (or even influence on) states thus gives organized groups power and many other benefits, which justifies our focus on the ways in which such control is maintained against other groups.

But states did not always exist – even today many spaces around the world can hardly be said to have them – a fact that limits the temporal scope of our project in this book. And they also vary considerably in their ability to maintain order and enforce laws, or more generally in what we might call their capacity to govern. Indeed, wherever there is no central-ized organization worth struggling over – no enduring institutions whose action can be harnessed to regulate social life in a given territory by suc-cessfully occupying a limited number of social positions, such as an office named 'the presidency' – patterns of political competition for control of states may not be the most important thing to understand when thinking about the politics of particular countries.

Differences in state capacity – or, in Michael Mann's (1984) terms, high levels of 'infrastructural power', in contrast to mere 'despotic power' or the ability to extract resources by the threat of violence – are typically manifested in the presence or absence of relatively high-quality impersonal bureaucracies with low levels of what we ordinarily call 'corruption'. These

Table 1.1   *Political regimes and state capacity*

	Democratic regimes	Non-democratic regimes
High infra-structural power	Incumbent office holders can use their power to effectively regulate the activities of the population, imposing binding rules (laws and regulations) for a variety of purposes, ranging from taxation to infrastructure provision to education. But they cannot in general impose substantial costs on other groups to prevent them from organizing to compete for state office.	Incumbent office holders can use their power to effectively regulate the activities of the population, imposing binding rules (laws and regulations) for a variety of purposes, ranging from taxation to infrastructure provision to education. In addition, however, they can also place effective barriers to political competition for central state power and office.
	These are typically 'consolidated' or 'advanced' democracies, such as the contemporary United States, South Korea, Denmark, and Japan.	Examples include the Soviet Union from the mid 1920s until its breakdown in 1989, the Egyptian regime since 1952, the Chilean military dictatorship of Augusto Pinochet, and many others.

bureaucratic structures have very deep historical roots; for that reason, a state's level of infrastructural power ('state capacity') appears to change only very slowly (Pritchett, Woolcock, and Andrews, 2012), and is to some extent *independent* of the pattern of political competition for their control, whether democratic or non-democratic (Fukuyama, 2013). Though 'consolidated' democracies tend to display high levels of infrastructural power, some states with democratic patterns of political competition show low levels of state capacity (for example, Jamaica, Malawi, and Guatemala today), while some states with non-democratic patterns of political competition have very high levels of infrastructural power (for example, Singapore, whose successes we will explore in more detail in Chapter 9). Thus, although some research suggests that differences in state capacity may be affected (in the long run) by the practices, norms, and institutions that regulate the struggle for power (Carbone, 2015; Carbone and Memoli, 2015), the degree of state capacity is *not* identical with the degree of democracy.

We shall call the combination of norms and institutions that govern *both* state capacity *and* the political competition for control of the state the 'political regime'; but we will focus in this book mostly on the norms and institutions that regulate the struggle for power, since changes in state

| Low infra-structural power | While in power, incumbent office holders cannot fully regulate the state's territory and population for many purposes, because, for example other groups retain independent authority and can impose binding rules on particular groups, or the population can effectively evade state regulation. Moreover, they also cannot impose substantial costs to prevent groups from contesting and winning elections.

These are often seen as 'lower quality democracies'. Examples include modern Jamaica, Colombia, and India. | Incumbent office holders can place many barriers to political competition for central state power and office, ranging from rigging elections to physically restraining potential competitors. Nevertheless, while in power, they cannot fully regulate the state's territory and population for many purposes, because, for example other groups retain independent authority and can impose binding rules on particular groups, or the population can effectively evade state regulation.

Examples include most pre-modern monarchies, Russia between 1917 and 1920, Zaire (modern Democratic Republic of Congo) under Mobutu Sese Seko, and perhaps contemporary Venezuela. |

capacity take place mostly over the *longue durée*. Political regimes thus vary along two dimensions: the democracy–non-democracy dimension and the state capacity dimension (see Table 1.1; see also Tilly (2007)). Both aspects of a regime – state capacity and democracy – may matter for a population's welfare, but we should also keep in mind that, to the extent that states have low capacity to govern, the forms taken by the competition for their control (democratic or non-democratic) may not make much difference to the outcomes that matter to people.

The Dimensions of Non-Democratic Politics

Saying that non-democracies have one thing in common – relatively large barriers to entry into political competition by groups who do not control the state – does not mean that they are all the same. The world of non-democratic regimes is very diverse, ranging from regimes that look almost like democracies and work almost like them to regimes that have almost nothing in common with them and work in completely different ways. To organize this variety, we shall focus on four dimensions of non-democratic politics:

1. **Legitimating norms and institutions**. Some non-democracies are 'republics', claiming to accept some form of popular sovereignty; others are 'monarchies', claiming that sovereignty resides in a particular family. Accordingly, non-democracies also differ in the extent to which they use electoral and plebiscitary means (however rigged) to regulate selection to executive office and legitimate state action. In Chapter 2 we examine the evolution of these norms and institutions over the past two centuries, and show how it came to be that most modern non-democracies, like modern democracies, claim to accept popular sovereignty and make extensive use of electoral institutions.

2. **The degree of social 'pluralism' permitted by the regime**, or more specifically the extent to which ruling groups attempt to control society in pursuit of an ideological project (Linz, 2000 [1975]). Some non-democracies are 'authoritarian' regimes that are content with preventing particular groups from gaining power but do not have a well-defined ideology that demands extensive control over society (or cannot achieve such control); others are 'totalitarian' or 'ideocratic' regimes that attempt to exercise far more ideological control over society. In Chapter 3 we explore the factors that made it possible for some important non-democratic regimes in the twentieth century to exercise a large degree of ideological control over society, as well as the reasons why most modern non-democracies are today merely authoritarian regimes.

3. **The degree of 'personalism' within a ruling elite**, or more specifically the extent to which rulers are forced to share power with an elite that can impose binding normative constraints on their actions (Svolik, 2012). Some non-democratic regimes are 'personal dictatorships', where a single figure concentrates power and the rest of the elite cannot substantially or consistently constrain his actions; while others are 'institutionalized' regimes, where an elite can impose consistent constraints on the ruler's actions, and reasonably clear norms regulate political competition within the regime. We shall explore how power has been concentrated, or shared, in non-democratic regimes over the past century in Chapter 4.

4. **The key organizations through which power is exercised**. In some non-democratic regimes, political parties are the primary institutions organizing political competition, ensuring elite cohesion, channelling information about society, and in general retaining control over the state. In others, military organizations are more important for these roles, while political parties, if they exist, are subject to military control. And in yet others dynastic families control parties (or dispense with parties) and military organizations. We shall explore these differences, and their consequences for non-democratic politics, in Chapters 5 to 7.

These aspects of non-democratic politics can be used to roughly classify non-democratic political regimes in two different ways. First, we can focus on the *outcomes* of struggles over legitimating norms, social control, and power-sharing. Such a classification distinguishes primarily among more or less authoritarian, and more or less personalized regimes. Second, we can focus on the *institutions* that are used to regulate and channel these conflicts over social control or power-sharing. Such a classification distinguishes regimes primarily on the basis of the primary organization a ruling elite uses to control the state, which over the last century has typically been a political party, a military organization, or (in a few cases) a dynastic clan. Each of these classifications represents a distinct (though complementary) view of *political power* in non-democratic regimes: the first emphasizing the forms of power that rulers and ruling elites can actually exercise, and the second emphasizing the *vehicles* through which that power is exercised.

Social Control and Personal Power in Non-Democratic Regimes

On the first view, we can place non-democratic regimes in a two-dimensional matrix of ideal types according to the degree to which ruling elites succeed both in controlling and directing social pluralism according to a singular vision, and in sharing power with a ruler (Table 1.2). (We omit complications derived from struggles over basic legitimating norms, as most regimes today, with some small exceptions, share a basic republican orientation, as we shall see in Chapter 2.) It is important to stress that though struggles over social control and power-sharing are often related, they are distinct: the degree to which power becomes personalized in a struggle within the ruling elite is not always tightly connected with the degree through which that same elite can exercise control over society in pursuit of an ideological project.

The different non-democratic regimes combine three basic kinds of social control – competitive authoritarian, authoritarian, and totalitarian – with two basic forms of 'personalization' – dictatorships and non-personalized or institutionalized regimes. These are all ideal types, but real life is messy, and no regime fits exactly any given category for all time. Struggles over social control and power-sharing are rarely settled clearly and definitively. We might thus be better off imagining a continuous space through which states move over time rather than a 3-by-2 table. Consider Figures 1.1 and 1.2. Figure 1.1 shows an illustrative trajectory through the two-dimensional space of social control and personalism for Russia and Venezuela, two countries which we will be discussing in more detail at various points in this book, plus the trajectory of New Zealand – a

Table 1.2 *A typology of non-democratic political regimes*

	Competitive authoritarian	Authoritarian	Totalitarian or ideocratic
Personal rule (dictatorships)	Executives are elected, and there is genuine electoral competition for power, but opposition groups labour at a significant disadvantage, and other institutions have little control over the executive. Examples in this book include the Chávez regime in Venezuela from 2006 to 2013.	Executives may or may not be elected, but political competition for power is tightly restricted, and independent organization for political purposes is very difficult. Examples in this book include the Franco regime in Spain and the Pinochet military regime in Chile.	Executives may or may not be elected (though without opposition), but the elite cannot constrain the ruler, and society is tightly controlled in pursuit of an elite-endorsed ideological project. Examples in this book include the Soviet Union under Stalin and Germany under Hitler.
Institutional control	Executives are elected but are significantly constrained in their actions by elites and other institutions. There is electoral competition for power, but opposition groups labour at a significant disadvantage. Examples in this book include Mexico until 2000.	Executives may or may not be elected but are significantly constrained in their actions by elites and other institutions. Independent political organization is difficult or impossible, yet some space for autonomous social (but non-political) organization exists. Examples in this book include the current Saudi regime.	Executives may or may not be elected (though without opposition) but are significantly constrained in their actions by elites and other institutions. Society is tightly controlled in pursuit of an elite-endorsed ideological project. Examples in this book include the Soviet Union after Stalin's death.

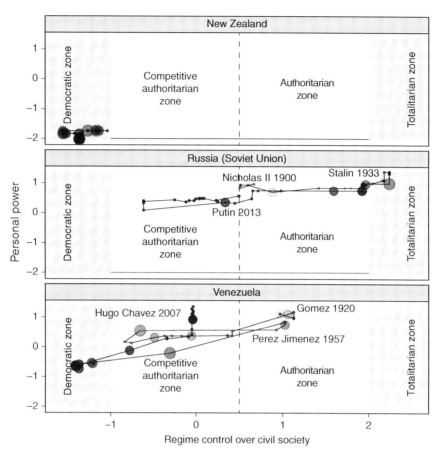

Figure 1.1   *Sample trajectories through regime space. The* y *axis shows an index of 'personal power' constructed from a latent variable analysis of a number of existing measures of personalism. The* x *axis shows an index of how tightly controlled a society is, derived from the v2x_ccsi variable in the V-dem dataset (Coppedege et al., 2015); higher values mean more control over society. Labels indicate local peaks in personal power; the size of the points is proportional to the number of observations for a particular combination of personal power and social control. The index of personal power is constructed from the V-dem indexes of legislative and judicial constraints on the executive and of executive corruption; Polity IV's measure of executive constraints (Marshall, Gurr, and Jaggers, 2010); Geddes, Wright, and Frantz's (2014) indicator of personalism; Kailitz's (2013) indicator of personalism; Magaloni, Chu, and Min's (2013) experimental measure of personalism; and Wahman, Teorell, and Hadenius's (2013) measure of mean executive turnover in non-democratic regimes.*

country generally considered an institutionalized democracy – for comparison. Figure 1.2 shows the trajectory of Russia in each of these dimensions separately. (The trajectories are merely illustrative because the data on 'personalism' and 'social control' are not ideal; but they shall serve our purposes here. A complete package with replication data and code for all the many charts in this book is also available from this book's website at www.palgravehighered.com/companion/politics/marquez; figures for other countries can easily be generated.)

Note first that in Figure 1.1 New Zealand spends all of the last century (the data goes back to the 1900s) in the lower-right corner: a state with a vibrant civil society that is not highly controlled by the state, and where individual prime ministers, for all their power, are subject to a variety of effective institutional controls. This is the typical pattern for democratic, institutionalized regimes – even though New Zealand's head of state is technically the British monarch.

By contrast, Russia has both experienced a wide variety of forms of social control and had rulers who have exercised different degrees of personal power (see in particular Figure 1.2). The country began the 1900s as a monarchy legitimated by divine right rather than by appeals to popular sovereignty, and where elections or other institutions of popular participation accordingly did not exist. At that time, Tsar Nicholas II was at the peak of his autocratic, personal power; no institutions could formally control him. Yet Russian society, though repressed, was not mobilized or controlled in the service of an ideological state project, and groups independent of the state, including groups that attempted to exercise political influence, could and did exist. Russia was then an authoritarian monarchy whose ruler had a medium–high level of personal power.

With the Russian Revolution in 1917 Russia became a republic, and elections and plebiscites were henceforth widely used to legitimate state action, though these were never free and fair and soon became completely non-competitive. As the Communist Party consolidated control in the aftermath of the civil war, and the Soviet Union emerged from the Russian empire, personal power first decreased, especially during the Lenin era – when the principle of collegial leadership was generally respected, despite Lenin's undoubtedly great prestige (Tumarkin, 1983) – but then increased after Lenin's death, reaching its peak with Stalin's 'Great Terror' in 1937. Simultaneously, after a brief moment of openness following the February Revolution, where many groups independent of the state could compete for power and influence, Soviet control over society in the service of the Communist ideological project steadily increased (Kotkin, 2014).

By 1933 the Soviet Union was a totalitarian dictatorship, that is, a regime which could tightly control society in the service of an ideological project, and whose ruler had a very high level of personal power, unconstrained by the rest of the ruling elite. Indeed, the Communist Party elite not only was unable to control Stalin's actions, they were even substantially decimated by him during the 'Great Terror' of the 1930s (Conquest, 2008). This situation changed after Stalin's death in 1953, when Soviet rulers lost some personal power as the principle of collegial leadership became more fully institutionalized again and ideological controls relaxed, but social control

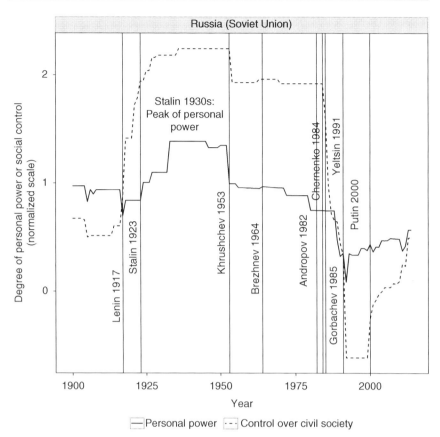

Figure 1.2 *Personal power and social control in Russia over time. The y axis shows an index of 'personal power' constructed from a latent variable analysis of a number of existing measures of personalism (solid line) and an index of control over society (dotted line). The index of social control is derived from the v2x_ccsi variable in the V-dem dataset (Coppedge et al 2015); higher values mean more control over society. The index of personal power is constructed from the V-dem indexes of legislative and judicial constraints on the executive and of executive corruption; Polity IV's measure of executive constraints (Marshall, Gurr, and Jaggers 2010); Geddes, Wright, and Frantz's (2014) indicator of personalism; Kailitz's (2013) indicator of personalism; Magaloni, Chu, and Min's (2013) experimental measure of personalism; and Wahman, Teorell, and Hadenius's (2013) measure of mean executive turnover in non-democratic regimes. Vertical lines indicate start years for various rulers according to the Archigos dataset of Goemans, Gleditsch, and Chiozza (2009), updated to 2014.*

only slackened substantially in the 1980s, as Gorbachev's 'perestroika' and 'glasnost' policies allowed for the reinvigoration of an independent civil society. The post-Stalin Soviet Union thus became slightly less totalitarian (moving towards the authoritarian side of the spectrum), and power in the state became less personalized and more institutionally controlled.

With the break-up of the Soviet Union, both social control and personal power continued to decrease, the former drastically, the latter less so, as the Russian constitution approved in the early 1990s ensured that the president would remain personally powerful (Kotkin, 2008). Finally, after a brief period of genuine openness in the early 1990s, the current president, Vladimir Putin, began to increase both the regime's social control (without reverting to Soviet levels of social control) and (to a lesser degree) his own personal power, leading to a regime that today combines medium–high levels of personalism with authoritarian levels of social control.

Venezuela exemplifies another way in which power can become personalized more or less independently of social control. The country became a republic in the early 1800s, after independence from the Spanish monarchy, and elections (limited and not always competitive) thus began to be used as ways to legitimate power and select rulers. Nevertheless, these electoral norms were fragile and often violated by people who took power by force. Indeed, the state itself did not always monopolize legitimate violence over the entire territory. In the early 1900s Juan Vicente Gómez ousted the previous president, Cipriano Castro, pacified the country, and accumulated a great deal of personal power. But though his rule was repressive, it was not highly ideological or able to fully control society, and political groups autonomous from the state continued to exist. At the time, Venezuela was thus an authoritarian dictatorship in a state with relatively low levels of infrastructural power.

After Gómez's death, social control relaxed, pushing the country into the democratic zone in the 1940s. Rulers were much more constrained, and political parties flourished. This period was cut short by a military coup, led by General Marcos Pérez Jiménez. Pérez Jiménez, however, was not a purely personal dictator; he was instead accountable to a junta of other officers, and never accumulated as much personal power as Gómez. His regime was overthrown in 1958, and social control was relaxed much further as Venezuela transitioned to a long period of democracy. During this period, most presidents were constrained by other institutions, though they were less constrained than New Zealand prime ministers. But the multiparty system experienced a crisis in the 1990s (see the online materials for more detail, as well as Box 3.2), leading to the rise of an outsider, Hugo Chávez, who won the presidency in 1997 in a free and fair election. Chávez, who was enormously popular, soon accumulated great personal power, and his regime engaged in practices that made it increasingly difficult for opposition groups to compete for power. But he never attempted, or managed, to tightly control civil society in pursuit of his ideological visions. Indeed, the regime's control over society was close enough to 'democratic' forms of social control that there can be controversy about whether this was a genuinely non-democratic regime, as we shall see in Chapter 5. Thus at best the regime became 'competitive authoritarian', even if by some measures Chávez was the most powerful leader the country had had in nearly a hundred years.

We will explore in more detail these and other examples at various points in this book. (Additional narratives for several other regimes are also available at this book's website at www.palgravehighered.com/companion/politics/marquez.) The key point to note here is that though personal power and social control are often related (it is harder to accumulate personal power without some degree of social control), they are not always tightly linked. Though Venezuela has experienced several periods where power has become concentrated in a single person, it has never come close to the extremes of social control found in Soviet Russia; and though Russia has had many 'strong' leaders, the degree of social control it has experienced has varied widely.

Authoritarian Institutions

The second way of understanding variations among non-democratic political regimes focuses on the primary organizations used by ruling elites to exercise power – in particular to engage in social control and manage power-sharing with a ruler. Three kinds of institutions have been historically important in this connection: political parties, military organizations, and dynastic families. Depending on which of these institutions is dominant, most recent scholarship on non-democratic regimes (Geddes, Wright, and Frantz, 2014; Wahman, Teorell, and Hadenius, 2013; Magaloni, Chu, and Min, 2013; Kailitz, 2013) distinguishes among military, party, and monarchic non-democratic regimes (including some hybrid combinations). This book follows this line of research in arguing that political power in modern non-democracies is usually built on the basis of one of these organizations, though other institutions – the Church in medieval Europe, or the state bureaucracy elsewhere, for example – have also occasionally played important roles in the past. Accordingly, as we shall see in Chapters 5 to 7, many aspects of non-democratic politics are related to which of these organizations is dominant within a regime. In particular, the repressiveness and durability of a regime, and its ability to exercise social control or to produce prosperity, depend in part on whether parties, military organizations, or dynastic families exercise primary control over the state.

It is nevertheless important to note that, though there are affinities between forms of social control, degrees of personal power, and particular organizations and institutional settings, these are not the same thing. While (as we shall see in Chapter 4) in the most personalized regimes institutions tend to decay into simple patronage networks, and the least personalized regimes usually have strong parties capable of imposing important restraints on top leaders, in between these extremes many institutional combinations are possible. Military rulers can be restrained by juntas of officers, party leaders can be held to account by strong politburos, and kings are often accountable to family councils. As several scholars have noted (Geddes, Wright, and Frantz, 2014; Wahman, Teorell, and Hadenius, 2013; Magaloni, Chu, and Min, 2013), all sorts of regimes can be more or less personalized, regardless of the main institutions used to control the state.

Similarly, it is true that as we move towards the competitive authoritarian extreme, non-democratic regimes will tend to organize the competition for power through multiple political parties and competitive but not fair elections, whereas as we move to the totalitarian extreme ruling elites will tend to exercise power through a single party and to avoid competitive elections. But these forms of party rule, and the regimes to which they give rise, are poorly captured by the number of parties in the political sphere. Totalitarian regimes, in particular, are not well conceptualized simply as 'single party' regimes, not least because totalitarian episodes have taken place in some regimes without much mediation from ruling parties, or even against them (for example, the chaos of the 'cultural revolution' in China, discussed briefly in Chapter 8, or similar episodes in Libya's own cultural revolution in the late 1970s); what makes a regime totalitarian is not the number of parties, but the fact of ideologically driven control. Moreover, in between totalitarian and competitive authoritarian extremes a wide variety of institutional combinations are possible, ranging from monarchies such as Saudi Arabia, where power is concentrated in the hands of a dynastic clan, to military regimes where the army controls the state, to regimes where a single party is highly dominant but other parties exist; no purely institutional classification matches exactly with the degree of social control exercised by a regime.

This is an important reason why this book makes use of the older distinction between 'totalitarian' and 'authoritarian' regimes in addition to the more recent distinctions between more or less personalized regimes and between party, military, and monarchical regimes. Though current scholarship has tended to de-emphasize the totalitarian-authoritarian distinction, primarily due to its perceived politicization during the Cold War (Linz, 2000 [1975]) and its apparent vagueness and limited applicability today (perhaps only North Korea and Eritrea qualify as totalitarian regimes, though some other 'non-state' movements, such as the so-called 'Islamic State', display totalitarian tendencies), I argue for its continuing relevance as an analytical tool. Ideology and the forms of social control it enables, not just the organizations through which power is exercised or the degree to which power is personalized, matter to non-democratic politics. For this purpose, I draw especially on the work of Linz (2000 [1975]; 1976 [1964]), who has done much to make the ideal types of totalitarian and authoritarian rule sociologically useful, as well as on the more recent work of Kailitz (2013), who has argued for the value of a category of 'ideocratic' rule applicable not just to the great Communist regimes of the twentieth century but also to other regimes with a highly ideological component, such as the Qaddafi regime during certain periods in its history. This is of course not to argue that the newer focus in the study of non-democratic regimes on institutions is misplaced, but that it is best supplemented with a perspective that emphasizes the way in which ideological commitments shape the possible uses of these institutions.

It is also worth noting that it is often quite difficult to identify which institutions – parties, military organizations, or dynastic families – are genuinely dominant in a non-democratic regime at any given time. Consider, for example, the regime that emerged from the victory of Francisco Franco in the Spanish Civil War of 1936–39, a regime to which we will return in this book several times. In this book's terminology, the Spanish post-civil war regime (1939–75) was clearly an authoritarian dictatorship (Linz, 1976 [1964]): Franco had a great deal of personal power, and the regime tightly limited political organization and competition, but (except very early in the regime's life) it did not attempt to fully control society in pursuit of an ideological project. Yet scholars have often disagreed about how to make sense of the regime in institutional terms. Some scholars emphasize its 'personalistic' character (Geddes, Wright, and Frantz, 2014), since Franco held undisputed personal power with few formal constraints, while others characterize it as a military regime (Cheibub, Gandhi, and Vreeland, 2010), since Franco came to power at the head of a military insurrection and the military provided the most important support for his regime, especially early on. Other scholars choose to stress instead the fact that the regime only allowed a single political party, the Falange (Wahman, Teorell, and Hadenius, 2013), which played important roles in social control and the management of political competition within the elite (Preston, 1995; Payne, 1987). Finally, others consider it a hybrid, combining features of military and party regimes with a healthy dose of personalization (Kailitz, 2013) in proportions that varied over time.

The reason for this variety of classifications is not that scholars are confused, but because institutions play different roles within a regime over time, and researchers devise specific classifications by focusing on some of these functions at the expense of others (Wilson, 2014). For example, if the focus is on the ability of institutions to constrain leaders, then the Franco regime is best conceptualized as a personalized authoritarian dictatorship, since the ruling elite could not use regime institutions to constrain him; if the focus is on the institutions through which the regime managed social pluralism or access to state power by non-elite groups, it is perhaps best to conceive of it as a single party regime; and if the focus is on the way it ensured elite loyalty and legitimated itself, it is best to conceive of it as a kind of hybrid with multiple institutions playing supporting roles at different points in time and with different constituencies. As Svolik (2012, p. 38) notes, regimes can use all of these institutions to exercise power, and it is not possible to make mutually exclusive classifications by trying to assess which of them is really primary.

Thus, rather than putting too much stress on the question of whether a specific regime is a 'party' or 'military' regime, this book focuses instead on the factors that determine when and how parties, military organizations, or dynastic clans can be used effectively (individually or in combination) to both manage elite power-sharing and exercise social control. In particular, I argue that these organizations work best when they can provide sufficient incentives for *elite cohesion*, manage the *loyalty* of supporters through appropriate rewards and punishments, and *mobilize* supporters beyond the ruling class. As we shall see (Chapters 5 to 7), the ability to provide incentives for elite cohesion and to mobilize supporters in a disciplined way shows why the most successful ruling organizations in non-democratic contexts over the last century or so have been *political parties*, whereas military organizations, for all their control over force, have been far less able to retain power than one might have predicted.

Problems and Outcomes of Non-democratic Rule

Regardless of their organizational bases, most elites in non-democratic regimes face a number of common problems concerning their preservation in power. Precisely because non-democratic regimes depend on excluding, if need be forcibly, other groups from control of the state, they must constantly consider the possibility of both internal and external challengers, including popular uprisings. As a result, all non-democratic regimes must be able to both discourage opposition and secure sufficient popular support or acquiescence to deter these challenges. In Machiavelli's famous formulation, all non-democratic elites must be able to inspire both fear and love if they want to remain in power, though at a pinch fear alone will do. In Chapter 8 we focus specifically on the tactics most authoritarian regimes use to demobilize challengers ('fear') and mobilize supporters ('love').

The production of fear and love depends on two interrelated activities: the gathering and manipulation of information, and the use of symbolism and ritual to amplify or dampen emotion and legitimate state action. While all regimes, democratic or non-democratic, engage in these activities, I show that non-democratic regimes face some unique challenges that are directly related to the degree to which they control public space (how 'totalitarian' they are) and the degree to which power is concentrated in a single person (how 'personalized' they are). In particular, many very powerful non-democratic regimes have difficulty gathering credible information about both elites and society at large, since fear of the regime induces people to dissemble. Worse, such regimes cannot always easily make their statements credible, or their symbolism effective, since the population knows they can lie with impunity.

This problem of credibility has sometimes been called the 'dictator's dilemma' (Wintrobe, 2008). A ruler who can punish with impunity may induce people to tell him only what he wants to hear, but this is not always what he needs to hear if he wishes to maintain his position. Yet the problem goes much further, for power affects also the credibility of the dictator's own messages and commitments. Chapter 8 thus specifically examines the mechanisms through which non-democratic regimes attempt to mitigate these credibility and commitment problems, exploring how they build intelligence organizations, use censorship in ways that still allow them to understand what is really going on in society, and attempt to make sure their messages are believable and effective.

One important reason to care about whether a regime is democratic or non-democratic is whether they produce policies that in general benefit the population. Indeed, a great deal of ideological debate today is about whether 'democracy' (understood in the Western liberal sense exemplified by the United States or European states) is better or worse than other forms of political organization, especially for less developed countries or in 'non-Western' cultural contexts. From this point of view, the problems faced by non-democratic regimes in gathering and using information affect their ability not only to retain power, but also to make rational policy decisions on behalf of their populations.

In Chapter 9 we thus examine the question of whether, and under what conditions, non-democratic regimes are able to produce policies that are broadly for the benefit of the population. As we shall see, while democracies are on average better than non-democracies at producing the sorts of things that we care about, there are important exceptions to this generalization. Successful non-democratic regimes typically have institutions that allow them to gather and process relevant information and opinion in accurate and timely ways, to co-opt and discipline those who have access to productive resources, and to adjust policy as circumstances change. More interestingly, these regimes resemble democracies in some functional respects, allowing for reasonably open discussion of many issues, even if they otherwise tightly control the political sphere.

Regime Change, Revolution, and Democratization

One key theme of this book is that political regimes are not static. Indeed, they not only change gradually as circumstances change, but sometimes disintegrate in spectacular revolutionary upheavals. In Chapters 10 and 11 we thus explore the processes through which non-democratic political regimes change and sometimes even democratize.

Two distinct kinds of explanations of regime change are evaluated. First (Chapter 10), some explanations stress long-term structural changes affecting cultural values, economic interests, and/or geopolitical environments. These are 'macropolitical' or 'structural' explanations: they tell us much about the conditions under which regime change is likely, but little about the specific circumstances, decisions, and activities that actually bring it about. Other explanations (Chapter 11), by contrast, de-emphasize precisely these structural factors, focusing instead on the actions of elites and masses at particular points in time, and in particular those actions and decisions that make collective action possible. These are 'micropolitical' explanations, which tell us much about how regime change happens but less about the long-term changes that have made certain sorts of regime transitions (for example, transitions towards democracy) more likely today than in the past.

Macropolitical and micropolitical theories of regime change are not necessarily mutually exclusive. They simply refer to different levels of analysis: one pointing to the conditions that make enduring regime change likely; another indicating the factors that actually trigger regime change and the activities that typically produce such a change. Nevertheless, specific explanations are sometimes in tension with one another. This is particularly the case for theories that stress cultural factors in the explanation of regime change, as opposed to theories that stress economic conflicts of interests or geopolitical changes. These theories are sometimes presented as claims that authoritarian regimes are more suited to some cultures than others. In Chapter 10 I take a sceptical look at these theories, stressing that although cultural values do seem to matter for regime change and persistence, they do not determine whether a country is democratic or not, and indeed that they tend to change in predictable ways with economic development. The key idea here is that regime change is at bottom a conflictual, not a consensual, process, even if all such social conflicts are mediated by culturally specific values about fairness; and the kinds of conflicts that produce regime change ultimately depend less on purely cultural than on economic and geopolitical factors.

As we shall have occasion to see throughout this book, most significant transformations in non-democratic regimes do not lead to democracy. Nevertheless, regime change often involves significant participation from ordinary people demanding more political influence (even if not always specifically democracy). And given the long-run trends (documented in Chapter 2) that have not only made democracy far more common in the world today than a century ago, but have also ensured that it no longer has any ideological competitors, it is no surprise that political scientists today are especially concerned with the conditions that lead not only to regime change, but also to democratization. This book thus devotes significant space to discussing both the structural conditions that lead to democratization and the forms of 'contentious politics' that tend to make it possible. In particular, Chapter 11 discusses the opportunities that allow people to protest for regime change, the mechanisms through which protest develops and grows, and the particular forms (violent and non-violent) it takes, as well as the consequences of these forms of contentious politics.

Conclusion

The general perspective of this book can be summarized in the idea that non-democratic regimes are always the product of struggles. These are first of all struggles to control the state and exclude challengers (making it possible for some groups 'not to lose elections', at least for a time), but also struggles to control society in pursuit of particular projects and struggles within the ruling group for power. These struggles are waged with the help of specific organizations, of which the modern political party and the modern military are the most important ones, as they provide powerful mechanisms for ensuring elite loyalty and controlling society. And the temporary outcomes of these struggles shaped the spectrum of non-democracy in the last two centuries, from the quasi-democratic regimes that form the bulk of non-democratic political systems today to the harsh totalitarian regimes of the early twentieth century, and from tightly constrained corporate leaderships to nearly all-powerful dictators.

The substantive content of these struggles has been shaped by history: first and perhaps most importantly, the great global shift away from monarchical forms of legitimation towards democratic ones, aided and abetted by important geopolitical changes in the past two centuries, but also the many more local changes in values, resources, and interests that have shaped the world since the Industrial Revolution. While these changes have by no means led to the triumph of some ideal form of democracy, they have shifted the distribution of power in the world in ways that have forced non-democratic regimes to adapt and change, becoming, if not more democratic, at least more likely to be mistaken for democracies than before. We thus begin by sketching these 'big picture' changes in the norms of legitimation and the forms of political competition over the last two centuries.

Chapter 2

The Changing Face of Non-Democratic Rule

Will the Real Democracies Please Stand Up?

No country today wants to be thought undemocratic. So powerful is the allure of democracy today that the vast majority of countries in the world call themselves 'democratic' – regardless of whether or not they actually *are* democratic in any recognizable sense. Non-democratic regimes do not typically advertise themselves as such in their major legal documents, and perhaps do not even believe themselves to be non-democratic.

Indeed, by 2013 more than 90 per cent of the world's population lived in independent states with constitutional documents that asserted their democratic character (see Figure 2.1), and most of the people who lived in countries with constitutions that did not mention democracy nevertheless understood themselves to be living under democracy (see Box 2.2). Even more strikingly, the vast majority of countries not only describe themselves in constitutional documents as democracies, but also assert most of the 'liberal' rights and freedoms we normally associate with the concept (see Box 2.1 for a good example). Over and over, from the Egypt of Mubarak to the China of the Chinese Communist Party, from the Syria of the al-Assad clan to the Russia of Vladimir Putin, from the Mexico of the Institutional Revolutionary Party (PRI) to the Venezuela of Chávez, from the Zimbabwe of Mugabe to the Cuba of the Castros, everywhere we find high-flown proclamations of the democratic character of society, the dignity of the individual, and the importance of civil rights. It is actually very difficult to distinguish between the constitutional commitments of a human rights abuser and of a working democracy (Ginsburg and Simpser 2013).

If we took their public declarations at face value, almost every regime in the world is democratic and holds 'liberal' rights in the highest esteem. And yet we know this cannot be right. At least by the standards of contemporary political science, only about half of all countries, comprising about half of the world's population, can be reasonably identified as roughly democratic today (Figure 2.2). How did it happen that almost every state in the world today wants to clothe itself in democratic garb?

In this chapter, I sketch the historical context that led to the current dominance of 'democracy' as a universal norm, and the consequent transformations in the forms of non-democracy over the last two centuries. The first

Box 2.1   A highly progressive constitution

Can you guess from whose constitution this passage comes from?

Article 64. […] The state shall substantially guarantee all citizens genuine democratic rights and freedom, and happy material and cultural lives. […]

Article 65. Citizens shall have equal rights in all spheres of the state and social life.

Article 66. All citizens who have reached the age of 17 shall have the right to vote and the right to be elected, irrespective of sex, race, occupation, length of residence, property and intellectual level, party affiliation, political view, or religious belief. Citizens serving in the armed forces shall also have the right to vote and the right to be elected. […]

Article 67. Citizens shall have freedom of speech, press, assembly, demonstration, and association. The state shall guarantee conditions for the free activities of democratic political parties and social organizations.

Article 68. Citizens shall have freedom of religion. This right shall be guaranteed by permitting the construction of religious buildings and the holding of religious ceremonies. Religion shall not be used in bringing in outside forces or in harming the state and social order.

Answer: North Korea!

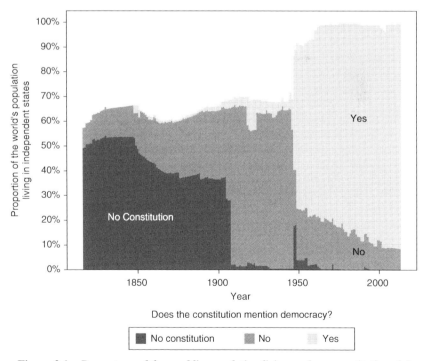

Figure 2.1   *Percentage of the world's population living under a constitution claiming to be democratic. Constitutional data from the Comparative Constitutions Project; population data from Gleditsch (2010) and the World Bank. Author's calculations.*

Box 2.2   Which countries do not call themselves democratic?

Out of around 200 sovereign entities in the international system today (give or take a few), only 16 today fail to mention the democratic character of their government and society in any of their constitutional documents: Australia, Brunei, Denmark, Japan, Jordan, Malaysia, Monaco, Nauru, Oman, Samoa, Saudi Arabia, Singapore, Tonga, the United Kingdom, the USA, and Vatican City. (Countries that do not mention democracy are identified from data made available by the Comparative Constitutions Project at http://www.comparativeconstitutions.org.)

Even this number is overstated. The proclamations of the independence of Malaya (1957) and of the formation of Malaysia (1963), as well as the proclamation of independence of Singapore (1965) all stress the 'democratic' character of these nations; the European Convention of Human Rights, which counts Denmark and the United Kingdom as signatories, also mentions the democratic character of all the convening parties. And among the remaining countries, the United States, Australia, Denmark, Japan, and the United Kingdom would normally be considered – by insiders and outsiders – to be long-standing democracies. Today, only absolute monarchies such as Brunei and Saudi Arabia really advertise the fact that they are *not* democracies.

Moreover, this rhetorical triumph of democracy is not even a recent development, or a specifically Western one. The first mention of 'democracy' in constitutional documents occurred in the French revolutionary constitution of 1848 and in the Swiss constitution of the same year. But the next set of mentions occur in the nineteenth-century constitutions of most Latin American and Haiti, followed by the constitutions of several Eastern European countries that emerged from the breakup of the Austro-Hungarian Empire in the early twentieth century, as well as those of several countries in Southern Europe, and Russia. And the founding constitutions of most countries that gained independence after the Second World War in Africa, Asia, and elsewhere almost all stress their democratic character. Indeed, the practice of constitution-making (the drafting of 'explicit' social contracts) and the widespread acceptance of democratic principles were closely associated in the twentieth century.

---

section describes how modern non-democratic politics took shape against the background of great changes in the legitimation of political authority. The second section shows how this change in legitimating principles was accompanied by significant institutional transformations in the 'shape' of non-democratic regimes. And in the final section I identify three great 'moments' in the development of modern non-democracy: first, a 'totalitarian' moment after the First World War; second, a 'dictatorial' or simply 'authoritarian' moment beginning with the post-Second World War process of decolonization; and finally, a 'competitive authoritarian' moment beginning with the end of the Cold War.

This account is more descriptive than explanatory, showing that modern forms of non-democracy are deeply entangled with the development of modern democratic institutions, but postponing in-depth consideration of their causes until later chapters. And the story is told in part through charts and graphs, in order to stress that the striking changes that have occurred in the legitimating norms of political authority and the mechanisms for regulating political competition over the past two centuries have global, not merely 'Western', scope, and that they have roots going back to the nineteenth century. Data and code for all charts is available in this book's data supplement; I encourage readers to play with it and produce their own charts.

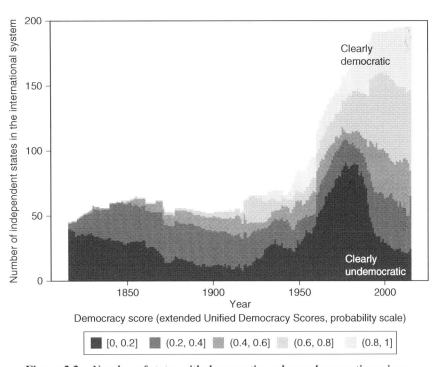

Figure 2.2   *Number of states with democratic and non-democratic regimes. Democracy data from Pemstein, Meserve, and Melton 2010, extended by the author to the nineteenth century and transformed to a probability scale (Márquez 2016a). Values close to one indicate that the country is almost certainly a democracy according to current scholarly standards, values close to zero that it is almost certainly not a democracy, and values in between indicate that the regime may have characteristics of both democracy and non-democracy, and as a result there is disagreement among scholars as to how democratic the regime is, or whether it is democratic.*

Democracy, Dictatorship, and the Legitimation of Political Authority

The words we use to describe political phenomena are typically imprecise and contested; and the words we use to describe the 'non-democratic' political phenomena that are the focus of this book are doubly so. Words such as 'tyranny', 'despotism', 'dictatorship', 'authoritarianism', and 'totalitarianism', easily become weapons in struggles for power, especially today when the word 'democracy' has come to acquire such a positive connotation. But it was not always so. In fact, 'democracy' until very recently was generally thought to be a bad form of government, not something to be imitated, and some of the most common terms we use to refer to non-democratic regimes, such as dictatorship, had positive connotations.

Much of our terminology to describe political regimes comes from Greek and Roman antiquity. Classical writers tended to divide political arrangements in terms of the *number* of people who exercised power (one, a few, many, sometimes as a proxy for social classes like the poor or the rich), the *purposes* for which power was used (the common good vs. the private interest of the ruler, for example), and the *form* in which it was used (according to law or arbitrarily). From this perspective, democracy was just one of many possible political arrangements, not necessarily the best or the worst one. And while classical writers differed in many respects about the merits of different political regimes, all of them nevertheless agreed that 'tyranny', understood as the government of a bad or unjust monarch, was the worst form of government. (To echo the English philosopher Thomas Hobbes many centuries later, tyranny was 'monarchy misliked'.)

Tyranny was not only associated with monarchy, however, but was also often understood by elites in the Greco-Roman world as a pathology of democracy. Since democracy was understood as the direct government of 'the many' – the poorer and less educated citizens, assembled together to decide on all of their common affairs – their poverty and lack of education were thought to make them especially susceptible to deceptive persuasion leading to tyranny. The popular, demagogic leader was always a potential tyrant. The susceptibility of democracy to tyranny in turn contributed to a sense of democracy as something at best ambiguous, at worst downright dangerous.

But if democracy was not seen by theorists as an unambiguously good form of government (something which did not happen until the late nineteenth century; see Dunn (2005)), neither was monarchy. A good regime was neither, or rather, it was a mixture of democratic and non-democratic elements, or a 'republic', as it came to be known later. The paradigmatic example of such a regime in pre-modern times, the Roman Republic, incorporated into its constitution an element of popular participation by free male citizens that was understood by theorists as a 'democratic' aspect of an otherwise 'mixed' regime (Márquez, 2011a).

The fall of the Roman Republic and its transformation into a more straightforwardly monarchical system ended any currency democracy might once have had even as an element of a 'mixed' system of government. Over the centuries that followed, the basic understanding of legitimate political authority was monarchical almost everywhere, even if political power was in fact often tempered informally both by elements of popular participation and by the need to secure elite cooperation. (The legitimation of political authority had almost always been monarchical in the great empires beyond Rome.) With few exceptions (for example, the Renaissance city-republics of the Italian peninsula), we must wait until the great republican revolutions of the late eighteenth and early nineteenth century to observe widespread rejections of monarchical authority.

The nineteenth century also saw a revival of interest in another term the Romans had invented: the 'dictator', a term we have already used to refer to rulers with great personal power. In early Republican times, the dictator was a magistrate appointed in times of crisis to an office with enlarged emergency powers, for a strictly limited period, in order to 'save the republic' unfettered by the slowness of collective deliberation or the inflexibility of ordinary laws. But the dictator could not change fundamental institutions, and at the end of the day he was accountable to the aristocrats who populated the Roman Senate; his office was essentially temporary and time-limited, deriving most of the legitimacy it may have had from a concern with the common good, not from its ties to particular noble families or divine authority.

By late republican times, however, the office of dictator had fallen into desuetude, and attempts to revive it changed its meaning substantially. The Roman general Sulla (138 BCE–78 BCE, dictator in 82 BCE), and then Julius Caesar (100 BCE–44 BCE, dictator 48 BCE), made it into something more threatening, less temporary and limited. These examples gave a bad name to dictatorship already in antiquity, though theorists later still occasionally used the term to refer to a temporary magistrate, accountable to some other body of people but not bound by normal procedures, and given the task of resolving an emergency situation (Schmitt, 2014 [1921]). With the fall of the Republic, the point of using 'dictatorship' to refer to a potentially tyrannical ruler was also lost; when speakers of many European languages wanted to refer to a bad monarch, they would use words derived from 'tyrant' or (later, in the eighteenth century), 'despot', which refer to a ruler who treats his subjects as slaves or uses power for his own private purposes rather than the common good (Figure 2.3). Such an understanding accepted the basic legitimacy of monarchy.

Nevertheless, the re-emergence of republicanism in the nineteenth century gave the word a new lease on life. In particular, the acute problems

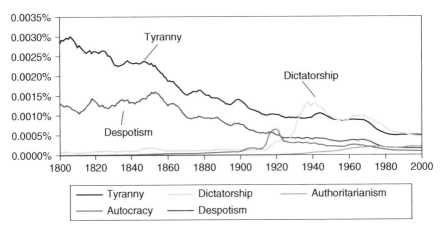

Figure 2.3 *Changing frequency of terms referring to non-democracy in the corpus of English books digitized by Google. Similar patterns can be observed in other European languages.*

faced by many of the new Latin American republics made 'dictatorship' useful in political struggles, justifying the assumption of supreme power 'to save the republic'. Indeed, the early rulers of many of these republics still occasionally took on the title of 'dictator' without embarrassment: Simón Bolívar was dictator three times during the wars of independence in the territories that eventually became Venezuela, Colombia, Ecuador, Bolivia, and Peru, and the first leader of independent Paraguay, José Gaspar Rodríguez de Francia, declared himself its 'perpetual dictator' in 1813, ruling the country until his death in 1840 (Przeworski, 2010, pp. 63–4).

Moreover, though the term 'dictator' eventually re-acquired a negative connotation (the example of Rome was ambiguous, especially if rulers showed any signs of wishing to remain in power forever), the idea that it is sometimes justifiable to disregard the constitution in order to 'save the republic' was extremely common in the many justifications for coups in the modern world. Indeed, the idea of a special magistrate who might need to rule without constraint in times of crisis still survives, by other names, in the many provisions for emergency powers of modern constitutions; and like their ancient equivalents, these provisions have been much abused. In Egypt, for example, constitutional rights were almost continuously suspended under such emergency rule provisions from the 1950s until shortly after the overthrow of Mubarak in 2012. The invocation of crisis situations to suspend the constitution, typically 'temporarily', remains one of the many tactics modern rulers have used to restrict political competition and secure their own position.

The positive connotation of the term 'dictatorship' also re-emerged for a time in the late nineteenth and early twentieth centuries in Marxist and fascist circles. For Marx, and later Lenin (Lenin, 1965 [1920]), the dictatorship of the proletariat was not the problematic rule of a single individual or group, but the power of the working class, organized to crush its enemies without the constraints of law. This usage still survives in the Chinese constitution, which speaks of the Chinese Communist Party leading the 'People's Democratic Dictatorship'. Yet in these cases dictatorship remains tied to democracy as a transitional phase towards a deeper, fuller democracy; indeed, it is even associated with the main organizational innovation of republican politics, the political party (see Chapter 5). Similarly, some early twentieth-century fascists spoke of 'dictatorship' in positive terms, drawing on its classical sense as a tool for resolving what they saw as great national crises (see the classic discussion in Schmitt, 2014 [1921]). Yet fascists also tended to accept that in the modern era political regimes must derive their legitimacy not from god or tradition, but from the people; and they, too, organized their politics around parties.

Ideas about dictatorship thus remained parasitic on 'republican' ideas about the sovereignty of the people, rather than providing an essentially different source of legitimacy for alternative ways of organizing politics. 'Dictatorship' came to signify an impairment of popular sovereignty, either temporary or permanent, and thus eventually became a catch-all term for all regimes that were not democratic. A similar story could be told about the term 'authoritarianism', which also became a catch-all term for referring to such regimes through the idea that non-democratic regimes abuse their authority (Márquez, 2014). In other words, we speak today of dictatorship and authoritarianism, rather than of tyranny or despotism, precisely because 'democratic' ideas about legitimate authority, and the republican institutions with which they became associated, have become dominant in the world today. But though republican institutions eventually became the norm, these can and have been adapted to restrict political competition in non-democratic ways all over the globe.

A Very Short History of Republican Institutions

In 1788, no country in the world guaranteed universal suffrage, and most had no tradition of suffrage at all. Most people could not vote, and voting was not generally recognized as something that needed to happen before rulers could rule; rulers could and did claim to have authority to rule on other grounds. No 'suffrage norm' (a norm that rulers must be elected) existed; norms of hereditary selection structured the symbolic universe in which political competition took place, and defined its ultimate boundaries for most people.

Yet by 2013 there were only four or five countries in the world that did not publicly acknowledge at least male voting rights for most major offices, and nearly 100 per cent of the world's population lived in countries that claimed to guarantee at least male suffrage, even if they did not hold elections or held only one-party meaningless 'elections'. Most strikingly, more than 75 per cent of the world's population lives today in countries that not only have universal suffrage, but hold elections with some competition, as we can see in Figures 2.4 and 2.5 (for a fuller story, see Przeworski, 2010).

Of course, the meaning of this new, emerging norm of universal suffrage varied with the context. The fact that all adults could vote in the Soviet Union or in Libya under Qaddafi had different political implications, and provided people with different options than the fact that all adults can vote today in New Zealand or Venezuela, as we shall see in Chapter 5. But few people now dispute the norm of universal suffrage, which was once new and terrifyingly radical. Large-scale class conflict over the scope and extent of the suffrage, with elites expressing great fears that if the lower classes were admitted to the suffrage, widespread expropriations would follow, was common in the nineteenth century, especially in Latin America (Przeworski, 2010). Overall, however, the tide slowly turned to favour the enfranchisement of non-elites everywhere.

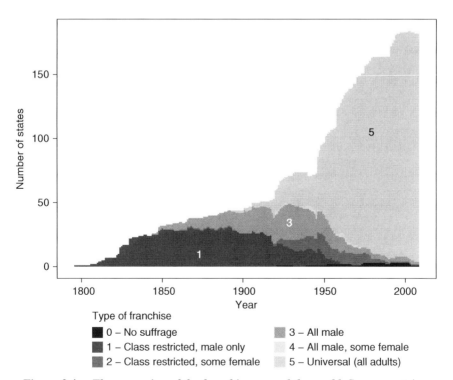

Figure 2.4   *The expansion of the franchise around the world. Some countries with franchise rules set at the sub-national level (for example, the USA in the nineteenth century) are excluded. Data from Przeworski (2013).*

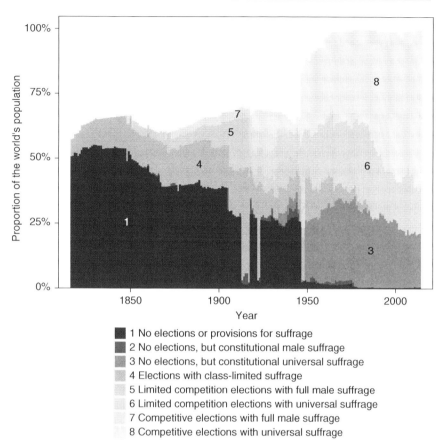

Figure 2.5   *Types of electoral regimes around the world. Data from Skaaning, Gerring, and Bartusevičius (2015), extending the PIPE dataset from Przeworski (2013). Population data from Gleditsch (2010).*

Widespread expropriations (or even large reductions in inequality) did not usually follow. The intuition powering the conflicts over the franchise was that democratic institutions with a larger franchise should be more redistributive than non-democratic institutions, or democratic institutions with a smaller franchise. But though the expansion of the suffrage did, at times, succeed in changing the balance of power between economic and political elites and poorer citizens, elites often learned to adapt to the new norms or capture the new institutions. (And those elites that did not adapt were sometimes swept away in great revolutionary upheavals.)

We shall explore these conflicts in more detail in Chapter 10. For the moment, we merely note that although neither the worst fears of opponents nor the greatest hopes of proponents of franchise expansions ever materialized, the quality of political competition did change. New symbols and rituals of power displaced old symbols and rituals; and new political tactics and justifications had to be invented and tested by trial and error.

Most importantly, as suffrage expanded, other institutions also changed. Not only were people given formal voting rights; they were increasingly selecting rulers with real authority. Over the course of the last two centuries, the number of *effective* rulers that came to power via election (however unfair) rather than by inheriting their position or being selected by a narrow group increased radically (Figure 2.6), as did the number of elected legislatures with real powers; almost all countries today have a legislature, and almost all such legislatures are staffed by elected representatives. The shift between the world of the eighteenth century, where politics was structured around norms of hereditary selection, and today's world, where politics everywhere is structured around electoral norms, is nearly complete.

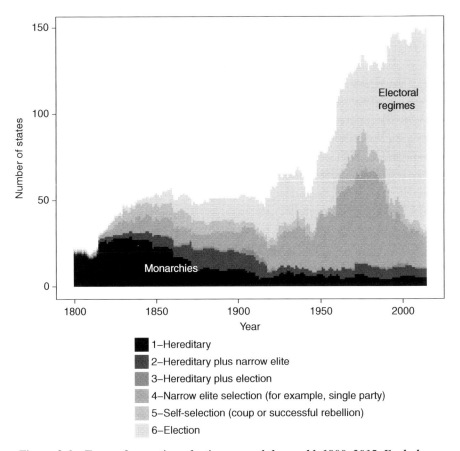

Figure 2.6   *Types of executive selection around the world, 1800–2015. Excludes transitional or anarchic periods and periods of foreign occupation, and countries with populations smaller than 500,000 people. Data from Polity IV project, Marshall, Gurr, and Jaggers (2010).*

To be sure, the shift towards electoral forms of ruler selection has been halting, and it has experienced many reverses. We would be hard-pressed to say that most early adopters of the suffrage norm – for example, Haiti in 1804, most Central and Latin American countries after their wars of independence, and so on – were or became especially democratic; the majority were plagued by coups, dictatorships, and other forms of civil strife for much of the nineteenth century. Indeed, the long-term trend towards democratic forms has not always been correlated with greater constraints on the use of executive power (see Figure 2.8); elected leaders claiming democratic legitimacy can of course be dictators. But ruling elites wishing not to lose elections had to adapt to these new realities; and as we shall see in the next section the twentieth century offered a number of opportunities to do so.

Waves of Democracy and Non-democracy

Democratization – understood as the emergence of genuinely competitive elections with wide suffrage that effectively regulate the competition for state power – has happened in distinct 'waves' since the nineteenth century (Huntington, 1993): a period from around the mid 1820s to the 1920s, from the mid 1940s to the early 1960s, and from the mid 1970s until the late 2000s (see Figure 2.7). Each of these waves represents periods when the number of transitions to political systems with competitive elections and widespread participation outnumbered the number of transitions to political systems without such features, thus increasing the number of democracies in the international system from zero at the beginning of the nineteenth century to around 106 today (depending on how one counts them).

This process has not been linear; as Huntington noted, from the 1920s to the end of the Second World War and from the early 1960s to the mid 1970s, there were two 'reverse waves' of de-democratization (periods where transitions to non-democracy outnumbered transitions to democracy), and some political scientists believe that a new wave of de-democratization or 'democratic backsliding' has begun in the last ten years (Puddington and Roylance, 2016).

Each of these waves and reverse waves has been driven by different processes and led to distinctive forms of democracy and non-democracy. During the first wave of democratization, which coincided with the first great decolonization – the independence of the USA from Britain and of most Latin American nations from Spain – the key processes involved the de-legitimation of monarchy by the great American and French revolutions and structural changes brought about by economic development (Huntington, 1993; Boix, 2011). (We shall say more about the latter

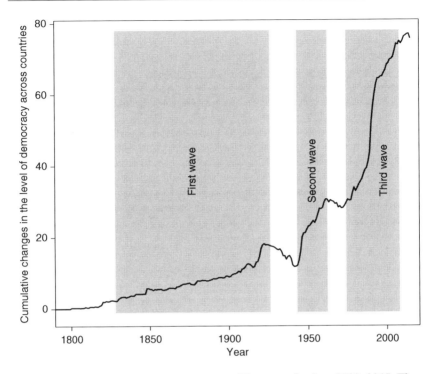

Figure 2.7   *Huntington's Three Waves of Democratization, 1800–2015. The exact beginning and end of each wave depends on how we measure transitions to democracy. Shaded areas indicate Huntington's own periodization of the waves of democracy. Data from Pemstein, Meserve, and Melton (2010), extended by the author into the nineteenth century (Márquez 2016a).*

process in Chapter 10). Purely political factors also played a role, such as the changes in the international system that came about due to the victory of the Western Allies in the First World War, which created a number of new national states from the remains of several empires.

The first wave of democratization also saw increasing alignment between types of executive selection, types of political competition, and degrees of executive constraint. While in the mid nineteenth century there was no great correlation between, for example, the degree to which the executive was constrained by formal norms or institutions and the degree to which political competition was conducted via electoral means, by the 1930s this relationship was much stronger as suffrage expanded and electoral institutions began to 'bite'. Political regimes polarized; they either selected constrained executives via open electoral competition, or they were ruled by unconstrained and unelected executives which suppressed political competition. Though this correlation declined a bit with the emergence of authoritarian and totalitarian regimes with significant electoral institutions during the first reverse wave of non-democracy, it never returned to nineteenth-century levels, and even increased slightly during the second wave of democratization.

Allied victory in the First World War severely undermined the remaining legitimacy of monarchy in Europe and led to the formation of many new democracies. But many of these democracies were soon discredited by the economic crisis of the Great Depression. The punitive treatment of the losers of the war (Germany especially) and the birth of the Soviet state, which seemed to many to provide an appealing alternative to squabbling oligarchical parliaments, also played a role. Thus, though the full story of what happened is complicated (see, for example, Paxton, 2006; Linz, 1978), crisis in Europe both de-legitimated multiparty democracy and increased support for the great totalitarian movements – Fascist and Communist – which claimed to represent a new way of acting on behalf of the people or the working class, and which were to cause so much pain in their name. The first reverse wave of non-democracy thus saw the emergence of the first totalitarian regimes (a story we will explore in more detail in Chapter 3), climaxing in the horrors of the Second World War.

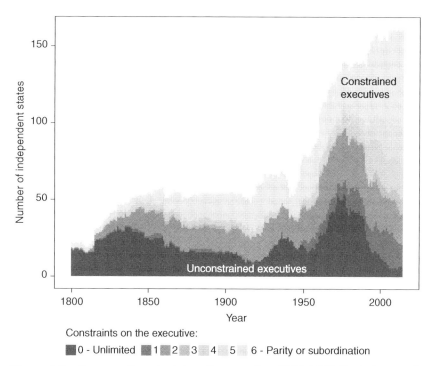

Figure 2.8   *Degrees of constraint on the executive, 1800–2015. Excludes transitional or anarchic periods and periods of foreign occupation, as well as countries with fewer than 500,000 people. Data from Polity IV project, Marshall, Gurr, and Jaggers (2010).*

Allied victory in the Second World War in turn discredited the Fascist (but not the Communist) alternative to democratic competition and installed a number of new democracies, the most important of them in Japan and West Germany. It also triggered a second decolonization period that led to the entry of many new states from Africa and Asia into the international system. Most of these states chose 'democratic' justifications of rule for their inaugural constitutions and held multiparty elections very early in their post-colonial history, though the single-party Soviet alternative to multiparty democracy had a great deal of prestige among many post-colonial elites. But when the geopolitical environment changed with the beginning of the Cold War, many of these democracies failed. Constitutions proved not to be very binding, and many elected leaders were able to monopolize power, or else were overthrown by ambitious challengers, in the highly uninstitutionalized environments of the immediate post-colonial period.

The dynamics of the Cold War led both superpowers to support regimes they could control, and to undermine those they found ideologically opposed. The Soviet Union thus supported and encouraged single-party regimes in its own image (like the East German regime), while the USA preferred military regimes with convincing anti-communist credentials (the Chilean military dictatorship of 1973, supported by the USA in its inception, is one classic example here). In practice this led to the suppression of political competition in a great number of new countries and to many opportunities for emergence of 'unconstrained' or 'personal' rulers (Figure 2.8), as well as to the emergence of a large number of military-led regimes (Figure 2.9). The second reverse wave was thus the heyday of the classic authoritarian dictatorships, taking power in the name of some emergency or another, and ruling with few constraints in a repressive manner (a story we will explore in more detail in Chapters 4 and 6).

Strikingly, however, the language of democracy and the norms of suffrage and election to power were not rejected during this time; they were merely reinterpreted, often in absurd ways. The Chilean dictator Pinochet, for example, claimed to be promoting a particular kind of 'authoritarian democracy' (Constable and Valenzuela, 1993, p. 71), the Franco regime in Spain the 1950s and 1960s insisted on its character as an 'organic democracy' (Payne, 1987, pp. 355, 401), and Trujillo referred to his brutal dictatorship in the Dominican Republic as a 'neodemocracy' (Wiarda, 1968, p. 116). Even as constitutions were often disregarded or suspended for the sake of some imagined emergency situation (an unconscious reversion to the ancient roots of dictatorship as emergency rule), the basic norms of republican life remained untouched, exercising a small but constant pressure on institutional change.

By the middle of the 1970s, these normative pressures, in conjunction with other changes, had begun to de-legitimate and undermine the

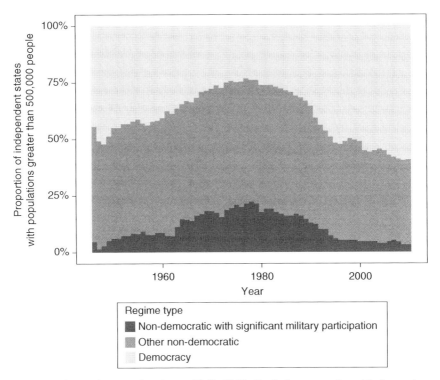

Figure 2.9   *Military-led regimes, 1945–2010. Excludes countries with fewer than 500,000 people (n = 150). Data from Geddes, Wright, and Frantz (2014).*

authoritarian regimes of the second reverse wave (Huntington, 1993). The rhetoric of democracy and human rights came back to bite many of these regimes after long periods of economic growth weakened their social bases and justifications for power. (Many military regimes, in particular, had taken power in the name of 'development', but development either had been achieved or had failed). Changes in the policies of influential national and transnational actors (such as the Catholic Church, the European Union (EU), and the USA) made it difficult for overtly authoritarian regimes to find external support. Finally, the 'demonstration' effects of successful democratization, as in Eastern Europe, pushed even more regimes to democratize. To these factors we might add the economic exhaustion of the Soviet model, which led to a search for new patrons and encouraged oppositions in many post-colonial contexts.

But though many nations did democratize during the 'third wave', many merely adopted the forms of democratic competition without the substance. And many of these new democracies have recently failed, or shown signs of becoming more authoritarian (Puddington and Roylance, 2016). History is not a one-way ratchet towards ever-greater democratic competition. Indeed, as we shall see in more detail in the next chapter, rulers and ruling elites in many of these countries soon learned to manipulate multiparty competition for their benefit. The third wave of democratization is thus also the competitive authoritarian moment.

Conclusion

Modern non-democracies do not claim to legitimate their authority in fundamentally different ways than modern democracies. With few monarchical exceptions, they claim at worst to be forms of emergency rule, transitional periods *en route* to more democratic societies. Accordingly, they have also learned to live with institutions associated with republican ideas, especially elections and parties – and even when they have eschewed these, they typically claim to have done so 'to save the republic', as the ancient Roman phrase had it. Modern non-democracies are thus recognizably 'dictatorships' in the classical sense of the term, even if they no longer refer to themselves as such.

Non-democracies have, however, changed over the past century in specific ways. Just as there have been three waves of democratization, we have seen that we can also identify three waves of non-democracy, or perhaps better three non-democratic moments: a totalitarian moment that promised to overcome multiparty democracy with something better, a dictatorial or authoritarian moment which presented itself as a transitional or emergency phase, and the current moment, in which non-democratic regimes are mostly content with mimicking democracy. In the next two chapters we analyse in more detail the specific characteristics of these forms of non-democracy, as well as their causes and consequences.

Chapter 3

The Struggle over Social Control: Totalitarian and Authoritarian Rule

Some of the most vivid images of dictatorship come from 'totalitarian' regimes: goose-stepping soldiers and gigantic mass rallies in Nazi Germany, extraordinary propaganda art from the Soviet Union or the Chinese Cultural revolution, the horrendous crimes of the Holocaust or Stalin's 'Great Terror'. Many other non-democratic regimes, by contrast, appear drab and boring; they may be repressive, even occasionally criminal, but they are often unexciting. Is there an important difference between the 'totalitarian' regimes that caused so much suffering in the twentieth century and the more ordinary 'authoritarian' regimes that populate the non-democratic bestiary? How should we understand this difference, and what accounts for it?

In this chapter, we shall see that the distinction between 'totalitarian' and merely 'authoritarian' regimes is rooted in the degree to which a single highly articulated ideological vision directs the activities of the state and destroys any space for alternative ideologies or interests. Totalitarian regimes are the outcomes of struggles over social control in which one group, the bearer of a single ideological vision, achieves (nearly) complete victory over all other independent groups and views. The ideological monism of the totalitarian state thus stands in sharp contrast to what Juan Linz called the 'limited pluralism' of the authoritarian state, where the winning groups cannot or will not achieve such total victory. After a description of the ideal type of totalitarianism, we shall thus also describe both the conditions that give rise to totalitarian and authoritarian regimes, and the different varieties of totalitarianism and authoritarianism social scientists have identified. We close the chapter with a discussion of the most common variety of authoritarianism today, the 'competitive' form.

Totalitarianism

The modern study of non-democratic rule emerged from the traumas of the Second World War. Scholars surveying the wreckage of political life during the 1930s and 1940s saw the Nazi and Stalinist dictatorships, in particular, as new phenomena in need of explanation. These two ideologically opposed regimes showed disturbing similarities: an unheard-of capacity for large-scale repression and terroristic control over their populations, highly ideological political projects, and enormous levels of political centralization. Taking their cue from Mussolini's description of his own regime in the Italy of the 1930s as 'totalitarian', several scholars (for example Arendt, 1973; Friedrich and Brzezinski, 1965 – both originally published in the 1950s) argued that these two regimes represented the most important examples of a genuinely new category of non-democratic rule: the totalitarian regime.

Though these scholars often disagreed about the specific criteria defining totalitarianism, they agreed that the key distinction between totalitarian and other non-democratic regimes lay in the ideological nature of their rule. Unlike other regimes, totalitarian regimes attempted to thoroughly control and transform society in pursuit of ideologically defined goals; the state was meant to be (even if, in practice, it was not always) *total*. Politics was meant to embrace all areas of life, yet no alternative political projects, or even any hint of disunity in pursuit of the typically utopian goals of the ideology, were to be tolerated. More formally, totalitarian regimes displayed a particularly toxic combination of three characteristics (adapted from Linz 2000 [1975], p. 70):

1. A single party 'and its dependent, affiliated organizations' control all social and political space. No genuinely independent groups are allowed to exist.
2. The actions of this party and its leaders are always justified by reference to 'an elaborate and often utopian ideology', whose interpretation is monopolized by the ruling group, and which constrains what can and cannot be said in almost every social setting.
3. Political participation through ideologically sanctioned channels is not merely encouraged, but required, since the ideology typically demands 'the total transformation of society' and even of human nature as such.

Totalitarianism properly speaking typically requires the triumph of a party deeply committed to an ideological project over all potential competitors in society, and thus it can also be analysed as a form of party rule (see Chapter 5). (It is possible for something like totalitarian domination to occur without or against a ruling party, as during the Chinese or Libyan 'cultural revolutions', but this seems to be very rare, for reasons we shall discuss shortly.) But, unlike most forms of party rule, it is characteristic of genuinely totalitarian regimes that even apparently non-political organizations are placed under the control of the ruling party. The ruling party is not just intolerant of alternative political organizations (all of which are banned or made wholly subservient to the ruling party in every totalitarian regime); it is intolerant of any independent form of social organization.

For example, soon after securing power in 1933, the Nazis embarked on a policy of 'co-ordination' that put enormous pressure on all independent organizations to become officially 'Nazified' or face dissolution, including singing clubs, shooting societies, all sports clubs, and local civic associations (Evans, 2004, Kindle loc. 7179–7199). All associational life had to be conducted in the name of Nazism, and under Nazi supervision. Similarly, during most of the life of the Soviet Union, the only organizations a person could join were controlled by the Communist Party, from youth leagues and sports clubs to labour unions. Soviet-influenced regimes sometimes even had 'political parties' governing in a 'united front' with the ruling party (for example, in East Germany, the ruling Socialist Unity Party was supposedly the senior partner in a coalition with the Christian Democratic Union, the Liberal Democratic Party, the Democratic Farmers' Party, and the National Democratic Party); but these parties were, in fact, always totally controlled and utterly dependent on the ruling party. Even purely economic enterprises tend to become subordinated to the party – most obviously through state control of the economy in the Soviet-inspired regimes, which involved the appointment of 'political commissars' in every enterprise, but also in Germany, where the autonomy of economic enterprises was eventually subordinated to Nazi war plans.

By the same token, however, to the extent that independent organizations could not be destroyed or made dependent on the totalitarian party, as the Church and the monarchy in Italy after Mussolini's Fascists came to power, projects for totalitarian control faltered. The resulting regimes could at best be characterized as 'authoritarian', even if (as in the Italian case) they insisted on describing themselves as totalitarian.

Totalitarian regimes do not merely espouse an ideology; they insist on politicizing all aspects of human life on the basis of this ideology, no matter how remote they may appear to be from politics. In genuinely totalitarian regimes, there is thus a 'politically correct' art, sport, science, music, and even cuisine, and people who produce 'politically incorrect' work in any of these domains (as determined by the ruling party) run sometimes quite severe risks of repression. For example, the Nazis insisted that there was such a thing as correct music (Wagner and Orff), painting (realist, vigorous, 'Germanic'), sculpture (manly and warlike, as in the works of Arno Breker), science (racist), and went to great lengths to ban 'degenerate' art (most of the work of the modernist artists in the Weimar era). The Soviets were equally insistent on the existence of a correct socialist culture and science. Soviet scientists in Stalin's time were even forced to reject modern genetics as 'bourgeois science' under the baneful influence of Trofim Lysenko. By contrast, most merely authoritarian regimes do not have ideologies elaborate enough to regulate every aspect of social life; as long as an activity is not directly threatening to the ruling elite, it is generally allowed to proceed.

Ideological commitments also lead totalitarian regimes to spend more resources than other regimes on propaganda and indoctrination. Indeed their popular image (shaped by such books as Orwell's *1984*) often stresses precisely this aspect of totalitarian life: newspapers are not merely censored, but forced to print only ideologically approved content; the airwaves transmit nothing but regime-approved programmes, and severe penalties may exist for circulating, listening to, or watching unapproved sources (as in North Korea today); and adults are occasionally forced to attend political indoctrination classes and self-criticism sessions where their adherence to regime values is monitored (as in many Soviet-influenced regimes).

Although all sorts of non-democratic regimes attempt to shape the information their citizens can see in order to thwart popular challenges, genuinely totalitarian regimes are interested in shaping the consciousness of their subjects far more than other regimes. Propaganda is conceived as a form of education into the values of the regime, and the education and socialization of children become topics of intense interest. For example, the Nazis not only re-oriented the school curriculum in accordance with their anti-Semitic ideology and anti-intellectual predilections (increasing the amount of physical education and decreasing the amount of 'formal learning' in schools), but they also created elite schools (the 'Adolf Hitler Schools', 'Order Castles', and 'National Political Educational Institutions') to shape a new generation of Nazi leaders (Evans, 2006, Kindle loc. 5412). Education in most Soviet-influenced regimes was also highly politicized, and promising party members were channelled into special party schools.

It is nevertheless easy to overstate the effectiveness of propaganda and indoctrination, as we shall see in more detail in Chapter 8; the reality of Nazi and Soviet propaganda often fell far short of the popular image of scarily effective brainwashing. Indoctrination and propaganda have often produced tedium and alienation rather than enthusiastic commitment, and education has never been the efficient machine for socialization it is sometimes portrayed to be, even in the most tightly controlled totalitarian regimes. Yet the combination of an all-encompassing ideological project and complete party penetration of society is the key to understanding how these political regimes can even aim at 'total control'.

If an ideology is elaborate enough, it can in principle be used to determine whether any given action, no matter how private, should or should not be allowed, or to justify any amount of repression in pursuit of the 'politically correct' action. And though the content of actual totalitarian ideologies varied – ranging from the highly coherent and intellectually demanding versions of Marxism that developed in the Communist dictatorships after the Russian Revolution of 1917 to the incoherent racist ramblings of Nazism – they were similarly all-encompassing in their intent.

The fact that Communist and Nazi ideologies had such different content has been used as a criticism of the coherence of the 'totalitarian' category (Kershaw, 1993). During the Cold War in particular some people argued against the 'false equivalence' implied by characterizing both the Nazis and the Soviets as equally totalitarian regimes. But though the differences in content had some obvious implications for the ways in which politics differed in these regimes, making possible different 'varieties' of totalitarian domination (Linz, 2000 [1975]), they do not imply that the category is meaningless.

But without a party – an organization of the committed – that reaches everywhere in society (down to the block level in every totalitarian regime, with party tentacles extending to every enterprise and social organization) and monopolizes the interpretation of the ideology, control can rarely if ever even aim to be total; autonomous spaces remain too large. This is one reason why highly ideological parties who seize control of the state do not always succeed in creating totalitarian regimes. As noted above, the Italian Fascists, who gleefully embraced the 'totalitarian' label, were constantly forced to compromise with social institutions that they could not control (Paxton, 2006), and some communist regimes (for example, in Poland, where the Church and, later, the labour union Solidarity were strong and independent) also failed to fully subordinate independent social forces to the ideological project of the regime. They remained merely authoritarian insofar as they did not achieve complete victory in the struggle for social control.

Totalitarian regimes properly speaking are incapable of leaving people alone. Not content with a demobilized and apathetic population, they demand constant proof of popular commitment to their ideological project by forcing ordinary people to participate in various public rituals of affirmation. Both the Nazi Party in Germany and the Communist Party of the Soviet Union insisted on holding plebiscites and elections they could not possibly lose, and spent a surprising amount of effort mobilizing people to vote. For example, in April 1938 the Nazis staged a plebiscite for union with Austria (the famous 'Anschluss'). The cause was genuinely popular on both sides of the border; a fair vote would have easily approved it. Yet in order to turn out the vote,

> Gangs of brownshirts toured every street at regular intervals, forcing people out of their homes and carting them off to the polling stations. The sick and bedridden were made to cast their votes at mobile polling stations that visited them at home. People who refused to vote, or threatened to vote 'no', were beaten up, forced to parade through the streets with a placard round their neck with words such as 'I am a traitor to the people', dragged round pubs to be shouted at and spat upon, or consigned unceremoniously to lunatic asylums. (Evans, 2006, Kindle loc. 2159)

But coerced participation in totalitarian regimes does not end on voting day. In most Communist countries from the Soviet Union to North

Korea today, participation in certain public rituals of regime affirmation (from parades to demonstrations and funerals) is expected and coercively encouraged in various ways which we will explore in Chapter 8; and the Nazi dictatorship was of course famous for its rallies at Nuremberg and other public extravaganzas. Even greetings became signals of commitment ('comrade' in the Soviet dictatorships, the 'heil Hitler' of the Nazis).

High levels of apparently enthusiastic popular mobilization for regime rituals give these regimes the appearance of popularity despite high levels of repressiveness. It is again easy to overstate their actual popularity; under repressive conditions, people do not always find it safe to disclose their true feelings, a phenomenon social scientists have called 'preference falsification' (Kuran, 1997). And, as we shall see in Chapter 8, fear can make people identify with a regime that they would not genuinely love under less terroristic conditions. But the appearance of popularity is not always false, for reasons ranging from the apparent 'charisma' of a leader to genuine ideological appeal, especially when the regime appears to be successful. The historian Ian Kershaw argued that 'few, if any, twentieth-century political leaders have enjoyed greater popularity among their own people than Hitler in the decade or so following his assumption of power on 30 January 1933' (Kershaw, 1987, 1), though he also noted that Hitler's popularity was in many ways purchased at the cost of the popularity of his own party (Kershaw, 1987, 83). Similarly, even at the height of the Great Terror Stalin appears to have been quite popular; there are even stories of people who suffered heart attacks on hearing of Stalin's death (Plamper, 2012, p. xiv). Some scholars have even *defined* totalitarian regimes as precisely those regimes which combine high levels of loyalty with high levels of repression, thus maximizing their power over their populations (Wintrobe 1990, pp. 58–68).

Unlike repression in many authoritarian regimes, however, totalitarian repression often targets people who are not actual threats to the regime, merely because the ideology identifies them as a 'category' of enemies, obstacles to the ideological project pursued by the ruling party: Jews in Germany, or 'class' enemies and their families in the Soviet Union (Getty, 2002) or North Korea today. The sources of repression are to be found not (just) in a tyrant's suspicion of opposition but in the regime's abstract ideological commitments. Indeed, the most 'terroristic' forms of repression in such regimes – the killing of the Jews, the mentally ill, Communists, Gypsies, and other groups in Nazi Germany; the Great Terror in the Soviet Union under Stalin in the 1930s; the systematic killing of intellectuals in Cambodia – were not merely cynically justified in the name of the ruling party's ideology, but (by and large) directed by people fanatically committed to it, even if in some cases (the purges of the Soviet Communist Party by Stalin) they also served to consolidate the dictator's position.

Perhaps not surprisingly, the greatest 'democides' and 'politicides' (mass murder conducted for political reasons) of the twentieth century were almost certainly committed by totalitarian regimes (Rummel, 1994; 1995b). As far as anyone can tell – and counting deaths from political action is by no means straightforward or uncontroversial – Communist Cambodia under the Khmer Rouge earns the dubious distinction of having been the most lethal regime of the twentieth century, having 'exterminated', according to estimates collated by Rudolph Rummel, about 31 per cent of its population in the four years it lasted (Rummel, 1994, p. 4). This is not to say that highly ideological regimes always engage in mass killing – the German Democratic Republic, for example, did not (Pfaff, 2001) – or that non-ideological regimes never do – many non-totalitarian regimes have committed democide and politicide (see Rummel, 1994, p. 4, for a useful list). But ideological projects, held with sufficient conviction by a party whose tentacles reach throughout society, have often facilitated terror and mass killings.

It should be clear from this brief discussion that fully totalitarian regimes are, mercifully, quite rare; few regimes meet the criteria Linz and other theorists of totalitarianism proposed. The vast majority of non-democratic regimes have not been totalitarian; and students of totalitarianism often found it necessary to distinguish between 'pre-' and 'post-' totalitarian phases even *within* supposedly totalitarian regimes, such as the Soviet Union. After all, total domination was not achieved in a day – it took time to overcome the resistance of independent social groups – and ideological domination had a tendency to decay into 'ritualized adherence to ideological formulae' while popular participation became purely 'formalized' (Linz, 2000 [1975], p. 252). Most non-democratic regimes have not aimed to occupy all social and political space with a single, highly elaborated ideological project, and they have often been content with a demobilized population. Even before the fall of the Soviet Union, most scholars of non-democratic regimes avoided the category, sometimes because of its associations with Cold War polemics (Linz, 2000 [1975], pp. 129–36). Instead, scholars focused on the broader category of 'authoritarian rule'.

Authoritarianism

Properly speaking, an 'authoritarian' system is a political system where the rulers routinely use their authority in illegitimate ways (Sartori, 1987; Márquez, 2014), for example by illegitimately appropriating public powers (Brooker, 2014). But the usage we shall be focusing on here contrasts mere authoritarianism with totalitarianism. According to Linz, authoritarian regimes are:

political systems with limited, not responsible, political pluralism, without elaborate and guiding ideology, but with distinctive mentalities, without extensive not intensive political mobilization, except at some points in their development, and in which a leader or occasionally a small group exercises power within formally ill-defined limits but actually quite predictable ones. (Linz, 2000 [1975], p. 159)

Authoritarian regimes, unlike totalitarian regimes, do not come about through struggles over social control resulting in the triumph of one ideology enforced by a single party. Instead, several distinct and independent groups come to have a share of political power and influence over political decisions, but there are more or less sharp limits on which interests can be represented and on which organizations can take part in the political process (unlike in democracies).

In a continuum ranging from zero pluralism (the totalitarian extreme) to maximal pluralism (the democratic extreme), authoritarian regimes can take many intermediate forms, depending on the particular circumstances that made it possible for political elites to limit pluralism and the particular ways in which they managed political competition among themselves. Among these, Linz described a veritable bestiary of political institutions, including 'bureaucratic-military' regimes (for example, the regimes in Brazil and Argentina in the late 1960s and early 1970s, first described in O'Donnell (1973)); corporativist 'organic statist' regimes (for example, the Portuguese dictatorship of Salazar); 'mobilizational post-democratic' regimes (fascist but non-totalitarian regimes); 'postindependence mobilizational regimes' (like the Tanganyika African National Union (TANU) regime led by Nyerere in post-independence Tanzania); 'racial democracies' (for example, Apartheid South Africa); 'defective and pre-totalitarian' regimes (like the early Franco regime in post-civil war Spain); and 'post-totalitarian' regimes (for example, the Soviet Union after Stalin) – all of which sometimes blended into one another, producing many hybrid forms (Linz, 2000 [1975], pp. 173–4).

These categories were not deduced theoretically by Linz, but were inductively derived from close analysis of the politics of many countries. Linz paid special attention to the circumstances under which ruling coalitions formed, the social and political consequences of particular alliances, and the institutions created to manage interest competition within the authoritarian coalition. Bureaucratic-authoritarian regimes, for example, emerged from alliances of professional militaries with the bureaucratic apparatus for the purpose of 'modernizing' a country after a coup, while post-independence mobilizational regimes typically emerged from the decolonization struggles of many African countries and developed into single-party regimes which, however, could not become totalitarian due to the vagueness of nationalist ideology and the heterogeneity of the groups fighting for independence. This set of categories was thus not easily oper-ationalized for the purposes of quantitative research; they were guides for analysis requiring concrete knowledge of social conditions in particular countries, not ready-made labels that could be easily applied to particular cases, and they were certainly not simple institutional distinctions.

Nevertheless, authoritarian regimes can be understood generally as 'cartels' of distinct but mutually dependent groups that prefer to limit political competition despite many differences in values or preferred poli-cies. These authoritarian coalitions may be united only by vague commit-ments to 'defending order, modernizing the nation, overthrowing a corrupt regime or rejecting foreign influences' (Linz, 2000 [1975], p. 173), while differing over the specific mechanisms for achieving these objectives. As Linz saw, the ideological vagueness of authoritarian regimes was not incidental; on the contrary, it was the result of efforts to hold diverse groups together in a coalition. Moreover, in such circumstances, 'the lack of an assertion of specific, articulated, and specific commitments facilitates adaptation to changing conditions', especially when the external environ-ment was hostile, and allowed ruling coalitions 'to neutralize opponents, co-opt a variety of supporters, and decide policies pragmatically' (Linz, 2000 [1975], p. 164). The ideological pronouncements of such regimes are thus frequently inauthentic and imitative, borrowed from the dominant ideas of the time and the region. For example, though the Franco regime in Spain used the symbols and language of fascism during the 1930s, such mimicry did not denote a deep commitment to fascist ideology, as the Falange – the fascist party that formed part of Franco's coalition – would find out to its great chagrin when the implementation of its ideological programme was first postponed and eventually abandoned (Payne, 1987).

The Franco regime in Spain from 1939 until 1974 illustrates well other aspects of authoritarian rule (Linz, 1976 [1964]). The regime had its roots in a military coup against the Republican government that turned into a brutal civil war lasting from 1936 to 1939, thanks in great part to the highly polarized circumstances of Spanish society at the time. Eventu-ally the forces led by Francisco Franco triumphed; but these forces were not themselves tightly unified ideologically. Though the military played the predominant role in the winning coalition, Fascists (the Falange), tra-ditionalist monarchists, and other conservative Catholics, also played a role. And they all had very different views concerning the major political issues of the time: the restoration of the monarchy, the desirability of pop-ular mobilization, wealth redistribution, the role of the Church, and so on (Payne, 1987). Franco proved a skilful manipulator of this coalition, even-tually transforming what had begun as a regime dominated by the military into a highly personalistic dictatorship. Indeed, his success resulted in part from his ability to *refrain* from commitment and thus definitively alienate any of the members of his coalition.

One might think that Franco's lack of ideological commitment and apparent penchant for procrastination would have been bad for his regime; but, as sociologists Padgett and Ansell (1993) have argued, vagueness, procrastination, and ambiguity are especially useful tactics for the management of ideologically heterogeneous coalitions. A successful leader in these circumstances is often better off postponing commitments that can alienate core supporters, being everything to everybody as far as possible, and generally being the 'hub' of the coalition – the point through which all interests must be articulated. If they are skilful, such leaders can often acquire significant powers.

By the same token, the lack of specific ideological commitments limits the appeal of these regimes for those groups of people who make ideas their business, or who for some other sociological reason have a need to find meaning in politics; without a clear ideology, as Linz notes, they have a limited 'capacity to mobilize people to create the psychological and emotional identification of the masses with the regime' and little appeal for 'intellectuals, students, youth, and deeply religious persons' (Linz 2000 [1975], p. 164). The totalitarian leaders, by contrast, were anything but vague, even if they changed their views often, and their regimes had often surprising appeal to intellectuals. Intellectually influential people such as the jurist Carl Schmitt and the philosopher Martin Heidegger were card-carrying Nazis, and a large number of well-known thinkers, from Sartre to Althusser, remained faithful to the Soviet project even after the worst excesses of Stalinism had become widely known.

Ideological vagueness in authoritarian regimes is nevertheless not a mistake, but a rational response to the trade-offs involved in mobilizing a supporting coalition. Insisting on the specificity of an ideological system may encourage more committed activists (fascists, communists, and so on) but it also intensifies conflicts within an already heterogeneous coalition, whereas vague symbolic commitments can maintain a larger coalition but decrease the degree to which the coalition members can coordinate on specific actions. Vagueness thus 'works' as a policy to hold together a diverse coalition when members believe that their goals cannot be achieved 'outside the tent' but also believe that they have a chance to push specific policies in their favoured direction. The first belief is strengthened when rival coalitions are deeply mistrusted (for example, the left and the right after the Spanish Civil War); the second when coalition members have long-term projects (perhaps themselves vague) rather than one-off specific demands.

In these circumstances, the problem for coalition leaders is that the moment specific actions are actually undertaken, members learn information about the chances of their preferred outcomes actually happening, threatening the unity of the coalition. Leaders interested in political survival thus have an incentive to procrastinate and act in ambiguous ways (as Franco did), so long as they do not have the resources to definitively resolve ideological conflicts in their favour. By contrast, when leaders expect to win such conflicts (as in totalitarian regimes), or when coalition members come to see that their chances of achieving their deeper objectives are as good outside the tent as inside, vagueness loses value: either the leader demands commitment to specific programmes or vague symbols fail to keep coalition members in line.

Their lack of clear ideological commitments also accounts for the fact that authoritarian regimes typically prefer not to mobilize the population to any great degree, except in exceptional circumstances; they would much rather have apathetic but acquiescent populations to ideologically committed ones. Franco is not atypical here; save for a brief period of time in the late 1930s and early 1940s when the fascist elements of the regime seemed dominant, and fascism was globally ascendant, he preferred that the population retreat to private life, and allowed for a certain degree of autonomy to many groups so long as they did not engage in overtly political activities or otherwise threatened the regime. The regime was not (for the most part) interested in a highly politicized populace; and though it was highly repressive, especially in the first few years after the end of the civil war, it typically attempted to target only specific opponents of the regime, not ideologically determined categories of enemies.

The Franco regime was both authoritarian and 'personalistic'; devoid of genuine ideological commitments, but ultimately dominated by a single person who rose to the top by manipulating the conflicts of a diverse coalition. We will discuss the idea of a 'personalistic' regime in more detail in Chapter 4; for the moment we only note that authoritarian regimes need not be personalistic. In many such regimes it is not easy to find a single figure that is utterly dominant, and in fact sometimes we find formal institutions that allow for interest representation of the members of the ruling coalition and prevent a single person from acquiring absolute power, as in the Brazilian military regime of the 1970s and 1980s, with its controlled parliament and rotation in power of the military candidates for president.

The methods through which authoritarian regimes manage interest representation and allow some pluralism in the competition for power and influence are various. For example, though the Franco regime was highly personalist, international and domestic pressure eventually led Franco to introduce 'corporatist' institutions of interest representation – based on occupational groups rather than on universal suffrage – which both expressed the pluralism of the regime and yet tightly limited any competition for power. But elections with universal suffrage are now one of the key mechanisms by which most modern authoritarian regimes manage their limited pluralism; and many such regimes have prospered by learning to manage limited forms of multiparty competition, though to the extent that they intentionally limit the degree to which interests and ideas can be articulated and influence the direction of state policy, they remain authoritarian. Such regimes have been called by many names: hybrid regimes, competitive authoritarian regimes, managed democracies, and so on. We shall explore these electoral authoritarian regimes in more detail in the next section.

Competitive Authoritarianism

As we have already noted, most authoritarian regimes after the third wave of democratization do not look very different from democracies. Political parties of many ideological stripes compete, often fiercely, for the presidency of a country or seats in its legislature. Elections take place at regular intervals, and the vast majority of adults are able to vote in them. The media provide a colourful display of opinion, fact, and entertainment, including the occasional, titillating corruption scandal. The constitution and other important legal documents claim to protect civil liberties, including basic rights of assembly, expression, religious freedom, and the like, and street protest, dissent, and other forms of political expression are not hard to find.

Yet something is not quite right; a closer look makes us uneasy about describing the patterns of political competition we observe in many parts of the world today as 'democratic', even if we are also unwilling to call these regimes 'dictatorships' – with all that the term connotes. In places such as Zimbabwe, Russia, Romania, Armenia, Georgia, Ghana, Guyana, Venezuela, and many other countries, elections may be bitterly contested – opposition figures may occasionally win them and come to hold political office in the legislature or at the subnational level, but they compete against incumbents in a playing field that is neither free nor fair. Incumbents may persecute or harass their opposition by legal or illegal means, intimidate or buy the media, pack supposedly 'independent' judicial institutions with their supporters, use state resources without restraint for campaign purposes, and even occasionally steal elections in an effort to secure their position.

Consider a few quick examples. In Ukraine in the 1990s, 'businesses that financed the opposition were routinely targeted by tax authorities' and in Ghana similarly 'entrepreneurs who financed opposition parties "were blacklisted, denied government contracts, and [had] their businesses openly sabotaged"'. In Taiwan, the ruling Kuomintang (KMT) used to outspend its opponents 50–1 in elections during the 1990s, and in Russia the Yeltsin campaign spent 'between 30 and 150 times the amount permitted the opposition in 1996'. In the Peru of Alberto Fujimori, private television stations 'signed "contracts" with the state intelligence service in which they received up to $1.5 million a month in exchange for limiting coverage of opposition parties' (all quotes from

Levitsky and Way, 2010, pp. 10–11). Selective prosecution of political opponents is common in Russia; with local variations, the tactic can be found elsewhere, from Malaysia, where Anwar Ibrahim, a former finance minister, was prosecuted for sodomy when he began to express opposition to the ruling party, to Singapore, which has perfected the art of the libel suit against critics of government policy (Mauzy and Milne, 2002, ch. 10). Such libel and defamation suits are the tool of choice for shutting down critical forms of media; according to Levitsky and Way, in the 1990s newspapers in Croatia were sued for libel more than 230 times; in Cameroon at around the same time the use of defamation suits forced the closure of several newspapers. Sometimes media restrictions even get a decent veneer of justification, as when the Chávez government in Venezuela refused to renew the 'over the air' licence of RCTV, an opposition-leaning TV station, in 2007, for having supported the coup against his government in 2002.

All of these actions are of course made easier if the government takes care to pack supposedly impartial or independent institutions (constitutional courts, electoral commissions, and so on) with government supporters. In Venezuela today, for example, most members of the Supreme Court and the electoral commission make no secret of their allegiance to the Chavista government; even after the opposition won a supermajority in the national assembly in 2015, the Supreme Court brazenly nullified most of their legal initiatives (Hawkins, 2016). In some cases, onerous registration or eligibility requirements for political parties or candidates prevent opposition groupings from effectively contesting elections; for example, despite being one of the most popular organized political forces in Egypt since the 1950s, the Muslim Brotherhood could not register as a political party, due to regulations banning religiously based parties (Blaydes, 2010, p. 40), and in Iran candidates are scrutinized by the 'Council of Guardians' for fidelity to the principles of the Islamic revolution before they can contest elections.

Finally, there are the more obvious tactics to suppress political competition, to be used when all else fails: voter intimidation and beatings and imprisonment of opposition members by security forces (as in Zimbabwe under Mugabe, where activists from the opposition Movement for Democratic Change (MDC) were key targets in waves of repression during the 2002 and 2008 elections); attempted murder of political opponents (as in Ukraine in 2005, where Viktor Yushchenko, the popular challenger, was apparently poisoned in an attempt to prevent him from contesting the election); old-fashioned ballot box stuffing (in Egypt, people used to say that 'they never had to vote because the government did it for them' (see Salah and Mayyasi, 2013)); and vote falsification of varying degrees of sophistication, as in Ukraine in the 2005 election, or in Serbia under Slobodan Milosevic. To put the difference in stark terms, incumbents in many of these countries often seem to be able to (literally) get away with murder in their quest to hold on to the state, unlike incumbents in countries conventionally thought to be democratic.

All of these regimes are pluralistic in that many different ideological groupings are able to compete for control of, and influence over, the state. Moreover, they manage their pluralism by means of multiparty elections, rather than through factional competition within a single party or through corporative systems of group representation. Yet they are *authoritarian* in Linz's sense of the word, insofar as their pluralism is limited either by making electoral victory deliberately impossible for some groups, or by otherwise insulating the most important offices of the state from the reach of electoral competition.

Let us step back for a moment from the dazzling variety of tactics governments can use to disadvantage their electoral opponents and think more carefully about how elections might fail to be fully democratic while still retaining some degree of genuine competition. (Nobody today thinks of single-party 'elections' in North Korea as a genuine sign of democracy or political competition, though they do pose questions that are worth discussing; more on these electoral rituals in Chapter 5). Begin with the 'standard' account of democratic elections, which we discussed in Chapter 1: at some more or less set interval, an election is held, in which multiple parties compete for votes. These parties – groups of people voluntarily bound together by common interests, ideology, or identity – can easily form without arbitrary or onerous interference from the current holders of executive power; and they have reasonable opportunities to make their case to a broad electorate, within the constraints given by the basic costs of attracting the attention of people who may not be especially interested in politics. Impartially enforced regulations attempt to level the playing field among parties, ameliorating to some extent the ability of some groups to leverage economic power into political power; and reasonable vote-counting rules determine the main groups who can negotiate over a share of state power, the 'winners' of the election.

Importantly, no party or organization can unilaterally change the rules regulating electoral competition to favour itself or to prevent other parties from winning. Parties who emerge victorious thus gain a share of state power; and their use of this power cannot be arbitrarily negated by unelected bodies that control the state but do not need to compete in the election. In this idealized picture, elections therefore serve as the means by which a population *selects* the people who can make use of state power (or supervise those who do), keeps these people *accountable* by the threat of selecting other parties at the next periodic interval, and produces more or less *representative* government, that is, government that is presumed to act in ways that reflect the interests and values of major groups in the population. Authoritarian systems with multiparty elections may depart from this idealized model of democratic competition in at least one (but sometimes more than one) of three ways.

First, multiparty elections may not alter who controls the state, because the state is controlled by groups who do not need to compete in elections. In this case, elections may be reasonably free and fair affairs involving a multiplicity of groups, but their results do not directly change the composition of the group that controls the levers of state power, even if they influence policy in some ways. The most obvious examples of this situation are countries where a monarch has ultimate power over the policies and personnel of the state, despite the existence of an elected parliament, as in Jordan today; but there are other examples of unelected organizations whose ultimate control over the state coexists with lively electoral competition.

Post-revolutionary Iran, for example, developed a political system in which ultimate decision-making power is vested in the 'Leader of the Islamic Revolution' (today, Supreme Leader Ali Khamenei), who in turn controls various independent organizations and economic resources that make him in fact supreme over the elected part of the government. This system did not develop all at once, and there has been, and continues to be, a great deal of struggle between the unelected and the elected branches of the government (Brownlee, 2007a); but over time the 'deep state' (controlled primarily by clerics) has achieved supremacy over the 'elected state' (controlled mostly by lay politicians). Thus, though the elected president of Iran has a great deal of influence on policy and controls real resources of his own, he can always be overruled by the Supreme Leader. At the end of the day, the results of electoral competition in Iran cannot dislodge the group that ultimately controls the state (up to and including the Supreme Leader), because popular elections simply do not serve to select the personnel of these offices, and elected politicians do not have sufficient power to overrule or supervise them. Levitsky and Way (2010, p. 14) call regimes like the Iranian one 'tutelary regimes', where 'elections are competitive but the power of elected governments is constrained by nonelected religious …, military …, or monarchic … authorities'.

Second, multiparty, competitive elections may occur in contexts where major social groups are disenfranchised, either because they cannot vote, as was the case for black and coloured citizens in South Africa during the Apartheid period, or because major parties representing them are banned, as in Argentina from 1957 to 1976, when the Peronist party, the most popular in the country, was outlawed but electoral competition was allowed. Levitsky and Way (2010, p. 14) call these regimes 'constitutional oligarchies' and 'restricted or semi-competitive democracies', respectively. In these contexts, elections do determine who controls the state, but the resulting governments are (by design) incompletely representative.

Finally, multiparty elections may occur in contexts where the incumbent party can unilaterally manipulate or disregard the formal rules and informal norms regulating electoral competition so as to make it very hard for opposition parties to win elections, regardless of their underlying popularity (Magaloni, 2006, pp. 35–6). In these regimes, the incumbent party can leverage its power – through supermajorities in legislatures, disproportionate influence over the media, control of state resources, and so on – into a nearly impregnable electoral position. And though opposition parties may still be able to influence policy to a greater or lesser extent, they are very unlikely to be able to seize control of the state through electoral means alone.

These regimes are the most common and widely studied authoritarian regimes with multiparty competition; notable examples are Mexico under the PRI from 1929 until at least 1994, when an electoral reform restored some independence from the PRI to the Federal Electoral Institute, the body in charge of administering Mexican elections (Magaloni, 2006, p. 38); Zimbabwe under Robert Mugabe and the ZANU-PF Party; Singapore under the People's Action Party from 1959 until today; post-Soviet Russia; and Egypt from the introduction of multiparty competition under president Anwar Sadat in 1977 until the fall of president Hosni Mubarak in 2012. Levitsky and Way (2010, p. 14) call these regimes 'competitive authoritarian' regimes (so long as there is some opportunity for the opposition to gain a genuine share of state power through electoral means – Levitsky and Way prefer to speak of simply authoritarian regimes in many cases where multiparty elections exist, because they do not think such elections are always meaningful); Magaloni (2006) calls them 'hegemonic party autocracies', or simply 'multiparty autocracies'.

These regimes differ from basically democratic polities such as Japan under the long dominance of the Liberal-Democratic Party (LDP) or India under the Congress Party from independence until 1977. In these cases, we have highly dominant parties that were nevertheless unable to unilaterally manipulate electoral and other rules to ensure their maintenance in power. Their maintenance in power is to be attributed, not to institutional manipulation, but to some combination of genuine popularity and clever yet mostly 'constitutional' politicking. By contrast, competitive authoritarian regimes, though unable or unwilling to completely suppress or control all organized electoral opposition, remain in power at least in part by manipulating the rules regulating electoral competition.

The three 'failure modes' of multiparty elections just described are not mutually exclusive. It is possible for multiparty electoral competition to be unable to alter control of (much of) the state, and simultaneously for some parties or candidates to be excluded; and these restrictions on political competition can in turn coexist with abusive behaviour by the incumbent party. Restrictions on political competition can 'pile up', as they did in the 2009 presidential election in Iran, which combined a powerful deep state that could not be dislodged solely by electoral means, the disqualification of 'liberal' candidates by the Council of Guardians, and abusive electoral behaviour by the incumbent government of President Mahmoud Ahmadinejad, including credible allegations of fraud (Sahliyeh, 2010; Kamrava, 2010). But in general, the abuse of incumbent advantage is the most common form of competitive authoritarianism today, and there is considerable evidence that authoritarian regimes that hold reasonably competitive multiparty elections are more lasting than authoritarian regimes that do not, and this 'duration advantage' has increased since the end of the cold war (Kendall-Taylor and Frantz, 2015). How did this form of authoritarianism emerge?

Origins of Competitive Authoritarianism

As we saw in the previous chapter, the heyday of authoritarian and totalitarian regimes without any kind of multiparty electoral competition was during the Cold War, when the Soviet Union and the United States struggled for global influence, and dictators on both sides could count on the support of a superpower. With the collapse of the Soviet Union, the single-party model of autocracy lost much of its appeal, especially in poorer, aid-dependent countries. And the loss of Soviet patronage created conditions under which many previously closed regimes were put under increased pressure to show conformity to norms of multiparty competition. This was true not only of Soviet-allied regimes, but also of American-affiliated autocratic regimes (such as the military dictatorship of Pinochet in Chile, or the kleptocratic regime of Mobutu in Zaire), whose 'excesses' could no longer be simply justified in the name of providing a bulwark against communism.

Not all of these regimes introduced multiparty competition as a result of the end of the Cold War – Cuba and North Korea are two obvious exceptions – but most experienced crises that led to political changes (see Box 3.1). Depending on factors including the strength of the ruling group and the coherence of the state, as well as the degree of internal and external pressure for democratization, some of these regimes democratized (for example, the military dictatorship of Pinochet), some eventually collapsed (for example, Zaire – now the Democratic Republic of Congo – after 1997), some became more or less stable multiparty authoritarian regimes, and only a few hung on as closed authoritarian regimes.

Scholars differ about which regimes should be considered true multiparty authoritarian regimes, which should be considered full democracies,

Box 3.1   How did Cuba and North Korea survive after the end of the Cold War?

In Cuba, the loss of subsidies and preferential trade agreements with the Soviet Union led to what Cubans call the 'special period' (a time of scarcity and forced economic reform). More drastically, the loss of Soviet subsidies in North Korea contributed to the great famine of 1993–94, which in turn triggered a process of 'marketization from below' (Haggard and Noland, 2012) and ultimately weakened the state's control over individuals. But both regimes eventually found ways of restoring some of the lost Soviet patronage: Cuba turned to Venezuela, flush with oil money in the early 2000s, and North Korea turned to China, which had by then become an economic success story and was interested in preventing the collapse of the Kim Jong Il regime. Had they not been able to find such patronage, they may well have experienced some form of regime change.

and which should be described using some other terminology, but we can get a general idea of the magnitude of the change the end of the Cold War produced by taking a look at the variation in restrictions on multiparty competition since the Second World War among a large sample of non-democratic regimes (Figure 3.1).

Before 1990, the majority of non-democratic regimes either banned parties outright, or allowed only a single official party to exist; only around 30 per cent of all non-democratic regimes had multiple parties in the late 1970s and early 1980s, according to the data presented by Svolik (2012). Afterwards, most of these non-democratic regimes either transitioned to some form of democratic competition, or allowed for multiparty competition without democratizing fully; today, more than 70 per cent of all authoritarian regimes allow for multiparty elections.

These multiparty elections were not all introduced at the same time or in response to the same pressures, of course. In some cases, multiparty elections were introduced after the collapse of a previous regime, as in Russia and the Eastern European countries where single-party Communist regimes fell apart suddenly under popular pressure. In other cases, a single-party regime introduced multiparty elections voluntarily in order to manage international demands or tamp down domestic pressures, as in Egypt in the late 1970s (Blaydes, 2010). Some authoritarian regimes had long used multiparty elections for reasons that predate the end of the Cold War, as in South Africa (where the conflict between the white minority and the black and coloured majority shaped exclusive political institutions during the Apartheid period) or Iran (where the 1979 revolution created a hybrid system, mentioned above, including both competitive elections and strict limits on competitors). And many 'new' multiparty authoritarian regimes emerged after the end of the Cold War through the abuse of existing democratic

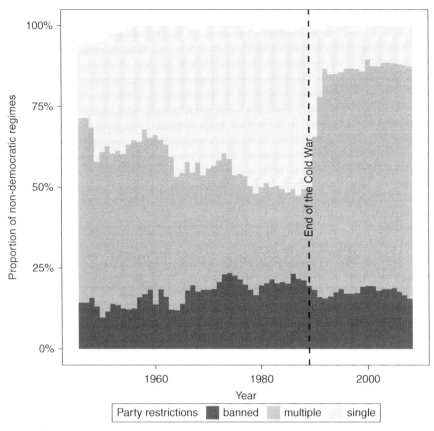

Figure 3.1 *Restrictions on party competition in a large sample of non-democratic regimes in the post-Second World War era. (Excludes countries with fewer than 500,000 people.) Svolik counts 'united fronts' as single parties when the parties involved are not genuinely independent, as in China and the German Democratic Republic (GDR), where ruling Communist parties supposedly rule (or ruled, in the case of the GDR) in a 'united front' with other parties. (Data from Svolik (2012); the bars do not reach to the top of the figure because for some cases in the dataset there is no information).*

institutions by incumbents; in fact, while new authoritarian regimes typically emerged through coups in the immediate post-Second World War period, the vast majority of them (some 85 per cent) have emerged through incumbent takeovers of formerly democratic regimes, which have typically left in place 'democratic-seeming' institutions like multiparty elections but co-opted them for their own purposes (Kendall-Taylor and Frantz, 2015).

The reason why many authoritarian regimes did not democratize despite allowing for multiparty competition has much to do with the advantages incumbents can derive from shaping the 'rules of the game' to their benefit in weakly institutionalized contexts. This is especially easy when single-party regimes decide to introduce multiparty elections from a position of strength, as was the case in Sadat's Egypt, where they helped strengthen, not weaken, the regime (Blaydes, 2010; Brownlee, 2007a). But even when regimes collapse suddenly and apparently completely, multiparty competition often favours former ruling parties. Dictators are sometimes surprisingly easy to overthrow; deep power structures are typically very difficult to change.

Consider the example of Romania, which we will revisit in later chapters. The regime of the hated dictator Nicolae Ceauşescu suddenly collapsed over four days in December in 1989, during the great wave of Eastern European anti-communist revolutions of that year; Ceauşescu himself was shot on 25 December after a hasty trial. The regime had been so repressive, however, that no organized opposition existed; genuine dissidents could be counted on the fingers of one hand, and civil society groups were basically non-existent. In the power vacuum that emerged in the aftermath of the regime's sudden collapse, an ad hoc coalition of regime opponents called the National Salvation Front (NSF), including well-known dissidents and people who had participated in the revolt, took power with a mandate to transition away from Communism. Yet this group was quickly 'captured by ex-Communist officials' (Levitsky and Way, 2010, p. 98) who had no commitment to genuine democracy, even though most of them had been marginalized by Ceauşescu, but who *did* have control over the organizational assets of the Romanian Communist Party, the only organization that reached deep into the Romanian countryside (Tismaneanu, 1993). Other parties also quickly formed, but the NSF's organizational advantages and control of the state (including the hated Securitate, the Romanian secret police, which the NSF decided not to dismantle) made it difficult for them to compete on a level playing field.

Thus, when multiparty elections first took place in 1990, the NSF candidate for president won 85 per cent of the vote, aided by a rhetoric that successfully connected with the population's fears about a quick transition from Communism, as well as their ability to abuse state resources, harass opposition, mobilize voters in remote areas of the country, and manipulate the media. Unsurprisingly, opposition forces had difficulty making their message known to the population, especially in the countryside, and they were mercilessly slandered as the agents of foreign forces by state TV (Tismaneanu, 1993).

The Romanian story has a relatively happy ending. Romania's dependence on the EU and the prospect of integration made routine violations of democratic norms costly for the regime, not only at election time, but also in between elections; as Levitsky and Way (2010) argue, Romania was more susceptible to Western influence than many similar countries. Despite some problems, the 1992 elections were fairer than the 1990 elections, and (perhaps more importantly) deprived the governing party of a majority in the parliament, which made it harder for them to manipulate electoral norms. And later elections were even fairer, to the point that today Romania is a member of the EU and is widely considered a democracy. There is positive feedback here: constraints (in part externally imposed) on the power of the NSF and its successor parties to manipulate the rules of political competition led to fairer competition over time.

The more general point is that regimes that are forced to use multiparty elections for whatever reason have often run real (if sometimes small) risks of losing them, or at least of triggering large popular mobilizations if they are seen to break the norms of electoral competition too obviously (Tucker, 2007), as happened in the so-called 'Colour Revolutions' in Serbia (2000), Georgia (2003), Ukraine (2005), and Kyrgyzstan (2006), all of which led to the fall from power of the government (Beissinger, 2007). But yielding power in the face of popular pressure is not sufficient to make such regimes democratize, as the first group to control the state afterwards can reap increasing rewards from this control, making it increasingly difficult for the opposition to have a chance at power. Indeed, this is perhaps the more likely outcome: power breeds power, as money breeds money.

More interesting cases are those initially democratic regimes that become more authoritarian over time without ever abandoning multiparty elections. In such cases, we often find a great deal of controversy over whether the particular country is or remains democratic, as any changes leading away from open political competition are often small and justifiable taken one by one, and incumbents can and do point out that they are elected in reasonably competitive elections when their democratic credentials are questioned. The case of Venezuela, which we have briefly mentioned earlier in this chapter, is especially interesting in this regard, as opinion – both popular and scholarly (Ellner, 2010; Corrales and Penfold, 2010; Hawkins, 2016) – is sharply divided over whether Venezuela is a democracy, and (if not) when it ceased to be one. Moreover, Venezuelan politics presents features that suggest both a move towards a less inclusive, more restricted form of political competition *and* simultaneously towards more inclusive forms of political engagement (see Box 3.2). (For a fuller discussion, see the online materials included with this book.) The key point is that political competition in Venezuela became more difficult for some groups due not to international influences, however, but to the dynamics of its highly polarized internal conflict.

Box 3.2 Venezuelan politics in the Chávez era

Venezuela's political history over the past 15 years has been profoundly shaped by the breakdown of the relatively democratic two-party system that emerged after the overthrow of military dictator Marcos Pérez Jiménez in 1958. (It is worth noting that even the question of how democratic the post-Pérez Jiménez '4th republic' was is fiercely disputed in Venezuela. Chavistas often argue that the system was scarcely democratic, even though it was characterized by elections that were free of fraud). More than fifteen years of economic crisis associated with declining oil prices led to failed coups in 1992 that brought the charismatic military leader Hugo Chávez to public attention. After a brief period of imprisonment for his participation in one of these coups, Chávez entered electoral politics as an 'outsider' candidate, and buoyed by his appeal to the poorest Venezuelans, convincingly won election in 1999.

The traditional parties were crushed, and Chávez and his supporters immediately set out to remake Venezuelan institutions in what they claimed was a more participatory and democratic direction. Among other things, Chavistas produced a new constitution that included more opportunities for the use of referenda, and over time they added new participatory institutions, such as communal councils, and new social programmes that helped decrease inequality and increase the income of many poor citizens. Nevertheless, Chávez's fierce rhetoric and some of his actions (which included increasing the length of the presidential term and making immediate re-election possible, packing important institutions with his supporters, and constantly compelling private radio and TV stations to carry his often very long messages) raised fears among a broad swathe of Venezuela's upper and middle classes about the direction of the country.

Public opinion was quickly polarized, and things came to a head in 2002, when a short-lived coup briefly removed Chávez from power by taking advantage of violent incidents after huge anti-Chávez protests. A strike at the state oil company and a boycott of legislative elections followed. Chavistas drew the lesson that they needed fuller control over the military and the media to achieve the objectives of the 'socialist revolution', and set out to do both. By 2009, buoyed by increasing oil prices and new social programmes, the Chávez regime had won many more elections (including a recall referendum), while increasing its control over the military and state institutions (through means that included imprisoning one judge who acted contrary to Chávez's wishes) and slowly reducing the number and reach of genuine opposition media by a combination of means (including the creation of government-allied community radio and TV, the use of threats to deny licences or other resources to opposition media, the political rationing of scarce newsprint to some publications, and the outright purchase of hostile media through obscure shell companies controlled by government supporters). And while the opposition had been marginalized within formal institutions to the point that many members of the opposition no longer believed a fair electoral contest was possible, the Chavista regime consistently pointed to the 2002 coup as evidence of the opposition's anti-democratic nature and to its social programmes, election wins, and 'participatory' institutions as evidence of its democratic credentials.

Today, more than three years after the death of Chávez from cancer in early 2013, the controversy over Venezuela's democracy persists. Despite the fact that the Venezuelan opposition won a big victory in legislative elections in late 2015, most scholars agree that Venezuelan political competition no longer works in the way that political competition in liberal democracies works; the barriers to political competition placed on the opposition are large, even if the Chavista regime remains popular among some sectors of the population, as the systematic disempowering of the new legislative assembly shows. Indeed, the regime is often cited as an example of a competitive authoritarian system, where elections matter, an opposition exists, and opposition media can be found, but the opposition is unlikely to achieve power by electoral means alone.

Conclusion

Non-democratic regimes vary in the degree to which a single, highly articulated ideological view dominates the state. At one extreme, we find the ideological monomania of totalitarian regimes; at the other, we find regimes that are almost democratic in the extent to which they allow electoral political competition. With the exception of North Korea and perhaps Eritrea, most totalitarian regimes have mercifully disappeared today; most non-democratic regimes are authoritarian, rather than totalitarian, falling in the middle of the continuum between the total lack of pluralism of totalitarianism and the wide pluralism of democracies. Their ruling elites cannot or will not completely eliminate independent groups and the views they represent; they do not hold highly articulated ideological views; and they prefer populations to be demobilized, or to be mobilized only in very particular ways.

These authoritarian regimes attempt to manage the competition for power and influence among different groups within their supporting coalition through various means, ranging from factional competition within single parties to 'corporatist' institutions of group representation to multiparty elections. Since the end of the Cold War, however, multiparty elections have emerged as the means of choice for managing this pluralism. 'Competitive authoritarian' regimes, though not altogether new, have thus become the most common form that authoritarianism takes today, originating in part from international pressures to provide credible signals of democratization, and in part from incumbent takeovers of democratic systems.

Chapter 4

Personal Rule

Political regimes differ not only in the degree to which they enable the representation of a variety of views and interests; they also differ in the degree to which any particular individual – the ruler – has power. In particular, some non-democratic regimes, though perhaps repressive and odious, act according to public norms and make their leaders accountable to other elites, as in East Germany from 1949 to 1990, or in China after the death of Mao; in others, leaders are at best constrained by the de facto armed resistance of other people, and are free to act on their every whim, no matter how bizarre, as in the regime of Mobutu Sese Seko in Zaire (1965-97), or François Duvalier in Haiti (1957-71). Power in the latter regimes is *personalized*: concentrated in a single person, and exercised in ways inconsistent with publicly recognized norms.

Though the personalization of power is not a danger unique to non-democratic regimes – scholars sometimes speak of 'delegative democracies' (O'Donnell, 1992) to refer to democratic regimes where executive power is highly concentrated – it is more common in such regimes, for reasons we shall explore in this chapter. At any rate, whenever power becomes highly personalized in a democracy, political competition tends to break down; delegative democracies often cross the line into 'competitive authoritarianism'. And the excessive concentration of power in a single person is what most people mean by 'dictatorship'.

This chapter examines the many forms of 'personal rule'. I begin by contrasting 'personal' rule with 'institutionally constrained' rule, showing how these two ideal types can be understood in terms of the principal-agent relationship obtaining between a ruler and the organizations through which he exercises power in society. I then discuss the typical process by which power becomes personalized, stressing the ways in which rulers can exploit the advantages of their position to accumulate power at the expense of other members of the ruling elite, and consider the factors that lead to different outcomes in this struggle over power-sharing, ranging from consolidated personal rule to institutionally constrained rule.

The chapter then moves on to consider the distinction between regimes that display a high concentration of power in the hands of single individuals ('personal' dictatorships) and regimes where the exercise of power happens primarily via personal relationships of patronage ('patrimonial' or 'neo-patrimonial' dictatorships). Though these two forms of 'personalism' often go together, as we shall see, since personal power typically depends on some form of patronage, they are not quite the same thing

(Svolik, 2012; Guliyev, 2011). The chapter closes by examining how personal rulers typically manage such patronage relationships, and considers the factors that sometimes enable them to remain in power despite horrendous economic and social costs.

Personal Rule vs. Institutionally Constrained Rule

The most colourful and morbidly entertaining images of non-democratic rule come from people who have achieved complete personal power. 'Personal rulers' are the original 'crazy dictators' – the men (and it has nearly always been men) – who have succeeded in escaping the constraints of norms or institutions, and who are thus able to subject state policy to their whims. These are the men who can get away with holding farcical 'elections' that make them presidents for life; who can treat the state as their personal patrimony; and whose personal eccentricities or prejudices are magnified by the possession of apparently unlimited power. Consider just a few examples:

1. Hastings Kamuzu Banda, self-appointed 'president for life' of Malawi in the 1970s and 1980s, once boasted: 'Anything I say is law. Literally law' (Jackson and Rosberg, 1982, p. 166, citing Philip Short's biography). He not only monopolized the naming and firing of every significant official in the country, but took over many important ministerial portfolios himself, saying in 1972: 'Nothing is not my business in this country ... Everything is my business. Everything' (Jackson and Rosberg, 1982, p. 165). And he made it clear that he was not bound by ordinary legal decisions, reserving to himself the right to modify the decisions of the courts at will, or to take the property of anyone he thought a 'subversive'.
2. Idi Amin Dada, the criminal ruler of Uganda from 1971 until overthrown by a Tanzanian invasion in 1979, bestowed on himself not only the title of President for Life, but also 'Lord of All the Beasts of the Earth and Fishes of the Seas and Conqueror of the British Empire in Africa in General and Uganda in Particular', and claimed to be 'the uncrowned King of Scotland'. During his time in office, all administration broke down in Uganda, its Asian community was dispossessed and expelled from the country, and more than 100,000 people of all ethnic groups were killed (Decalo, 1985).
3. Muammar Qaddafi, ruler of Libya from 1969 until overthrown by rebels with help from NATO forces in 2011, did not technically have an official position in the regime (he was merely the 'Brother Leader of the Revolution'). Yet his every pronouncement, no matter how seemingly absurd, had a way of turning into policy:

[In 1977] the Libyan leader suggested that in order to achieve self-sufficiency every Libyan family had to raise chickens in the home. The cages and birds were imported and, for an obligatory fee of fifty-seven Libyan dinars ($150 at the 1977 exchange rate), were distributed by the government to Libyans. To many city dwellers in small apartments raising chickens in their kitchens was a difficult if not impossible affair. The result was that many ate the birds and found other uses for the cages.

... General Qaddafi's declaration that Libya must achieve food self-sufficiency was justification enough for his aid[e]s to institute that controversial plan of raising chickens in the home. The Libyan leader found the idea novel enough to encourage its implementation. On another occasion the General commented on the high cost of new automobiles. Soon after, the government agency entrusted with importing and selling cars to the public began to import only used cars and ironically sold them at new car prices. The policy was reversed only after a great number of people complained. He remarked about the proliferation of Western musical instruments in the country. The result was the gathering and burning of musical instruments. While driving through an area in the suburbs of the city [of] Benghazi he wondered whether the area would be suitable for agriculture. Within a month all residential buildings in that area were demolished. (El-Kikhia, 1997, p. 106)

As these examples indicate, 'personal rule' is first of all a form of rule where one person rules unconstrained by specific norms and institutions (Jackson and Rosberg, 1982). Personal rulers are not necessarily all-powerful, but their power is constrained only by the de facto power of other people, rather than by more or less impersonal rules, norms, or customs. To the extent that constitutional or legal rules exist that pretend to constrain the ruler, they are either blatantly disregarded or can be changed at will to suit his purposes. Indeed, forms of personal rule are often marked by a striking disjunction between a sometimes imposing façade of 'formal' rules and the utter disregard for these rules in practice (see Box 4.1 for a good example from the Dominican Republic).

Personal rule thus stands in contrast to 'institutionally constrained' rule, in which the ruler is accountable to some body of people, such as an army, a party, or a dynastic clan, who can constrain his actions in accordance with some set of formal or implicit norms. In institutionally constrained systems of non-democratic rule, presidents or general secretaries retire at the end of their legal terms; need to consult with other powerful individuals before making major policy changes; and in general cannot simply make policy on their own. For example, under the PRI in Mexico, presidents succeeded each other with regularity every six years, naming their successors at the end of their

---

Box 4.1   Constitutional parodies

The personal ruler of the Dominican Republic from 1930 to 1961, Rafael Trujillo, was not always the 'official' President – sometimes he would have his
brother Hector, or some sycophantic crony, like his friends Jacinto Peynado
Reinoso or Joaquín Balaguer, elected to the office – but he was always its ruler,
continuing to attend to all government business from his home office while his
puppet presidents merely signed documents or endured the most boring ceremonial duties of the presidency (Wiarda, 1968, p. 74). No Dominican citizen
was confused by these arrangements; everybody knew that the 'real' head of
state was always Trujillo, and indeed the press barely bothered to mention the
existence of the 'official' president while Trujillo was technically not in office.
And though Trujillo prided himself on always sticking to the letter of the constitution, he not only controlled its interpretation through his power over the
Supreme Court, but could change it at will when its reinterpretation would have
been too cumbersome; the Dominican Republic had four constitutions during
his tenure. Though on paper these constitutions, modelled on the American
system, with its elaborate checks and balances, always appeared to constrain
the presidency, in practice the system was aptly described by Jesús de Galíndez
as a 'constitutional parody' (Galíndez 1956, pp. 99, 189; incidentally, Galíndez
was murdered by Trujillo for publishing this book).

---

terms (Magaloni, 2006). Similarly, in China, after Deng Xiaoping's death in
1997, formal rules and implicit understandings came to effectively limit the
terms of General Secretaries of the Communist Party of China (CPC), and
even during his lifetime party bodies met regularly to make policy, in contrast to the situation during Mao's lifetime, who could not be forced to retire
and did not need to consult with any of his colleagues before launching major
campaigns (Teiwes, 2001). And the Brazilian military had strictly enforced
rules for rotation in power between 1964 and 1985 that prevented any specific individual from accumulating too much power (Skidmore, 1988).

We can think of the relationship between a ruler and various institutions
which may be able to constrain his actions in terms of what economists
call 'principal-agent' relationships (Brooker, 2014, pp. 63–66). In institutionally constrained systems of rule, the ruler is the agent, and some other
organization is the principal, which 'uses' the ruler to achieve its own goals.
Agents (rulers) may cheat and attempt to act in their own interests, but the
organization can still hold them to account in a reasonably effective way.
In 'personal' systems of rule, by contrast, the ruler is the principal, and the
organization is the agent; the ruler 'uses' the organization to achieve his
goals, rather than vice versa. A fully institutionalized system of rule prevents the ruler from misappropriating the power of the organization, as the
Al Saud family has ensured with regards to the Saudi King (see Chapter 7),
or the Chinese Communist Party Politburo has done with regards to the
General Secretary of the Party since the death of Deng Xiaoping.

By the same token, a system of rule becomes personalized when rulers succeed in inverting the principal-agent relationship between them and their 'launching organization' – the organization that brought them to power, be it an army or a party or a dynastic clan (Haber 2006). Stalin did this in the Soviet Union during the late 1920s and early 1930s (Svolik, 2012), Mao achieved this in China after 1958 (Teiwes, 2001), and Pinochet managed a similar feat in Chile by 1978, when he forced General Leigh out of the ruling military Junta (Constable and Valenzuela, 1993, pp. 68–69). Personal rule and institutionally constrained rule form a continuum, of course: particular rulers are more or less able to escape the constraints of the organizational structures that brought them to power or through which they rule. But it is worth stressing that, in this sense, personal power does not exclude the existence of effective institutions; it only means that power is exercised *through* those institutions by a ruler, rather than *by* the institution and its members.

The Personalization of Power

Generally speaking, the sorts of political competition that result in personal, concentrated power are *unregulated* by formal institutions. Leaders acquire or lose power not because of constitutional provisions or laws, but by skilfully managing *personal* relationships with other people. It is thus not surprising that extensive 'personalization' of power has been found often (but not only) in post-colonial contexts (such as Africa's new states in the 1950s and 1960s), in which the norms regulating the competition for power were still in a state of flux, constitutions had not been tested, and colonial institutions had at best dubious acceptance (Figure 4.1).

The process by which power is concentrated in the hands of a single person usually follows a basic script. A new regime comes to power – perhaps through a coup, a popular uprising, the death of a previous personal ruler, or even a democratic election – in which several people play important roles, but one person has some important advantage over his colleagues – perhaps he has control over appointments to key bodies, or has great personal prestige that can be exploited to mobilize the masses, or can control the flow of information, or is simply more cunning and ruthless than they are. In the poorly institutionalized context of the new regime (especially if the norms of political competition have just been broken), this person may be tempted to seize more power for himself (not always for purely selfish reasons; they may sincerely believe that they know better how to best promote the revolutionary cause or the national interest), while his colleagues would prefer to prevent this from happening. This is what Svolik calls the 'problem of authoritarian power-sharing' (Svolik, 2012, ch. 3).

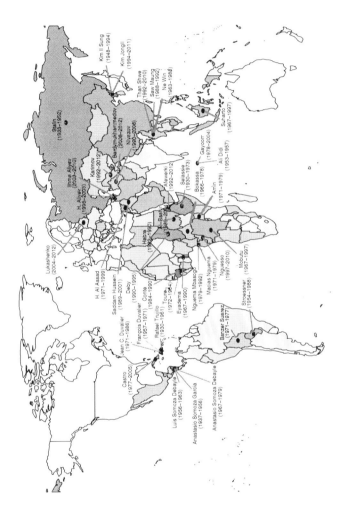

Figure 4.1 *Personal rule around the world, 1900–2012. The darker shading represents those countries that have experienced more personal rule in this period. Illustrative leaders were in the top 5 per cent of personal power according to the index used here. Years in the label represent the years of maximum personal power, not necessarily the years of the ruler's tenure. This index of personal power is constructed from a latent variable analysis of the following sources: the V-dem indexes of legislative and judicial constraints on the executive and of executive corruption (Coppedege et al., 2015); Polity IV's measure of executive constraints (Marshall, Gurr, and Jaggers 2010); Geddes, Wright, and Frantz's (2014) indicator of personalism; Kailitz's (2013) indicator of personalism; Magaloni, Chu, and Min's (2013) experimental measure of personalism; and Wahman, Teorell, and Hadenius's (2013) measure of mean executive turnover in non-democratic regimes.*

The specific advantage exploited to personalize power varies from case to case. For example, Stalin controlled the organizational apparatus of the Communist Party of the Soviet Union (CPSU) at Lenin's death in 1924, but he was not especially charismatic, nor did he have great personal prestige everywhere in the party. Similarly, Pinochet had more control over the information necessary to the policy-making process than his colleagues, and could use his position as head of the army to also manage the promotions process and ensure his loyalists always occupied key posts, though he had little charisma. By contrast, Mao had immense prestige in China after the People's Liberation Army triumphed in 1949, and could exploit this prestige to mobilize the masses outside the communist party (and even against the party), despite the fact that other people controlled the 'formal' offices of the state. Qaddafi, similarly, could use his personal charisma and authority to mobilize groups outside formal state structures, so that he remained in power even though he lacked formal position within the regime (Pargeter, 2012). Whatever the advantage, if a leader decides to press it to concentrate power, the only way that he may be stopped by his colleagues is if they can credibly threaten to depose him, a risky course of action. (Some of the leader's colleagues may wish to grab power for themselves, or expect benefits from betraying plotters; conspiracy in the absence of regulatory norms of political competition always involves existential risks.)

Moreover, any individual power grab by the leader may look justifiable – for example, Pinochet demanding to be made President by the junta as a way to achieve legitimacy for the regime or demanding Leigh's resignation in order to preserve the unity of the junta, Franco being made Generalissimo to ensure the continuing flow of aid to the rebel side during the Spanish Civil war (see Constable and Valenzuela, 1993; Preston, 1995) – but over time, they may accumulate to make a revolt extremely unlikely to succeed. Former peers may be reduced to abject dependence, and sometimes even purged or killed after humiliating trials, as the ruler comes to control more and more resources. For example, Stalin went from one among many powerful individuals at the top of the CPSU, who on occasion had to apologize to his colleagues for rudeness, to the master of their fates; more than half of all politburo members were killed during his time in office, including formerly powerful potentates such as Trotsky, Zinoviev, Kamenev, and Bukharin (Svolik, 2012, p. 54). At some point, then, a revolt by the leader's peers may simply be impossible, and known to be so; the personal ruler has then 'consolidated' his power, and can expect to die in his bed, or at worst to be overthrown only by exceptional events like a foreign invasion or an unlikely popular uprising (Svolik, 2012, p. 63).

In this high-stakes game, the leader's colleagues may nevertheless sometimes succeed in working together to enforce emerging norms of power-sharing, creating more or less formal institutions that facilitate their ability to monitor a leader's power-grabs or to punish him if he attempts them. These institutions may include unambiguous constitutions limiting terms in office or enforceable requirements for consultation through regular meetings of party politburos or military juntas. For example, after the death of Mao Zedong in 1976, the victorious faction in the struggle for the succession (led by Deng Xiaoping) sponsored reforms to the party constitution intended to eliminate the possibility of one individual accumulating too much power. These reforms eliminated the position of Party Chairman; imposed formal term limits on the presidency of the People's Republic of China (PRC) and informal expectations of retirement from the post of General Secretary and Chairman of the Central Military Commission after ten years; and revived formal mechanisms of consultation that had gone into disuse during Mao's long tenure in power (Svolik, 2012, pp. 91–2).

But institutional control does not emerge merely from the existence of some document stating that the president is term-limited or that he must consult with appropriate party bodies; rather, it emerges from the willingness of influential elites to 'bandwagon' against power-grabbing insiders. When Jiang Zemin dragged his feet on giving up the offices of General Secretary and Chairman of the Central Military Commission in 2002 (for which there were no formal term limits, only informal expectations), enough influential party members protested that he eventually gave up these offices (the last one by 2004); if they had not done so, he might have got away with violating these informal expectations, and thus grabbing a little bit of power from his successor, Hu Jintao. And though, as Svolik (2012, p. 94) notes, clear, unambiguous statements of term limitations or consultation requirements can be useful in facilitating such bandwagoning (by, for example, clearly signalling when the leader has violated power-sharing norms and expectations), they are not enough to make them stick, due to the way in which personal power is normally exercised. Indeed, today in China Xi Jinping appears to be reversing this process, accumulating much greater power for himself than his predecessor did.

Power-sharing and Leader Exit in Non-democracies

Whenever the competition for power is ultimately uninstitutionalized ('personalized'), it always occurs 'in the shadow of violence' (Svolik, 2012, p. 2). In such circumstances, rulers typically worry about coups, plots, and other forms of 'political instability' much more than when power is not so personalized, precisely because they cannot count on other people respecting their right to hold on to an office. Conversely, it is a good sign that power is personalized when coups and coup plots are common, since such events indicate precisely that norms regulating political competition have no force. In these circumstances, issues of succession also loom large, since even if a ruler has conclusively defeated his rivals, his successor cannot count on particular norms or institutions to ensure a smooth transition (Jackson and Rosberg, 1982, pp. 58–73). Wherever power is personalized leaders of all kinds are accordingly more vulnerable to 'irregular' ouster than those in democratic regimes; indeed, very few leaders with great personal power leave office in a regular manner (Figure 4.2).

Non-democratic politics in general tends to be more personalized than democratic politics. (The correlation between indicators of personal

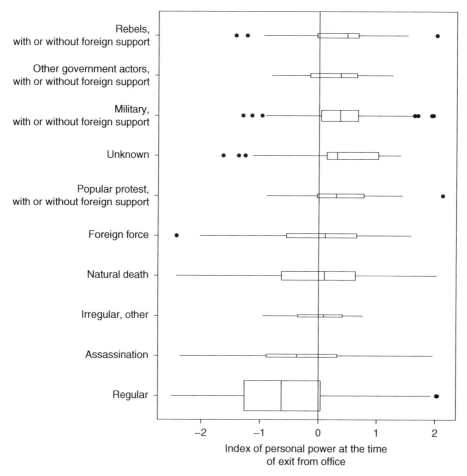

Figure 4.2 *Manner of exit for all political leaders, 1871–2014, by their degree of personal power. (The index of personal power comes from a latent variable analysis of diverse indicators of personal power; higher values indicate rule is more personalized. Note that this measure is highly uncertain for years before 1900. See previous figure for details of its construction. Leader data from the Archigos dataset of Goemans, Gleditsch, and Chiozza (2009), updated to 2014.)*

power and indexes of democracy is around 0.8.) The difference is especially evident in the manner in which leaders in different regimes leave office; while few democratic leaders lose office in an unregulated or unconstitutional manner, a conservative estimate suggests that nearly half (and perhaps up to 60 per cent; see Figure 4.3) of all non-democratic leaders have lost power in an unregulated manner in the post-Second World War period.

Whether or not a non-democratic leader is deposed by a coup or leaves office in some other way depends on the outcomes of the power-sharing conflict described in the previous section. Leaders who have succeeded in consolidating power tend to lose it either by natural death or by the action of actors external to the elite, such as by popular revolution or foreign intervention. After 42 years in power, Qaddafi lost power by the combination of popular revolt and North Atlantic Treaty Organization (NATO) intervention; without the latter, he might still be in power (Chorin, 2012). Similarly, Mobutu Sese Seko was overthrown by the military activities of the Rwandan-supported Alliance of Democratic Forces for the Liberation of Congo-Zaire (ADFL), led by Laurent Kabila. In both cases, regime 'insiders' played little role in their ouster, and in the Qaddafi case many insiders fought to the bitter end, a sure sign that he had in fact succeeded in fully consolidating power.

Though no personal ruler is ever completely safe from overthrow by regime insiders, Figure 4.2 indicates that leaders who are least restrained by any elites are more likely to die in their beds of old age than leaders who are more restrained. And there is substantial evidence that when power is both highly personalized and highly concentrated leaders are extremely unlikely to be forced out of power except by outsider-led revolts (Snyder, 1992; Brownlee, 2002); only around 5 per cent of all non-democratic leader exits (Figure 4.3) occur via mass revolts or armed insurrection, and most of these – for example, against Marcos in the Philippines or Qaddafi in Libya – occur in regimes where power is both personalized and concentrated.

It is also possible, indeed common, that a leader may be unable to consolidate power, and that conflict among insiders remains chronic. Short tenures and frequent coups d'état by insiders, as in Iraq before the rise of Saddam Hussein or in Syria before the rise of Hafez al-Assad, are typically the result. In fact, as Figure 4.3 indicates, by far the most common way in which non-democratic leaders lose power is through a coup; nearly a third of all non-democratic leaders in the 1946–2013 period lost power at the hands of elites supported by the military, and the majority of these coups were led either by other regime insiders, or by military personnel not associated with any opposition figures; only a tiny minority of all coups d'état (less than 20 per cent) are clearly led by opposition ('outsider') figures who somehow manage to enlist the support of the armed forces. Moreover, the vast majority of these coups occur within a few years of a leader's seizure of power, before they can accumulate sufficient power. In such regimes power remains *personalized* (since it is not regulated by public rules) but not *concentrated* in any particular person; they lack institutionalized mechanisms for resolving elite conflicts, and they may not be able to fully control society, unlike some highly personalized regimes.

As we have noted, a third outcome, where an authoritarian elite succeeds in institutionalizing rules regulating the competition for power, is also possible, as in modern-day China or PRI-era Mexico. As we see in Figure 4.3, some non-democratic leaders do lose power via regularized succession procedures. Yet this outcome is surprisingly uncommon; Svolik's data suggests that only about 10 per cent of all non-democratic leaders either stepped down due to term limits or elite consensus (a sure

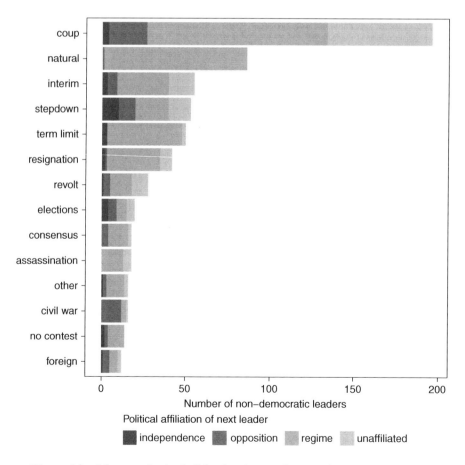

Figure 4.3   *Manner of exit of all leaders in non-democratic regimes, 1946–2008, and political affiliation of successor. Data from Svolik, 2012.*

sign of institutionalization), another 7.5 per cent stepped down for other reasons, and about 2.5 per cent were defeated in elections. Indeed, even apparently institutionalized non-democratic regimes remain vulnerable to ambitious insiders, though less so than non-institutionalized regimes.

Personal Power and the Structure of the Ruling Elite

Whether struggles over power-sharing among insiders end in one or another of the outcomes discussed in the previous section depends on many factors, including such idiosyncratic considerations as the personalities and characters of the people involved, the specific tactics deployed by them, and unexpected events that give the advantage to one or another side. Nevertheless, some influential theoretical models (Bueno de Mesquita et al., 2001; Bueno de Mesquita et al., 2003) suggest that two structural features of this struggle are especially important for whether or not power tends to become personalized in a political system: (1) the size of the insider group, what Bueno de Mesquita and colleagues (2003) call the 'winning coalition' and Svolik (2012) calls the 'ruling coalition'; and (2) the kind of people who can be *recruited* into this ruling coalition, what Bueno de Mesquita and colleagues (2003) call the 'selectorate'.

The winning or ruling coalition comprises the people whose support and loyalty is *essential* to retain control of the state, and who (if they act in concert) can easily overthrow a particular ruler. These are typically the people who control key offices of the state and the army, or large and important economic resources, and who have regular access to the leader (see also Gerring et al., 2013). By contrast, the selectorate comprises the set of people who can be *selected* as members of this ruling coalition by means of meritocratic promotion, personal connections, ascriptive characteristics, or anything else, and who in turn play some role in *selecting* the leadership of the state.

Exactly how to draw the boundaries between these groups in particular cases is a complicated question without a satisfactory theoretical answer (Gallagher and Hanson, 2015). For one thing, both the ruling coalition and the selectorate change over time as a result of the goals pursued by top leaders, the intended or unintended consequences of their struggles, and various other institutional features of society. Leaders who are committed only to personal enrichment, for example, may require a much smaller 'winning coalition' to retain control over the state than leaders who are committed to larger ideological projects. And the *effective* size of the selectorate ultimately depends on the *criteria for recruitment* into the winning coalition (which Bueno de Mesquita and colleagues (2003) model, imperfectly, as 'affinity'); not every member of a potential selectorate is immediately eligible to become minister of defence, for example, whatever their loyalties. But for our purposes a rough conceptualization of these groups is sufficient. For example, the key people in Gaddhafi's Libya (the Libyan winning or ruling coalition) were a very small group (perhaps no more than a hundred people; see El-Kikhia, 1997 and Brahimi, 2011) drawn primarily from his immediate family, childhood friends and RCC comrades, and members of the Gadhafa, Warfalla, and Megaraha tribes. Similarly, the ruling coalition in China is comprised of members of the Central Committee of the CPC, senior army officials, and some others, all of whom are drawn from the general membership of the party.

The key point of Bueno de Mesquita and colleagues' argument is that the kind and extent of the resources needed to ensure the loyalty of the people who are *essential* to hold control of the state vary according to whether they can be easily replaced by others. Leaders need to expend resources to secure the loyalty of a coalition to control the state. To the extent that members of the winning coalition can be *excluded* from these benefits effectively, they will tend to be more loyal to the leader. And the leader's ability to exclude them from benefits increases with the size of the effective pool of alternative recruits and decreases with the absolute size of the winning coalition. The larger the effective pool of potential recruits, the more dispensable any given member of the ruling coalition is, and thus the more 'cheaply' their loyalty can be bought, whereas the larger the winning coalition, the harder it is to 'pay' its members with goods from which others can be excluded, such as direct bribes or business opportunities. As a result, the smaller the winning coalition, and the smaller the ratio between the size of the winning coalition and the selectorate, the more likely it is that power will become personalized. Conversely, the larger the absolute size of the ruling coalition, and the smaller the effective pool of potential replacements, the greater the resources required to keep them loyal, and the smaller the effectiveness of purely private goods to ensure loyalty. In such cases, we should expect power to become less personalized, and thus rulers to become more beholden to their selectorates (Besley and Kudamatsu, 2007); we could speak here of the leader's 'constituency'.

This model is clearly too simple to explain all the detail of real cases, and has been criticized for its emphasis on the mere size of the winning coalition rather than on the relationships between insiders (Gallagher and Hanson, 2015). At any rate, much depends on how we conceptualize the effective pool of potential members of the winning coalition. For example, though it might seem that in China today the selectorate is much larger than the winning coalition (many millions of party members versus a few hundred or thousand people in the Communist Party's major committees), the *effective* number of people who can replace Central Committee members is much smaller, given the need for specific abilities and demonstrated loyalties at the top of the CPC apparatus. In other words, in practice, given the kinds of objectives to which Chinese leaders are committed today (economic development and foreign prestige), the effective selectorate of current CPC leaders is quite small, making them significantly dependent on other elites. By contrast, Mao's personal power came from the fact that he could in fact appeal *beyond* the party through his charismatic authority to recruit people committed to his utopian projects. In other words, Mao controlled a resource that effectively decreased a small elite's security of tenure, thus effectively expanding his 'selectorate'. Yet the basic structure of the conflict between a ruler and his selectorate does tell us something about the circumstances under which personal power can be accumulated, namely wherever control of the state depends on few people, the ruler can distribute some valued resource as payment to these people, and yet elite members are relatively replaceable. These are the conditions that give rise to what political scientists and sociologists call *patronage relationships*.

Personal Dictatorships and Patrimonial Regimes

All concentrated personal power depends on 'patron-client' or 'patron-age' relationships (Snyder, 1992; Jackson and Rosberg, 1982, pp. 38–48; Guliyev, 2011). A patron-client relationship is a private bargain that establishes mutual obligations on unequally situated individuals: the patron undertakes to provide valued resources (for example, jobs in the government, access to expropriated property, and so on) and protection in exchange for loyalty (for example, votes in elections, violence against enemies of the patron, and so on). The private bargain may be reinforced by non-material factors – the charisma or prestige of the patron, ascriptive characteristics such as kinship or ethnicity that reinforce trust – but at bottom all patronage relationships are forms of unequal private exchange, based on the patron's monopoly over some valued resource. Such relations can have multiple levels, since higher-level clients can be patrons to lower-level clients, and tend to produce 'pyramidal' hierarchies of personal dependence.

Though patronage relationships are a basic social structure, present in all societies (Martin, 2009), in political systems where power is highly personalized they underlie every 'formal' institution (such as elections and constitutions) and subvert their functioning, substituting their private logic of personal loyalties for the public logic of loyalty to the 'formal' rules of the game. In patronage relationships what matters are always personal connections, not what the formal rules say; and where such relationships underlie formal institutions, they can ensure that appointees to them – party members, legislators, and so on – do the bidding of the patron. (For a good example of what such relationships can achieve, see Box 4.2.)

Box 4.2   Personal power and elections in Haiti

François 'Papa Doc' Duvalier, the personal ruler of Haiti from 1957 to 1971, shows well how patronage relationships can be used to subvert the clearest and most unambiguous rules. Duvalier had been first elected to the Presidency of Haiti in 1957 for a six-year term in a rigged but reasonably competitive election, and had since consolidated his power. According to unambiguous constitutional rules he was not supposed to stand for re-election until April 1963. Yet in 1961 his electoral council argued, absurdly, that because his name had been *printed* on every ballot of a scheduled congressional election, Duvalier had been 're-elected' to another six-year term, despite the fact that nobody knew this in advance (Diederich and Burt, 1973, 169–70). (By 1964 he would dispense entirely with elections, declaring himself 'President for Life' in a referendum so rigged as to verge on parody; the ballot only had a 'yes' option (see Diederich and Burt, 1973, 277)). These were violations of clear, unambiguous rules; yet despite US condemnation and some ineffectual plots (mostly by exiles), no one within the elite was able to act against Duvalier, because everyone who 'mattered' within Haiti's formal institutions – the attorney general, the electoral board, and the entire national assembly (which meekly rubber-stamped his power grab) – was dependent on him through patronage relationships. Not doing the bidding of Duvalier would have meant dismissal from plum positions in a very poor country, and (more likely) beatings or even death at the hands of other clients (for example, the Tonton Macoute militia). People with a conscience tended to run for the nearest embassy.

Where the core political structures in a society are patronage relationships rather than bureaucratically organized parties or militaries, scholars speak of *patrimonial* or *neopatrimonial* regimes (Snyder, 1992), or in extreme cases of *sultanism* (Chehabi and Linz, 1998). Not all regimes where power is highly concentrated are patrimonial, and power is not always highly concentrated in patrimonial regimes, since there may be many powerful patrons in a single regime (for instance, feudal barons in medieval monarchies). Stalin, for example, became an all-powerful personal dictator by exploiting his patronage power as General Secretary of the CPSU, which allowed him to place his loyalists in key positions throughout the sprawling party-state apparatus, just as earlier Russian Tsars had also accumulated personal power by exploiting their role as chief patrons in society (Hosking, 2000). But patronage merely enabled Stalin to control the CPSU, which remained a complex bureaucratized party organization, whereas it was the *key* structure of rule in the Russian state before the 1917 revolution. Stalin was thus a personal ruler in a non-patrimonial totalitarian regime, whereas Nicholas II was a personal ruler in a patrimonial monarchy.

The more complex the society and the goals of the ruler, the more likely it is that a structure more complex than a patronage hierarchy (such as a political party) will be required to control it (Martin, 2009). Only those tyrannies without ideological visions beyond the gratification of the ruler, such as those of Idi Amin or Macías Nguema, can do without such institutions; and in these cases it is even misleading to speak of 'rule', since the state is then nothing other than a loose network of patronage relationships between predatory warlords with extremely limited ability to do anything other than steal resources and wreak havoc (Decalo, 1985). By contrast, the great totalitarian dictators, for all their control, required more complex and bureaucratized organizations to achieve their goals. Such considerations have led some scholars to propose to restrict the terminology of 'personal' rule only to patrimonial or neo-patrimonial states (Guliyev, 2011). But in every regime where power is highly concentrated patronage relationships represent the primary lever through which a ruler can control the operation of other institutions, even when these other institutions are not themselves mere patronage networks. We thus distinguish between forms of personal rule in which otherwise bureaucratized institutions are tightly controlled by a single person, in part through patronage relationships (concentrated power, as Stalin had in the Soviet Union), and forms of personal rule in which institutions are thoroughly riddled with patronage (patrimonial rule). Patrimonial rule is a 'thick' rather than a 'thin' conception of personal rule (Guliyev, 2011).

In 'patrimonial' regimes all important political relationships are *personal* rather than *institutional*. Most pre-modern monarchies were patrimonial states, but the form has never completely died out, as the term 'neo-patrimonial' indicates. Neo-patrimonial regimes seem to have the core bureaucratic institutions of the modern state, such as political parties and bureaucracies (hence the 'neo-'), but these are so thoroughly transformed by patronage relationships that they cannot operate on the basis of impersonal criteria. The regime of Haile Selassie in Ethiopia from 1930 until his overthrow in 1974 was a classic patrimonial regime; but many other regimes – Ferdinand Marcos in the Philippines, Mobutu in Zaire, 'Papa Doc' Duvalier in Haiti, Idi Amin in Uganda, Iraq under Saddam Hussein, the Shah of Iran, Syria under the al-Assads – fall into this category to some greater or lesser extent, according to the degree to which purely personal patronage 'chains' penetrate formal institutions and the rest of society (Brownlee, 2002; Snyder, 1992). Papa Doc's Haiti is an exemplary case; at the time of his death, 1 in 20 people in Haiti were members of his Tonton Macoute militia (a pure patronage organization), dwarfing the regular army, which only had about 7,000 people and was also full of patronage relationships (Snyder, 1992, p. 388).

Patrimonial regimes are marked by a conflation of the ruler's private domain and the public interest (Guliyev, 2011), so that the state is treated as an extension of the ruler's household, and its offices as his personal property, to grant and dispose as he sees fit on the basis of personal loyalty, constrained merely by tradition or the similarly personalized power of other patrons in society. Though they may be (and often are) highly repressive, their repressiveness is not based on any elaborate utopian ideology, but dependent more than anything else on the ruler's suspicions and prejudices. The hundreds of thousands of people that died in the Idi Amin or Macías Nguema regimes did not die because Amin or Macías Nguema were pursuing any particular utopian project to an extreme, but through the sheer criminality of the one (who reportedly enjoyed participating in violence himself) and the irrational hatred of the other for 'intellectuals'.

With a few exceptions, the main interest of patrimonial rulers is their preservation and self-aggrandizement in power rather than any sort of separately defined 'public' interest. Their self-centredness can be striking; in the early 1990s, as the state was visibly falling apart, Zaire's currency, printed in Switzerland, was sent directly to Mobutu's yacht to use as he saw fit (Bratton and van de Walle, 1994, p. 475). But even less venal patrimonial rulers tend to treat their state as a personal possession, which gives their states a highly 'corrupt' appearance. Yet short of foreign invasion, some patrimonial rulers appear to endure in power for incredible lengths of time, skilfully preventing elites from constraining them, domestic oppositions from coalescing, and external patrons from sanctioning them. How do they manage these feats of sheer survivorship?

The Personnel Management Techniques of the Personal Ruler

Because patronage relationships are private bargains between patrons and clients, the effective personal ruler is constantly concerned with personnel management, and political life in personal dictatorships is a constant round of appointments, promotions, demotions, and dismissals designed to maximize the loyalty of followers. All rulers of highly personalized political systems thus have extensive powers of appointment and dismissal underpinning their ability to act as 'chief patrons'. In the Dominican Republic in the 1940s, for example, Trujillo was able to appoint and dismiss at will not only central government officials and military leaders, but members of congress, judges, and even local government officials. He was said to keep a file with signed but undated resignation letters from all government officials, so that 'officials frequently arrived at work only to learn that they had "resigned"' (Wiarda, 1968, p. 62); the undated resignations obviated even the need for explicit powers of dismissal. Often, these extensive patronage powers are even formally stated in constitutions, where they may represent the only 'real' aspect of an otherwise ignored document (Jackson and Rosberg, 1982, pp. 11, 54–55).

Yet the personal nature of patronage relationships means that, in the absence of uncommon personal charisma, they are exceptionally vulnerable to sudden drops in the flow of resources the ruler controls, requiring the ruler to be constantly on the lookout for new sources of revenue to reward his followers. He must thus also be a fundraiser, extorting financial aid from external patrons or exploiting his ability to say what 'the law' is to create opportunities for enrichment. For example, Duvalier used to masterfully play on American fears of communism to receive aid with few strings attached by threatening to switch allegiance to the Soviet camp – meeting with the Polish legation, allowing the minuscule communist student union to stage a protest, and so on – despite being greatly disliked by Washington (Diederich and Burt, 1973). Similarly Mobutu was almost uncannily able to extract resources and aid regardless of his behaviour in office (Young, 1994; Turner, 1988), eschewing reliance on a single patron such as the United States and playing potential helpers against one another (Snyder, 1992). And at the domestic level, many post-independence African rulers used justifiable 'Africanization' policies to reward their followers and cement patronage relationships; in recent years, Robert Mugabe of Zimbabwe, for example, managed to keep many followers loyal despite the country's horrendous economic performance by rewarding them with land expropriated from white farmers.

However, mere control over the levers of patronage is not enough to secure a ruler's hold on power when norms regulating political competition are weak or non-existent. Personal rule, more than any other form of rule, is dependent on the personal skills of the ruler; and in order to remain in power, they must be able to use their patronage powers intelligently to develop the loyalty of key clients, prevent them from developing power bases of their own, and make it difficult for them to organize against him. Indeed, precisely because the personal ruler cannot count on impersonal norms to retain the loyalty of his clients but must rely on his personal prestige and his ability to distribute valuable resources, he may suspect overly competent followers (who are most likely to be able to successfully plot against him) and to prefer less competent but more clearly loyal followers, leading to the common spectacle of inept but sycophantic ministers and military commanders under a personal ruler (Egorov and Sonin, 2011).

For example, during Mobutu's rule in Zaire, loyal generals were greatly preferred to competent ones (who might have been able to organize a coup), with the result that when genuine armed resistance to his rule emerged in the east of the country, Mobutu had to be saved by foreign mercenaries, since his army was useless for actual fighting (Wrong, 2000). And under the more extreme forms of patrimonial rule – for example, the rule of self-declared 'Emperor' Jean Bédel Bokassa in the Central African Republic (1965–79), or the tyranny of Macías Nguema in Equatorial Guinea – only the most sycophantic opportunists have any chance of receiving rewards from the ruler (Decalo, 1985), making these regimes utterly unable to engage in any form of rational policy-making. In Equatorial Guinea under Macías Nguema entire ministries simply closed down; the only function of the state to which he paid attention was internal security (Wood, 2004). Systems based on pure patronage (patrimonial or neo-patrimonial regimes) can thus present the strange spectacle of all-powerful rulers who cannot get anything productive done except remain 'in power', unlike personal rulers who control highly institutionalized parties, like the great totalitarian dictators.

'Loyalty' in personal systems of rule means less the affective bonds between the ruler and his followers (which are often of little importance in the poisoned atmosphere of a ruler's court) than the proper alignment of the interests of the ruler and his clients. Though charisma and personal prestige rooted in past achievements can sustain the loyalty of followers without material rewards for a time, even highly charismatic rulers will lose their personal connection to their followers if the latter perceive that their fundamental interests are threatened by remaining with the leader. For example, though Hitler was a classically charismatic leader, enormously popular with rank-and-file Nazis, it is clear that the final defeat of the German armies at Stalingrad in 1942, on which he had staked his credibility, seriously eroded his popularity and ultimately his authority (Kershaw, 1987). Successful personal rulers – those with the 'Machiavellian' political skills to remain in power for long periods of time in the absence of norms regulating political competition at the top of the political system – thus tend to pursue varied strategies to promote the alignment of the interests of their followers with their own. Three distinct strategies are common, which we may call *dependence*, *complicity*, and *division*.

Dependence

Personal rulers often attempt to maximize the personal dependence of their clients by such classic tactics as the rapid rotation in office of civil servants, ministers, and military commanders; the appointment of officials far from their home districts or their 'promotion' to ambassadorships in distant places; and recurrent 'purges' of party members (if there is a government party) – all of which make the day-to-day politics of personal rule resemble a giant game of musical chairs. (The analogy is common in accounts of patrimonial rulers; Turner (1988, p. 215) applies it to Mobutu, and Jackson and Rosberg (1982, p. 164) apply it to Banda, for example.) Histories of personal rule show a great deal of uniformity on this point, as rulers who wish to accumulate power often arrive at similar solutions to ensure the dependence of their clients. For example, Pinochet, like Trujillo, also kept a file of undated resignations (Constable and Valenzuela,

1993, p. 58), which obviated the need to use explicit and cumbersome dismissal procedures.

These tactics exploit people's natural loss aversion to ensure that the interests of clients remain aligned with those of the patron. But they also prevent clients from developing power bases of their own by using the resources of their offices to develop their own clienteles. Their dependence on the patron is maximized to the extent that they have both more to lose from disloyalty and fewer political resources to attempt any disloyal activity. These tactics are thus most effective when the state is the main vehicle for economic advancement in a society, as it was in the immediate post-colonial period in many African countries, where the threat of dismissal from a government post carried very large economic consequences.

Dependence is also maximized to the extent that there are few if any alternative sources of patronage in the state. Personal rulers are jealous of their role as patrons; their chief rivals are the rich and powerful in their societies, who can use their own resources to maintain alternative clienteles. These people can be made dependent, however, to the extent that the ruler can credibly signal to them that their wealth and power depends on his continued good will. For example, in Russia, Vladimir Putin has been able to make the 'oligarchs' (people who became immensely wealthy after the end of the Soviet Union by exploiting their contacts with the state) dependent on him by showing them that political activity (for example, the creation of political parties) would result in severe financial repercussions via targeted investigations of their (often shady) financial deals; those insufficiently docile, such as Mikhail Khodorkovsky, quickly find themselves in legal difficulties (Gill, 2006).

Complicity

Dependence results not only from the monopoly over opportunities for economic enrichment that the patron may hold, but also from the possibility of punishment. Rulers intent on accumulating power often ensure that their subordinates can be punished for actions that they themselves might have ordered or encouraged, thus ensuring their *complicity*. Here we find, for example, the practice of allowing followers to enrich themselves illegally, turning a blind eye to atrocities by security forces, or collecting what Russians call 'kompromat' (compromising material) on powerful individuals. The ever-present threat of possible punishment, which hangs always like a sword of Damocles over the heads of people who might otherwise allow their heads to get too big, ensures loyalty; indeed, because punishment is in some cases independent of whether the ruler is in office, these tactics may even ensure that at least some people (for example, members of the security forces with 'blood on their hands') will fight for the ruler in case of popular insurrection.

Techniques of complicity tend to produce 'structural' corruption – corruption that is encouraged by the ruler as a way of keeping followers in check. The most salient fact about Mobutu's regime was the 'corruption' of the state; Zaire has been called a 'kleptocracy'. But 'corruption' in Zaire was a policy, not a problem that the ruler was unsuccessful in solving; Mobutu reserved to himself the right to denounce corruption selectively to 'rotate and remove many officials' (Jackson and Rosberg, 1982, p. 178) while appropriating the lion's share of the state's revenues. And while Mobutu's own venality was legendary – a French official once memorably referred to Mobutu as 'a walking bank account in a leopard skin cap' (Young, 1994, p. 247) – most non-totalitarian personal rulers encourage a certain amount of corruption as a matter of course. Alfredo Stroessner, the personal ruler of Paraguay from 1954 to 1989, is alleged to have said once that 'it is necessary to foment criminality, because criminality produces complicity and complicity produces loyalty' (Sondrol, 1991, p. 619), which sums up the basic idea neatly.

Even rulers who were not especially corrupt personally, like Francisco Franco in Spain, were quite aware of the value of corruption in inducing complicity and hence loyalty; according to Paul Preston, Franco 'often repaid those who informed him of corruption not by taking action against the guilty but by letting them know who had informed on them' (Preston, 1995, Kindle loc. 14795–14797). Like many other rulers who have accumulated a great deal of personal power, he was also aware of the value of temporarily unpunished complicity in binding those who did the 'dirty work' of the dictatorship to him, failing to punish some of his most bloodthirsty subordinates, despite protests by his military colleagues, as a means of binding them to him (Preston, 1995, Kindle loc. 5169–5174).

Division

When powerful people nevertheless cannot be made utterly dependent on the ruler – because, inevitably, they control important resources – they can often be divided in ways that prevent them from joining forces to constrain the ruler. The tactics involved here depend most of all on the 'Machiavellian' abilities of the ruler, but they are often surprisingly simple – for example, receiving ministers separately rather than as a group, exploiting personal rivalries or other social cleavages, creating multiple security agencies with overlapping responsibilities and reporting, and so on. Wrong (2000, pp. 97–9), for example, reports that Mobutu preferred never to hold open cabinet meetings (where he would have been forced to 'endorse a single point of view'), instead receiving his ministers separately, encouraging them to inform on each other, and making them feel like they were always right.

Everywhere one looks, the multiplication of security agencies is a common 'coup-proofing' tactic (Quinlivan, 1999), but it is especially important in dictatorships that concentrate power in the ruler's hands, from Hitler to Trujillo to Mobutu. The point of these tactics is to prevent coordination by stimulating rivalry among those who could be dangerous if they joined forces. Thus, in personalized systems of power political competition is typically 'factional' – competition for the influence and favour of the ruler, often under the umbrella of a ruling party or some other organization, that does not attempt to displace him, and which the ruler can judiciously manipulate to remain in power. Depending on the ruler's views, he may even seek to encourage such competition; in Hitler's Germany, where ideological considerations were paramount, it was consciously promoted and often led to the radicalization of policy, as Nazis competed to gain the favour of Hitler. (The historian Ian Kershaw (1993) called this phenomenon 'working towards the Fuhrer' (p. 117.))

Personal rulers also cultivate 'external' sources of power. As mentioned earlier, Mao and Qaddafi, for example, retained the option of undermining their own 'formal' supporters (the Revolutionary Command Council in Qaddafi's case and the Communist Party in Mao's case) by using their prestige and charisma to appeal to the 'masses' (in practice, idealistic young people who were receptive to revolutionary messages). The successful personal ruler refuses to rely on a single force, and is constantly on the lookout for groups that can be used against one another.

Conclusion

Personal rulership is the most colourful as well as the most tragic form of non-democratic rule. It is most likely to emerge as a result of struggle between many strongmen in a new regime where the norms regulating political competition have not yet been institutionalized and hence cannot be enforced, but it is a permanent danger in every regime where rulers can exploit informational or other advantages to accumulate power at the expense of other members of the elite. And successful personal rulers can survive for very long periods of time in office, despite sometimes horrendous social and economic policies, because they succeed in making all potential elite rivals dependent on them.

As we have seen, personal rulers remain in power through the skilful exploitation of patronage relationships. But though all rulers who accumulate great personal power tend to do so via carefully constructed patronage structures, and to use similar tactics to preserve their predominant position, 'personal' power can nevertheless take a number of different forms. For one thing, there are, as we have seen, differences in the degree to which patronage relationships pervade all of society, or are merely the instruments through which rulers control otherwise effective institutions such as political parties. Personal rulers in totalitarian systems, like Hitler or Stalin, required largely institutionalized, bureaucratic parties and armies to implement their ideological visions; but even non-ideological personal rulers have made use of relatively institutionalized organizations to control societies and enact policies of some degree of complexity. We thus now turn to the institutions that channel political power in both personalized and institutionally controlled contexts.

Chapter 5

Parties

Power relationships in non-democratic regimes are not always highly personalized. As we saw in the previous chapter, the struggle for power in many non-democratic regimes may result in the establishment of some institutional framework which, though never perfectly effective, is capable of imposing some limits on rulers and of regulating the competition for state power. Moreover, even personal rulers unconstrained by their elite colleagues often exercise power *through* particular organizations that enable them to control society and achieve their goals. Two institutions have played especially important roles in how non-democratic regimes are ruled in the modern world: the political party and the modern bureaucratized army. Both of these emerged from the transformation of certain patronage relationships (Martin, 2009, chs. 7–8) into functionally specialized and normatively regulated hierarchies – the party as an organization for mobilizing large numbers of people, and the army as an organization for the use of violence.

This chapter focuses on the role of political parties in non-democratic regimes, while the next two chapters focus on armies and other institutions through which political power has been exercised in non-democratic regimes. We begin by surveying the diversity of ways in which non-democratic regimes have made use of parties. This diversity raises the question of whether there are any particular characteristics of parties that make them useful for non-democratic regimes even in contexts in which they do not serve to contest elections. The answer, I argue, is that (some) parties are particularly effective at ensuring elite cohesion, managing the loyalty of supporters through appropriate rewards and punishments, and mobilizing groups beyond the ruling elite in support of the regime. In particular, parties ensure elite cohesion and manage the loyalty of supporters when they are able to give their members important *career opportunities* that are not available outside the party, and thereby a stake in regime survival.

Insofar as parties ensure elite cohesion, they are not particularly different from other institutions of non-democratic rule. Effective vehicles of power – parties, armies, and dynastic clans – all provide such incentives, even if (as we shall see) in different degrees. What makes parties distinctive as ruling organizations is that they specialize in the mobilization of the broader population in elections, even when elections cannot serve to determine who holds power. The chapter thus considers next the question of the meaning of non-democratic elections: what are elections for when they do not determine who rules? The answer, I suggest, often has more to do with strengthening ruling coalitions and marginalizing potential opposition than with the legitimation of governments and the selection of policy-makers. More generally, elections in non-democratic regimes typically function as *signals of strength*, though they can also help such regimes gather information about the population, manage international demands, and even (on occasion) legitimate the regime.

The Diversity of Parties and Party Rule

The political party is a peculiarly modern institution, unknown before the nineteenth century (Martin, 2009, ch. 8). Its emergence can be attributed to the functional imperative of *contesting elections* in large, territorially based states, which accounts for their non-existence before control or even influence over the state through electoral contests was a live possibility. Nevertheless, political parties today exist even in contexts where elections either do not exist or do not serve to regulate the competition for state power, as in the current Chinese regime. Indeed, political parties are popular in non-democratic regimes. As we saw earlier in Chapter 3 (Figure 3.1), only about 10-20 per cent of non-democratic regimes have consistently banned all political parties in the post-Second World War period. These have been mostly led by the military (for example, the military regime led by Onganía in Argentina between 1966 and 1970) or have been dynastic monarchies (for example, the Saudi or Qatari monarchies). But most military-led regimes, and many monarchies, have happily coexisted with one or more political parties; and as we noted in Chapter 3, even the proportion of regimes that have allowed only one party to exist decreased greatly in the post-Cold War era from a high of around 50 per cent of all non-democratic regimes in the late 1980s to around 10 per cent towards the end of the first decade of the twentieth-first century (Figure 5.1). But why are parties so popular in non-democratic regimes, especially where elections do not matter?

Scholars typically argue that the key advantage of parties in non-democratic contexts is that they serve to keep ruling elites in power; regimes with parties appear to be more durable than regimes without, and regimes that allow only a single party seem to be the most long-lasting of all (Svolik, 2012; Geddes, 1999; Geddes, Wright, and Frantz, 2014), though the mechanisms for this durability are disputed. Yet non-democratic regimes do not use parties always in the same way, suggesting that elites build parties, and use them, in response to different pressures and for different purposes, with different consequences for regime stability. Some allow only a single, highly ideological regime party and either do not hold elections or hold only single candidate 'elections'; others permit some degree of multiparty competition, sometimes keeping tight control over the legislature, sometimes failing to prevent opposition parties from gaining control over a significant legislative bloc (see Figure 5.1); in some cases the regime may even endorse more than one party, as in Brazil in the 1960s under military tutelage. And the importance of the party may vary quite a bit over the life of a regime. In the Franco regime, for example, the importance of the Falange steadily diminished over time (Payne, 1987).

Parties also vary greatly in structure, size, and purpose, ranging from small but highly disciplined and ideologically coherent conspiratorial organizations (such as the Bolshevik Party shortly after the Russian Revolution) to sprawling patronage mills (such as the PRI in Mexico before the 1990s). Even parties committed to similar ideologies vary greatly: communist parties, for example, had memberships

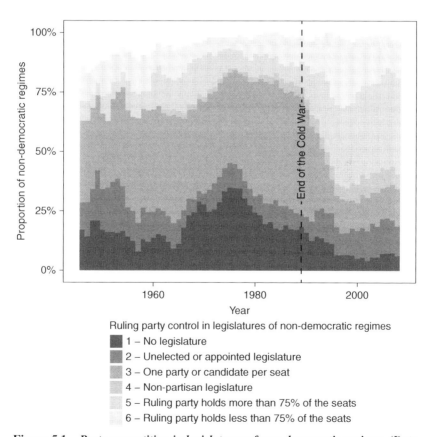

Ruling party control in legislatures of non-democratic regimes
- 1 – No legislature
- 2 – Unelected or appointed legislature
- 3 – One party or candidate per seat
- 4 – Non-partisan legislature
- 5 – Ruling party holds more than 75% of the seats
- 6 – Ruling party holds less than 75% of the seats

Figure 5.1 *Party competition in legislatures of non-democratic regimes. (Data from Svolik 2012.) The bars do not reach to the top of the figure because for some cases in the dataset there is no information.*

that varied from a low of around 0.7 per cent of the population in Cuba in 1969 (Leogrande, 1980, p. 399) to about 25 per cent of all adults in Czechoslovakia in the 1940s (Grzymała-Busse, 2001, p. 446), though most averaged between 5 per cent and 10 per cent during their time in power, as in today's China, where around 5-6 per cent of the population are members of the CPC (McGregor, 2010, p. xiv). Ceteris paribus, less ideological parties tend to be larger; the PRI in Mexico, for example, comprised up to 23 per cent of the entire population of the country in 1963 - more than 8 million people (Purcell, 1975, p. 163) - while the Arab Socialist Union claimed, on paper, about one in six Egyptians as members in the early 1960s (Brownlee, 2007a, p. 86). And regime parties also differ in the degree to which their organizations 'saturate' the country they rule over. For example, in Communist East Germany and Czechoslovakia there were very few communities without a party committee, while in Communist Poland more than a quarter of all communities lacked one (Grzymała-Busse, 2001). The question then becomes why some regimes invest resources in creating tightly disciplined parties, or parties with branches throughout the entire country, whereas others are content with sprawling patronage organizations, or parties with little coverage beyond the capital.

Part of the answer is that whether a regime bans all parties, uses a single party, or allows for some form of multiparty competition may not be entirely under its control. Social conditions impose limits on the degree to which a regime can extend party control or eliminate parties altogether. As we have noted, during the Cold War, single party regimes emulated models from the Soviet Union and other Communist powers and received support from them, but the end of the Cold War forced many of these regimes to allow multiparty competition. Some of them democratized, but others seem to have adapted well enough to the new world order, so that nowadays authoritarian regimes with multiple parties are both extremely common (more than 75 per cent of all authoritarian regimes hold multiparty elections, according to Brancati, 2014, p. 314) and appear to be increasing in durability (Kendall-Taylor and Frantz, 2015) and control – more of them have large majorities in the legislature (Figure 5.1). The fact that a regime bans all multiparty competition, or regularly produces huge supermajorities in elections, in other words, may be a *symptom* of its underlying strength rather than a cause of it. And the fact that single-party regimes seem to be very durable may have more to do with underlying social or political conditions that allow ruling elites to restrict political competition than with the mere fact of having a single party. We must thus ask not only about what accounts for the greater durability of party-based non-democratic regimes, but also about the constraints faced by elites wanting to rule through parties, or wishing to eliminate them.

Parties as Devices for Elite Cohesion

Nevertheless, elites do invest resources in creating parties, and effective parties do help them to exercise social control and achieve other goals. The reason for this is that parties are voluntary organizations that screen potential elite members for commitment to the regime and give them incentives to stick with it in the hopes of achieving high position, while selectively punishing the disloyalty of outsiders (Svolik, 2012, ch. 6). In doing so, they tend to ensure that the elite remains unified in a crisis.

Screening

The key fact about parties in non-democratic regimes is that they are for the most part *voluntary* organizations; people apply to join because there are material or other advantages to joining, or because they agree with their ideological projects and would like to help bring them about. But membership is rarely automatic; regime parties usually engage in *selective recruitment* in order to discriminate between the loyal and the disloyal (Svolik, 2012, p. 162). Candidates are thus typically screened for ideological compatibility before admitting them to full membership status, sometimes via long 'probationary' periods during which they have to prove their worth to the party by performing costly political service (see Svolik, 2012, p. 168, who cites the seven-year probationary period for prospective members of the Iraqi Baath party).

Parties may also conduct regular 'purges' to expel opportunists who join merely to gain material advantages, and require their members to give some of their time and money to the party; strikingly, even some of the most powerful parties ever to have held power, such as the CPSU, have been funded in great part by member dues rather than taxes (Belova and Lazarev, 2007). Since, if everyone is in the party, party elites cannot discriminate between the committed and the uncommitted, compulsory membership – as, for example, in Nasser's 'National Union' in Egypt in 1956 (Blaydes, 2010, pp. 30–1) or in Mohammad Reza Palahvi's 'Resurgence' party in Iran in 1975 (Katouzian, 1998, p. 193) – is rare, and usually supplemented by a variety of 'levels' of membership that distinguish between degrees of commitment. (Compulsory regime parties can still serve to exclude some people if the act of *joining* is not automatic and genuine opponents of the regime find it repugnant to go through with its requirements; in the Iran of the Shah, some opponents of the regime opted for exile rather than joining the regime party. But in general the point of a party is to *screen* the committed from the uncommitted.)

The degree to which ruling parties have high or low standards for admission, or demand greater or lesser ideological purity from members, nevertheless varies greatly over time and across political systems. The more 'totalitarian' the system, in particular, the greater the demand for ideological purity and party service, the more stringent the standards for admission, and the more frequent the purges, whereas parties in 'authoritarian' systems, in which the regime party is at best one among many interest groups, often require little more than payment of dues (Linz, 1976 [1964], p. 175). Resistance from other social groups, as well as the party's need for particular skills, can also impose limits on the degree to which ruling parties can afford to be more or less selective.

For example, the Communist Party in Poland always had fairly lax standards of admission, partly because it could not fully penetrate Polish society or completely obliterate independent organizations, which provided ambitious and competent people with many outside options for satisfying careers (Grzymała-Busse, 2001). The Polish Workers' Party, seen as a creature of Moscow, could not hope to govern without the cooperation of many different non-party groups, and thus did not make party membership a prerequisite for many important offices or attempt to enforce rigid ideological conformity within its ranks. By contrast, the East German Communist Party (the 'Socialist Unity Party' and its United Front allies, technically) controlled society more thoroughly thanks in part to the presence of the Soviet army, but also because, obsessed with subversion from West Germany, it never felt that it could relax its standards of ideological purity (Grzymała-Busse, 2001). Over time, however, even highly ideological ruling parties, like most communist parties in Eastern Europe before 1989 or in China today, have tended to de-emphasize ideological purity in favour of technical expertise and education (Bian, Shu, and Logan, 2001; Walder, 1995; Hanley, 2003).

Career Ladders

Parties may supervise armies and party members may staff security agencies, but they are primarily organizations for the management of popular loyalty, not for the infliction of violence, despite the existence of the occasional party militia like the Nazi SS and the Fascist Squadristi. The work of party activists (or 'cadres', as they were called in Communist countries) typically involves turning out people to vote or encouraging them to participate in other public rituals, agitating and propagandizing in favour of particular policies or campaigns, carrying out ideological work or surveillance activities, and only occasionally participating in repressive actions. Such work is typically a requirement for advancement through the hierarchy, ensuring that only 'reliable' members with demonstrated commitment to the party become influential.

In return for party service, ruling parties offer individuals a 'career path' in which advancement up the party hierarchy is correlated with access to political influence, better jobs, economic opportunities, and prestige

(Belova and Lazarev, 2008; Bian, Shu, and Logan, 2001; Svolik, 2012; Walder, 1995). The classic case here is the Soviet *nomenklatura* system (Rigby, 1988), adopted with slight variations by most communist parties the world over – a list of high-level jobs for which loyal party service was essential, and which received exclusive benefits unavailable to other people. Many other regimes where parties play a big role have adopted similar systems. Moreover, though advancement in party careers is typically facilitated by the patronage of higher-level party leaders, institutionalized parties do put some weight on more or less impersonal criteria of party service for promotion, such as the ability to increase revenue, turn out the vote, or achieve other goals necessary to the preservation of party control (see, for example, Shih, Adolph, and Liu, 2012 on promotion within the CPC). Even under Stalin's personal rule advancement within the CPSU was not totally subject to his whims (Harris, 2005), though party rule under the Nazis did eventually degenerate into what some historians have called 'feudal anarchy' (Kershaw, 1993, p. 107), a network of relationships of pure personal loyalty to Hitler.

The fact that regime parties provide a more or less clear career ladder for the opportunistically ambitious or ideologically committed is one of the key features that distinguishes them from the pure patronage relationships common in patrimonial regimes, or from the ad hoc attempts to 'buy' the support of the masses that all rulers use in times of crisis (Svolik, 2012, p. 162). Because patronage relationships are *personal* bargains, they cannot facilitate 'careers' in the proper sense of the term. In extremely patrimonial regimes, the most powerful minister can be destroyed, and the most abject sycophant promoted far beyond his abilities, at a moment's notice. Accordingly, patronage relationships are highly sensitive to changes in immediate resource flows; the moment the flow of economic resources dries up, there is little reason to stick with the patron short of a belief in his personal charisma.

By contrast, effective parties turn into more or less impersonal hierarchies in which party members who *credibly* signal their loyalty to the party by doing useful work to preserve its monopoly on power are in turn rewarded later with appointments to jobs whose prestige and power is relatively *independent* of the top leader. Party members thus make an *investment* into the organization that gives them incentives to 'hang together' rather than to bolt at the first sign of difficulties. In particular, by giving important social elites a stake in the organization, they make it possible for them to resolve their disagreements without threatening corporate control over the state (Brownlee, 2007a). Like all successful institutions of non-democratic rule, parties thus enable elite cohesion, the capacity of elites to act together even in crises. This seems to be one reason why regimes that depend on parties that are closer to pure patronage organizations, based on the exchange of jobs and other economic benefits but demanding little party work in return, are less resilient to economic crisis than regimes that depend on parties with more stringent service requirements, such as Zimbabwe's African National Union, which emerged from armed struggle and has survived economic crises large enough to fell many other regimes in the region (Levitsky and Way, 2012).

The Management of Disloyalty

In order to provide proper career incentives, all parties must be able to control a large number of appointments to state positions that can be held out as a reward for party service (Svolik, 2012, ch. 6). In this way all ruling parties resemble patronage relationships; without some way of aligning the interests of members with the interests of party leaders, it is ultimately difficult for the latter to discipline or control the activities of the former. At the totalitarian extreme, every position in society that can bring prestige, influence, or wealth is controlled by the party, and granted as compensation for loyal service. In this situation, party membership is extremely valuable, and party members are easily disciplined by the prospect of losing it.

Most of the time, however, parties do not achieve this degree of pervasiveness. Alternative careers outside the party remain possible and desirable, and may serve as platforms of influential opposition. Moreover, the greater the number of positions a party attempts to monopolize, the more likely the attempt will arouse resistance from society. Party rule in non-democratic regimes thus unavoidably requires some greater or lesser degree of selective repression (Svolik, 2012, ch. 6); as organizations for the management of loyalty, parties not only reward the committed, but also punish the disloyal.

Such punishment can take many forms, ranging from simple denial of benefits to non-party members to physical repression. An interesting case here is the 'punishment regime' of the Mexican PRI, described by Magaloni (2006). The PRI's monopoly on power required winning elections, which it did by providing government transfers to voters in exchange for votes (as well as a certain amount of fraud). Because the party could credibly withdraw these benefits from areas of opposition strength, poor voters, who were most dependent on them, found it very difficult to vote for the opposition. These 'legal' opposition parties were thus permanently marginalized, which in turn made them less attractive vehicles for disgruntled elite PRI members; only the most violent ideological disagreements would result in splits in the PRI.

The selective punishment of voters thus generated elite cohesion. For the most part, it made little sense for influential members of the party to seek to resolve their disagreements by creating new parties. Yet this system began to break down when economic development made poorer voters less dependent on government transfers, and thus more willing to vote for the legal opposition, which in turn increased the chances of opposition parties and made them into more plausible vehicles for the ambitions of disgruntled PRI members, which in turn weakened the incentives for elite cohesion. Eventually, the PRI faced the choice of either allowing genuine opposition to emerge or becoming more repressive; and at the end of the day, the path of repression was not taken.

The Mexican case also illustrates another way in which effective ruling parties manage the career incentives of the loyal: by making sure people at the top of the hierarchy retire on time. Term limits at all levels (including the presidency) served to increase career mobility, opening up positions for lower-level activists (Svolik, 2012). Similar retirement norms have developed today in the CPC, whose top leaders are restricted by convention to two five-year terms at the helm, as we saw earlier. Where such incentives for retirement do not exist, parties can turn into 'gerontocratic' organizations, as was the case in the Soviet Union under Brezhnev, where the average age of the Politburo in the late 1970s was over 70 (Kotkin, 2008, p. 49). This 'government by invalids' – Brezhnev occasionally drooled on himself in TV appearances, and worked no more than two hours a day – fuelled disappointment among ambitious younger members of the party, such as Gorbachev, and blocked any reforms to a system that barely worked.

It has sometimes been argued that the reason why non-democratic regimes promote party formation is that parties may serve to co-opt opposition (Magaloni and Kricheli, 2010; Gandhi, 2008, ch. 3). But this is only true for marginal cases; parties do not typically recruit implacable ideological enemies (Svolik, 2012, p. 183). Instead, parties attempt to co-opt those ideologically closest to them, or at worst opportunistically minded people willing to do party work in exchange for enrichment opportunities, while repressing, or at least marginalizing, more principled opponents. It is better to conceptualize parties as organizations that provide incentives for elites representing important constituencies to work together by giving them a stake in organizational control of the state; an effective party makes 'opposition' a less rational option for them than working through their disagreements through party forums, ranging from the ubiquitous politburos of communist parties to other councils (including, in some but not all cases, parliaments).

In other words, the party does not so much co-opt opponents as prevent the emergence of opposition from within the ruling elite by providing incentives for elite cohesion. Yet it is important to note that incentives for elite cohesion are present in all successful ruling organizations, including militaries and dynastic clans, as we shall see in the next two chapters. Parties differ from other institutions of non-democratic rule not so much because they provide incentives for elite cohesion, but because they typically specialize in the mobilization of the broader population in rituals of regime support, such as elections and public demonstrations. How does such mobilization help non-democratic regimes retain power?

Varieties of Electoral Experience

The vast majority of regime parties in non-democratic contexts take part in elections, just as their counterparts do in democracies, though in non-democratic regimes elections are *not* the primary means by which power changes hands. Elections in such regimes do not serve primarily to select leaders, keep them accountable, or produce representative governments. But this does not mean that they are pointless. Even elections without any opposition at all can serve important regime ends, and are often introduced or maintained for purposes that have little to do with democracy. They are important tactics for the 'management of loyalty' that non-democratic regimes can use in order to prevent the emergence or growth of mass-based threats to their rule.

Consider first an extreme case: 'elections' without choice, as the elections for the Supreme People's Assembly in North Korea (see Box 5.1). Such elections are not as common today as they once were, but they were once common enough. Most elections in the Soviet Union, for instance, were not substantially different from the latest North Korean election, though they were more frequent. According to the National Elections under Democracy and Autocracy (NELDA) dataset (Hyde and Marinov, 2012) there have been 11 such elections in North Korea before 2014, more or less every five years, though in at least one case (the 1990 election) there was an eight-year gap before the next election took place. By contrast, the Soviet Union had an average of one election per year, for offices at all levels of the federation (Karklins, 1986). But why bother? Any state powerful enough to produce victories with 100 per cent of the vote can clearly dispense with elections; yet the North Korean regime, like almost every other state in the world, apparently sees some advantage in retaining public electoral rituals.

One obvious answer to this question is tempting, but incorrect: that these elections are meant to 'legitimate' the regime by providing a 'veneer' of democracy. This idea is commonly found in press accounts of these elections (Talmadge, 2014), but sometimes political scientists also argue that elections must in general legitimate regimes even in the absence of political competition (Brooker, 2014). The problem is that there is no evidence that anyone is fooled who did not already want to

Box 5.1 Elections in North Korea

Elections in North Korea are held more or less every five years, last on 9 March 2014. These do not involve any choice among parties, platforms, or candidates. Voters are presented with only one candidate per district, all of them belonging to the Korean Workers' Party (KWP), and expected to vote 'yes'. Though technically voters can mark 'no' on their ballot papers, voting is not genuinely secret, and North Korean defectors report feeling that there are considerable risks in voting against the party's candidates, so much so that it appears that practically no one does it (New Focus International, 2014).

Moreover, even if people's votes were secret, the deputies they elect have no real power, since the Supreme People's Assembly is the most perfect example of a rubber-stamp parliament still existing today; experts on North Korean politics cannot recall a single instance in which a deputy has ever voted against a bill introduced by the government. To paraphrase an old Soviet joke, citizens in North Korea pretend to vote, and their representatives pretend to rule them.

You might think that this would be reason enough for most citizens to skip the election; but voting is not optional, and failure to show up to vote also carries considerable risks. North Korean defectors report that the elections in recent years have become the occasion for a crackdown on 'missing individuals' – people who have migrated to China, army personnel who are AWOL, and people without proper resident permits (North Koreans cannot settle freely within the country's cities):

> At any other point in the year, family members of missing persons can get away with lying or bribing surveillance agents, saying that the person they are looking for is trading in another district's market. But it is during an election period that a North Korean individual's escape to China or South Korea becomes exposed. [...]
>
> In the mid-2000s, state surveillance and security agents [...] requested families to give up information about missing persons by saying that they knew the person was in China, but that if he or she returned to North Korea to vote in the next election, all would be forgiven by the Workers' Party. There were threats too: if the missing person did not return for the election, the treacherous penalty of abandoning the homeland would be paid by the remaining family members. (New Focus International, 2014)

> Coercion is not the only thing on the state's menu, however. Candidate posters are printed, agitators enlisted to give talks at workplaces emphasizing the importance of the elections, and a festive atmosphere is created on the day of the event. And after the election is over, North Korean news agencies dutifully report the expected results: turnouts above 99 per cent, with 100 per cent support for the KWP and its leader. 'Man on the street' quotes from voters explain how happy voters are to be voting the KWP into power yet again, and how grateful they feel for its leadership; and editorials praise the unity of the country and the loyalty of the citizens.

be fooled, and certainly not anyone with any genuine influence – not the international community, not the leaders being 'elected' (who are presumably well informed about where real power lies), and not the voters, who 'generally have no interest in who their candidate is as many already live their lives apart from the state, and don't bother to find out the name of the person they have just 'voted' into office' (New Focus International, 2014).

Indeed, it is not obvious that elections would make any difference to the North Korean state's claims to be democratic, since the Chinese state, which does not have direct popular elections for its supreme legislative assembly, also claims to be just as democratic, with about as much (or as little) justification. The 'veneer' of democracy that elections provide in this particular case is just too thin to do any genuine work producing political support for the regime. In some other cases, such as the 're-election' of Duvalier in 1961, described in Chapter 4 (Box 4.2), the 'electoral parody' was so obvious that if anything it *de-legitimated* the regime in the eyes of both international and domestic audiences: the United States and the Organization of American States insisted that the election was 'a sham', and the United States even put out the message in 1963 that it would welcome a coup to oust him, as it considered his legal term to be over (Diederich and Burt, 1973, p. 192).

This is not to say that elections without competition cannot serve to 'legitimate' a regime in some sense, as we shall see. But we must be careful when we use this word; it tends to conceal more than it illuminates. 'Legitimation' is a coarse concept, subsuming a wide variety of disparate and even contradictory processes through which attachments to a regime are generated and maintained or lost and reversed (Márquez, 2016b). It is thus best to avoid the term when thinking about the specific function that electoral institutions serve in authoritarian states, since it may lull us into seeing spurious parallels between their workings in democratic contexts and their workings in non-democratic regimes.

But if not all elections in authoritarian contexts 'legitimate' the regime, what are they for instead? The scholarly literature on elections under authoritarianism (for useful reviews, see Magaloni and Kricheli, 2010; Gandhi and Okar, 2009; Brancati, 2014) suggests at least the following (not mutually exclusive) possibilities: elections can serve as signals of invincibility, as forms of loyalty management, as information-gathering mechanisms, as rituals of power, and as international mimicry.

Elections as Signals of Invincibility

Autocrats may stage elections that they proceed to win by huge margins in order to signal invincibility and thus discourage opposition (either from the ruling group or from outsiders). Here the election serves, above all, as a display of power; the more complete the victory, the more futile resistance to the ruling group might seem. What is the point of fighting against a state that can apparently garner 100 per cent support in elections? And even if opposition parties exist (unlike in North Korea), why would a voter waste his or her vote on parties that self-evidently cannot win, or support the incumbent anyway?

Mexico from 1929 until 2000 is a good example of this dynamic. Widely considered a non-democratic country throughout this period, the country was ruled by the Partido Revolucionario Institucional (PRI), which emerged from the pacts that ended the Mexican revolution. Elections for all levels of government - Mexico is a federal republic - occurred throughout this period. Opposition parties (with the partial exception of the Mexican Communist Party, banned until 1978) could compete in these elections without undue interference (though with limited access to media or state resources). Nevertheless the PRI always won these elections, and until the late 1980s won them by huge margins (the PRI vote share in presidential elections was usually upwards of 75 per cent), thoroughly marginalizing the opposition. Yet the key to the PRI's success was not so much that it was widely loved (though it was popular), or that it practised fraud and repression (though the party was not above using these tools); it was its aura of invincibility. When voting for the opposition carried no benefits, and might even involve some financial loss, poorer voters were highly unlikely to switch their vote to one of the untested opposition parties. As a peasant from the state of Morelos put it in 1994 (quoted in Magaloni, 2006, p. 64):

> I have always voted for the PRI because only this party can win. Why would I support the opposition if it can't win? They told me that this time they would also give us checks [he was referring to cash transfers within the then recently instituted Farmers Direct Support Program (PROCAMPO) designed to support small-scale farmers]. I must thus vote for the PRI to get my check.

The signal of invincibility provided by the PRI's overwhelming victory margins was not just directed at voters; it was also directed at ambitious politicians from the ruling party itself. Because the Mexican constitution prohibited re-election, ambitious politicians from within the PRI who failed to get the presidential nomination at the end of a president's term could in theory split from the party and compete on their own - indeed, the two other big political parties in Mexico today, the PRD and the PAN, started out as splits from the PRI. But splitting was less appealing when they knew that they would be completely crushed in an electoral fight.

One interesting implication of the idea that elections can serve to provide signals of invincibility is that elections in strong authoritarian states should tend to use fraud less to get the ruling party to the winning threshold (50 per cent plus one, so to speak) than to pad the margin of victory. In these cases, ruling parties may use fraudulent elections not because they are unpopular, but because they want to nip all opposition in the bud, so to speak. Thus, in Mexico until the late 1980s fraud was generally used to increase the margin of victory, not to steal elections that the opposition would have won. When in 1988 the PRI appeared to have stolen the presidential election (it is very likely that the opposition candidate for president, Cuahtémoc Cárdenas of the Revolutionary Democratic Party (PRD), won that election), this was a huge shock to the system, and it triggered a political crisis that led to the eventual opening of political competition in the 1990s. Having to outright steal the election (and having this fact become common knowledge) showed that the party was *weak*, not strong.

Russian elections since the fall of the Soviet Union, especially under Vladimir Putin, also appear to function as a way of signalling the regime's invincibility. Krastev and Holmes (2012, p. 35) report that 'most Russians have known that elections are rigged' yet also believe that 'had the electoral process been free and fair, Putin would have come out on top anyway'. And as in the Mexican case, many voters support Putin today less because they genuinely like him than because he appears invincible. Krastev and Holmes quote a story that the political scientist and political consultant Gleb Pavlovsky used to tell that illustrates the point well (though it refers to Putin's predecessor, Boris Yeltsin). A woman 'reported that she supported Zyuganov, the Communist Party candidate, but was planning to vote for Boris Yeltsin. When Pavlovsky asked her why she would not be voting for Zyuganov, she replied: 'When Zyuganov is president, I will vote for him." (Krastev and Holmes, 2012, p. 35).

This image of invincibility is not harmed by the fraud 'everyone knows'; it is precisely because Putin can convincingly show that he can get away with it that voters come to feel it is pointless to support alternatives, even if it is in theory open to them to support these. The 'elections' in Duvalier's Haiti (described in Chapter 4) or in Trujillo's Dominican Republic, which were marred by much more extreme forms of fraud, also seem to have served to send signals of invincibility rather than to genuinely gauge their political support, though in these cases the signals may have been intended for potential (armed) opposition groups rather than the voters.

Elections as Loyalty Management

To be sure, many other factors, not just fraud, also help to discourage citizens from voting against ruling parties in similar authoritarian systems with elections. For example, a divided and unappealing opposition (as in Russia today) or a strong record of accomplishment (as in Singapore under the PAP) may lead voters to stick with the strong devil they know, even if they do not like him much, rather than take a chance with devils they do not know (or with devils they associate with previous bad experiences, as in the Venezuelan case discussed at length in the online material for this book and in Box 3.2). And if the ruling party can credibly target benefits precisely to supporters, or threaten to punish non-supporters, the incentives to stick with the ruling party are of course more convincing; only people who have little to lose are likely to vote against the ruling party.

Again, the Mexican case is exemplary, as poorer voters received very specific benefits by voting for the PRI, and stood to lose them by voting for the opposition. The opposition National Action Party (PAN), in a fit of desperation, even coined a slogan pleading with voters to take the benefits offered by the PRI but vote for the PAN: 'agarra lo que te dan, y vota por el PAN', that is, take what the PRI gives you and vote PAN (Magaloni, 2006, p. 67); 'vota por el PAN' is also a pun in Spanish, 'vote for bread'. Yet this was not always possible, especially in rural areas where ballot secrecy was easily compromised. Similar dynamics were found in Egypt under Mubarak, where the poor and economically insecure voters that constituted the vast majority of the Egyptian population received immediate small benefits from voting for the ruling National Democratic Party (NDP) –including outright cash bribes – but were punished when they did not through neglect of opposition areas in the allocation of state resources (Blaydes, 2010, pp. 5, 11).

Highly dominant parties often have many ways of punishing voters who do not show sufficient support. In wealthy Singapore, for example, wards that elect opposition MPs tend to be 'last in line' for upgrades to their infrastructure (Mauzy and Milne, 2002, p. 149), and funds for other services are often withheld from them as well (Verweij and Pelizzo, 2009, p. 19), which of course makes voting for the opposition much less desirable, given the unlikelihood of such parties winning the election. (The People's Action Party (PAP) in Singapore has used a variety of tactics, ranging from intimidation of opposition leaders to creative gerrymandering, to ensure its control of upwards of 80 per cent of all parliamentary seats since independence.) As one analyst quoted by Mauzy and Milne quipped, 'Singaporeans who want opposition voices in Parliament usually want the Opposition to represent someone else's constituency' (Mauzy and Milne, 2002, p. 146). Moreover, the PAP manipulates the rules of electoral competition and the media consciously in order to project an image of invincibility:

> The PAP does not view politics as a game; on the contrary it looks upon it more like war, and it can be ruthless in an election. It does not mind being accused of using a "sledgehammer to kill a gnat"; it wants to remind the people of the consequences of taking on the PAP. (Mauzy and Milne, 2002, 147)

As the philosopher Thomas Hobbes wrote in his famous book *Leviathan*, 'the Reputation of Power, is Power' (chapter 10).

Elections as Information Gathering Mechanisms

The most convincing demonstrations of invincibility are, of course, the 100 per cent voting margins that Soviet and North Korean elections regularly produced (and produce, in the North Korean case). Yet such incredible margins pose a different problem for the regime: estimating how much of this support is genuine. This is a particular instance of a more general problem faced by all authoritarian regimes, and which we will have occasion to encounter again and again; the more power you have to make people *say* that they support you, the less you know about the genuineness and strength of this support. This presents authoritarian rulers with a dilemma: should one relax control, to observe how much genuine support there is, and risk open opposition? Or should one increase control, to discourage opposition, and instead risk covert opposition? Wintrobe (2000) called this problem the 'dictator's dilemma'.

Elections can serve to mitigate this problem in two ways. First, even choiceless elections produce some information about the commitment of citizens to the regime, and in multiparty contexts, even very unfair elections can produce information about the relative popularity of different social forces. Second, elections produce information about the mobilizational capacity of lower-level officials.

Consider first choiceless Soviet elections (Karklins, 1986). As in North Korea today, Soviet voters could only choose to vote 'yes' or 'no', but voting 'no' entailed some risk and could not be properly done secretly. And as in North Korea today, the regime enlisted party cadres and ordinary citizens as 'agitators' to produce maximum turnout (agitators were made responsible for bringing 20-30 voters to the polls), and there was enormous social pressure to vote. All of this meant that elections always appeared to result in nearly unanimous verdicts - over 99 per cent support for the party in most cases, with turnouts similarly over 97 per cent. But these 97 per cent turnouts are not the whole story. By the 1970s, the turnout numbers excluded people who were not properly registered to vote, as well as prisoners (who supposedly had the right to vote); people without residence permits for the cities where they lived (as in North Korea and China today, Soviet citizens could not settle freely within the state's territory); and people who requested absentee ballots but did not actually fill them (a popular tactic to avoid voting). Actual voter turnout in the 1970s and 1980s seems to have been closer to 90 per cent than to 100 per cent, and in some of the major cities like Moscow may have reached as low as 75 per cent in some elections. And among those who voted between 1 per cent and 5 per cent made use of their right to enter an election booth to cast a negative vote or to write something on the ballot.

Though these turnout numbers and voting margins are still impressive, they represented a decline in commitment to the Soviet project from earlier years, and the Communist Party did its best not to publicize them; rumours of a decline in voting fed into perceptions of the weakening of the system. And as in North Korea today, information about who failed to vote was useful to identify potential troublemakers, even though punishments for non-voting were relatively rare in the waning years of the Soviet Union. (Indeed, the increased prevalence of non-voting and the lack of punishments for it were a symptom of the regime's exhaustion.)

More usefully, multiparty competition can provide information about which social forces in a regime are relatively popular, and which are not, even when elections are wholly unfair. This information can help an autocrat avoid disastrously unpopular policy mistakes and to make more informed decisions about how to distribute resources within his supporting coalition. For example, in Singapore the ruling party does sometimes adjust policy in response to perceived changes in its levels of electoral support, despite the PAP's unwillingness to allow serious political competition. In response to an unexpected result in a 1981 by-election, for example, the PAP even introduced, in 1984, a class of seats in parliament designed to go to non-PAP voices - 'Non-constituency members of parliament' (NCMPs) - but with fewer powers than regular MPs - NCMPs cannot vote on no-confidence motions, constitutional amendments, or supply and money bills. Opposition leaders like J. B. Jeyaretnam of the Singapore Worker's Party have since then used such seats to influence the direction of policy by raising questions in parliamentary debates (Mauzy and Milne 2002, p. 144). From the perspective of the PAP, such opposition voices increase the quality of policy-making without actually risking a loss of power.

Less benevolently, the ruling party in Egypt during the Mubarak era, the NDP, used information from elections to determine who should receive spoils and access to corrupt business opportunities:

> Highly contested elections in Egypt closely resemble an all-pay auction, with bidders (parliamentary candidates) paying for a shot at the prize (the parliamentary seat). The bid that candidates pay is the cost of the electoral campaign, which is not financed by the hegemonic party. Rather than payment going to the regime directly, however, the largest expense associated with a campaign involves side payments [anything from outright bribes to more subtle forms of vote buying] to supporters as part of election mobilization. (Blaydes, 2010, p. 10)

Successful candidates – people who, by definition, are influential insofar as they have shown they can mobilize voters – then received Egypt's powerful guarantees of parliamentary immunity, which (because they were so difficult to lift) essentially functioned as a licence to print money. In other words, the regime rewarded proven ability to influence voters with a great opportunity for enrichment. At the same time, because these opportunities for enrichment were mostly illegal, parliamentarians were vulnerable to legal attack if they defected from the ruling party. Unless they were highly ideologically motivated (like the few members of the Muslim Brotherhood that managed to get themselves elected), MPs were thus disinclined to attack the government in any way, which cemented the legislative supermajorities that allowed the NDP to change the rules of the game at will. Corruption was not simply an unfortunate side effect of this system; it was the glue that held it together.

In a similar way, according to some analysts, elections in Russia have also served to reward and punish subordinates on the basis of their ability to mobilize voters:

> Rigged elections … are functioning gears in the machinery by which Putin has exercised and maintained his power … elections have served as the principal instrument for controlling and renewing the country's political elite while minimizing the risk of dangerous splits in its ranks…. Local officials should not simply profess their loyalty but also demonstrate their capacity to exercise control. Their ability to stuff ballots or falsify tabulations can be field-tested, as can their capacity to force-march students or public-sector workers to the polls. (Krastev and Holmes, 2012, p. 36)

Failures to reach appropriate 'targets' in the vote sometimes result in the replacement of officials; Krastev and Holmes (2012, p. 36) report that 'after United Russia [Putin's party] received only 35 percent of the vote in the 2010 regional elections in Tver … Governor Dmitri Zelenin lost his job. … Where United Russia performed poorly in the December 2011 parliamentary elections, sitting governors likewise got the sack'. Here the important function of the elections is to identify officials who are able to contribute to the maintenance in power of the regime, not the officials who are most competent at the task of governance.

Elections as Rituals of Power

Elections are, among other things, elaborate ritual performances in which the symbols of the regime appear as key objects of attention and which can be used to mobilize or amplify emotions and normative commitments (Kertzer, 1988). It is through the mobilization and amplification of emotion that elections can serve to 'legitimate' a regime, though care must be used when we make this claim, for elections can mobilize emotions in a variety of ways, including ways that de-legitimate, rather than legitimate, a regime.

For example, elections in Haiti under the Duvaliers were festive occasions, even though they were hardly determinative of the outcome (Diederich and Burt, 1973); if nothing else they generated some temporary positive emotions associated with the regime, though most people were quite aware that they did not represent credible attempts to meet democratic standards. And elections in the Soviet Union were similarly festive, always on a Sunday, and they sometimes included ceremonies in which new voters were given flowers. As in North Korea today, the regime reported the results of the elections as a demonstration of the unanimity and total emotional commitment of the population to the communist project:

> The results of the elections to the USSR Supreme Soviet and the unanimous election to the country's supreme body of state power of the candidates of the indestructible bloc of Communists and non-Party people provide striking new evidence of the monolithic unity of the Party and the people and of the working people's full support for the domestic and foreign policy of the CPSU [Communist Party of the Soviet Union] and the Soviet state. The elections have convincingly shown the thoroughly democratic nature of the world's first society of developed socialism and the working people's firm resolve to persistently strive for new successes in all sectors of communist construction. (*Pravda*, 7 March 1979, as quoted in Karklins (1986); the language the Korean Central News Agency uses today to report on the North Korean elections is strikingly similar.)

Yet all evidence suggests that even if elections in the early years of the Soviet Union helped to mobilize positive emotions towards the communist project – serving as a means through which ordinary citizens affirmed their genuine commitments to the construction of communism – in the long run they produced not legitimacy or enthusiasm but *alienation* and *resignation*. This is not to say that the elections did not serve a purpose; as the regime ritually triumphed over the citizens by forcing them to participate in a mass charade, boasting of its ability to get citizens to approve of it even when everybody knew of the falsity of these claims, it simultaneously signalled its invincibility and produced apathetic and privatized citizens who were unlikely to participate in political opposition. The 'legitimation' involved in Soviet elections was less something granted by citizens on rulers (through enthusiastic emotional attachment to regime symbols, including the party and its candidates) than a kind of ruler self-legitimation (Barker, 2001, ch. 3), in which party leaders convinced themselves of their own right to rule by ritually 'winning' these elections by absurd margins.

Multiparty elections can similarly fail to produce positive emotional attachments to a regime's symbols (that is, to 'legitimate' the regime), in part because the positive emotions and attachments generated among partisans of the winning party may be counterbalanced by the negative emotions of partisans of the losing parties (Anderson et al., 2005). It is no secret that long-standing factional competition, gridlocked government, and corruption may make people yearn for the simplicity of rule by a single party or for a temporary dictatorship; but the more important point for our purposes is that in these cases elections may not be able to legitimate the system, because the symbols that become the focus of attention in each election belong to particular parties and groups, rather than reflecting the value of the system as a whole. The European dictatorships that emerged from the ruins of parliamentary quasi-democracies in the interwar period are perhaps the best examples of this 'legitimation failure'; the polarization brought about by irreconcilable visions of the polity discredited electoral politics as such, not just particular parties (Paxton, 2006; Linz, 1978). Accordingly, most of the fascist movements that emerged during this period declared themselves to be against parties and elections as such, because parties and elections were unable to symbolize the unity of the nation, and whenever such parties were able to seize power they proceeded to eliminate them, sometimes with considerable popular support.

But the failure of elections to legitimate a regime can still be seen in somewhat less spectacular fashion in places such as Venezuela or Thailand today, which combine an apparent mass commitment to democracy (as measured by the World Values Survey and other international surveys) with a very large degree of ideological and emotional polarization, whose causes we will explore in more detail in Chapter 10. In these circumstances, losing factions in electoral contests have tended to reject the 'legitimation' provided by elections to the winning faction; the fact that these regimes are 'elected' has not made political conflict any less fierce, or reconciled the losers (in both cases approaching half of the population) to the continued existence of the regime. Indeed, in both cases the opposition has gone so far as to welcome short-lived military coups (2002 in Venezuela, 2006 in Thailand), justified in the name of protecting democracy from elected leaders.

The case of Venezuela (see online materials for a full description and background, as well as Box 3.2) is instructive. International opinion surveys indicate that Venezuelans are in general highly supportive of 'democracy' in the abstract, and they understand elections to be an important part of democracy. Moreover, during the last 15 years there have been 15 major elections in Venezuela, including five presidential elections, elections to a constitutional assembly, a recall referendum, and a referendum on several important constitutional amendments. But though most of these elections have been judged reasonably free of fraud by independent observers, this has not led the opposition to reconcile itself to the regime or, indeed, the regime to reconcile itself to the opposition. On the contrary, with each new election the conflict between Chavistas (supporters of the late president Hugo Chávez, first elected in 1999, and his socialist 'Bolivarian revolution') and anti-Chavistas has become more and more entrenched, with the regime insisting on its electoral legitimation, and describing the opposition as 'golpistas' (coup-mongers) and 'fascists' and the opposition insisting on the unfairness of these elections and describing the regime as a 'dictatorship'. Indeed, Venezuelans today are surprisingly willing to condone coups that favour their own side, despite their apparent support for democracy and electoral norms in the abstract.

Elections have thus certainly served the Chavista regime as the main ritual through which the emotional investments of its loyal followers have been produced and renewed. The mass meetings and other campaign activities typical of electoral campaigns are well suited to producing charged symbols of identity and emotional bonds to individuals and parties, especially in the hands of a skilled practitioner like Chávez, who was routinely described as 'charismatic' (Merolla and Zechmeister, 2011). But while these symbols produced very positive emotions in a fluctuating group (often a majority) of Venezuelans, they have also produced very negative emotions among the rest. In these circumstances, we cannot say that merely holding multiparty elections has served to 'legitimate' the Chavista regime, except in the (trivial) sense that the vast majority of Venezuelans agree that elections are a necessary (but not sufficient) aspect of democracy. Mere agreement on an abstract norm - democratic governments need to be elected - has not produced any sort of further agreement on whether a particular election was fair or truly legitimate, or reconciled opposition supporters to being consistently on the losing side of election contests they do not consider sufficiently fair. Thus, despite the fact that elections do serve to energize core regime supporters and allow it to recruit international allies, it is a mistake to think that they have had a straightforwardly legitimating effect, since they also serve to energize negatively core opposition supporters and allow them to recruit like-minded supporters.

Nevertheless, elections *can* sometimes serve to produce emotional attachments to a regime (and thus 'legitimize' it) even when they are neither free nor fair, and known to be neither free nor fair among the population (as they also do in many consolidated democracies, where elections represent occasions in which the people reaffirm their unity despite their differences). Elections that can mobilize national symbols and dramatize the unity of a nation, such as constitutional plebiscites or secession referenda, are especially well suited to this task; perhaps even Soviet and North Korean elections functioned in this way in the early years of these regimes. Krastev and Holmes (2012, p. 38), for example, report that in

Putin's Russia 'periodic elections have served to demonstrate (that is, to exaggerate) Russia's national unity and to dramatize the imagined coherence and solidarity of Putin's nation'.

An election, at the end of the day, is first of all a big party; and if the party is well run it can serve to stimulate positive emotions and normative commitments to a regime. But the conditions under which this happens are less common than we might think; electoral rituals can divide and alienate as much as they can unify and legitimate. And there is no particular reason why a regime will look to use elections to maximize mass support, rather than to divide or demoralize potential opposition.

Elections as International Mimicry

Finally, sufficiently credible multiparty elections can today 'legitimate' a regime in the eyes of a relevant international audience; but the sense of legitimation involved here has less to do with the emotional attachments of citizens to the regime or the ritual character of elections than with the workings of norms in the international arena.

The democratic norms whose ascendancy we documented in Chapter 2 have been increasingly interpreted by powerful states like the United States and the countries of the EU to require multiparty elections, and made a precondition for receiving various forms of aid. Especially since the end of the Cold War (but even before then), regimes that can mount a sufficiently credible, if sometimes flawed, show of multiparty competition thus benefit relative to regimes that cannot do so, and many regimes appear to have introduced such competition in response to these pressures (Levitsky and Way, 2010). As we have noted, this does not mean that they democratized; but the introduction of multiparty competition was often a useful signal of conformity to this international norm, especially when it could be presented as part of a *process* of slow democratization or 'political reform'.

For example, Egypt abandoned single-party elections for multiparty elections in 1976 during the Anwar Sadat presidency, partly as a way of signalling closer alignment with US values and priorities (Brownlee, 2007a; Blaydes, 2010); Mobutu Sese Seko of Zaire (today the Democratic Republic of Congo) did the same in the early 1990s under pressure from the United States and France, his main patrons (McNulty, 1999, pp. 57, 67). In neither case did the introduction of multiparty competition lead to substantive democratization, as both regimes were perfectly able to manage their opposition in this changed institutional context. (Mobutu's preferred tactic involved the creation of hundreds of weak political parties, most covertly sponsored by his own Mobutist organization, which kept 'the opposition divided and weak' (McNulty, 1999, p. 74); we have already seen some of the tactics used by the Egyptian state to manage multiparty competition.) Elections in these cases may or may not have 'legitimated' these regimes from the point of view of their populations – it is dubious, to say the least, that the 'burlesque of democratization' in Zaire increased the desire of ordinary citizens to support the regime, which was eventually overthrown by an armed rebellion in 1997 – but they did provide some cover in the international arena, where 'organized hypocrisy' (Krasner, 1999) reigns supreme, and the introduction of multiparty 'elections', however dubious, could be seen as part of a slow 'transition' to more democratic forms of government.

Nevertheless, it is worth noting that some non-democratic regimes are not able to manage even this sort of transition to electoral competition without collapsing, especially where state capacity is low (Levitsky and Way, 2010). From the point of view of an autocratic regime considering whether to signal conformity to global democratic norms by introducing multiparty competition, elections are sometimes risky, and they do not always pass a sober cost-benefit analysis. Moreover, the signal of conformity to international norms they send has a tendency to decay over time (that is, become less convincing to international audiences) if further movement towards democracy is not detected after some time, or if the elections are insufficiently credible; yet regimes do not always move further down the path of democratization, and may instead become more repressive.

Conclusion

Modern non-democratic regimes, from the competitive authoritarian extreme to the totalitarian one, make much use of parties as instruments of rule. Though parties differ widely in structure across regimes, and are used in different contexts, the particular mechanisms that make them work are always similar: parties serve to ensure elite cohesion by screening prospective elite members for loyalty, and giving them clear career paths that incentivize them to remain loyal in the hopes of eventually receiving high position. Parties also play an important role in social control by selectively punishing disloyalty and helping the regime signal its strength to potential opposition groups.

The main way through which parties signal a regime's strength is by staging, and winning by large margins, elections that require them to mobilize large numbers of people. Nevertheless, elections can be risky, and regime elites are sometimes forced to use repression. But as regimes become more repressive, they often come to depend more and more on the military, which is typically the only agency that can contain mass-based threats to a regime (Svolik, 2012, ch. 5). We thus now turn to regimes where the military plays a predominant role in the next chapter.

Chapter 6

Armies

The popular image of many non-democratic regimes is dominated by the military dictator. From Charlie Chaplin's *The Great Dictator* to Woody Allen's *Bananas* to Sacha Baron Cohen's *The Dictator*, authoritarian rulers are often shown in uniform in movies and other forms of entertainment. Real dictators, from Hitler to Saddam Hussein, have often worn military garb, even if they had not risen up through the ranks of the military (Hitler was only a corporal in the First World War; Saddam Hussein was never accepted into the military academy of Iraq). And it certainly seems as if military rule should be the most common form of non-democratic rule, given the fact that military officers control force. In his seminal study of military intervention in politics, *The Man on Horseback*, Finer (1962) posed the question thus:

> Instead of asking why the military engage in politics we ought surely ask why they would ever do otherwise. For at first sight the political advantages of the military vis-à-vis other and civilian groupings are overwhelming. The military possess vastly superior organization. And they possess arms. (Finer, 1962, p. 5)

Yet, despite the fact that the military possesses arms, military rule properly speaking is both less common and more fragile than a naive view of the political advantages of military force might suggest. This chapter shows why. It begins by examining the main way in which the military has come to power in the twentieth and twenty-first centuries, the coup. Though the military can often exercise influence without staging a coup, specific conditions of the post-colonial context in many areas of the world tended to encourage the military to attempt to seize power directly. We shall also see that these factors have become less salient in recent times, and thus coups and military regimes have declined in number and importance.

The chapter then moves on to consider how military regimes typically attempt to consolidate their power and rule through the military organization. It stresses that despite their many apparent advantages in the use of repression, military organizations often have difficulty maintaining elite cohesion and securing the cooperation of essential civilian forces. Unlike parties, military organizations are not very good at mobilizing support beyond the ruling elite, and they do not always provide sufficient incentives to elites to stick together in the face of policy disagreements. Military rule properly speaking is thus surprisingly fragile, and to the extent that it endures, it tends to shed its purely military character.

The Coup

The most spectacular form of military intervention in politics is the coup. A coup is the forcible seizure of state power by military leaders (or other 'insiders', such as members of the ruling elite) in defiance of the existing constitutional framework. Though coups do not always involve high levels of violence, they always involve at least the *threat* of violence to displace existing power-holders. And though coups do not always result in military rule properly speaking – some coups are led by non-military actors, and after some coups the military quickly retreats to barracks after installing a new civilian government – most coups have been led by military leaders (Goemans, Gleditsch, and Chiozza, 2009), and they usher at least a transitional period in which rulers exercise power primarily through the military.

That military leaders are able to easily seize power is not, at first glance, surprising. As Finer (1962) noted, the political advantages of the military are significant. Modern militaries are typically disciplined corporate bodies with a particular professional *ethos* and a hierarchical organization which can act quickly and decisively to coerce other actors. Moreover, they normally have high social prestige and are seen as 'custodians of the nation', rather than as simply another interest group. Unlike, for example, the Pretorian Guard in late Imperial Rome, which at times auctioned the empire to the highest bidder, modern militaries typically claim to intervene in politics in the name of the Nation, not in the name of the narrow self-interest of the soldiers (Finer, 1962, pp. 205–7), and this claim, though not always true (modern militaries are not above intervening in politics for reasons of narrow or corporate self-interest), is often credible to the public and is in any case firmly believed by coup makers (Singh, 2014). Hence military intervention against discredited and incompetent governments, however democratically elected, very often appears initially popular; and it is not uncommon to see people celebrating in the streets after a coup.

Military coups were in fact relatively common throughout the second half of the twentieth century, especially in countries in Africa and Latin America during the Cold War (see Figure 6.1). They were particularly common in states facing political crises of one sort or another, and they tended to recur in the same states; one coup bred another. Some states (for example, Paraguay and Syria) went through long periods of near-constant military intervention – coups succeeded each other with monotonous regularity, as if military intervention were the only means of replacing

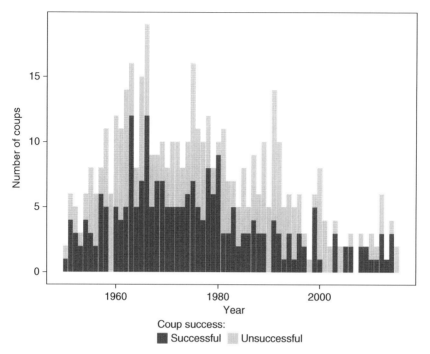

Figure 6.1   *Successful and unsuccessful military coups, 1950–2015. The data used to construct these figures slightly overstate the frequency of genuine military coups, since they include coups led by non-military insiders. (Data from Powell and Thyne (2011), updated to 2015.)*

governments. Yet, like closed authoritarian regimes, coups have declined in frequency since the end of the Cold War, due to the same processes that made openly authoritarian regimes less palatable throughout the world in this period (see Chapter 2). Indeed, coups today tend to lead to elections more quickly than before (Marinov and Goemans, 2014).

Nevertheless, coups have not gone away, even if they have become rarer and tend to result in shorter-lived military regimes. And thus we need to consider what factors might explain such a drastic form of military intervention in politics. The key factor, it turns out, is intractable political conflict, which tends to increase the 'demand' for military intervention while increasing the military's freedom of manoeuvre.

Determinants of Military Intervention

Most of the countries where coups have taken place are poor. And scholars have repeatedly found that poverty and underdevelopment greatly increase the risk of coups (Finer, 1962; Londregan and Poole, 1990; Luttwak, 1969; O'Kane, 1981; Belkin and Schofer, 2003). But it is not poverty *per se* that makes some countries coup-prone, but a lack of consensus among powerful groups in a society on the scope and location of political authority. As Finer put it: 'Where the parties or trade unions are feeble and few, where the procedure for the transfer of power is irregular or even non-existent, where the location of supreme authority is a matter of acute disagreement or else of unconcern and indifference: there the military's political scope will be very wide' (Finer, 1962, p. 21). Accordingly, some very poor countries, like India, have not suffered from military coups (though they have suffered other forms of political instability) because the principle of civilian supremacy is firmly established – there are many organized civilian parties and other groups that are willing to defend the political system, and there is a reasonable consensus among powerful groups on the location of political authority and the procedures for transferring power from one party to another.

By contrast, Latin America has historically had a higher rate of coups than Africa, despite higher levels of economic development. And several middle-income countries, such as Thailand and Argentina, have been prone to coups (Thailand last had a coup in 2014; Argentina experienced eight successful coups and at least twelve coup attempts in the period 1943–84). In Greece, democratically elected governments were overthrown by the military in 1967 and again in 1973, when it was firmly a middle-income country whose economy was growing strongly. In all of these cases (and many more from the first part of the twentieth century and late nineteenth century), political crisis – insurgency, conflict with radical ideological parties, and so on – not poverty, was the key factor disposing militaries to intervene. These political crises were sometimes related to economic crises – in Argentina, for example, the military typically intervened in periods when inflation was getting out of control and the Peronista labour movement was agitating for higher wages – but they were not identical with them. Accordingly, most research on the structural determinants of coups fails to find a strong influence of economic growth on coup risk (Singh, 2014; Belkin and Schofer, 2003; Londregan and Poole, 1990).

Though economic growth does not appear to be a major determinant of military intervention, it appears to be the case that high levels of economic inequality do matter (Svolik, 2012, ch. 5). The reason seems to be that high levels of economic inequality produce high levels of mass conflict (large-scale protests, and so on), which lead governments to become dependent on the military, since the army is typically the only organization with the repressive capacity to deal with large-scale protest. But the more dependent governments become on the military, the easier it is for the military to push them aside. Indeed, Svolik (2012, pp. 134–135) notes that at very high levels of inequality, we should see *less* direct military rule than at middle levels of inequality, simply because governments then are so utterly dependent on the military that the latter need not intervene directly to make its preferences prevail.

This is not to say that military rule is necessarily 'right wing'. Many military coups have been staged by impeccably socialist leaders, some of whom have moved on to attack entrenched elites, such as the 1952 coup that brought the Revolutionary Command Council and Gamal Abdel Nasser to power in Egypt, or the 1968 coup that brought General Velasco Alvarado to power in Peru. (Both of these coups, incidentally, were greeted with great enthusiasm by the masses when they happened; see Woodward (1992) for a description of the atmosphere in Egypt after Nasser's coup.) High levels of social conflict, fuelled by large structural inequalities, make the military more autonomous from the government, and more able to intervene on *either* side of a conflict.

Societies with strong, organized civilian movements committed to the defence of representative institutions have nevertheless often proved surprisingly able to resist military coups, even in conditions of persistent political conflict, and despite the overwhelming advantages of the military in terms of weapons, speed, and organization. Consider the failure of the Kapp Putsch in 1920s Germany, which aimed to overthrow the Weimar Republic. Here we have a society undergoing an extreme economic and social crisis brought about by defeat in the First World War – conditions which favoured military intervention – yet the coup failed after political parties, trade unions, and many other organizations in Germany's dense civil society followed a call by the legitimate government for a general strike.

By contrast, in largely rural societies with few national organizations other than the army, military intervention could happen apparently at will; the dismal story of Paraguay between 1935 and 1954, before General Stroessner succeeded, after a successful coup, in consolidating his personal rule for the next 35 years, can be told as a bleak succession of coups and countercoups where governments of all kinds were unceremoniously evicted by military leaders if they did not like their policies, and sometimes for no particular reason at all save the desire for power (Finer, 1962, pp. 131–2).

Authoritarian Consolidation after Coups

Structural factors are not destiny, however, and many rulers succeed in 'coup-proofing' their regimes (Quinlivan, 1999). General Stroessner survived for 35 years in power not because the Paraguayan military suddenly became much less likely to intervene in politics, or even because he himself was a military man, but because he was able to prevent coups by skilfully managing his relationship with the army. Similarly, in Syria, a country that Edward Luttwak (the writer of an influential 'practical handbook' on coups in 1968) once called 'the coup country *par excellence*' (Luttwak, 1969, p. 80), there were nine successful coups and some unknown number of unsuccessful coup attempts between independence in 1946 and 1971, after which Hafez al-Assad, himself coming to power in a coup, managed to rule uninterruptedly for nearly 30 years, died in office, and passed power on to his son Bashar al-Assad. The latter is still in power despite a rebellion that has raged since 2011; and though there have been a couple of coup attempts in this long span of time, none has succeeded. The reason for this relative stability is that both al-Assads, father and son, have made it very difficult for the military to act against them – creating parallel military organizations, filling the high command with members of trustworthy groups, rotating personnel frequently, and so on.

Once begun, coups have tended to continue until a sufficiently skilful leader manages to domesticate the military or consolidate power in his own person. Indeed, one of the best predictors of the risk of a coup is another recent coup (Belkin and Schofer, 2003), since, as Finer noted, 'the claim to rule by virtue of superior force invites challenge; indeed it is itself a tacit challenge, to any contender who thinks he is strong enough to chance his arm' (Finer, 1962, pp. 17–18). In 1968, then Iraqi prime minister Abu Zuhair Tahir Yahya is reported to have said, 'I came in on a tank, and only a tank will evict me' (Luttwak, 1969, p. 149). But though Tahir Yahya did not, at the end of the day, wait for the tanks to evict him (he shortly thereafter resigned his post, complaining that his warnings of an impending coup were not being taken seriously), the Baath Party quickly obliged, overthrowing the government of president Abdul Rahman Arif only a week later, and paving the way for Saddam Hussein's rise.

Iraq, which had three successful coups and several more unsuccessful coup attempts between the overthrow of King Faisal in 1958 and the Baath Party's rise to power in 1968, is the typical case; coup attempts only ended with the consolidation of the personal dictatorship of Saddam Hussein in the 1980s, whose regime survived defeat in the first Gulf War (1992) and was finally dismantled only with the American invasion of Iraq in 2003 (Quinlivan, 1999). Coups are thus a symptom of what we might call 'normative fluidity': they are rare in both consolidated democracies and consolidated authoritarian or totalitarian regimes, in the former because the norms regulating political competition are well established and have many organized defenders (Lehoucq and Pérez-Liñán, 2014), and in the latter because the regime has succeeded in 'coup-proofing' itself, or can draw on many organized defenders beyond the military, such as a political party or a parallel armed organization (Haber, 2006).

Thus, the majority of military coups in the twentieth century occurred in poorly consolidated authoritarian regimes suffering from political crises, and have typically resulted in the substitution of one authoritarian regime by an even more authoritarian one (Figure 6.2), as in the overthrow of

Libya's monarchy by the Free Officers' movement in 1969, which eventually led to the personal rule of Qaddafi. By contrast, a regime where there is relative consensus among powerful groups about the norms of political competition is basically invulnerable to coups, though such norms can be disrupted by severe political crises. The famous military coup of 11 September 1973, against the democratically elected president of Chile, Salvador Allende, was unusual, since it overthrew the leader of an already fairly democratic country with a highly developed civil society and a long tradition of representative institutions; it speaks to the depth of the political crisis in 1973 that the coup was able to succeed (Constable and Valenzuela, 1993, ch. 1).

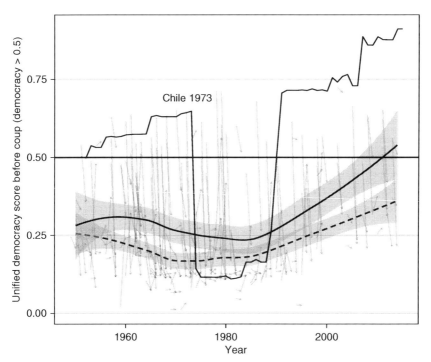

Figure 6.2   *Level of democracy before and after coups, 1950–2015. The smooth solid black line represents a smoothed line of fit for the average level of democracy in a country before a successful coup took place; the dashed line represents a smoothed line of fit for the level of democracy after the coup took place. Each small grey arrow represents the change in the measured level of democracy in a given country produced by a successful coup. Scores above 0.5 can be considered more or less democratic. Chile's democracy scores for the entire period are provided for illustrative purposes. Data on coups from Powell and Thyne (2011) updated to 2015; data on democracy by Pemstein, Meserve, and Melton (2010), extended by the author to 2015 and transformed to 0-1 scale (Márquez 2016a).*

The Fragility of Military Rule

In practice, though men with arms have often ruled – in historical aristocracies and aristocratic monarchies, the nobility was composed of the main specialists in violence in society – modern military rule is more fragile and less violent than one might expect (Geddes, Frantz, and Wright, 2014). Purely military regimes have tended to be brief affairs, lasting fewer years than other regimes (Geddes 1999; Geddes, Frantz, and Wright, 2014). For example, while nearly half of all non-military regimes classified by Geddes, Wright, and Frantz (2014) survive for 20 years or more, fewer than a quarter of the regimes with significant military involvement survive that long, and the proportion of military regimes surviving to any given length of time is consistently lower than the proportion of non-military regimes surviving to the same length of time (Figure 6.3). Moreover, military regimes not only present themselves as 'temporary' – in keeping with the original meaning of 'dictatorship', as we saw in Chapter 2 – but in fact often attempt to extricate themselves from power voluntarily, or at least to transform themselves into 'civilian' regimes, in keeping with their promises.

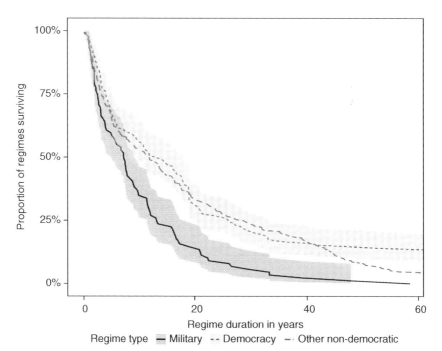

Figure 6.3   *Estimated duration of regimes with substantial military participation vs. other regimes, 1945–2010. Shaded areas denote 95 per cent confidence intervals. Data from Geddes, Wright, and Frantz, (2014).*

For example, the Brazilian military regime of 1964, after seizing power and dissolving the old political parties (in 1965), nevertheless soon encouraged the formation of two political parties to contest congressional elections and influence (but not control) policy-making. Though these elections were not free, and one of the parties in particular – the Brazilian Democratic Movement (MDB) Party – was consistently hamstrung in its attempts to engage in opposition to the regime, they nevertheless were not pure puppets of the military, and by 1974 were playing a relatively independent role, with one of them consistently being identified with the government, and the other with the opposition (Mainwaring, 1995). Even those rare military regimes that do not begin with promises of impermanence, such as the Argentine military dictatorship of Videla (who seized power in 1976), are often forced by events to disengage from direct rule, or, what amounts to the same thing, to engage in politics. Soldiers who wish to become rulers must become politicians; yet there are few reasons to think that most soldiers make good politicians (Finer, 1962, p. 196).

Scholars have proposed several reasons for the failure of 'pure' military rule under modern conditions. First, professional military men are often ill-prepared to run a complex modern economy without the cooperation of civilian forces (Finer, 1962, p. 15). Their training and separation from civilian society prepares them for war, not for peace. They are specialists in coercion, but this is rarely enough to govern. Second, and relatedly, military regimes just find it hard to secure this cooperation after the immediate political crisis that brings them to power is past and their failures to solve the main problems of governance faced by the countries they rule become apparent. They are 'born in sin', as it were. To secure sufficient civilian cooperation they must share power; and genuine power-sharing rekindles the separation between the political and the military leadership that makes it possible for the latter to overthrow the former. The 'civil-military problematique' – essentially, the problem of who will guard the guardians (Feaver, 1999) – re-emerges with a vengeance the moment military leaders are compelled to become full-time politicians.

Finally, and perhaps most importantly, the more professional the military – the more its members are socialized into a distinctive ethos of military service – the more likely they are to prefer military unity over remaining in power (Geddes, 1999; Geddes, Frantz, and Wright, 2014). If the choice is between splitting the military into politicized factions that will fight one another or returning to the barracks, military rulers have often preferred the second option. In more technical terms, the incentives of professional military men often predispose them to 'bandwagon' – to side with the leaders of a coup when it looks like they are winning (rather than to fight against them) – but also to retreat to civilian life when it looks as if political division might lead to fighting. The incentives for elite cohesion that the military organization provides thus work to shorten the life span of purely military regimes.

Consider the example of Argentina, where recurrent divisions within the army led to periodic retreats from direct rule. In 1961, reasonably free elections for the Argentinian Congress produced the triumph of 'Peronista' forces unacceptable to the army. The Peronistas were loyal to the former president, Juan Domingo Perón, himself a military man who had been removed by a coup in 1955 after developing an independent power base in the organized labour movement. A classic charismatic 'populist' politician, he was in some respects the model for a figure we have already encountered in this book, the later (and late) Venezuelan president Hugo Chávez in the 2000s. When Arturo Frondizi, the civilian president at the time, refused to annul the elections, the army unceremoniously evicted him from the *Casa Rosada* and imprisoned him (Rock, 1985, p. 342).

Yet soon enough the army found itself divided on whether to remain in power or to quickly turn over the reins of power to a civilian government. On one side, the 'Azules' ('blues') wanted to quickly return to the barracks after manipulating the labour movement into supporting a suitable military man; on the other side, the 'Colorados' ('reds'), or as they were also known, the 'gorillas', rejected all compromise and wanted to remain in power for as long as possible. The conflict between these factions at times came close to erupting into 'open war' (Rock, 1985, p. 344); though some fighting is recorded, eventually the Colorados pulled back from the brink and grudgingly supported the Azules rather than risk full-scale civil war. Similar divisions are reported among the officers that overthrew the Egyptian monarchy in 1952, though in that case the problem was resolved through the creation of a regime party that served to marginalize pro-democracy army officers (Brownlee, 2007a; Woodward, 1992), making the regime less dependent on the military.

To the extent that purely military regimes endure, it is thus typically either because some external threat unifies the military (as in Myanmar, formerly called Burma, where a long-running insurgency has made the military reluctant to yield power until very recently), or because they are transformed into something else: the personal dictatorship of one of the coup leaders (as in Spain under Franco or Libya under Qaddafi), or a regime with parties and elections (as in Brazil after the 1964 coup). The key point is that, to endure, military dictatorships need to develop extra-military sources of support (Haber, 2006), like political parties that can be mobilized in defence of the regime and can ensure civilian collaboration (as in Egypt), or else figures within the military must be able to accumulate enough personal power to become more or less invulnerable to coups, in the process ceasing to be regimes where the military rules as an institution and become regimes where a person (the dictator) rules *through* the army.

A few military regimes are able to construct institutions ('juntas') that avoid these outcomes by institutionalizing rules for the transfer of power, representing military interests, and monitoring incumbents (Brooker, 2014, pp. 122–4), but these are fragile (juntas in 1952 Egypt and 1973 Chile were quickly reduced to irrelevance by Nasser and Pinochet, respectively; see also Figure 6.4) and are typically combined with some degree of civilianization, even if the latter simply involves the retirement of active-duty officers and their conversion into civil servants. In any case, pure military control has typically proven hard to 'legitimize' (O'Donnell and Schmitter, 1986); since, like most modern authoritarian regimes, modern military regimes are or pretend to be 'the rule by the few in the name of the many', rather than the 'rule by the few in the name of the few' (Perlmutter, 1981, p. 2), they soon require more credible disguises. And the forces pushing military organizations to extricate themselves quickly from power have only grown since the end of the Cold War (Marinov and Goemans, 2014).

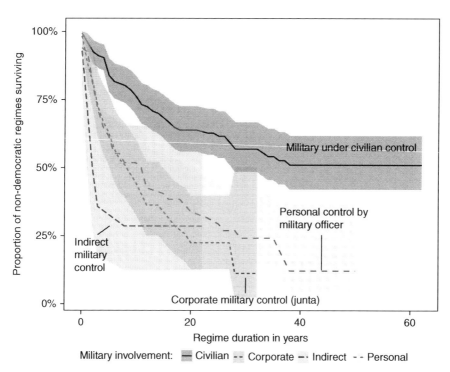

Figure 6.4 *Estimated duration of non-democratic regimes by type of military involvement in politics. 'Civilian' means the military is under the firm control of civilian authorities; 'personal' means the military is under the control of a military figure who has concentrated power; 'corporate' means a junta or some other military body rules; and 'indirect' means the military does not rule directly but has veto power over civilian authorities. Shaded areas denote 95 per cent confidence intervals. Data from Svolik (2012).*

Conclusion

Military coups have tended to happen in places where substantial political conflict increases the demand for 'solutions', but military organizations have often proved unequal to the task of governing, unless they cease to be purely military. And given the normative pressures favouring electoral regimes today, they have found it increasingly hard to justify their authority once the immediate crisis that triggered a coup is past. Thus, despite the fact that they control the means of violence, military regimes are surprisingly fragile and typically short-lived. In particular, military organizations seem to have difficulty maintaining elite cohesion in the face of disagreements about governance, leading them to prefer extrication from power to the possibility of civil war.

Chapter 7

Dynastic Families

Some modern authoritarian regimes do not pretend very hard to rule in the name of the people. Instead, they claim to derive their legitimacy from more traditional sources, such as a holy and exalted lineage. These are the 'absolute' monarchies. Monarchies in this strict sense are rare today, and they are mostly concentrated in the Middle East; but their longevity and geopolitical importance make it worthwhile to examine them in more detail.

As we shall see in this chapter, though the number of genuinely ruling (as opposed to constitutional) monarchies has declined greatly, consistent with the broad normative changes towards republican forms described in Chapter 2, most of the remaining monarchies have survived by institution-alizing certain kinship structures to produce surprisingly resilient regimes. In these regimes, the key institution through which power is exercised is neither the army nor the party, but the *dynastic family*. After describing the decline of monarchy in the modern world, we thus explore the conditions under which monarchical regimes have managed to endure in the modern world, as well as the distinctive ways in which they have held power through institutions that neither incorporate significant numbers of ordinary people into the regime (as parties do) nor specialize in the use of violence (as armies do).

The Decline of Monarchy

Observers of politics have historically applied the term 'monarchy' to a variety of superficially similar but sociologically often quite distinct regimes. Etymologically, monarchy is of course 'rule by one', but this does not get us far in understanding how (or if) the current Saudi monarchy differs from a personalistic dictatorship, let alone from a medieval French monarch or the British constitutional monarchy. A more promising approach suggests defining monarchies as regimes where there is a recognized norm of selecting an effective ruler with *lifetime tenure* from a specific family. This sort of 'ascriptive' selection process (selection by birthright), as sociologists sometimes call it, typically goes hand in hand with legitimating claims that do *not* appeal to the ultimate authority of the people (the king has authority not because he is the representative of the people, but because he is the representative of God, comes from an exalted lineage, and so on) and with an exalted status for the effective ruler. The titles 'King' or 'Queen' and their various equivalents – Prince, Sultan, Emir, Emperor, Caesar, Shah, and so on – are first and foremost markers of status, not only elevating the person of the monarch above the common run of people and entitling them to special visible honours, but also signifying their lifetime possession of political power.

To be sure, 'republican' titles such as 'President', 'Prime Minister', and so on are also markers of status, but they typically do not connote lifetime tenure; self-styled 'presidents for life' like Hastings Kamazu Banda of Malawi (in power 1964–94), François Duvalier of Haiti (in power 1958-71, 'president for life' from 1964), or Jean Bédel Bokassa of the Central African Republic (in power 1965–79), have to explicitly indicate that their office is not subject to re-confirmation at more or less regular intervals. With kings, that goes without saying. The combination of an ascriptive norm of selection to offices with effective political power (rather than more or less ceremonial positions, such as the British Queen), lifetime tenure, and a particular set of person-centred rituals and symbols defines monarchy.

Given the magnitude of the shift towards democratic norms of justification documented in Chapter 2, the survival of effective monarchies today presents a bit of a puzzle. Though ascriptively selected rulers were extremely common before the nineteenth century, nowadays the number of national states with monarchies in this sense is tiny; using data from Polity IV (Marshall, Gurr, and Jaggers, 2010), we find no more than 11 countries (Bahrain, Bhutan, Jordan, Kuwait, Morocco, Oman, North Korea, Qatar, Saudi Arabia, Swaziland, and the United Arab Emirates) where there is a norm of selecting members of a particular family for the top executive offices, and one of them is North Korea, which is not (normally) considered to be a monarchy. Moreover, in six of these (Bhutan, Jordan, Kuwait, Morocco, Swaziland, and the United Arab Emirates) monarchs share some power with other institutions, such as parliaments. We have to go back to the beginning of the twentieth century to find a substantial number of regimes where ascriptively selected rulers wielded substantial powers, and most of these died out after the First World War, when a large number of monarchies were overthrown all over the world (see Figure 7.1).

Once overthrown, older forms of monarchic legitimacy have proven difficult to resurrect, even if we broaden our scope to include ostensibly 'republican' leaders who have tried to ensure that control over the state passes to their sons or other family members after their death or retirement, as Mubarak tried to do in Egypt and Qaddafi attempted in Libya. 'Transitions to monarchy' are quite rare, even though many highly personalistic regimes have shown a tendency to turn into family enterprises. But these family regimes have also been fragile beyond the second generation when succession happens in the context of ostensibly 'republican' norms of justification.

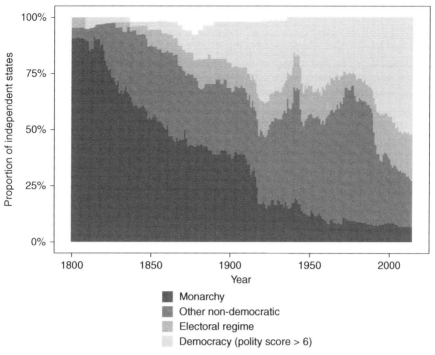

Figure 7.1   *Proportion of monarchies around the world, 1800–2015. All countries whose executive is selected through 'ascription' (whether or not it is paired with other forms of selection) are identified as monarchies. Excludes periods of foreign occupation or anarchy, and countries with fewer than 500,000 people. Data on executive selection from Polity IV.*

For example, though the self-declared 'president for life' of Haiti, François Duvalier (also known as 'Papa Doc'), was succeeded upon his death by his son Jean Claude ('Baby Doc') in 1971, the latter was overthrown in 1986; and though the Trujillo regime in the neighbouring Dominican Republic was by most accounts dominated by his immediate family, Trujillo was assassinated in 1961 before he could ensure a smooth succession (Wiarda, 1968). Brownlee (2007b) counts only ten hereditary transitions in republican contexts in the period 1946–06 from a possible total of 258; and only one of these transitions (the North Korean transfer of power from Kim Il Sung to Kim Jong Il) has now continued into the third generation (when Kim Jong Un succeeded Kim Jong Il in 2011). To be sure, more remote historical examples (for example, the transition from the Republic to the Principate and later to the Empire in ancient Rome) could also be adduced to show that transitions *to* monarchy are rare but not impossible. And it is also worth noting that some supposedly 'ceremonial' monarchs, such as the Thai king, have managed to strengthen their real political powers even in the context of representative institutions and occasional military rule (McCargo, 2005). But in general, monarchy in the strict sense of the term seems to have declined quite substantially, and transitions to monarchy seem to be extremely rare.

The scarcity of monarchies today, along with the rarity of transitions to ascriptive selection processes in the modern era, has led some commentators to consider monarchies as 'antiquated' political systems, 'traditional' survivals doomed to extinction. Already in 1968 Huntington (1968) argued that monarchies were peculiarly ill-suited to dealing with the stresses of economic development due to their inability to include emerging social groups into the ruling coalition. And his case certainly seemed compelling at a time when most remaining monarchies were falling victim to new republican regimes. Yet Huntington's predictions did not come to pass, since some monarchies still remain even in the information age, and show few signs of dying. We could thus conclude that the remaining monarchies are precisely the most resilient examples of a once common political form; whatever the Saudi monarchy is doing, for example, it has served it well for over 70 years, despite enormous geopolitical and economic changes. Indeed, surviving monarchies appear to have weathered the protests of the 'Arab Spring' better than nominally republican regimes, and to have been freer of various forms of political instability than their non-monarchical neighbours (Menaldo, 2012).

Lynchpin vs. Dynastic Monarchies

In any case, most contemporary monarchies are not truly traditional. Instead, they are for the most part the legacies of British imperial policies in the early part of the twentieth century, when most of the states of the Middle East were shaped (Anderson, 1991). Though not every monarchy still remaining today is the result of British policy (Saudi Arabia was forged in the late 1920s and early 1930s by Ibn Saud through the conquest of nominally independent parts of the Arabian peninsula, for example), Europeans, 'taken with what they believed to be political and cultural precedent, endowed the Middle East with an unusually large number of monarchies' (Anderson, 1991, p. 3). Imperial policy helped particular lineages consolidate control over nascent proto-states, especially in the Gulf, and even created a number of new states from whole cloth after the Second World War, strongly encouraging the emergence of regulated forms of hereditary succession in them (Menaldo, 2012, p. 717).

To be sure, not all of these monarchies survived the upheavals of decolonization in the 1950s and 1960s, despite the best efforts of imperial powers. The Egyptian and Iraqi monarchies, for example, were overthrown in the 1950s by left-wing nationalist forces led by the military, while the Libyan monarchy lasted longer, until overthrown by Qaddafi and the Free Officers group in 1969. But the monarchies that survived were quite distinctive. They seem to have been of two types: 'lynchpin' monarchies in which the king stands aloof from the day-to-day governing process while forging alliances with parties and social groups outside the royal family, such as the Jordanian monarchy (Lucas 2004); and 'dynastic' monarchies, in which senior family relatives typically constrain the ruler and monopolize key state offices (Brooker, 2014; Herb, 1999).

In lynchpin monarchies, the king keeps power by successfully *mediating* between competing social forces which have independent power bases (for example, non-Bedouin Jordanians, Bedouin, and Palestinians in Jordan), a task that requires genuine political skills but is also helped by economic subsidies – provided today both by the United States and by other monarchies in the region (see Yom and Gause, 2012) – and by skilfully deploying the symbolic capital that monarchic symbols can provide (for example, descent from the Prophet Mohammed, as in the Jordanian case). Dynastic monarchies, by contrast, can be compared to closely held 'family firms', with the family business being the corporate control of the state (and the enjoyment of its oil rents, in the Gulf monarchies), the king as the family CEO, the senior male relatives as the key executives and company board, and most of the remaining family members as shareholders and lower-level employees.

Dynastic Monarchies as Family Firms

The Saudi monarchy fits the dynastic model quite well. Senior members of the family monopolize all important state positions, such as the defence, interior, and foreign ministries, and they play a role in determining the king's successor. Since 2007 there is even a formal institution, the 'Allegiance Council', staffed entirely by senior princes, that is supposed to select and confirm a new king and crown prince. Like a responsible company board, the senior princes have on occasion deposed rulers deemed to be irresponsible, and bypassed unsuitable candidates for the succession. For example, they briefly eased King Saud bin Abdulaziz from governance after he blundered with an ill-conceived plot to kill the immensely popular president, Gamal Abdel Nasser, of Egypt in 1958, and then more permanently in 1964, when they formally deposed him in favour of his brother Faysal. And the family chose not to make Muhammad bin Abdulaziz king in 1975, despite the fact that he was the most senior of the surviving sons of Ibn Saud after the death of King Faysal, probably due to general agreement within the family that his temper and drinking habits made him a bad candidate (Herb, 1999, p. 102). (Abdulaziz was briefly crown prince in 1964, but resigned quickly from this position under pressure from his brothers.)

Moreover, because the family is so large – Yamani (2009) estimates there were 22,000 royals in 2009, a ratio of about one per thousand inhabitants – it can control not only what in Arabic are sometimes called the 'ministries of sovereignty', the most sensitive positions in the state, but also place its members throughout the state apparatus, and in particular the armed forces, where they serve to deter coups (Quinlivan, 1999). (The large number of royals is partly due to polygamous practices. And not all royals are directly descended from King Saud.) The family also serves as an information-gathering mechanism through the practice of 'audiences' with royals, which it uses both to understand what the population is thinking in the absence of a free media and to provide particularized favours:

> The ruling families, and especially the Al Saud, use the size of the family to extend the *majlis* [audience] system to as many citizens as possible ... Like American members of Congress the princes of the Al Saud act as intermediaries between citizens and the bureaucracy, earning personal credit for solving the problems that arise out of a bureaucracy that is, in the first instance, a creation of the Al Saud. (Herb, 1999, p. 43)

The royal family in Saudi Arabia has also developed many of the institutions of successful political parties. Its internal culture is highly hierarchical (deference to older members is strictly enforced, even when the difference in age is only of a few days), though consultative; major decisions are supposed to be made by consensus, and princes are expected to speak candidly about what they learn through their contacts with the population (princes who develop a reputation as liars are unlikely to go very far). Furthermore, it has created effective private disciplinary and dispute-resolution mechanisms (including, on occasion, special jails for misbehaving princes outside the regular legal system). In return for lifetime submission and service, all royals receive an allowance and (in Saudi Arabia) a state job, calibrated to their seniority and political importance. These rewards are difficult to estimate, since the Saudi state is understandably not keen to publicize the amount of state oil revenue that goes straight into the pockets of Al Saud family members, but Herb (1999) cites estimates that suggest that at the height of the oil boom, in the 1970s, the family received at least 12 per cent of all government revenue - an unimaginably large sum, given the many billions of dollars earned by Saudi Arabia from high oil prices at the time (1999, p. 31). In percentage points, the Al Thani of Qatar received an even larger amount, an astonishing 32.8 per cent of all oil revenues, and the Al Thani are a much smaller royal family than the Al Saud.

Succession Rules

One of the key things that makes family governance work is, paradoxically, the indefiniteness of the succession rule in the dynastic monarchies. The succession norm in Saudi Arabia, for instance, only establishes that the kingship should pass to the most senior 'able' male descendant of Ibn Saud, rather than simply to the eldest son or brother of the current king. One might think that this would exacerbate the succession conflicts common in many monarchies – almost half of all Romanovs in Russia from Peter the Great to Nicholas II died in family disputes over succession issues (Kotkin, 2014, Kindle loc. 1943), and the Ottoman Sultans even formalized their right to kill their surviving brothers on acceding to power in a 'Law of Fratricide' in the sixteenth century (Herb, 1999, p. 27). But the very indefiniteness of the succession norm, combined with the emergence of the modern state with its many positions to fill, actually incentivizes family members to 'bandwagon' against ambitious princes who threaten the corporate hold of the family.

Though ambitious princes may prefer to rule unconstrained by the 'company board' of their senior brothers and uncles, they will typically prefer that the state remain in family hands over one of their brothers ruling alone or with the support of outsiders. And those from cadet branches of the family who are not contending for the rulership have little incentive to jeopardize their position by supporting candidates who take 'extreme' measures in their quest for power, such as threatening intrafamily violence or directly appealing to outsiders for support. For example, when King Saud bin Abdulaziz did a tour of the realm in 1963 distributing money to tribal chiefs in an attempt to salvage his position and undermine his brother Faysal by securing the support of 'outsiders', uncommitted family members quickly switched to Faysal's side; as Herb (1999) says, the only effect the trip had was 'to enrich some bedouin shaykhs and to further alienate his brothers, who sought a decree from the *ulema* [the religious establishment] declaring Faysal the ruler and making Saud king in name only' (1999, p. 97). Shortly afterwards, Saud threatened violence against Faysal, which sealed his fate; the senior princes now deposed him for good.

Since different contenders will normally tend to offer similar 'bargains' to influential family members in return for support, there is little point for uncommitted princes to strongly support candidates that threaten to overturn the family monopoly on power, while the losing contenders can expect to be rewarded with money and influence even if they do not inherit the kingdom. Thus, despite not being made king in 1975, when his brother Faysal died, Muhammad bin Abdulaziz remained an immensely wealthy, respected, and influential member of the family. By contrast, a rigid succession rule provides incentives for ambitious royals to use more extreme measures (for example, poisoning their brothers, appealing to the people) that risk the family monopoly on power.

The Importance of Elite Cohesion

On this account, the Saudi family does not remain in power because of special family bonds, the certainty provided by a clear succession rule, or some Saudi cultural predisposition towards monarchy, or even the fact that Saudi Arabia is a key US ally and one of the world's largest oil producers, but through the incentives for elite cohesion provided by dynastic rule. To be sure, Saudi oil wealth certainly helps the king buy support among both family members and the rest of the population, but the price of support is subject to inflationary pressures; more oil revenues mean potential contenders must pay more for support. King Idris of Libya was overthrown when oil revenues were flooding state coffers, partly because he had no family members who had incentives to defend him. US support – another factor usually cited to explain the Saudi monarchy's longevity (Yom and Gause, 2012) – can also be a mixed blessing; on the one hand, it provides the family with access to intelligence and resources otherwise unavailable; on the other hand, it provokes a cultural backlash that challengers outside the Al Saud can and have mobilized (like the famous Saudi Osama bin Laden).

Instead, the family's endurance in power is due to the fact that there are few incentives for family members to mobilize outsider support in their disputes; attempting to do so merely makes family members bandwagon against you. Hence, despite many minor divisions, on crucial questions the family tends to remain united; and a ruling class that is unified on these questions – meaning, a ruling class that does not seek to bring in outsider support to settle its major disputes – is very hard to overthrow. Like successful party-based regimes, the Saudi monarchy endures because dynastic clan control over the state provides many incentives for elite cohesion.

This is not to say that the Al Saud and other Gulf Royal families do not have anything to fear from outsiders, or that they do not try to obtain support among other social groups. All successful non-democratic regimes have supporters beyond the ruling class, and the Gulf monarchies are no exception. They, too, distribute resources to favoured social groups in response to threats, and attempt to mobilize their financial resources and their symbolic capital ('legitimacy') to try to achieve the support of influential groups, such as the religious establishment. For example, when protests started spreading in the region in 2011, 'Kuwait announced a US\$5 billion domestic program that provided \$3,500 in cash to every citizen along with free foodstuffs for a year; the Saudi monarchy committed \$130 billion to job creation, salary increases, and development projects; and Qatar announced massive pay and benefit hikes for public servants and military personnel' (Yom and Gause, 2012, p. 83).

Saudi Arabia has also consistently attempted to co-opt the support of the religious establishment in the face of recurrent threats from radicals going back many years; in 1979 religious radicals even seized the Grand Mosque in Mecca for a few months. In response, Saudi rulers have consistently favoured certain schools of Islamic thought, providing them with great influence in educational matters, and appealed to religious symbols to establish their legitimacy (Menaldo, 2012, p. 711). Finally, the wealthy monarchies have also helped the poorer ones in moments of crisis; Saudi Arabia sent 1,500 troops to help put down a massive surge of protest in neighbouring Bahrain in 2011, and it provided more than $5 billion to oil-poor Jordan to help its Hashemite rulers deal with unrest (Yom and Gause, 2012, p. 83).

But none of these actions are particularly distinctive. Non-monarchical regimes that endure also develop 'cross-cutting' coalitions, use resources to try to prevent threats, attempt to legitimize themselves with whatever symbolic capital they command, and sometimes receive substantial foreign support. In any case the effectiveness of these tactics in monarchies is predicated on *family unity*. If incentives pushed ambitious princes to mobilize outsider support on their own, 'escalating' fights by, for example, courting the army or the clerical establishment as individuals, the Gulf monarchies would not be nearly as stable as they have proved to be.

Finally, it is easy to overestimate the mobilizing power of monarchical symbols and legitimating claims; even in the early twentieth century their hold on people was not nearly as strong as it might seem. Certainly the Arab countries that overthrew their kings in the 1950s and 1960s showed no particular attachments to 'monarchical' justifications, and though proper measurement of public opinion is impossible in the Gulf we do know that the royal families have sometimes needed to use coercion against the mass of the population – most spectacularly in Bahrain in 2011 – to remain in power. At best, monarchical symbols and political culture serve to 'coordinate' elite expectations (Menaldo, 2012, p. 711), which probably adds to their stability, but in this respect they do not greatly differ from other ideologies that have been used for the same purpose.

In some respects the Saudi system (and to a lesser extent the system in other dynastic monarchies) has more in common with systems of single-party rule than with medieval European kingship. The Al Saud are an odd party, to be sure; only women can join voluntarily (by marrying into the family) but without gaining any formal power (though they may have influence through their sons). But, with its internal dispute-resolution mechanisms, its intelligence networks, and its 'service' requirements, the family basically mimics the institutions of an effective (if small) party on the Leninist model, though without an elaborate guiding ideology. And thus the incentives that keep it in power are not dissimilar from the incentives that kept the PRI in Mexico or the CPC in China in power – they are reasons for insiders to stick together and not seek outsider support, and thus to prefer corporate control of the state to going alone.

Conclusion

As we have seen over the past three chapters, effective institutions of authoritarian rule typically work in similar ways everywhere. They mobilize the support of larger constituencies, generate incentives for elites to work together, and provide rewards for the committed and loyal while punishing the disloyal. When these institutions work, authoritarian regimes usually last beyond the life of any particular leader.

Successful monarchies are no different in this respect, despite being apparently out of step with the democratic norms of the modern world. The mere fact that a ruler calls himself 'king' is no guarantee of longevity, unless he and his family have sufficient skill to create a cohesive elite, manage the loyalty of family members, and secure the acquiescence or support of groups beyond the ruling elite.

Chapter 8

Problems of Non-Democratic Consolidation and Control

Political power in non-democratic regimes is never wholly secure. Ambitious insiders may plot to achieve absolute power; and outsiders may gather enough support to supplant an existing ruling elite. Even the most complete personal autocrat still fears the possibility of a popular uprising, and needs to always to be on his guard against ambitious subordinates. Though, as we have seen (Chapters 4–7), the most important risks to rulers and ruling elites in non-democratic regimes usually come from *within* the ruling elite, leaders and other authoritarian elite members do spend significant resources trying to avert challenges from outsiders. This chapter focuses on the tactics rulers and ruling elites use to prevent such challenges and ensure their control over the broader population.

These tactics range widely, from simple repression to the sophisticated manipulation of information and emotion, depending on the objectives leaders pursue and the environment in which they must act. Among the means rulers and ruling coalitions use to secure popular support or acquiescence, this chapter describes the uses and limits of surveillance, propaganda, and cults of personality. We shall argue that, in general, these tactics have two primary functions: making it difficult for people to mobilize *against* the regime, typically by demoralizing and scaring them (tactics of 'fear'); and increasing their attachment to the regime (tactics of 'love'). Yet, as Machiavelli noted many centuries ago (*The Prince*, chapter 15), there are important trade-offs between 'fear' and 'love'. Though all rulers would wish to be both loved and respected, it is not always possible to ensure this; and in the final instance, fear turns out to be a more reliable guide to the preservation of a regime than love, as Machiavelli argued.

The production of both fear and love depends fundamentally on the gathering and manipulation of *information*. All successful political regimes require accurate information to function, and in turn use information (or mis-information) to achieve a variety of objectives. First, all regimes need reliable information about the activities, characteristics, and moods of the population they rule over in order to make rational decisions. Second, all modern states, like all large organizations, also need reliable information about the activities of their lower-level agents – bureaucrats, party workers, and so on. Third, all political leaders require reliable information about potential challengers within and outside the ruling elite in order to effectively defend their position. And fourth, all regimes attempt to shape public opinion by selectively releasing or distorting information, or privileging certain narratives over others.

Though these uses of information are common across all regime types, non-democratic regimes face several challenges that, though not unknown in democratic regimes, are far more acute in political systems that explicitly attempt to restrict political competition and concentrate power. Simplifying greatly, we might say that the people lie more to their rulers (and to each other) the more totalitarian the regime, and that in turn more totalitarian regimes lie more to the people. The challenge from the regime perspective is thus how to figure out the truth behind the lies of the people, while making its own lies reasonably credible, or at least capable of holding people's attention. We shall call these the *information management challenges* of non-democratic regimes. In the first two sections of this chapter, we thus begin by exploring the specific ways in which the use and management of information is distinctive in non-democratic regimes.

Information is not the only thing that rulers need to use well; they also need to manipulate emotion, primarily via the deployment of symbols and the staging of various 'rituals of power'. In the last section, we look at the variety of ways authoritarian rulers make use of symbolic politics, noting both its powers and its limits.

The People's Lies

The task of gathering information about a population is never straightforward. In fact the whole development of the modern state is bound up with the development of new ways of producing knowledge about populations (Foucault, 2008; Foucault, 2007); the very word 'statistics' betrays its origins in this process of state development. Depending on the goals pursued by state elites, the production of this information will require making the population more or less *legible*, a process that may involve various degrees of coercion (Scott, 1998), and which may be resisted by people for a wide variety of reasons. Beyond this very general problem faced by all modern states, every regime is also interested in information about which groups support it, as well as about the quality of that support.

The Totalitarian's Dilemma

In reasonably democratic regimes, there are many sources of information about this sort of regime support: polls, independent media, and the like provide a reasonably accurate (though not always perfect) picture of the regime's (and its leadership's) political support among a variety of groups. The same cannot always be said of authoritarian and totalitarian regimes, however, since their very power gives many groups in the population incentives to *hide* their true feelings (cf. Wintrobe (2000), who calls it the 'dictator's dilemma', as well as Kuran (1997), who speaks about 'preference falsification'). Indeed, the more powerful the leader and the regime – the more they are the main source of rewards and punishments in society – the more it pays to say only what the powerful want to hear; it is not for nothing that classic treatises on the education of personal rulers, such as Machiavelli's *The Prince* or Xenophon's *Hiero* strongly warn of the dangers of flattery. Effective non-democratic leaders are quite aware of this problem; as Mao wrote to Ho Chi Minh in June 1966, just as he was about to hit the peak of popular adoration in the Cultural Revolution:

> I advise you, not all of your subjects are loyal to you. Perhaps most of them are loyal but maybe a small number only verbally wish you "long live," while in reality they wish you a premature death. When they shout "long live," you should beware and analyze [the situation]. The more they praise you, the less you can trust them. This is a very natural rule. (Quoted in Leese, 2011, p. 186)

The closer a regime is to the 'democratic' side of the spectrum, the less pressing this problem will be. In competitive authoritarian regimes, there are enough independent (if sometimes harassed and biased) sources of information about popular opinion that the main problem will not be gathering such data but preventing opposition challengers from using it to effectively mobilize domestic or international opinion against the regime. But in personalistic and more totalitarian regimes the problems can be particularly severe. The personal ruler, for example, typically faces opponents who are especially interested in bringing about his 'premature death', and thus have the greatest incentives to hide their true views. And most of the Communist countries of the twentieth century, which espoused a particular ideological orthodoxy and credibly threatened to punish dissent from it, had to deal with preference falsification to some greater or lesser extent, since the appearance of orthodoxy was one of the preconditions for advancement in society, or even just for avoiding trouble. The Czechoslovak dissident Vaclav Havel powerfully captured the problem in his famous 'story of the greengrocer', written from prison in 1978 (Havel, 1992); the greengrocer puts up the Communist posters in his store not because he really believes in the slogans, but simply to 'avoid trouble', and because he is doing so just to 'avoid trouble' the fact that he mouths the slogans and puts up the communist posters is not a reasonable gauge of 'support' for the regime.

To be sure, 'as if' support (Wedeen, 1998) can help sustain a regime, since it makes it very hard for *opponents* to mobilize dissatisfaction. In a society where everyone is publicly indicating support for a regime, even in apparently insincere ways, potential opponents have a much harder time recruiting like-minded individuals to join their cause, and cognitive biases tend to demoralize them in any case, by making them *overestimate* the level of genuine support for a regime (Bicchieri and Fukui, 1999). But even though mere 'as if' signals of support may be sufficient to discourage the mobilization of opposition to a regime that strictly monitors the public observance of a particular orthodoxy, they complicate the task of gauging public opinion and mood, and thus can make negative surprises (from the point of view of the regime) more likely. Mere 'as if' support can, after all, be quite fragile (Kuran, 1991).

Surveilling the People

More totalitarian or personalized regimes typically attempt to solve the problem of gathering reliable information about popular opinion and moods, as well as about the activities of potential challengers, through the creation of surveillance organizations (for example, the KGB in the Soviet Union or the Stasi in the German Democratic Republic (GDR)) dedicated to the monitoring of both opponents and the general population. These organizations are not completely different from those intelligence agencies found in more democratic countries, but they are often larger and far more intrusive. The Stasi, for example, recruited more than 200,000 informants between 1950 and 1990 (Fulbrook, 1995, p. 228), and up to 2 million people - more than 10 per cent of the population - might have occasionally informed 'informally' on their fellow citizens. Indeed, the Stasi probably achieved the highest ratio of spies to population in history (Epstein, 2004, p. 322).

These organizations were often set up with the explicit purpose of spying on the population, and especially on potentially threatening groups. The Nazi Gestapo produced detailed reports of the public mood up to the very end of the Nazi regime (Kershaw, 1987). Similar reports were produced by intelligence units of the Falange in Spain and by the Cheka (later the KGB) in the Soviet Union. And they produced enormous amounts of information. For example, the Stasi gathered a staggering 174 kilometres of files on 6 million people, much of it stupefyingly banal (Epstein, 2004).

Nevertheless, the creation of dedicated surveillance apparatuses is not without trade-offs. For one thing, they are costly and not always reliable, since lower-level employees in these organizations often had career incentives to omit some negative information or to exaggerate positive information. Gestapo reports were often cheerier about the public mood in Nazi Germany than the reports produced by the underground organization of the Social Democratic Party, though both had their biases (Kershaw, 1987). In Spain during the early Franquista period – its most totalitarian period – reports on the public mood collected by the Falange were often perfunctory and uninformative.

(I speak from personal experience, having spent some time with these files at the Archivo General Administrativo near Madrid; see also Sevillano Calero (2000).) Perhaps more seriously, the Stasi failed to prevent the 1989 uprising in the GDR, or even to warn the leadership of increasing dissatisfaction with the system, despite having a wealth of public opinion data (including secret opinion polls), due in part to its ideological blinkers in reporting (Popplewell, 1992). To be sure, this was not all the fault of the Stasi; the top leadership of the SED (the East German ruling communist party) was rigidly committed to the triumph of socialism, and easily discounted information that did not fit within their ideological view of the world, an unfortunately all too human failing in many politicians. But the point is that the Stasi had incentives not to present the unvarnished truth to the leadership, or even to understand that truth properly.

Surveilling the State

More importantly, a too powerful intelligence service, just like a too powerful military, can become a threat to the leadership of a regime through its monopoly on information. The one man Stalin feared was Beria, the head of the NKVD (predecessor of the KGB); if Beria could condemn anyone to death, why not Stalin? After Stalin died, the rest of the members of the Politburo thus promptly banded together to arrest Beria before he could harm them (Svolik, 2012, pp. 132–3). Saddam Hussein nearly lost his life in a coup attempt in 1973 by Nadhim Kazzar, his hand-picked head of the Iraqi *Mukhabarat*, the security service or secret police of the Baath Party (Karsh and Rautsi, 1991, pp. 53–4). And in Peru in 1990–2000, Vladimiro Montesinos, the chief of the national intelligence service, basically ran the country behind the scenes through an elaborate web of bribery and corruption, making a puppet of Alberto Fujimori, the 'official' president, who was utterly dependent on him to govern (Mcmillan and Zoido, 2004). The more a ruler relies on his intelligence services, the more he is at risk of being under their thumb.

Leaders have attempted to deal with this threat in different ways. Some attempt to multiply intelligence services, setting them to monitor one another, and staff them with people of proven personal loyalty, engaging in coup-proofing against intelligence services as much as against armies (Quinlivan, 1999). But this strategy is costly and uncertain, given the difficulty of creating cohesive and efficient organizations; indeed, poorer authoritarian regimes sometimes prefer to encourage some measure of press freedom (with all its attendant risks of fuelling opposition) just so they can acquire accurate information about social conditions (Egorov, Guriev, and Sonin, 2009). For example, despite his tyrannical tendencies, the press was never very efficiently controlled in Mobutu's Zaire; and in the waning years of the Soviet Union Mikhail Gorbachev decided to liberalize the public sphere (the famous policy of 'glasnost') in part because information about what was really going on in the Soviet Union was increasingly difficult to obtain (Kotkin, 2008).

The problem in the Soviet case was less to understand the mood of the population – although that, too, was difficult – than to monitor the agents of the state, who were increasingly engaged in the most brazen forms of corruption:

> Widespread fictitious economic accounting was foiling planners to the point that the KGB employed its own spy satellites to ascertain the size of the Uzbek cotton harvest, but the spy agency itself suffered from internal falsifications. (Kotkin, 2008, p. 67)

Career incentives to lie are strongest in planned economies that reward meeting arbitrarily set production targets (like the Soviet Union), but they are common in all systems where most economic resources are controlled by the state. The results can be tragic; for example, there is substantial evidence that during the Great Leap Forward in China, ambitious apparatchiks could advance their careers by reporting fictitious crop numbers in line with Mao's optimistic expectations, leading to a great vacuum of information about the developing great famine at the top of the party apparatus (Kung and Chen, 2011; Leese, 2007; Walder, 2015).

The Regime's Lies

The flipside of the problem of *gathering* useful information is the problem of *using* information – making it public, shaping it into narratives, even inventing it – to shape public opinion: to energize and increase the number of supporters, while demoralizing and reducing the number of non-supporters. If the problem of gathering information in authoritarian systems is about figuring out the truth behind the population's (or the bureaucracy's) lies, the problem of using information is basically about how to lie (or at best, shade or hide the truth) in the most advantageous way possible. The dark arts of propaganda and public relations are of course used by politicians in all regimes, democratic or not, but authoritarian systems face some specific problems that are worth discussing: first, how much of the public sphere to control, and by what means; and second, how to ensure that the regime's message is credible and attended to. The solution to these problems has historically varied depending on geopolitical conditions, technological changes, and other considerations.

Regime Lies under Competitive Authoritarianism

Consider first the competitive authoritarian end of the spectrum. For a variety of historical reasons, ruling elites in these countries do not fully control independent sources of information, and opposition politicians can and do make use of the media to mobilize public opinion in their favour. When the ruling party is popular, this situation is not too threatening; indeed, a reasonably free media may help the regime maintain credibility as a democracy in the international arena. But when the regime becomes less popular, or feels particularly threatened by some opposition groups, it may wish to strengthen its control over the media. By some accounts, this is precisely the cause of increased 'communicational hegemony' in Venezuela (Corrales, 2015); the 2002 coup (where the private media played a key role in stoking anti-government protests and cheerleading the coup), and then the decline of oil prices in the waning years of the Chávez presidency, led to renewed efforts to push a pro-government message and to rein in anti-government media. Yet this could not be done directly without arousing too much domestic and international resistance; indeed, even the failure to renew the licence of the main private TV station, RCTV, in 2007, due to its anti-Chavista message and its role in the 2002 coup, triggered large anti-government student demonstrations.

So instead the government pursued a more indirect strategy. It increased its presence on the airwaves, creating new government-run channels, and slowly pressured private stations to self-censor (the example of RCTV had much pedagogical value) or to sell themselves to shadowy groups linked to the government; it sponsored new community radio stations and newspapers that were dependent for much of their funding on the government, and rationed newsprint to the most anti-government newspapers, reducing their circulation; and it made full use of laws and institutions that allowed it to pre-empt or punish recalcitrant private media (MacRory, 2013; Bennett and Naim, 2015; Corrales, 2015). Over time, this has meant that the government has come to control more of the message, especially away from the capital, where opposition media struggles to be heard. This has not meant that the population has become convinced of the government's claims – ratings for state TV are dismal, for example, in part because so much of its programming is considered boring and didactic – but it *has* meant that opposition parties have a harder time mobilizing the population around their message. Similar stories can be told about developments in Hungary, Turkey, Russia, and many other countries, as governments struggle to control the 'message' in the public sphere, either in the face of increasing opposition pressures, or for more ideological reasons (Bennett and Naim, 2015).

Regime Lies under Totalitarianism

The problem facing a regime that *already* controls the media and the education system, such as the North Korean regime, is slightly different – less about how to prevent opposition from using public information to mobilize opposition, and more about how to retain credibility in the eyes of the public. The less credible the government is, the easier it is for opposition to mount suddenly and unexpectedly, even in the absence of coordinating leadership (Lohmann, 1994; Bhavnani and Ross, 2003). Indeed, the very opacity of highly authoritarian and totalitarian regimes makes it difficult for them to make credible claims about their own strength. Minor changes in seating arrangements, the order of precedence at official ceremonies, the number of mentions of a person in the official newspaper, may all portend problems within the regime (or not), as the popularity of 'Kremlinology' (and its successor practices for North Korea and China) attest. This inherent lack of credibility is especially problematic during a succession crisis (Schedler and Hoffmann, 2016). Regimes must thus find ways to 'dramatize' that strength, usually through rituals that show the unity of the elite in a clear way: absurd denunciations of selected enemies, a refusal to speak anything but the ideological language, and so on.

One might think that total control over the information environment obviates the need for credibility – would not people reared on a constant diet of government lies simply believe whatever they are told, no matter how absurd? Yet the 'socializing' influence of media is often exaggerated, as we noted in Chapter 3. Nearly 40 years of Francoist propaganda did not turn Spaniards against democracy (Aguilar, 2009), and constant exposure to the cult of Ceauşescu did not turn most Romanians into his partisans (Tismaneanu, 1989). In China today – a country that, despite many changes liberalizing the public sphere, still maintains a large propaganda apparatus designed, in part, to persuade people of the 'legitimacy' of the CPC and its actions (Brady, 2008; Brady, 2009) – survey evidence suggests that more exposure to the most obvious forms of indoctrination, such as political education classes or newspapers like the *People's Daily*, is actually associated with more *negative* attitudes towards the government among university students and other groups (Huang, 2015b; Chen and Shi, 2001).

To be sure, people can be duped in particular cases, and control over the media does facilitate a certain kind of socialization. For example, in Soviet-style regimes of Eastern Europe, such as the GDR, people did absorb some of the egalitarian values of the official ideology to which they were exposed (Alesina and Fuchs-Schündeln, 2007), and today similarly many North Koreans appear to find the extreme nationalism pushed by the government propaganda machine at the very least congenial (Myers, 2010). But this socialization into a regime's values can be easily undermined when official claims come into conflict with lived experience.

When Ceauşescu prohibited Romanian media from reporting temperatures lower than 10 degrees Celsius to save fuel – the law required heating to be turned on when it was colder than 10 degrees – it did not improve the credibility of the regime (Sebestyen, 2010, p. 165). And unrelenting propaganda turned many East Germans into habitual cynics who did not believe anything the regime said (Pfaff, 2001), given the obvious failure of the promises of socialism. Indeed, this cynicism led many East Germans to habitually disbelieve claims that appeared in West German TV, which many of them received; they tended to view TV more as a source of entertainment than as a source of reliable information (Kern and Hainmueller, 2009). And ultimately, the very success of socialist socialization was the Achilles' heel of these regimes, as it ensured that their inability to fulfil their egalitarian promises would come back to haunt them in time.

The Censor's Dilemma

Regime credibility can only be maintained if regime messages do not habitually conflict with lived experience or deeply held popular values, or contradict other trusted sources of information. Rumour and gossip can often be deeply corrosive in authoritarian regimes; in China, for example, widely circulated anti-government rumours not only reduce trust in the government, but are very difficult to combat even when they are rebutted (Huang, 2015a). The problem is that the monopolistic control of the public sphere by the government may paradoxically reduce trust in its pronouncements, as people come to assume that anything communicated through 'public' channels is necessarily self-serving.

Thus, an authoritarian regime that is not utterly committed to preserving an ideological orthodoxy does not always have an interest in suppressing all public criticism. For one thing, criticism can be a source of information about lower-level malfeasance, popular needs and desires, and general policy feedback; for another, it might satisfy certain needs for expression, and allows it to modulate its own messages; and it also bolsters its own credibility on occasion. And though criticism sometimes makes collective opposition possible, not all criticism is immediately threatening. A sophisticated information management strategy thus does not attempt to silence all government criticism, but instead tries to prevent criticism from escalating into potentially uncontrollable collective action. This is precisely the sort of thing the Chinese government does today; it does not try to silence all criticism, but only those forms of criticism that threaten to produce unsanctioned collective responses (King, Pan, and Roberts, 2013). The Chinese public sphere is thus simultaneously lively and constrained; it produces much criticism but little coordinated action.

The same logic explains the apparently disproportionate efforts powerful governments expend silencing a few dissidents – from Vaclav Havel in Czechoslovakia to Aung Sang Suu Kyi in Burma to Andrei Sakharov in the Soviet Union to Ai Weiwei in China. These are typically people who have prestige and credibility that is independent of the state – they are great scientists (Sakharov), or the descendants of great independence figures (Suu Kyi), or recognized artists (Ai Weiwei), for example – which makes them able to speak authoritatively about matters of public concern. But their ability to 'speak truth' has greater potential to mobilize opposition forces than the voice of any other citizens. The problem with these figures is thus less the content of their speech – some may, in fact, accept the ideological orientation of the state, and see themselves merely as 'reformers' – than their ability to mobilize unsanctioned collective action; and it is this latter possibility that repressive responses attempt to quash, even in the face of strong international condemnation.

Even credible information from a regime will fail to have an effect on the population if it does not hold an audience's attention. The dullness of late-stage socialist propaganda was one of its weaknesses when considered as an instrument of persuasion, in contrast to the popular creativity of, for example, Cultural Revolution propaganda in China (Mittler, 2008; Mittler, 2012). Most modern Chinese propaganda is considered terminally dull by much of its audience, and appears to fail to persuade, as we noted earlier (Huang, 2015b; Chen and Shi, 2001). Similarly, many people in Franco's time (including Franco himself, who rarely read Spanish newspapers) drifted away from the rigidly controlled official media to unofficial sources or simply to private life (Payne, 1987), fatally undermining the regime's efforts to shape the souls of Spanish people.

One way of avoiding dullness is to encourage variety and free expression, as the Chinese regime does today – allowing lively, less controlled media alongside the duller official propaganda. But there are trade-offs here, which we might call the 'censor's dilemma': censor too much, and public life becomes dull, failing to shape people's values and opinions, but censor and control too little and alternate sources of information may become too threatening. During the early 1930s in Nazi Germany, for example, the *Frankfurter Zeitung* was given a bit of freedom not granted to most newspapers, due to its international reputation and the fact that it was owned by the industrial conglomerate I. G. Farben, which was important for Nazi plans. As a result the paper, formerly not that influential, quickly became the most important news organ in Germany, simply because it was the only place where credible information could be found. As the Nazi clampdown on the media intensified, however, the newspaper succumbed to political control, becoming just like all other newspapers. Most people then drifted away towards more stimulating but less informative forms of entertainment, like light music (Evans, 2006, Kindle loc. 2579–2595).

This is not to say that dull propaganda does not have its uses. For example, the sorts of propaganda the Chinese government still produces in great quantities – political indoctrination classes, prime-time TV shows like China Central Television's *Xinwen Lianbo* (Network News Broadcast) – though widely derided among the country's young as dull and formalistic, nevertheless send a signal that the government is 'strong', even if they fail to persuade. Survey evidence suggests that university students that remember more information from their political indoctrination classes are no more pro-government than other students, but they *are* more likely to think the government is strong and less likely to participate in dissent against it (Huang, 2015b). Obvious propaganda can be discouraging before it is persuasive.

In general, however, the tendency among authoritarian regimes today seems to be in the direction of avoiding dull and obvious propaganda while trying to manage the dangers of encouraging opposition. The current Russian regime, for example, appears to be determined that its propaganda be as unlike the ritualistic propaganda of the late Soviet regime as possible. Though it only controls the 'commanding heights' of the media, it fills the airwaves with an unrelenting stream of conspiracy theories and *risqué* reality shows that confuse and titillate the public (Pomerantsev, 2014). And though the regime cannot always achieve credibility (Russians may distrust Russian government pronouncements as much as they distrust any other source of information), it can nevertheless dent the credibility of alternative sources of information. This strategy is supplemented by such means as the use of paid Internet commenters, also found in many other regimes (the Chinese call them the '50 cent' party, in reference to the rate allegedly paid to the 'trolls' per post). The point of these tactics is less to ensure that the population is convinced of government claims than to muddy the waters and prevent the formation of cohesive anti-government public opinion. In other words, an authoritarian regime can *win* (that is, prevent opposition from coalescing) not necessarily by being the most credible source of information in the public sphere but by sowing enough confusion and distraction that coordinated action against it is very difficult.

From this perspective, 'winning' requires a certain degree of control over the main *mass* media – the broadcasting media, such as TV and radio, watched by the vast majority of the population – but it may not require any 'active control' over more fragmented media, like the Internet or 'high brow' publications. Consider again the case of Vladimiro Montesinos in Peru, mentioned earlier (Mcmillan and Zoido, 2004). Fujimori, a populist elected on a wave of anti-party sentiment in 1990, was widely thought to be a political novice, and did not command a parliamentary majority in a hostile congress. Montesinos then set about to make it possible for Fujimori to govern, primarily by bribing politicians, judges, and TV stations. He also documented all his bribes meticulously, videotaping them so that the people he bribed could not easily turn against him without being implicated themselves.

One of the striking findings uncovered by analysis of Montesinos' careful records was the importance he placed on controlling television; bribes paid to TV stations were more than a hundred times the amount paid to politicians, for the simple reason that information that became public via television was the most powerful means of mobilizing opposition. Indeed, the Montesinos regime unravelled when one of his videotapes found its way to the one TV station he had not thought worth bribing (given its small audience and interest in maintaining a 'clean' reputation). The same focus is clear in most non-democratic systems today. For example, the Venezuelan regime puts a lot more emphasis on controlling and creating its own mass media (primarily TV and community radio stations funded by the government) and pressuring existing TV stations to limit their criticism of the government than on controlling newspapers or Internet fora, which are more fragmented and less accessible to the vast majority of the population (Corrales, 2015).

Recently the argument has been made that the rise of new Internet 'social media' technologies makes classic information-management techniques less effective. Social media 'optimists' predict that social media will be more difficult to censor and manage than traditional media, perhaps due to what Ethan Zuckermann has called the 'cute cat' effect (Zuckerman, 2015), that is, the inability of governments to shut down social spaces used for many other purposes without incurring large costs to their authority. And there is some evidence that new social media technologies played a role in mobilizing opposition to the Ben Ali regime in Tunisia (Breuer, Landman, and Farquhar, 2014) and the Mubarak regime in Egypt in 2011 (Lynch, 2011).

But there is little evidence that these new technologies of communication have permanently changed the balance of forces in the struggle over information. Authoritarian regimes do not necessarily fear the Internet (Rød and Weidmann, 2015), and they have developed many tactics to pollute the information commons and monitor potentially dangerous people (Gunitsky, 2015; Tufekci, 2014). They have many resources for adaptation, and long practice in lying to the public. As we shall see below in more detail, the fact that social media played a noticeable role in the Egyptian uprising may have more to do with identity politics (disaffected young people were likely to gravitate to social media, just as in previous eras they were likely to gravitate to rock music) than with the intrinsic ability of social media to help mobilize opposition to authoritarian regimes (Slee, 2012).

Fear, Love, and Rituals of Power

Information management is typically deployed to prevent opposition and shape the views and values of a population; but it is also a part of a larger set of techniques of power intended to produce certain *emotions*. Authoritarian regimes, like all regimes, attempt to energize and increase the number of their supporters (to produce 'love', in short), while demoralizing and decreasing the number of their opponents (making them 'afraid', in short); and the deployment of information is only one part (though an important part) of a set of *rituals of power* for the management of emotion. Mass electoral meetings or anniversary parades, ruler adoration rituals, public trials and punishments, royal audiences, and even politicized soccer games are all part of the vast array of *interaction rituals* (Collins, 2004) that political elites can deploy to manage popular emotion and ensure the survival of the regime. Nevertheless, political rituals are not riskless for any regime; sometimes, as we shall see, political elites lose control of the dynamics of popular emotion, and the rituals they deploy end up being turned against them.

Rituals are part of all political systems, democratic or non-democratic, traditional or modern (Kertzer, 1988; Lukes, 1975). They come in many shapes and forms, not all of which are relevant for our purposes (see Goodin, 1978 for a useful typology). We are interested here in those rituals that are normally intended to 'legitimate' the state, or at the very least to increase attachments to political leaders and regimes. Such rituals range widely in scale, from spectacular mass gatherings requiring much organization (the Nazi rallies at Nuremberg, the mass receptions of the Red Guards for Mao at Tiananmen Square, the great pageants staged by Franco with the Falange in Spain, the May Day parades in the Soviet Union, large-scale election rallies in Chávez's Venezuela) to regular small-scale rituals in semi-public spaces and workplaces (for example, requiring students to salute the leader at school, self-criticism sessions in workplaces, rituals of initiation into youth organizations) to transitory and irregular rituals spontaneously emerging in some particular context (for example, loyalty dances during the Chinese Cultural Revolution (Jiang, 2010, pp. 208-10, photos 232-5)) or gift-giving on Stalin's birthday (Davies, 2004)) to 'private' rituals not required or monitored by the state (for example, burning incense in front of a shrine with a picture of Mao in place of the traditional 'stove god' (Steinmüller, 2010; Landsberger, 2002)).

The key feature that unifies these otherwise disparate phenomena is their ability to focus the attention of groups of people on regime-related symbols (the leader, the flag, slogans expressing the values to which the regime pretends to be committed, the heroes of the regime epic, particular episodes in its history, and so on) in order to amplify emotions associated with them. These regime-related symbols in turn circulate in chains of further rituals where their meaning and 'emotional charge' is constantly renewed (Collins, 2004).

Ritual is not mere propaganda, since it is not meant to be consumed passively by a population but requires some degree of active participation on their part. Such participation typically involves the production of appropriate signs of submission and support on the part of the population: cheering or being silent at the appropriate times; chanting certain slogans; using politically approved formulaic language; wearing appropriate clothing or carrying the right sorts of objects; performing some ceremonial action, like casting a vote; or even dancing and singing. Of course, some rituals are 'mediated' – only a small group may be physically present at a ceremony, while a larger audience may experience the event via television or other broadcast media – but to the extent that even the larger audience 'participates' in the ritual in some active way, it remains more than passively received propaganda.

Ritual and Resistance

Official ritual, like official propaganda, connects political symbols in elaborate and more or less coherent narratives that the powerful would like to be accepted, yet the political efficacy of ritual lies less in its cognitive content than in its emotional effects. In a ritual that 'works' properly, the group's 'emotional energy' increases, leading to a state of what the sociologist Émile Durkheim called 'collective effervescence', and making it possible for regime symbols to become deeply tied to a person's identity. Yet it is important to stress that, though official rituals are always intended to legitimate the state and its leaders, that is, to produce emotional commitments to the state by the people (Lane, 1981; Lane, 1984; Kertzer, 1988), we cannot assume that they automatically succeed in doing so. Rituals need not succeed in achieving 'political integration' (Lukes, 1975), and they can and do misfire, or fail to have much of an effect at all. For example, the many Soviet rituals consciously introduced in the 1960s and 1970s and documented in Lane (1981) failed to do much to arrest a loss of trust in the Soviet system and its leaders, despite confident assertions by some scholars, as late as 1984, that most people bought into them (Lane, 1984). Even early in the Soviet Union's life, when the revolution still commanded a great deal of popularity among the working classes, many rituals invented by the new regime to substitute for earlier religious rituals - like 'Octobering', a ceremony devised by the regime to mark the birth of a child with revolutionary symbolism in place of baptism - never had much popular support, and indeed were eventually abandoned due to their unpopularity (Gill, 2011, p. 74).

Moreover, though highly authoritarian states can flood public space with regime-related symbolism, they have no particular power to compel its acceptance in rituals if it does not 'resonate' with people's values or ideals. For example, in the 1950s, the Soviet-backed regime in East Germany made a concerted effort to promote the cult of Soviet leaders, printing hundreds of thousands of portraits and distributing them in rallies and parades. Yet these portraits were quickly discarded by ordinary people, who felt no particular affection for a regime many considered a foreign imposition (Tikhomirov, 2012, pp. 58–9). Many people also engaged in a wide variety of subtle acts of subversion of these official rituals and symbols: remaining silent when expected to cheer, refusing to buy the paraphernalia of the leader cults from shops, vandalizing statues and posters of Soviet leaders under cover of darkness, and the like. Such symbolic resistance culminated in an uprising in 1953 characterized by the 'iconoclastic' destruction of regime symbols, the only instance of large-scale protest in the GDR before 1989. As a result, the regime relented, toning down or abandoning the cult of Soviet leaders in favour of the promotion of rituals and symbols more in tune with popular feelings (Tikhomirov, 2012).

Resistance to imposed regime rituals and symbols is in fact quite common, though it is not always expressed so spectacularly as in the 1953 GDR uprising. Popular, even enthusiastic participation in regime rituals may coexist with an undercurrent of mockery that subverts the intended meaning of regime symbolism and the express purpose of the ritual. For example, in the Cameroon of Paul Biya and the Togo of Eyadéma, vulgar jokes at the expense of these two dictators were quite common, not just in the 'hidden transcript', away from the hearing of the powerful (Scott, 1985), as in the more repressive regimes of Romania under Ceauşescu or Syria under Hafez al-Assad (Tismaneanu, 1989; Wedeen, 1998), but in the double-entendres of popular responses in public events.

> [W]hen Togolese were called upon to shout the party slogans, many would travesty the metaphors meant to glory state power. With a simple tonal shift one metaphor could take on many meanings. Under cover […] of official slogans, people sang about the sudden erection of the 'enormous' and 'rigid' presidential phallus, of how it remained in this position and of its contact with 'vaginal fluids'. 'Eat your portion, Paul Biya,' echoed the Cameroonians, making allusion to the intensified prebendalisation of their state since 1982. (Mbembe, 1992, p. 6)

More often, however, the problem is less a population's resistance to regime symbolism than their lack of understanding of its meaning. When the Bolsheviks took power in Russia, the vast majority of the empire's population was illiterate, and could not understand the Marxist jargon their new rulers favoured (Gill, 2011, p. 21). Their symbols and rituals, from the Lenin cult to the May Day parades, were not always 'read' in the way that the political elite intended, not because people actively resisted, but simply because they did not understand them, or only vaguely grasped their meaning. As late as the 1920s people could be found who thought that Lenin was just the new Tsar (Tumarkin, 1983, p. 107). In fact, the vast majority of rituals in all political regimes have no univocal, easily understood meaning (Veyne, 1988), even where – as in the Soviet Union (see Lane, 1981, ch. 1) – ritual specialists expend much effort trying to design 'legitimating' ceremonies. As a result, ritual is only ambiguously effective as a socialization mechanism into regime values, since participants can often appropriate ritual symbolism for their own purposes.

The lack of univocal meaning for regime symbolism means that political elites are never in full control of the effects of ritual, as the population can sometimes 'turn the tables' on their rulers, especially when they participate in large groups and are expected to play symbolically defined roles, as Ceaușescu discovered in December 1989, when the mass meeting he called to signal his permanence in power turned into a televised mass protest against his rule, leading to his downfall only four days later (Sebestyen, 2010, ch. 48). The great rituals of capital punishment of the French monarchy before the French Revolution, public ceremonies intended to showcase the overwhelming power of the King, sometimes turned into riots due to the sympathies of the population with the condemned, and this was one reason they eventually disappeared (Foucault, 1995 [1975], ch. 1). And football matches in the Middle East, which have often been used to stoke pro-regime nationalist sentiment, have occasionally turned into uncontrollable displays of anger against those very regimes. In Libya in the first decade of the twenty-first century, crowds taunted Qaddafi's son Saadi (who fancied himself a professional football player) with the chant 'Saadi, don't think you are a big guy … Your destiny will be like Uday's' (Pargeter, 2012, p. 188). (Uday Hussein was, of course, Saddam Hussein's son, killed during the US invasion of Iraq.)

Ritual and Emotion

Yet despite these risks, mass gatherings are unmatched in their power to generate emotional linkages between particular groups in a population and their leaders, especially when participation is not compelled. The eight 'mass receptions' of the Red Guards by Mao Zedong at Tiananmen Square at the height of the Chinese Cultural Revolution led to ecstatic experiences among some participants, whose emotional bond with Mao was confirmed and amplified there (Leese, 2011); and the early Nuremberg rallies of the Nazi Party (immortalized in Leni Riefenstahl's film *Triumph of the Will*) were similarly received among some committed Nazis. This is not so much because Hitler and Mao were especially charismatic – Hitler was certainly an electrifying speaker in the opinion of many Nazis, but Mao mostly waved from the rostrum, saying little – but for similar reasons as a concert may produce ecstatic emotions among fans of a band, amplifying their reactions through co-presence and synchronized rhythmic activity (Collins, 2004).

Nevertheless, even 'successful' rituals – rituals that energize supporters and strengthen their emotional connection to a regime – need to be repeated if their emotional and cognitive effects are to endure; Collins (2004) speculates that the half-life of most rituals is about a week. Most political regimes thus celebrate various sorts of anniversaries – the leader's birthday, spectacular victories, glorious deaths, and so on – where a population's connection to regime symbols can be renewed, and the regime's 'metanarrative' (Gill, 2011) can be further elaborated. The great revolutionary regimes of the last few centuries went furthest in the direction of remaking the liturgical calendar as a way of breaking with their pre-revolutionary pasts, creating new feast days that commemorated important symbols of the regime to replace the feast days of the *ancien régime*.

For example, in the Soviet Union May Day (1 May) and the anniversary of the October Revolution (7 November by the new calendar) were major festive occasions; by 1930 many other events in the socialist 'epic' – including Bloody Sunday (9 January), Lenin's death (22 January), Red Army Day (23 February), Women's Day (8 March), the Day of the Overthrow of the Autocracy (12 March), Day of the Paris Commune, (18 March), the anniversary of 1912 Lena Massacre (14 April), the Day of the USSR (6 July), and the anniversary of 1905 Revolution (19 December) – had been officially recognized as special days of celebration (Gill, 2011, p. 74), while the holidays of the previous regime, such as Christmas and New Year, were de-emphasized. The French revolutionaries of the eighteenth century famously counted time from year 1 of the revolution, and for a time even attempted to substitute new, 'deistic' festivals (the short-lived 'festival of the Supreme Being') for the Catholic festivals to which the French population was overwhelmingly attached. But even non-revolutionary regimes have often instituted new ceremonial occasions. In Franco's Spain, for example, Victory Day (19 May, commemorating the victory of the Nationalist forces in the civil war), the Day of the Caudillo (1 October, commemorating the day when Franco became Generalissimo), and the anniversary of the death of José Antonio Primo de Rivera, the founder of the Falange (20 November), became major holidays in which huge public parades were staged (Payne, 1987). And in Paul Biya's Cameroon, 6 November (the anniversary of his ascension to power) was (and is) celebrated as a holiday (Mbembe, 1992, p. 18).

In most regimes, annual holidays and their associated large-scale public rituals are also supplemented by more frequent smaller-scale rituals, from very widespread practices such as singing the national anthem and pledging allegiance to the regime every morning at school to 'self-criticism' sessions at workplaces in Soviet-style regimes, specialized rituals intended to reinforce socialist values – and during the worst of the Stalinist period in the Soviet Union and the Cultural Revolution in China, to unmask and destroy 'class enemies'. Not all of these rituals have much of an impact on people's daily lives, and at any rate the extent to which the regime can compel participation in any official ceremony varies quite a bit. In many cases, compelling and monitoring large-scale participation in specific regime rituals is logistically unfeasible (only the committed, or those who hope to gain something from participation, show up), though the more totalitarian the regime, the more it is usually able to enforce and monitor general participation in great ritual occasions.

In North Korea today, for example, appropriate contributions to the mourning rituals for the deaths of Kim Jong Il or Kim Il Sung were apparently monitored by the local neighbourhood committee of the KWP, the 'inmiban' (see Demick, 2009); and in many other parts of the globe public participation in regime events has often been 'encouraged' by, for example, insisting that shops must close (Mbembe, 1992), or transporting public employees to them and conditioning their employment on attendance. Yet forcible participation in rituals does not appear to increase their emotional effectiveness, at least not if such participation is routinized and turned into a job requirement. Official celebrations in Franco's Spain became increasingly routinized and pro forma as time went on, never matching the intensity of the first few years of the regime, when thousands of people participated in carrying José Antonio Primo de Rivera's body to be interred at El Escorial (Payne, 1987, pp. 241–242). The early May Day parades in the Soviet Union, with their handmade signs and genuine popular involvement, appear by most accounts to have been much more successful demonstrations of popular commitment to the regime than the highly ritualized displays of military pomp of later periods (Gill, 2011; Tumarkin, 1983). Even the great Nuremberg rallies, attended by the most committed Nazis, 'lost their power to inspire' as time went on (Evans, 2006, Kindle loc. 4059). Emotional energy is generated by free participation in exceptional experiences, not by compulsory obeisance in routine and ossified ceremonies.

Cults of Personality and the Politics of 'As If' Support

Nevertheless, powerful social *expectations* of participation in official rituals, amounting to compulsion, can emerge even in the absence of explicit enforcement by the agents of the regime, long after all emotional links to the regime have been hollowed out; indeed, pressures to participate in regime rituals often emerge organically 'from below' even if few people identify with the regime or its leadership. This is most obvious in the case of many leader cults. A 'cult of personality' - a term popularized by

Soviet leader Nikita Khrushchev in his famous 'secret speech' denouncing Stalin's cult in 1956 (Khrushchev, 1956) - properly speaking consists not only in the propaganda surrounding the leader, but in the expectation to participate in ceremonies focused on showing one's loyalty to the leader. Much of the propaganda of the cult may be literally unbelievable and patently ridiculous, as when Hafez al-Assad was called Syria's 'premier pharmacist' by regime publicists (Wedeen, 1999, pp. 1, 12), or when the KWP's official newspaper, *Rodong Sinmun*, published an article in 2006 claiming that Kim Jong Il had perfected the art of teleporting himself instantaneously from one place to another, foiling US spy satellites (Hassig and Oh, 2009, p. 55), yet most people in those countries may still feel compelled to act *as if* they believed, by participating in leader adoration rituals (mouthing rote praise of the leader, keeping portraits of the leader in their homes, and so on), regardless of whether or not they 'buy' these claims.

In fact, there is a great deal of evidence that many people subjected to absurd leader propaganda do *not* believe these portrayals of their leaders in any straightforward way. Romanians under Ceauşescu, Spaniards under Franco, and Syrians under Hafez al-Assad certainly did not do so to any significant extent, despite an unrelenting barrage of inflated claims from state-controlled media about their leaders' godlike virtues (Tismaneanu, 1989; Wedeen, 1998; Fernández, 1983, pp. 311–324). Even most North Koreans, who are perhaps more isolated from outside sources of information than any other population in recent times, show few signs of literally believing their state's leader propaganda (Hassig and Oh, 2009; Chŏn et al., 2007); leader approval in North Korea, as in most countries, seems to be far more correlated with straightforward factors such as economic conditions or nationalistic associations than with the degree of flattery in their media. People are, for the most part, not dupes; the most that can be said for hyperbolic leader propaganda in North Korea (and elsewhere) is that it functions as a signal of the strength of the of the regime, like much other propaganda (Huang, 2015b), and that some of it appeals to particular national narratives that can be appreciated without being literally believed (Myers, 2010).

The problem, from the point of view of ordinary people, is that given the resources the elite is willing to spend on broadcasting absurd claims about the leader, no one can be sure that non-participation is not being watched and punished as a sign of disloyalty by more committed people; indeed, no one can be sure that non-participation in cult rituals cannot be used by cynical opportunists with no particular belief in the leader as an *excuse* to maliciously harm one's interests. This in turn may lead to general participation in the cult, which reinforces the expectation to participate, and so on, in a self-reinforcing spiral reminiscent of the old story about the emperor's new clothes (Centola, Willer, and Macy, 2005).

Some such process seems to have aided the formation of emperor cults in early imperial Rome, for example, as cynical and opportunistic senators had incentives to heap honours on the emperor and denounce for personal gain those who failed to show sufficient respect (Winterling, 2011); and in more recent times factional struggles at the top of the Communist Party in the Soviet Union (Gill, 1980, 2011) and China (Leese, 2011, 2007) led to the apparent 'deification' of Lenin, Stalin, and Mao among party members. Perfectly natural cognitive biases can further encourage cult participation, such as the fact that most think *other people* are more likely to believe propaganda claims than they themselves are (Bicchieri and Fukui, 1999), since one cannot observe directly their cognitive status but merely their participation in the rituals of the cult, or the fact that most attempt to manage the cognitive dissonance caused by the cult by at least acquiescing in its less absurd claims. And because general participation in cult rituals, even when most people lack any trust in the leader, also results in a lack of 'common knowledge' about the strength of *other people's* trust, it tends to felicitously (from the regime's point of view) discourage opposition mobilization, a situation that can be further encouraged by the occasional spectacular punishment of individuals for minor acts of disrespect against leader symbols (for a good example from North Korea, see Box 8.1).

Flattery Inflation

More interestingly, these signals of support can also be subject to a kind of 'inflation' even in the absence of official enforcement or encouragement (Márquez, 2013). During the Chinese Cultural Revolution, for example, supporters of Mao Zedong took to wearing 'Mao badges' - little metal badges with Mao's picture, produced by individual factories. These badges were at first only worn by the most hard-core supporters of Mao. However, both because Mao was genuinely popular and because there were some clear disadvantages to not being seen as a Mao supporter at the time (for example, being subject to harassment or worse by Red Guards, students, and factory workers who had pledged their loyalty to Mao and his ideas), everyone soon started wearing the badges. Soon enough, factories were producing billions of badges to meet the demand, and people who wanted to show that they were *really* committed to Mao had to distinguish themselves by wearing more badges, or wearing bigger ones, or wearing them in ways that showed more genuine love for Mao; badges as large as 30 cm in diameter were worn, or smaller badges were pinned directly on the skin (Leese, 2011, p. 216).

This fashion was not at all explicitly encouraged by Mao or other senior Chinese Communist Party figures. Premier Zhou Enlai would even grumble in 1969 about the waste of resources the production of badges involved. Similarly, entirely new rituals of support for Mao also appeared

Box 8.1   Rituals of mourning and the personality cult in North Korea

The apparently spontaneous rituals of public mourning when North Korea's founding president Kim Il Sung died in 1994 (and again when Kim Jong Il, his son and successor, died in 2011) sometimes strike people as showing that North Koreans must be very thoroughly 'brainwashed'. While some of this mourning was undoubtedly genuine (how much we cannot tell), some was certainly compelled, both by the explicit direction of the state, whose broadcasts indicated clearly what actions were expected from the population, and by the fear of being singled out as a dissident by one's peers. Stories from defectors attest to the compulsory nature of the mourning; one particular person noted that when he first heard the news of Kim Il Sung's death as a privileged student at one of North Korea's premier universities he at first felt nothing, but when he saw his classmates crying all around him, he suddenly realized that 'his entire future depended on his ability to cry: not just his career and his membership in the Workers' Party, his very survival was at stake. It was a matter of life and death' (Demick, 2009, p. 98). And the mourning quickly became organized by the Party:

> What had started as a spontaneous outpouring of grief became a patriotic obligation ... The inmiban [a neighbourhood committee] kept track of how often people went to the statue to show their respect. Everybody was being watched. They not only scrutinized actions, but facial expressions and tone of voice, gauging them for sincerity. (Demick, 2009, p. 101)

The point is not that nobody experienced any genuine grief at the death of Kim Il Sung. Other stories from defectors indicate at least some reservoir of good will for the founder of the regime, though no great deal of belief in the claims of superhuman ability concocted by propagandists. Indeed, privileged propagandists seem to have been more likely to believe in these claims than the ordinary people they were trying to reach, as we learn, for example, from the memoirs of Jang Jin-sung (Jang, 2014), which describe his rise to an important position in the regime's 'United Front Department' and his eventual disillusionment after meeting Kim Jong Il in person. Nevertheless, various social cues – including the fact that others were loudly mourning the leader, and the fact that party representatives were visibly present to monitor mourning – made people feel compelled to signal publicly and with sufficient show of tears that they, too, supported the dead leader, as there was the risk that *not* producing the expected signals would be punished, either directly by agents of the state, or by people who *did* genuinely love Kim Il Sung. In these circumstances, the mourning ritual was less a signal of genuine emotional attachment on the part of the population than a signal of the strength of the regime (Svolik, 2012, pp. 80–1), which was perceived as being able to easily punish non-participation.

at this time, also without much encouragement from above, such as 'quotation gymnastics', a series of gymnastics exercises with a storyline based on Mao's thought and involving praise of the 'reddest red sun in our hearts', and 'loyalty dances', which, like the quotation gymnastics, was 'a grassroots invention' designed to physically signal loyalty, and which spread 'even to regions where public dancing was not part of the common culture and thus led to considerable public embarrassment' (Leese, 2011, p. 205).

These practices emerged not because people were suddenly infused with much greater love for Mao than before, or even because they were being punished more strongly by the state for not signalling loyalty to Mao, but because the only way to show that one was *really* committed to Mao when everyone was supposedly loyal to Mao was to do something costly and distinctive. The situation was akin to what is sometimes called a 'Red Queen race' (after the Red Queen in *Alice in Wonderland*, who needed to keep running just to stay in place); people needed to increase the value of their signals of support just to avoid being singled out as insufficiently supportive by the groups of more fanatically committed people. In the factionalized atmosphere of the Cultural Revolution, where many groups outside and inside the state competed to show that they were Mao's most radical supporters, the result was a kind of *flattery inflation* – the phrase comes from Alois Winterling's account of the same process in his biography of the Roman Emperor Caligula (see Winterling, 2011).

The power of these rituals came from the fact that they induced tremendous social pressures to signal loyalty to the leadership by leveraging the emotional energies of committed minorities. For example, when members of the 'Capital Worker and Peasant Mao Zedong Thought Propaganda Team' took some mangoes that Mao had given them, put them in covered reliquaries, hoping to preserve them for posterity, and staged ceremonies to display them as a sign of reverence bordering on the religious, this was not because they feared any repercussions for not doing so (Chau, 2010). Their devotion to Mao was genuine; but their actions helped to trigger a veritable sort of 'Mango fever', as people competed to signal their allegiance to Mao, joining in parades and participating in other mango-themed ceremonies. The vast majority of participants in these rituals, though not necessarily opposed to Mao, were not fanatically committed to him. They participated for many reasons, from curiosity (few people had seen mangoes in 1960s China) to opportunism to (on occasion) fear of being thought insufficiently loyal.

The same is true of many other rituals in non-democratic settings; a small number of people may find their connection to the regime or the leadership strengthened through them, but a large majority may participate only out of opportunism or fear or even just the vague unease that 'something might happen' otherwise. At the end of the day, however, general participation in 'legitimating' rituals favours the regime even if most people do not do so out of love. As Machiavelli noted centuries ago, it is better to be both loved and feared; but if love does not result from regime rituals, fear will do nicely.

Conclusion

Leaders of authoritarian and totalitarian regimes, like leaders of all governments, attempt to gather information about the populations they rule over and use it to shape perceptions of their actions to their advantage. Similarly, they also stage spectacles and promote rituals intended to legitimate their position, or take advantage of rituals of loyalty and support created by grassroots actors in society. As we have seen in this chapter, however, authoritarian elites do face distinctive challenges in gathering and using information, since people under their control have powerful incentives to lie to them and to disbelieve what they say; and they are not always able to fully control the way in which propaganda and ritual shape the beliefs of the population to their satisfaction. And the more totalitarian the regime, the more acute these challenges; regimes that insist on controlling what people think have more difficulty in extracting credible information from their populations and making claims that are credible to them.

Most authoritarian and totalitarian regimes tackle their information challenges by developing special organizations to gather information (a 'surveillance apparatus') or allowing some independent sources of information to exist in a way that does not immediately threaten collective action. And authoritarian and totalitarian regimes sometimes forego the benefits of credible propaganda or convincing information for the sake of the signal of strength that even incredible propaganda or absurd rituals can produce. Yet these challenges never entirely go away. In particular, the information challenge faced by non-democratic regimes can be problematic for their attempts to achieve economic prosperity, as we shall see in the next chapter.

Chapter 9

Benevolent Authoritarianism

In a 1992 speech, the late founding prime minister of Singapore, Lee Kuan Yew, declared that:

> A country must first have economic development, then democracy may follow. With few exceptions, democracy has not brought good government to new developing countries … westerners value the freedoms and liberties of the individual. As an Asian of Chinese cultural background, my values are for a government which is honest, effective and efficient. (Lee, 1992, p. 376)

In Lee's view, democracy not only was unnecessary for good government, it was positively harmful under particular cultural and economic conditions. Though strictly speaking Lee did not consider the Singaporean system he had led 'undemocratic', only differently democratic, he did indicate in a 1994 interview that he was 'not intellectually convinced that one-man, one-vote is the best' system (Zakaria and Lee, 1994, p. 119), and certainly suggested many times that democracy was not necessary for economic development. Democracy was only good if it produced good government; and it could only produce good government under very specific cultural conditions. In societies where these conditions were not present, he thought, some other (more authoritarian, or more technocratic) political system would be preferable to democracy.

The idea that democracy is bad for good government, particularly good government conceived in terms of economic development, is thus sometimes called the 'Lee Hypothesis' (Sen, 1999b, p. 15). The hypothesis asks us to consider whether different political regimes have differential consequences for outcomes that matter, such as economic development. It is an inherently *evaluative* question; Lee is asking whether democracy is *better* or *worse* than (some particular form of) non-democracy under specific conditions. The idea is, of course, not original to Lee; in the nineteenth century, the liberal English philosopher John Stuart Mill both defended representative government with a wide franchise (what we today would call 'democracy') and argued that such a form of government was *not* appropriate for all societies (Mill, 1859). In societies that did not have what has come to be called the 'prerequisites' for representative government, some form of non-representative, authoritarian government (including, on occasion, imperial government) would be better for these societies.

153

Whether a country has a particular political regime or another one is not always subject to choice. Regimes are not like democratic governments; populations cannot always 'vote' to get rid of them, or to choose a different one, even if forms of government that are widely disliked are typically fragile. Instead, they often emerge from collective struggles that have sometimes unintended consequences; they 'grow' more than are 'designed', even if they are human creations, and of course they are sometimes imposed by more powerful countries. Nevertheless, to the extent that over time collective action may push regimes in particular directions (for example, towards democracy or authoritarianism), it is worth trying to understand whether or not different regimes have distinct consequences, and whether these consequences vary according to the broader social and economic context in which they are embedded. The question is especially pressing when considering the responsibilities that other, powerful states have to 'promote' democratization. If it turns out that democratization, as Lee argued, is positively harmful in some societies (that is, produces bad government), then it would not be a good idea to promote it; indeed, in such a case perhaps it would be a good idea to promote some *other*, more authoritarian form of government.

In this chapter, we thus explore the veracity of the 'Lee Thesis'. We first consider whether economic development is systematically associated with some particular form of non-democratic rule. Here the evidence shows that, though authoritarian regimes are over-represented among 'growth miracles', they are also over-represented among 'growth disasters'. Moreover, there is no evidence that democracy significantly retards economic development, even in East Asia, where most of the 'success stories' of authoritarian governance are located. Nevertheless, there is a very small number of authoritarian regimes whose distinctive institutions do seem to have played a role in helping their economies go 'from Third World to First' as Lee put it in the title of his memoirs. And the reasons for the success of democratic and (some) non-democratic regimes have to do with their ability to manage and process economically relevant information. Successful regimes are all alike in some important respects.

Economic growth is, of course, not the only thing that matters; and political regimes vary not only in the degree to which they are able to promote fast growth, but also in the degree to which their policies produce other outcomes: health, economic equality, education, and so on. As we shall see, the evidence here is equivocal; after accounting for the *level* of economic development and standard demographic characteristics, researchers often have difficulty distinguishing between the policies of democracies and the policies of non-democracies. Nevertheless, most researchers do find that democracies tend to govern in ways that benefit the majority more than authoritarian regimes, as we would expect on theoretical grounds. In particular, democracies are importantly different from most authoritarian regimes in the degree to which they protect the 'physical integrity' of their populations. Simply put, most democracies kill and torture their citizens less than authoritarian regimes, even though there are circumstances in which democratic regimes can be very repressive (especially of minorities).

We shall conclude the chapter with a brief discussion of one last potential difference between democratic and non-democratic regimes: their behaviour with respect to war. While it is clear that democratic regimes can be just as violent in their *external* relations as many non-democratic regimes (as examples from ancient Athens to the modern United States show), they appear to be less likely to engage in war against *other* democracies. This is the much disputed 'democratic peace hypothesis', mistakenly attributed to Immanuel Kant at least since Michael Doyle's classic two-part article on liberal legacies in foreign policy (Doyle, 1983a, 1983b). The controversies over this idea centre on whether the observed 'democratic peace' is due to causes other than democracy, or is even a spurious artefact of measurement. As we shall see, there is something to the argument that it is not democracy *per se*, but a whole constellation of 'liberal commitments', working together (not separately), that accounts for the facts of peace among liberal democracies. Yet we shall also see that much research indicates that at least some non-democratic regimes, specifically personalist regimes, are especially likely to engage in militarized conflict.

Democracy, Authoritarianism, and Economic Development

The question of how to promote genuine economic development – general prosperity, an educated and healthy population, and the other desirable material features of what is usually called, somewhat imprecisely, 'modernity' – has been one of the central political problems of the last century. Populations throughout the world demanded, and continue to demand, the kinds of economic opportunity and security associated with 'first world' countries. And though not every post-colonial leader was sincerely concerned with the problem of how to take their countries from, in Lee's phrase, 'Third World to First' (one thinks here of the anti-modernist attitude of Macías Nguema in Equatorial Guinea, or the kleptocracy of Mobutu), the vast majority paid at least lip-service to the broad goal of what came to be called 'economic development', even if some preferred the 'second world' (socialist) path to this goal to the 'first world' (capitalist) path. Whether socialist or capitalist, however, genuine economic transformation (the kind capable of transforming a poor country into a prosperous one) is inescapably tied to social transformation, and thus the economic problem is necessarily a *political* problem as well, involving questions about the sorts of institutions capable of carrying out the work of economic development.

Institutional choices are never made in a vacuum. Leaders and ruling elites do not simply 'choose' democracy or dictatorship; they must work from pre-existing institutional legacies, some of which may be hostile to the emergence of particular configurations of power. Moreover, the question of whether democracy is in some sense 'better' than other regimes is today inextricably entangled with thorny questions about Western imperialism, even though logically there is no relation between saying that democracy is better than some other political regime and saying that democracy must therefore be promoted at the point of a gun. At any rate, from the point of view of the ruling elites of many post-colonial, poor states, a highly institutionalized democracy has not been, at least initially, a real option. Instead, the choice facing developmentalist leaders has more often been between nurturing a poorly institutionalized democracy in the hopes that it will become more institutionalized later (perhaps with some external help), or attempting to create a stronger authoritarian state (again perhaps with some external help, though possibly from different patrons). From this perspective it is not clear that a more democratic system has many advantages for economic development and social transformation (Gilson and Milhaupt, 2011).

In theory, of course, democratic political systems ensure that the wishes of majorities are given some weight in policy-making, and regular elections are meant to keep politicians accountable to them. Voters should elect politicians that promise to produce economic prosperity for them, and dismiss those who fail to do so or make use of office for private purposes; and various constitutional constraints should reduce the ability of leaders to enrich themselves at the expense of the public, or to threaten the security of property rights. Simple game-theoretic models further suggest that leaders who depend for their political survival on large groups of people should be more likely to 'pay' their supporters with public goods (infrastructure investments, education, health care, and so on), while leaders who do not depend on their political survival on majorities of citizens may prefer to dispense private favours and opportunities for corruption to keep themselves in power (Bueno de Mesquita et al., 2001; Gerring et al., 2013). From this perspective, leaders who care about economic development should try to support democratic institutions.

But the theory is not always reflected in practice; even well-institutionalized democracies may fail to work in the ways predicted by simple models. And more complex models of how democracies actually work paint a more nuanced picture of their advantages and disadvantages. Voters may be ill-informed or misled by unscrupulous politicians, and thus rendered unable to accurately attribute responsibility for economic outcomes; politicians may be incapable of supporting unpopular reforms needed for economic development, given their short-term horizons; the cost of elections, and the ability of the wealthy to manipulate the political process in various ways, may favour the capture of the political process by the rich; and the many 'veto points' found in democratic system may give too much power to entrenched, particular interests at the expense of the broader public (for some evidence of these problems in the American context, see, for example, Gilens and Page, 2014; Page, Bartels, and Seawright, 2013; Bartels, 2005). Elections can become occasions for the opportunistic mobilization of ethnic prejudice (Collier, 2009), or for populist forms of redistribution that are ultimately self-undermining (Besley and Coate, 1998). It is thus plausible that democratic competition may prioritize current consumption over the sorts of capital investments that are required for genuine economic development, and that the kinds of compromises required of democratic politics may block or slow needed change (Huntington, 1968).

Moreover, despite the fact that most rich countries are now democracies, it is not clear that a country needs to *become* a democracy in order to become rich, and some reasons to think that democracy may *hinder* economic growth, at least in some circumstances. As an illustration, consider China and India today. Both countries are large and diverse, and in the 1970s both were very poor. But while China's post-Mao authoritarian system has steered the country through three decades of extremely fast economic growth, lifting millions out of poverty and virtually eliminating illiteracy, India's democratic system has presided under much more sluggish growth, and has failed to eliminate poverty, malnutrition, and illiteracy. China's successes today are thought to put in doubt the presumed superiority of the 'Western' democratic model (Bell, 2015), just as in the late 1950s observers worried about the Soviet model overtaking Western democracies (Ofer, 1987).

Regimes, Incentives, and Information

We can explore the question of the developmental advantages of different regime types more systematically. Scholars have proposed at least five different mechanisms through which political regimes may affect economic development (Knutsen, 2012; Przeworski and Limongi, 1993). The first three have to do with how regimes affect the incentives of political leaders and other actors; the last two with how political regimes process useful information:

1. Political regimes may affect economic development by giving leaders different incentives to respect the property rights of economically significant actors and to refrain from predatory behaviour. If stable property rights are needed for economic prosperity (because, for example,

they are needed to encourage investment, as most economists argue), then regimes that fail to respect such rights (by, for example, engaging in arbitrary expropriation and redistribution) will also fail to produce economic prosperity. To be sure, in some cases some forms of expropriation (for example, radical land reform) may be necessary to jump-start economic development (Albertus, 2015); but in general sustained growth cannot be achieved without stability of property rights. In highly unconstrained, personalistic regimes the property of anyone is at the mercy of the autocrat, which suggests that such regimes should do poorly. But from this perspective, democratic regimes do not have an obvious advantage over non-democratic regimes. While property rights under personal rule can be insecure, ancient fears (Aristotle, *Politics*, book 3) and modern game-theoretical models (Boix, 2003) suggest that property rights can *also* be insecure under the rule of democratic majorities, as poor majorities could use their votes to push their representatives to expropriate the rich. This argument does suggest that regimes that are credibly constrained in their ability to expropriate property in arbitrary ways should have some developmental advantages; and these regimes are more likely to be institutionalized rather than personalized, which favours 'consolidated' democracies over autocratic forms of personal rule.

2. Political regimes may also affect economic development by changing a political elite's time horizon for long-term investments. Two sorts of investments are relevant here: investments in *physical capital* that pay off in increased overall prosperity in the long run (for example investments in roads or ports), and investments in *human capital* (for example education or health). The classic case against democracy, from an economic point of view, makes the point that long-term investments in physical capital are unlikely to be made by vote-seeking politicians trying to please impatient voters. By contrast, leaders with long time horizons due to their security of tenure (such as hereditary monarchs) may have great incentives to help the country prosper, because they prosper when the country prospers. As an Italian monarchist put it in the 1920s, 'Monarchy is the best kind of government because the King is then owner of the country. Like the owner of a house, when the wiring is wrong, he fixes it' (cited in Olson, 1993, p. 567, from Banfield, 1958, p. 26; some form of the argument is at least as old as Hobbes – see *Leviathan*, chapter 20).

On the other hand, not every leader in a non-democratic regime has either security of tenure (as we saw in Chapters 4 and 6) or the patience to see his country prosper, especially if they think the increased wealth of others, or increasing education among the population, might imperil their hold on office. Moreover, voters in democracies seem likely to push for increases in education, health, and other forms of human capital, which might give democracies an advantage over more closed authoritarian regimes with respect to the second sort of investment. Elite behaviour in authoritarian regimes should thus vary widely, depending on their understanding of the security of their position and other factors. Singapore prospered by encouraging both high levels of savings and high levels of education. Zaire under Mobutu, by contrast, failed to do either; Mobutu feared maintaining or building roads because he thought they could be too useful to opponents wishing to overthrow him, and appropriated the majority of state revenues for his personal use, especially at the end of his time in office, when he felt his tenure was most uncertain (Knutsen, 2012; Wright, 2008). On the whole, therefore, authoritarian regimes do not seem to have a clear advantage over democracies with respect to their ability to promote long-term investments, though it is possible that some particular kinds of non-democratic regimes (for example, institutionalized monarchies) might.

3. Political regimes may differ with respect to the degree to which political elites have autonomy from vested interests. Some degree of insulation from vested economic interests may be necessary for the state to promote industrialization. For example, it has been argued that the great economic successes of East Asia all depended on the ability of the state to nurture industries producing for the world market through the right kind of 'infant industry' protection (Kohli, 2004; Gilson and Milhaupt, 2011). The idea here is that the state could help high-value industries to grow by temporarily sheltering them from competition. But it is in the interest of these industries for protection to continue indefinitely, or without conditions. If they have too much influence in the state, infant industry protection often degenerates into mere protectionism, where incumbents can earn 'rents' at the expense of the rest of society by charging higher prices and providing shoddier services to consumers than would be the case in the presence of competition. Authoritarian East Asian states managed to retain sufficient autonomy from the industries they regulated that they could avoid this problem, credibly conditioning protection on export success (Evans, 1995).

By contrast, economic policy-making in democracies may be subject to interest group capture, as protected industries or other influential actors may unduly influence policy-making in their favour (Olson 1993). To be sure, the same thing may happen in some authoritarian regimes; but it is at least plausible that *some* authoritarian regimes may have a developmental advantage insofar as their authoritarianism insulates them from vested economic interests.

Authoritarian government has also been seen as necessary to hold off demands for redistribution – from labour unions or the general public – that may conflict with long-term economic transformation or produce deadweight losses (see the 'skeptical' literature cited in Papaioannou and Siourounis, 2008; Knutsen, 2012). Many of the well-known 'economic miracles' in the twentieth century (for example the 1950s to 1970s in Spain under Franco, the Singaporean miracle under the PAP, or the Park regime in South Korea) repressed labour unions and held down wage growth. It is thus plausible that rulers committed to economic growth may need to curtail the power of many groups in society so as to increase the proportion of national income that is invested productively rather than consumed.

4. Political regimes may also differ in the extent to which they are open to economically relevant new ideas, or enable economically relevant knowledge to circulate in society. Economists have long argued that genuine economic development depends on innovation – the creation and diffusion of 'useful' knowledge, from improved production processes to entirely new technologies (Romer, 1990). But authoritarian regimes may face more trade-offs in allowing information to circulate freely (Knutsen, 2015b), since it is not always possible to distinguish between information and technologies that are only useful for economic purposes, and information and technologies that are *also* useful for political purposes. Consider, for example, the many forms of information exchange that are enabled by the Internet; a regime without much access to the Internet may avoid certain forms of anti-regime collective action, but it may also prevent the circulation of useful economic information. From this perspective, regimes with a relatively open public sphere should have greater long-run developmental advantages.

5. Finally, political regimes may differ in the extent to which they enable political elites to make decisions quickly or without much discussion. The classic case against democracy argues that decision-making in democracies can be slow or cumbersome, requiring much consultation with different groups. By contrast, non-democratic regimes may be able to make quicker decisions with less consultation. Yet it is not clear that this fact (if it is a fact) works to the advantage of non-democratic regimes. Decisions taken without sufficient consultation or deliberation may be very poor decisions, and deliberation may help improve the quality of decisions, even if they are taken more slowly (Landemore, 2013). Nevertheless, even if democratic regimes have some deliberative advantages, perhaps some non-democratic regimes can develop forms of consultation that effectively mimic them (Chandra and Rudra, 2015).

Overall, regimes that restrain the arbitrariness of policy-makers, enhance their temporal horizons, provide them some autonomy from vested interests, and allow for the free circulation of economically relevant information and the robust scrutiny of policy proposals should have a developmental advantage over regimes that do not do any of these things. From this perspective, theoretical arguments do not offer an airtight case for the virtues of democracy for economic growth and development – especially not when the choice is between a poorly institutionalized democracy and a stronger authoritarian state. Nevertheless, neither do they suggest that democracies are clearly bad for development; and on balance the informational advantages of democracies in theory probably favour them over less democratic alternatives, though this conclusion depends on how much we think these informational advantages matter relative to political incentives to invest or make decisions forcefully, or how well they can be reproduced by at least some non-democratic regimes.

Non-Democratic Growth: The Evidence

The aggregate empirical evidence suggests that democracies positively promote development on average, even if the effect is not always direct. The most robust fact about economic growth and political regimes is that growth is far more variable in non-democratic regimes than in democracies (Almeida and Ferreira, 2002; Rodrik, 2000; Chandra and Rudra, 2015). No matter how one looks at the data, or what factors one 'controls' for statistically, non-democratic regimes are over-represented both among the best and the worst performers in terms of economic growth. Post-Mao China, Singapore under Lee Kuan Yew, South Korea under Park Chung Hee, are all obvious examples of non-democratic (or, in the case of Singapore, not quite democratic) regimes that seem to have produced genuine economic development, lifting millions from poverty; Zaire under Mobutu, North Korea under Kim Jong Il, and Libya under Qaddafi are by contrast bywords for corruption, kleptocracy, squandered opportunity, and poverty.

More generally, authoritarian regimes tend to display more economic volatility than democratic regimes; sustained high (or low) economic growth rates in authoritarian regimes are much less common than high growth spurts followed by crashes. Democratic regimes, by contrast, seem to preside over more consistent economic growth. Such moderate but consistent growth has been argued to be of greater *quality* than higher but more volatile growth rates (Mobarak, 2005; Rodrik, 2000). Volatility hurts the poor especially (since they have low incomes to begin with, sudden downturns are more damaging to them), and extremely high rates of growth may not be socially optimal given the wrenching transformations they are typically accompanied by (Overland, Simons, and Spagat, 2005). We might say that even if democracies grew at a slower pace than authoritarian regimes on average, their growth has a 'goldilocks' quality (neither too much nor too little, as we see in Figures 9.1 and 9.2; the distribution of growth rate ranks in non-democratic regimes has 'fatter tails').

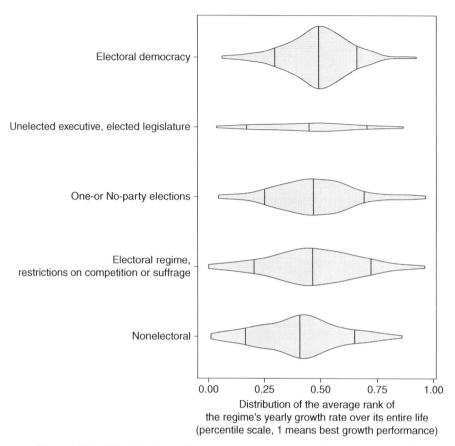

Figure 9.1   *Distribution of the average ranks of yearly growth rates of different regime types, 1950–2014. Since growth rates are volatile and affected by the total state of the world economy at any given time, we do not compare growth rates directly. Instead, we first calculate the growth rate percentile rank for each regime in each year (1 = highest growth in year, 0 = lowest growth in year), and then average these ranks over the entire life of the regime (so, for example, Singapore, an electoral regime with restrictions on competition, averaged a percentile rank of 0.7 from 1965 until 2014, a consistently high growth performer). Each violin then shows the distribution of these averages by regime type, with vertical bars indicating the bottom 10 per cent, the median, and the top 10 per cent of regimes. For example, we can see that the median democratic regime has produced growth in the top 50 per cent of growth rates, when averaged over the life of the regime, since the median democracy has had an average rank of 0.5 or above. Regime data comes from Skaaning, Gerring, and Bartusevičius (2015), extending the PIPE dataset from Przeworski (2013); economic growth data comes from Angus Maddison, the Penn World Tables, and the World Bank. There are a total of 793 regimes in the sample (median duration five years, though electoral democracies in the sample tend to last longer); areas are scaled to the number of observations in each category.*

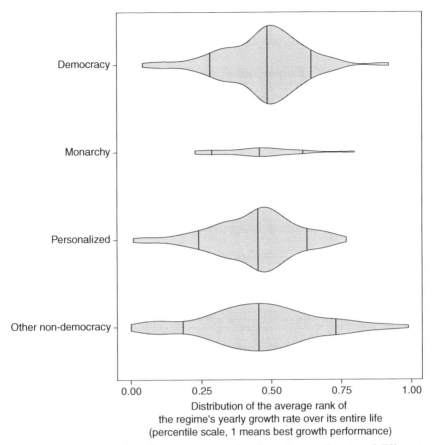

Figure 9.2 *Distribution of the average ranks of yearly growth rates of different regime types, 1950–2010. As in Figure 9.1, we first calculate the growth rate percentile rank for each regime in each year (1 = highest growth in year, 0 = lowest growth in year), and then average these ranks over the entire life of the regime. Each violin shows the distribution of these averages by regime type, with vertical bars indicating the bottom 10 per cent, the median, and the top 10 per cent of regimes. Regime data comes from Geddes, Wright, and Frantz, 2014; economic growth data comes from Angus Maddison, the Penn World Tables, and the World Bank. There are a total of 461 regimes in the sample (median duration ten years, though some last much longer); areas are scaled to the number of observations in each category.*

But in fact democracies do not appear to grow slower *on average* than non-democracies, though the difference between regime types is not large (Figures 9.1 and 9.2). On any given year, the median democracy grows faster than most non-democracies, and over the entire life of a regime the median democracy has tended to have better growth rates than the median non-democracy. (Monarchies have tended to have the second best performance, and personalized regimes and other non-democracies the worst.) But though democracy is *correlated* with slightly higher average growth rates (at least during the post-1950 era) the question of whether democratic political competition *causes* growth is difficult to answer affirmatively with any degree of certainty, since the same factors that cause economic development may also favour the emergence of democracy, while low growth may tend to cause the failure of emerging democracies, leading to selection effects (the democracies that survive and consolidate may tend to have higher growth rates than the average regime). More generally, it is possible that development causes democracy rather than the other way around, as some studies suggest (Murtin and Wacziarg, 2014; Boix and Stokes, 2003).

Yet although the statistical literature on growth and democracy is full of conflicting findings – some studies finding that democracy may be slightly positive for growth, especially over the long run (Gerring et al., 2006; Acemoglu et al., 2014; Papaioannou and Siourounis, 2008; Butkiewicz and Yanikkaya, 2006; Gerring et al., 2013), some that its influence may be slightly negative (Barro, 1996; Tavares and Wacziarg, 2001), and some finding no direct or clear effect of democracy on economic development (Przeworski and Limongi, 1993; Przeworski et al., 2000; Pinto and Timmons, 2005; Murtin and Wacziarg, 2014) – the preponderance of the evidence suggests that democracy does *not* harm economic development, and may well have indirect positive effects via the promotion of health and education (Doucouliagos and Ulubaşoğlu, 2008; Baum and Lake, 2003). Even in East Asia, where most of the authoritarian 'growth miracles' of recent times (China, South Korea, Singapore) are found, and in Africa, home to some of the world's newest and apparently most unstable democracies, sophisticated statistical analysis fails to find any particular disadvantage of democratization for economic development, even if it does not always find any particular advantage either (Knutsen, 2010; Rock, 2009; Narayan, Narayan, and Smyth, 2011). Chile actually grew *faster* shortly after transitioning to democracy, for example, than during Pinochet's 'developmental' military regime; and of course Japan's transformation into a developed country occurred under democratic rule.

Moreover, there is much evidence that many authoritarian countries, including China today, overstate their growth rates by as much as 1–2 percentage points per year (Magee and Doces, 2015; Wallace, 2016), an overstatement that is not found in most democracies. Indeed, growth estimates diverge more across existing datasets in authoritarian states than in democratic ones, probably due to the fact that bureaucracies in authoritarian countries have more incentives to report good news and downplay or even falsify bad news than bureaucracies in consolidated democracies, for reasons discussed in Chapter 8. Statistically speaking at least, authoritarian regimes thus have little to recommend them; democracies appear as good a bet as non-democracies in terms of their raw ability to produce statistically measurable economic growth.

Successful Authoritarian Regimes

The authoritarian regimes that do *succeed* in producing transformational economic development nevertheless appear to be very different from those that do not. Leaving aside some highly oil-dependent Middle Eastern authoritarian monarchies such as Saudi Arabia or Qatar (whose income per capita would be very high under any regime, and whose economic performance is at any rate highly dependent on the price of oil), or the generally overstated 'successes' of the Soviet industrial transformation under Stalin (which came at the cost of millions of deaths), most of the twentieth- and early twenty-first-century economic 'miracles' under authoritarianism have *not* been found among the most ideological, repressive, or personalistic regimes. China under Mao, a highly personalized and totalitarian regime, produced one of the greatest man-made famines in history (Dikötter, 2010), and managed the difficult feat of producing a depression in a planned economy (Walder, 2015). It is the more open China of the Deng years – both less totalitarian and less personalized – that achieved unprecedented economic growth rates, primarily by giving peasants secure control rights over the land, and allowing villages to organize themselves into companies that could benefit from economic activity without fear of expropriation (Huang, 2008). More generally, growth successes under authoritarianism – Indonesia under Suharto, post-Mao China, the 50s and 60s under Franco, the Park Chung Hee years in South Korea, Singapore under the PAP – have taken place in regimes with relatively open public spheres where economic policy (but not politically sensitive topics) could be discussed without too much fear.

These regimes have had leaders pragmatically committed to *development* rather than to their own private wealth or the implementation of some rigid ideological project (Gilson and Milhaupt, 2011), something that is not a given among politicians in any regime. But a pragmatic commitment to growth does not ensure that leaders will know what policies will actually foster economic development; indeed, even top development economists disagree about which policies effectively promote genuine prosperity (Easterly, 2011). Moreover, authoritarian rulers, like everyone else, are both cognitively constrained and susceptible to fashions and fads (Weyland, 2008). Consultative fora can help authoritarian regimes make more informed decisions about the complex problems of development; ruling elites who listen to informed arguments about the consequences of economic policies for various groups are less likely to make disastrous policy mistakes. Such regimes should thus result in less volatile and 'higher quality' economic growth, even if the public sphere is otherwise quite restricted, as some recent evidence suggests (Chandra and Rudra, 2015).

By contrast, when ruling elites operate in an information vacuum, either because lower-level bureaucrats have many incentives to falsify information (see Chapter 8), or because economic policy discussions are tightly constrained for ideological reasons, or because they need little support from important groups in society, they are more likely to make disastrous mistakes. The Great Leap Forward famine in China during Mao's time could only occur in an atmosphere where pragmatic development policy was discouraged by rigid ideological commitments and where lower-level officials thus had many incentives to misreport the truth about their consequences (Teiwes and Sun, 1999; Kung and Chen, 2011); and the absurd economic policies of 1970s Libya, which spent untold billions of oil revenue in wasteful infrastructure such as the 'Great Man-made River' project, could only be undertaken by a ruling elite that experienced no compulsion to listen to informed discussion of economic policy or to develop social support for their policies, given their total control over the oil revenues of the state (Pargeter, 2012). This is also one reason that democracies with a functioning public sphere tend to avoid famines and other disastrous policy mistakes, as Amartya Sen famously argued; it's not that politicians in democracies are necessarily better people, but that they are typically compelled to justify their actions in the public sphere (Sen, 1983, 1999a).

Moreover, in the 'successful' non-democratic regimes, the beneficial effects of public deliberation are combined with a respect for the property rights of a variety of economically important groups in society (Haber, 2006). Regimes with highly institutionalized parties thus tend to have higher 'quality of government' (Charron and Lapuente, 2011; Gandhi, 2008; Gandhi and Przeworski, 2006), including more robust economic growth, since these parties will typically need to incorporate a large number of groups while listening to and respecting their policy preferences (at least to some extent). Similarly, there is also evidence that regimes where the chief executive has great security of tenure, such as hereditary monarchies, also tend to respect property rights better than other regimes (Knutsen and Fjelde, 2013; Clague et al., 1996), and thus indirectly promote development. Most authoritarian regimes do not provide such strong guarantees; and the only case in which the greater ability of some authoritarian regimes to override property rights appears to give them a developmental advantage over democracies is with respect to land reform (Albertus, 2015). Such reforms (for example, in China after the victory of the Communist Party in 1949, or in both Koreas between 1945 and the outbreak of the Korean War in 1950) have sometimes been necessary to promote genuine economic development, yet have been very difficult to carry out under democratic regimes. Thus, transformative land reforms have mostly been carried out by revolutionary regimes of the left, or by military regimes that have felt strongly threatened by leftist movements. But beyond this very particular advantage, highly closed or ideological regimes have little to recommend themselves.

Consider, for a striking example of the developmental differences among non-democratic regimes, the diverging economic fortunes of the two Koreas after the Korean War. Everyone has seen the famous picture of the Korean peninsula from space, showing a South Korea ablaze with electric light and a nearly dark North Korea. It is less well known that most of the industrial capacity of unified Korea was retained by the North after the Korean War, and that for at least a decade after the conclusion of the 1953 armistice most people thought the North, with its revolutionary government, had a better standard of living than the South, with its corrupt elections and military strongmen. In fact, to the degree that economic output in North Korea is measurable (the numbers reported by Angus Maddison (1993) for North Korea's GDP are mostly educated guesswork), it probably grew at comparable rates to South Korean economic output during the first post-armistice decades (see Figure 9.3). Moreover, until the early 1990s the North Korean regime received much support from the Soviet Union, just as the South Korean regime received support from the United States. Yet, some time after the rise of Kim Jong Il in the 1980s, not only did economic output in North Korea decline, but hunger and eventually famine appeared. Though it is impossible to count the dead with any degree of accuracy, perhaps 200,000 people died in the 1993 famine, at a time when South Korea had already entered the ranks of 'developed' countries.

The key point to note is that, for much of the period between 1953 and 1993, both North and South Korea were under non-democratic regimes. (South Korea's transition to democracy is normally dated to 1988.) So the diverging fortunes of North and South cannot be attributed to democracy (or to culture, for that matter). But while the North Korean regime was a totalitarian one that became both more personalistic and more ideological over time, with its ruling elites insisting on central planning and control at the expense of economic dynamism, the South Korean regime became more open and less personalistic over time, eventually democratizing due to pressure from a thriving civil society in the late 1980s (Cotton, 1989). Whereas South Korean rulers from Park Chung Hee onwards were pragmatically committed to development, and allowed for genuine economic policy discussions, North Korean rulers increasingly preferred the consumption of wealth while clinging to ideological fictions that prevented public discussion of economic policy and ruthlessly suppressing all independent civil society actors. This is not to say that the military regimes of Park and his successors were highly tolerant of dissent, or free of

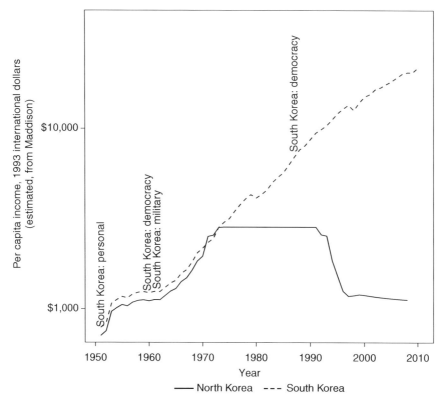

Figure 9.3 *Income per capita in North and South Korea, 1950–2010. Regime data from Geddes, Wright, and Frantz (2014). Income per capita data from Maddison (2013), in 1993 international dollars. Numbers for North Korea are educated guesswork; figures from 1970 to 1993 are likely interpolated.*

corruption. Many scholars have noted the cosy arrangements that developed between the South Korean government and the business conglomerates called *chaebol* during this period (Gilson and Milhaupt, 2011), and which have had corrupting influences on South Korean politics to this day. But the South's pragmatic commitment to development and its relatively more open public sphere (which included viable opposition parties and independent student and labour movements, however repressed) appears to have prevented the personalization and ideologization of power that seems to be primarily responsible for North Korea's development failures.

Corruption in Democracies and Non-Democracies

As the example of South Korea indicates, economic development in 'successful' authoritarian regimes can coexist with high levels of graft and other forms of bureaucratic corruption. Indonesia under Suharto was known for both rapid economic development and enormous corruption, and Suharto, his family, and his cronies grew immensely rich even as the Indonesian economy grew fast (Rock, 2009). China today is similarly characterized by both fast economic growth and much bureaucratic corruption (Rothstein, 2015). Though the quantitative literature on the political economy of development typically finds that bureaucratic corruption is a drag on economic growth (Aidt, 2009), graft may be less damaging to development when it is combined with mechanisms that ensure that state agents share a commitment to development goals and condition career advancement on the successful completion of development projects, as in China today (Rothstein, 2015). The key point is that economically successful authoritarian regimes keep their agents *accountable* for development failures, rather than (just) for violations of formal legal rules. In such conditions, graft acts as a kind of low-level tax, but 'the trains run on time', infrastructure gets built, and development projects get completed. By contrast, in highly personalistic authoritarian regimes where there is little genuine commitment to economic development on the part of the top leadership (for example, Zaire under Mobutu, or the Philippines under Marcos), corruption meant that infrastructure would not be built and other development projects would not be finished if it was profitable to the ruling elite *not* to complete them (see, for the Philippines, Overholt, 1986).

There is also some evidence that institutionalized single-party regimes tend to control graft better, at least in comparison to other non-democratic regimes in similarly developed countries (Charron and Lapuente, 2010). To the extent that poor people tend to be focused on day-to-day survival, politicians can ensure their support among lower-income groups through the provision of 'particularistic' goods (what are sometimes called 'handouts'), rather than the sorts of longer-term investments in public goods that may be more necessary for economic development. Hence 'corruption' in many forms tends to be more common in poorer countries, whatever the regime type, simply because there is less 'demand' for its control. The example of the Mexican PRI regime, discussed in Chapter 5, is illustrative here; poorer voters tended to support the PRI not because of its superior quality of governance, but because of its ability to provide particularistic benefits. Nevertheless, because such regimes are more sensitive to popular opinion and pressure than less institutionalized ones, they do tend to control corruption better as the country's income rises. The modern-day CPC's recurrent (and often serious) campaigns against corruption in recent times in China, as well as the PAP's enduring obsession with the control of corruption in Singapore, can stand as two important examples of the sensitivity of these types of regimes to the threat that corruption poses to their control over the state.

It is worth noting in this respect that new democracies are not always better than authoritarian regimes at controlling the most damaging forms of corruption to ensure that state agents actually work for the public, despite the fact that they contain built-in mechanisms of accountability in the form of elections and a (reasonably) free press. Indeed, transitions to democracy sometimes lead to increases in corruption, as centralized networks of patronage give way to a multiplicity of networks led by vote-seeking politicians, which compete with one another in the extent to which they predate on the public fisc (Rock, 2008; Campbell and Saha, 2013). Such decentralized corruption can in turn make it difficult for voters or other state agents to hold anyone accountable for development failures, with consequently deleterious effects on economic development. Over the medium term, such corruption may even increase the risk of democratic breakdown (Fjelde and Hegre, 2014); the more authoritarian aspects of the Chavista project gained popular support from the perception that political parties in Venezuela were terminally corrupt, and many military coups have successfully cited 'corruption' as a reason to overthrow elected leaders. Democratic consolidation and lowered corruption nevertheless tend to go hand in hand (Sung, 2004; Rock, 2008), probably because 'democratic consolidation' entails increases in the effectiveness of all kinds of accountability mechanisms, from a robust free press (Kalenborn and Lessmann, 2013) to the strengthening of the legal system, whereas many of the mechanisms of authoritarian control, especially personal rule, *depend* on the encouragement of some forms of corruption, as we have seen (see especially Chapter 4). Bureaucratic corruption in fact appears to be more damaging to the stability of democracies than to the stability of non-democracies (Fjelde and Hegre, 2014; Nur-tegin and Czap, 2012).

Other Public Goods in Democracies and Non-Democracies

Economic development, especially when measured in terms of GDP growth, isn't everything. In fact, some people think it has very little importance compared to things like improved health, poverty reduction, low inequality, and increased education. While these things are sometimes correlated with growth in GDP per capita, the correlation is by no means perfect; and there are certainly some authoritarian regimes, like the Cuban regime under the Castro brothers, that have been able to provide many such 'public goods' despite poor measured economic performance in terms of GDP growth. (The vaunted achievements of the Castro regime in the fields of health and education are sometimes exaggerated, but they do exist.) And some scholars have found that, after controlling for demographic and other characteristics, democracies do not have significantly different policies from non-democracies (Mulligan, Gil, and Sala-i-Martin, 2004). For example, democratization does not appear to reduce inequality very much, contrary to expectations that the expansion of political rights would lead to greater redistribution (Bermeo, 2009; Gradstein and Milanovic, 2004);

nor does it appear to have much of an impact on measured poverty (Ross, 2006) – though see Martel García (2014) for some important critiques of this particular study.

Nevertheless, the preponderance of the evidence suggests that the list of democratic advantages is long, especially for the poorest. Not only does an open public sphere, characteristic of democracies, seem to prevent famine (Sen, 1983, 1999a); democracies also seem to increase the calorie intake of the poor (Blaydes and Kayser, 2011). Moreover, industries in democracies have been found to pay higher wages (Rodrik, 1999); and democratic regimes improve access to health care and education (Baum and Lake, 2003). And though there is little evidence that democratization quickly reduces inequality, as we shall see in more detail in the next chapter, there is some evidence that democratic experience – the consolidation and deepening of democracy – does help reduce inequality in at least some cases (Gradstein and Milanovic, 2004b). To the extent that institutional mechanisms matter, the accountability induced by elections and an open public sphere seems to translate into better (though by no means perfect!) outcomes for the majority of citizens, including the poorest, than under most authoritarian regimes. And while there are indeed some authoritarian regimes that produce good economic outcomes for the majority of the population, such as post-Mao China and Singapore, they achieve such outcomes not so much because their rulers are especially benevolent, but more often because they functionally reproduce (though in limited forms) the mechanisms of accountability and information processing characteristic of democracies.

Democracy, Authoritarianism, and Violence

There is one outcome that should sharply differ across democracies and non-democracies: the protection of certain basic rights to 'physical integrity'. Democracies are not supposed to kill or torture their citizens; if they did so, then they would not be democracies. To be sure, if we define 'democracy' strictly enough to include the protection of basic rights, then democracies will of course be better than non-democracies at protecting basic human rights to physical integrity *by definition*. But if we think of democracies merely in terms of a particular form of political competition that ensures that multiple parties compete for state power, as discussed in Chapter 1, the picture is a bit murkier. Some regimes with lively political competition and other institutions associated with democracy, like India or the United States, sometimes engage in highly repressive activities against particular groups of citizens; and some regimes with more limited political competition, like Singapore or Oman, appear to protect the physical integrity rights of their population quite well.

Empirical studies do show that robust, consolidated democracies (measured in a variety of ways) protect the rights of their citizens to physical integrity better than non-democracies (Davenport and Armstrong, 2004; Regan and Henderson, 2002; Davenport, 2007a). Not only have democracies avoided the worst democides and politicides of the last two centuries, which were committed by totalitarian regimes, as we saw in Chapter 3 (Rummel, 1995b), but they have almost always been more internally 'peaceful' than almost all non-democratic regimes, as we can see in Figures 9.4 and 9.5. Sufficient democratization nearly always leads to reductions in repression and vice versa, regardless of how one measures or conceptualizes democracy, though there are some disputes about the 'threshold' of democracy that must be reached for this effect to take place.

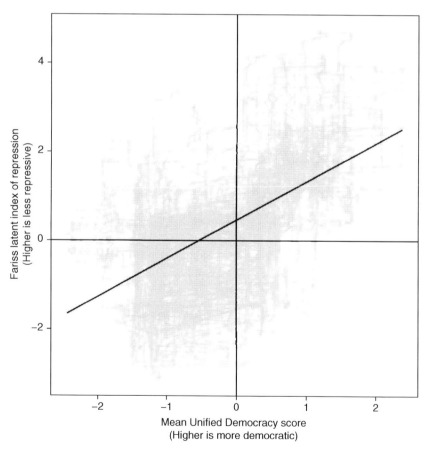

Figure 9.4   *Repression and democracy, 1949–2013. Each country's democracy-repression trajectory over this period is represented by a set of connected dots (light grey). The indicator of repression is from Fariss (2014); higher values indicate less repression. Democracy data from Pemstein, Meserve, and Melton (2010), extended by the author (Márquez, 2016a).*

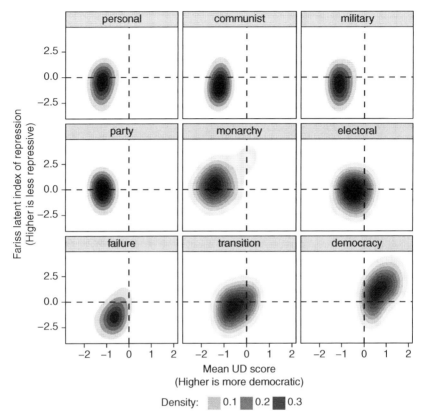

Figure 9.5 *Repression and political regimes, 1949–2010. Shapes indicate the density of the distribution of regimes; the darker shading means more concentration of regimes in this two-dimensional space (repression-democracy). The indicator of repression is from Fariss (2014); higher values indicate less repression. Regime data from Kailitz (2013).*

At the same time, mere electoral competition for power, even when robust and well developed, does not always promote respect for basic human rights, especially in the absence of other institutions normally associated with thicker conceptions of democracy (Davenport 1997). Specifically, political systems with some degree of democratic political competition for power may still repress their citizens with relative impunity when:

1. The target groups of repression are low-status minorities, physically or psychologically segregated from the 'core' members of the polity (for example, Dalits or Muslims in India, African Americans in the United States). Repression in democracies is hidden in prisons and other places away from the public glare; or it is directed at people who are not considered to be 'us' by the majority of the population.

2. The target groups can be credibly depicted as having unacceptable beliefs or deploying threatening tactics (for example, Muslims today, communists in the 1950s and 1960s, radical Black nationalists in the United States in the 1970s). State authorities in democracies, like state authorities elsewhere, attempt to construct internal enemies; when particular groups can be credibly painted as threatening to the majority or core members of the polity, their repression generates much less backlash than the repression of core members of the polity, especially when some legal justification that is credible to the majority can be found for the state's actions (for example, the Patriot Act).
3. The decentralized structure of the polity (as in India or the United States, both of which are federal systems) encourages a dispersion of responsibility. In these cases, lower-level, local state agents (for example, the municipal authorities) may engage in repression even when higher-level authorities do not sanction it (consider, for example, police violence in the United States). (Davenport, 2012)

In these cases, the checks and balances provided by electoral competition, a free press, and independent legal institutions, do not help much to constrain the state's repressiveness, because state authorities can exploit popular beliefs, fears, or lack of information to avoid accountability or credibly justify repression. This is not to say that non-democratic regimes would do better. After all, authoritarian regimes are much more able to repress their own citizens in the 'dark spaces of politics' (Policzer, 2009, p. 3) than democracies; and they more easily depict particular groups of people as internal 'enemies' deserving of repression, given the more closed nature of the public sphere in such regimes. The general point is thus that repressive state violence, in both democracies and non-democracies, is typically a failure of classically democratic principles; states get away with violence when they cannot easily be held accountable for it, which is easier to do when the public sphere is already constricted and internal enemies can be invented at will.

The level and kind of repression non-democratic regimes use against their own citizens varies widely. Though all non-democratic regimes restrict some civil liberties to prevent political competition (otherwise they could hardly be non-democratic), regimes that co-opt support from large groups of the population (such as single-party regimes) tend to be somewhat less physically repressive than other authoritarian regimes, at least on average (Davenport, 2007b). (Highly ideological single-party regimes have been, after all, responsible for some of the worst mass violence in twentieth-century history.) Monarchical regimes that enjoy sufficient legitimacy (and are not merely personal dictatorships) seem to also have been less repressive, on average, than other regimes (see Figure 9.5), just as they seem to protect property rights better, perhaps for similar reasons, namely the longer time horizons of their ruling classes (Davenport, 2007b). By contrast, as noted in Chapter 6, there is some evidence that military regimes are more repressive than other authoritarian regimes (Davenport, 2007b). The reason for this appears to be that military regimes are not only more isolated from society than other regimes, but also composed of people who are professionally trained as specialists in violence, which may lead them more willingly to use physical coercion in circumstances where other regimes would use alternative means of ensuring compliance.

Repression, Regimes, and Social Conflict

These 'static' facts about the relationship between political regimes and repression are all a bit rough and ready, since much violence, from police repression to civil and interstate war, arises from deep social conflicts that necessarily shape and even transform existing regimes. Decisions by the state to use violence against particular groups, or by organized groups to resort to violent means in pursuit of political objectives, are shaped by the same underlying distribution of power that gives rise to a particular regime, whether democratic or non-democratic. Deep social conflicts may thus give simultaneous rise *both* to repressive strategies *and* to non-democratic political regimes, while lower levels of conflict may in turn produce both less repressive and more democratic regimes (Boix, 2003), as we shall see in more detail in Chapter 10.

Nevertheless, there is reason to think that democratic institutions, if they can be established in a society (a big if!), may be better able to manage domestic conflicts in non-violent forms. In particular, democratic political institutions change the 'political opportunity structures' (Tilly, 2007) available to specific social groups, generally increasing their ability to organize and exercise influence on the state through formal channels, and encouraging substitution away from violent means of pursuing political objectives (Skrede Gleditsch and Ruggeri, 2010). More speculatively, consolidated democratic institutions are precisely those where an open public sphere and a culture of tolerance encourage the peaceful settlement of disputes over state power and policy (Przeworski, 2010).

Yet it is not immediately clear that democracies would be better able than non-democracies to manage sufficiently large-scale social conflicts, given certain features of democratic political competition. When social cleavages are deep-seated and irreconcilable (as, for example, in the United States before the civil war in the 1860s), elections may merely serve as 'group censuses' that vividly show the distribution of power within the polity. In these circumstances, some groups may fear they will turn into permanently excluded minorities, and they may therefore be tempted to resort to violent means to pursue their interests. Such fears of permanent marginalization appear to have been important for the decision of Bosnian Serbs to mobilize for violence after Yugoslavia began to break up, for example, and there is some statistical evidence that wherever ethnicity is salient and democratic institutions are new (as in many post-conflict situations), elections can 'trigger' civil conflict (Cederman, Gleditsch, and Hug, 2013; Cederman, Hug, and Wenger, 2008; Collier, 2009). The logic of nationalist mobilization in imperfectly democratic but democratizing states has even been argued to increase a state's propensity to external conflict, as elites resort to 'diversionary' war to hold together otherwise incoherent popular coalitions and preserve their position (Mansfield and Snyder, 1995).

By contrast, since many authoritarian regimes prefer to demobilize the population (as we saw in Chapter 3), they may be better able to tamp down ethnic or other sectarian feelings, as in Tito's Yugoslavia. Indeed, the argument that harmonious coexistence between groups is threatened by unfettered electoral competition has often been often used as a justification for authoritarianism, as in Singapore and China. To the extent that strong authoritarian regimes not only deny social groups the opportunity to influence state policy, but prevent them from organizing and mobilizing popular sentiment in the first place, they may thus be better able than democratic (or democratizing) regimes to keep a lid on social conflict.

These considerations suggest that the worst state repression, and the highest risks of civil war, should be found not in the most closed regimes (where the credible threat of repression is more important than actual repression, and serves to prevent opposition mobilization) or in the most open regimes (where the political opportunity structure encourages the use of peaceful means of bargaining and dispute resolution by all groups) but in hybrid regimes (the kinds discussed in Chapter 3). In such regimes, many groups can organize but are prevented from genuinely influencing state policy, which may diminish the expected return of non-violent means of political competition for them, while state elites concerned with the preservation of their own position have many incentives to further restrict political competition through nationalist mobilization or repression.

Many empirical studies do find that there is indeed more 'murder in the middle' (Regan and Henderson, 2002), that is, both more state repression on average, and higher risks of civil and interstate war, in states that are neither highly authoritarian nor highly democratic (Hegre, 2014; Mansfield and Snyder, 1995). But some of these findings emerge more or less *by construction*, since the most widely used measure of democracy, the Polity IV index (Marshall, Gurr, and Jaggers, 2010), tends to give middling ratings to countries where political competition exists but is characterized by violence and is poorly regulated by institutions; it is hardly surprising that political regimes where political institutions have failed to contain violent political competition are more at risk of civil war than regimes (authoritarian or democratic) where institutions are binding for all politically significant actors (Vreeland, 2008). Other measures of repression and democracy do not unambiguously show more murder in the middle (see Figure 9.4).

It is nevertheless the case that where state institutions are weak or incoherent, either because particular rulers have not been able to consolidate power or because democratization has destabilized them, we find a greater risk of civil war (Cederman, Hug, and Krebs, 2010; Skrede Gleditsch and Ruggeri, 2010). The problem is not democracy or even democratization *per se*, but the de-institutionalization that sometimes accompanies processes of democratization or 'autocratization'; where states remain strong during democratization, and thus can easily channel political competition through formal channels (for example, in most of Eastern Europe or in Chile in the late 1980s) there is little to fear from democratization.

There is also some evidence that suggests that strong authoritarian regimes are slightly more prone to civil wars than consolidated democracies (Hegre et al., 2001). Because authoritarian regimes *by definition* exclude some small or large groups of the population from political power through repressive means, they tend to be more at risk of civil war than regimes that are less exclusive, even if they manage to more or less temporarily put a lid on social conflict through repression. The logic of closed authoritarianism may encourage excluded groups to substitute violent for non-violent means, though so long as the state fully controls the territory armed rebellion is an unlikely prospect.

War and Political Regimes

War of any kind has been a rare event since the end of the Second World War, despite the impression one might get from watching the evening news. Most countries have not experienced either interstate or civil armed conflict of any great magnitude, and the numbers of both types of conflict have trended downward since 1945. But because war, and especially interstate war, has been responsible for some of the worst violence the world has seen, a great deal of scholarly attention has been devoted to the question of whether specific political regimes are more or less prone to starting wars or fighting them in specific ways. This research has led to the formulation of what has come to be known as the 'democratic peace' thesis.

Already in the late eighteenth century, when no regimes worth calling 'democracies' existed, Immanuel Kant speculated that republican forms of government – combining accountability to a broad public with the rule of law and the protection of certain rights – would be less likely to go to war (Kant, 1983 [1795]; Doyle, 1983a). His reasoning was simple: if 'the consent of the citizenry is required to determine whether or not there will be war, it is natural that they consider all its calamities before committing themselves to so risky a game' (Kant, 1983 [1795], p. 113). Kant never thought that 'democracy' by itself would be sufficient to prevent war. After all, he was well aware that regimes that had called themselves 'democracies' in the past (such as ancient Athens) had been quite warlike, and he was anxious to distinguish what he called 'republican' government (law-ruled polities) from such forms of 'democratic' government. But he did think that accountable and law-abiding government, in combination with federative structures across borders and the growth of cultural and economic exchange, would make war less and less likely over time through a historical learning process.

In the twentieth century, a number of scholars (Cederman, 2001; Doyle, 1983a; Doyle, 1983b) articulated Kant's views into a theory of the 'liberal peace'. The 'liberal peace' thesis says that peace is a complex, emergent outcome of the spread of 'liberal' institutions; it does not say that 'democratic' regimes, by themselves, are any more or less prone to war, much less that 'democracy' in some simple sense of the term prevents all war. But sometime in the 1980s, scholars started to research seriously the simpler question of whether *democratic* states (or more democratic states) were more or less likely to fight wars – which was only one aspect of the Kantian liberal peace thesis. And it soon became clear that, since the nineteenth century, countries that can be broadly described as democratic have fought few or no wars with one another (see Figure 9.6). This pattern is very robust to different measures of democracy and of war, but it is not what we might have expected from a simple-minded reading of Kant; democracies *do* go to war (one need only think of the United States in the twentieth century), but they appear to be less warlike among themselves. This is called the 'democratic peace' thesis.

The democratic peace thesis comes in two flavours, 'strong' or 'monadic' and 'weak' or 'dyadic'. The strong democratic peace thesis claims that democracies are, all things considered, *less likely* to go to war relative to other political regimes, though for a variety of reasons they are especially unlikely to go to war with other democracies. This is the more controversial form of the thesis, and though there is some support for it (Rummel, 1995a; MacMillan, 2003; Joshi, Maloy, and Peterson, 2015), most scholars endorse instead the 'weak' or 'dyadic' democratic peace, which merely claims that democracies, though just as warlike as other regimes, nevertheless are highly unlikely to go to war with other democracies (Quackenbush and Rudy, 2009; Maoz and Russett, 1993).

Moreover, though few scholars doubt that, as a matter of empirical fact, democracies (however measured) do seem to have fought fewer wars with one another, there is much controversy about whether this has anything to do with the nature of democratic political regimes, such as the fact that leaders in democratic regimes tend to be more constrained or the fact that

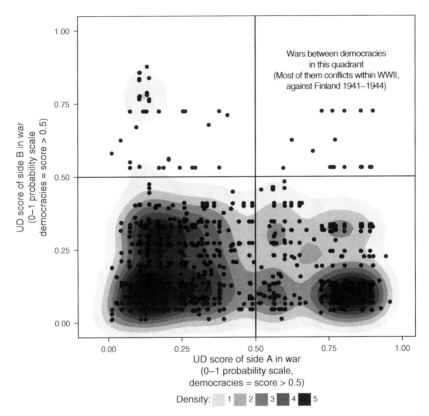

Figure 9.6 *War and democracy, 1816–2003. War data from Gledtisch's updated list of interstate wars. A war in this dataset is an armed conflict with more than 1,000 deaths. Democracy data from Pemstein, Meserve, and Melton (2010), extended by the author (Márquez, 2016a).*

democratic countries tend to share a common culture of compromise and negotiation (Rosato, 2003; Layne, 1994). Some scholars argue, for example, that democracies appear to be less warlike because economic development promotes the emergence of *both* peace and democracy within particular areas (Gartzke and Weisiger, 2014; Mousseau, 2009; Gartzke, 2007). Others suggest that democracy is more likely to emerge when states are secure in their borders, suggesting that peace produces democracy, rather than the other way around (Gibler and Tir, 2010). And yet others suggest that states with different regimes tend to go to war more often than states with similar regimes, so that the 'democratic peace' is matched by a 'dictatorial peace', at least among some kinds of non-democratic political regimes (Peceny, Beer, and Sanchez-Terry, 2002); certainly Figure 9.6 suggests that most wars have been between non-democratic regimes, so a strong version of the dictatorial peace hypothesis is unsupported.

The overall disciplinary consensus, however, seems to be in accord with Kant's original intuition: democratic regimes make leaders more (though not perfectly) accountable to broad publics, and their political cultures prize certain forms of compromise and negotiation, which in conjunction with other developments, such as the increasing economic and cultural interdependence of these states, lead to a general 'pacifying' effect among democracies. This does not mean that economic development or the consolidation of state borders (especially after the end of formal colonialism in the 1950s and 1960s) does not play a role in the emergence of a 'democratic peace', but it does seem to be the case that specific features of political democracy do play some role in sustaining peaceful behaviour among them. The importance of political accountability can be seen in studies of explicitly non-democratic regimes (Weeks, 2012); regimes whose leaders are less constrained by institutions (more personalized; see Chapter 4), and are more explicitly socialized to value military responses to problems (military regimes; see Chapter 6), appear to be more likely to go to war than regimes where leaders are more constrained by institutions and less socialized into military culture (such as single-party regimes).

It is worth stressing again that regimes are not 'chosen' in any straightforward sense by anyone. They emerge from very specific social and historical conditions, which include previous warfare, external intervention, and the like. In particular, the world system imposes severe constraints on the kinds of regimes that are likely to survive in particular historical periods, as great powers use force to shape the internal politics of many countries (Boix, 2011). The peace among Warsaw Pact members during the Cold War had more to do with the Soviet Union's hegemony than with any particularly pacifying characteristics of Communist states, though all Warsaw Pact countries sported similar single-party regimes.

By the same token, great powers, whatever their political regime (the United States and the Soviet Union, for example), are far more likely to be involved in warfare than other countries. Most interstate wars in the list compiled by Gleditsch (2004) involve great powers, while many countries in the international system have *not* been involved in war in the last two centuries, regardless of regime type. The fact that the United States has been involved in near-constant warfare since the Second World War despite being a democracy probably says less about democracy in general and more about the idiosyncratic politics of superpowers. The American state, in particular, appears to have developed since the Second World War a large 'military-industrial complex' that is highly insulated from political accountability and that provides political elites with a great deal of freedom to pursue military intervention around the globe – including the covert subversion of more or less democratic regimes, such as Allende's Chile or the Iranian government of Mossadegh (the elected prime minister during the 1950s 'liberal' period of the Shah's monarchy). But the point is precisely that the American state, for reasons having to do with its status as a global superpower in the wake of the Second World War, is *less democratic* in military matters – less accountable, and less bound by democratic norms – than other democratic states.

Conclusion

Overall, the empirical evidence reviewed in this chapter suggests that however we measure 'success', whether in terms of economic growth, education and health, internal peace, or even external war, more *accountable*, *deliberative*, and *institutionalized* regimes do *better* than less accountable, less deliberative, and less institutionalized regimes, especially over the long run. Not all of these regimes are democracies in the standard sense of the word; but all of them have come to resemble them. To paraphrase Tolstoy's famous opening lines in *Anna Karenina*, happy regimes are all alike; it's the unhappy ones that are all different.

Chapter 10

The Roots of Regime Change and Democratization

Regimes change. While significant regime change is rare, and most countries in the world have not experienced many regime changes in the recent past – out of 155 countries examined by Geddes, Wright, and Frantz (2014) for the period 1945–2010, 59 experienced no regime transitions, and 25 experienced only one transition – some countries have experienced many such changes since the Second World War, especially in the post-colonial world. These transformations have ranged from coups that merely change the personnel controlling the state to revolutions that comprehensively transform the normative and material bases of the state. They can be gradual, peaceful, and unspectacular, and they can also be sudden, violent, and spectacular; they can be forced by popular mobilization or led from the top; and they can be ephemeral or durable.

In this chapter, we begin to examine the factors that lead to regime change or stability, and in particular to enduring changes towards more democratic regimes ('democratization'). Though most forms of regime change in the post-Second World War era have not directly led to democracy (Table 10.1), the long-term trends we documented in Chapter 2 suggest that the arc of history in the last two centuries has bent towards democracy, even if it has occasionally taken long detours through various non-democratic regimes. Accordingly, political scientists have devoted considerable energy to trying to understand the factors that lead to democracy, consolidate authoritarian regimes, or lead to the sorts of instability that a few countries have experienced in the last century, with constant change between different regime types.

Two kinds of explanations for large-scale phenomena such as regime change are typically possible. The first kind focuses on structural factors, such as cultural norms or economic development, that may in turn shape political structures. Such explanations are 'macropolitical'. They do not attempt to explain the specific timing or the particular characteristics of the process of change, only the propensity for change or stability in particular societies, by linking one kind of structural change with another. The second kind is instead 'micropolitical'. These explanations focus on the specific timing and process of regime change, including the specific historical circumstances that enable identifiable agents to push for particular regime transformations. As we shall see, though these types of explanations can be in conflict, they are more often complementary, focusing on

Table 10.1   *Frequency of different types of regime transition, 1945–2010. This table counts only countries that have experienced transitions. Regime change is rare; in the period 1945–2010, only about 5 per cent of all country-years experienced regime transitions. Regime data comes from Geddes, Wright, and Frantz, (2014). 'Other' category includes instances of state breakdown, foreign occupation, and state termination (for example, after unification with a larger state).*

Initial regime	Transitions to democracy	To non-democracy	To other
Democracy		22.1%	0.3%
Non-democracy	23.9%	31.7%	10.3%
Other	7.3%	3.9%	0.6%

different levels of analysis of the same overall complex phenomenon. In this chapter, we focus on macropolitical explanations, leaving micropolitical explanations for the next chapter.

Macropolitical explanations of regime change and democratization typically come in two varieties. First, some explanations emphasize the role of values and culture. Such explanations start from the question of whether some non-democratic regimes are more likely to endure in some cultural contexts rather than others. In the first section of the chapter, we thus take a sceptical look at long-running debates over the compatibility between 'Islam' and authoritarianism, or between 'Asian Values' and 'Western liberal democracy' arguing that in general there is very little evidence that some cultures are specifically welcoming to authoritarian government, or that dictatorships are particularly appropriate in some cultural contexts. Nevertheless, we shall also see that there is a sense in which cultural change is a prerequisite to enduring regime change, and that many 'economic' processes of development can produce cultural changes that increase the propensity for regime change. In the second section of the chapter we shall thus review the more sophisticated versions of what has come to be called 'modernization theory', which links economic development and cultural change in a complex structural explanation for regime change.

The second important variety of macropolitical explanations of regime change emphasize the role of conflict over political power and especially economic resources. Regime change is viewed here primarily as a conflictive process in which different social groups contend with one another over the distribution of power in society (including the degree of social control and the degree of power-sharing among elites), and hence a process in which the structure of an economy, and specifically the kinds of inequality it produces, plays an important role. The third section of the chapter first surveys and then examines the strengths and weaknesses of several recent 'conflict theories' of regime change, arguing that conflict explanations of regime change make better sense when supplemented by 'cultural' explanations.

Culture and Authoritarianism

It is a commonplace of political commentary that culture matters for political regimes. Democracy is assumed to be 'Western', and many people take it for granted that this means it cannot work in 'non-Western' cultures, at least not without substantial modification. Lee Kuan Yew used to argue that while 'westerners value the freedoms and liberties of the individual', Asians 'of Chinese cultural background' valued efficient government more, and thus (he implied) did not value 'Western' democracy as much (Lee, 1992, p. 376). Similarly, during the last century many writers have claimed that the cultural peculiarities of this or that society (Catholic Spain, Muslim Indonesia, Asian Singapore) made it unsuited to the practices of 'Western representative democracy'. Indeed, the trope is very old: German writers argued in the nineteenth century that Germany's cultural distinctiveness necessitated authoritarian rather than representative democratic government (Thompson, 2001). On this view, democracy is less like money (an institution that has found uses in a wide variety of cultural contexts) than like ballet (a historically and culturally bounded practice that is appreciated, and makes sense, only in very particular contexts).

Nevertheless, though some people, especially in East Asia, still argue that cultural conditions sometimes necessitate explicitly non-democratic regimes, in which good government (achieved by meritocratic mechanisms) takes priority over self-government (achieved through public participation) and the right of all to vote is not taken for granted (Bell, 2015), most 'culturalist' discourses (including the 'Asian Values' rhetoric that was popular in the 1990s) do not in fact reject abstract principles of accountable and popular government. Indeed, such discourses often combine a rejection of 'Western' democracy with the praise of some other adjectivated form of democracy – 'socialist', 'organic', 'participatory', 'African', *'pancasila'*, 'sovereign', or even 'neo' – but certainly 'non-Western' or 'non-liberal'.

This praise of 'non-Western' forms of democracy can be a pretext for authoritarianism, to be sure, and it is sometimes used strategically by political leaders who wish to resist liberalizing pressures from the West. But it is nevertheless worth taking seriously as one aspect of a distinctively post-colonial project of asserting the value of one's own culture *vis-à-vis* current Western hegemony (Jenco, 2013), in part by attempting to claim a space for distinctively 'non-Western' understandings of democracy (Youngs, 2015). The rejection of 'Western democracy' is thus best understood less as a defence of authoritarian government (which hardly anyone endorses) than a rejection of a view that we might call 'Western democratic universalism'. This is the view expressed, among others, by former US President George W. Bush in a 2003 speech on the eve of the Iraq War:

> There was a time when many said that the cultures of Japan and Germany were incapable of sustaining democratic values. Well, they were wrong. Some say the same of Iraq today. They are mistaken. ... The nation of Iraq – with its proud heritage, abundant resources and skilled and educated people – is fully capable of moving toward democracy and living in freedom. ...

> The world has a clear interest in the spread of democratic values, because stable and free nations do not breed the ideologies of murder. They encourage the peaceful pursuit of a better life. And there are hopeful signs of a desire for freedom in the Middle East. Arab intellectuals have called on Arab governments to address the 'freedom gap' so their peoples can fully share in the progress of our times. Leaders in the region speak of a new Arab charter that champions internal reform, greater politics participation, economic openness, and free trade. And from Morocco to Bahrain and beyond, nations are taking genuine steps toward politic[al] reform. A new regime in Iraq would serve as a dramatic and inspiring example of freedom for other nations in the region. ...

> It is presumptuous and insulting to suggest that a whole region of the world – or the one-fifth of humanity that is Muslim – is somehow untouched by the most basic aspirations of life. Human cultures can be vastly different. Yet the human heart desires the same good things, everywhere on Earth. In our desire to be safe from brutal and bullying oppression, human beings are the same. In our desire to care for our children and give them a better life, we are the same. For these fundamental reasons, freedom and democracy will always and everywhere have greater appeal than the slogans of hatred and the tactics of terror. (Speech to the American Enterprise Institute, 27 February 2003)

Bush was asserting that democracy is a 'universal value', as the Indian economist Amartya Sen had put it a few years earlier (Sen, 1999a), viable in cultural contexts as diverse as those of Japan and Iraq. In his view, there was nothing inherently unlikely about the emergence of democracy in 'non-Western' societies, since human beings everywhere have similar aspirations for accountable government that protects their rights and freedoms. He rightly noted that varieties of democratic political life exist in many different cultures, and that a history of dictatorship (as in post-war Germany or Japan) does not immediately prevent a society from successfully developing democratic institutions, even when those institutions are 'imposed' by an occupying army. The practical conclusion he drew, however, was much more discomfiting, namely that the United States (as the leader of the Western world) should engage in democracy promotion (with democracy understood in American terms) as part of a comprehensive project of violent regime change in Saddam Hussein's Iraq.

The failure of the latter endeavour – Iraq's institutions today, destroyed by decades of war and dictatorship, and incapable of politically incorporating much of the Sunni minority that remains at war with the central state, are not exactly a shining example of democratic success – discredited the entire project of 'imposing' democracy by force in the twenty-first century. There was in fact little reason to think that such a project could succeed in the absence of supportive conditions that were totally absent in Iraq but not in Germany and Japan at the end of the Second World War (Downes and Monten, 2013; Beetham, 2009). Worse, it discredited the word 'democracy' in the eyes of many people as a pretext for Western hegemony, as if accountable self-government could only ever be a 'Western' idea, and Iraq should be condemned to live under the worst sort of personalistic dictatorship.

But Bush's basic democratic universalism is not so easily refuted. Many democratic practices and ideas have in fact flourished far from 'the West', in many different cultural contexts, even if they have not always been known by the name 'democracy' (Keane, 2009). It may be true that culture matters for political institutions, but it is not clear that it ever constitutes a great barrier to the emergence of democratic institutions, nor is there much reason to think that some cultures are only well suited to authoritarian government.

Cultural Explanations of Political Change and Stability

The question of how culture may affect political regimes is nevertheless difficult to answer rigorously, because the notion of 'culture' has often been used in ambiguous, contradictory, and tautological ways in the study of politics (Lane, 1992; Dittmer, 1977; Formisano, 2000). Before we proceed further, it is therefore necessary to clarify how culture can explain political change and stability.

A common understanding of 'culture' identifies it with the symbolic dimension of social action: the shared narratives, beliefs, and values embodied in a society's practices, rituals, norms, and institutions, including political institutions. In order to *explain* institutions in terms of culture without risking tautology, however, we must be able to distinguish between political institutions as emergent patterns of social action, and culture as the specific values and beliefs that guide individual people's actions and thus result in them supporting or rejecting particular political regimes. Moreover, explanations that appeal to culture must typically refer not just to the values and beliefs of small groups of people but to those of the broad masses; the culture that is supposed to explain macro-institutional change or persistence is the *national* culture, not simply the culture (beliefs and values) of the political elite.

It may seem obvious that what most people believe explains the institutions that develop in a society. Yet it is not clear that the values and beliefs of the majority of the people really matter for the emergence and stability of political institutions, since most of the time ordinary people are relatively powerless to affect institutions *unless* they are mobilized by elites. Moreover, a national culture is not a unified whole; people believe many different and even contradictory things. Indeed, sometimes extreme cultural divisions are invoked to explain why certain political regimes cannot consolidate in a given society; we shall say more on such 'conflict theories' of regime change and stability later in this chapter. And it is worth noting that what most people *claim* to believe and value (in public opinion surveys, for example) is not necessarily identical with what they *actually* value (as shown by what they do in concrete circumstances), much less with the real reasons behind their actions. Human beings are very good at rationalizing the pursuit of their interests on plausible-sounding normative grounds, and people sometimes misunderstand the meaning of their own (and other people's) social action. Finally, the politically relevant beliefs and values of most people in any society may themselves be determined or caused by deeper political and economic structures, and thus may not be the most important causal factor for explaining the emergence or stability of particular political regimes (Márquez, 2016b; Przeworski, 1998).

Nevertheless, even if elite actions are crucial for regime change and stability – the decision of the conservatives around von Hindenburg to offer the chancellorship to Hitler was clearly pivotal for the emergence of the Nazi regime, for example – mass values and beliefs may still constrain what elites can do, and therefore the sorts of regimes that can be stable. And even if what people claim to believe is not always identical with what they actually do believe, the former may still be generally a good guide to the latter. Accordingly, many scholars have attempted to use survey research to probe the correlations between the values that most people claim are important to them and the sorts of institutions that develop in their society. But since people value and believe many things, not all of which are plausibly connected to regime change and stability, we must thus ask *which* values and beliefs matter. What values, beliefs, and attitudes constitute a society's relevant 'political culture'?

There are three broad schools of thought on this question (Inglehart and Welzel, 2005). The first claims that a society's 'political culture' is manifested in those beliefs and values that are *directly about* the political system, such as beliefs about the legitimacy of democratic institutions, trust in parliaments or presidents, and preferences for democracy over authoritarianism. We can call this the 'legitimacy' theory of political culture. The second argues that a society's political culture is specifically manifested in people's beliefs and attitudes towards social interaction in everyday life, such as trust in one's fellow citizens, attitudes towards participation in voluntary activities, and so on, all of which have an impact on the density of associational life in a society. We can call this the 'civic capital' theory of political culture. The third argues that the relevant political culture for the explanation of regime change or stability concerns the relative frequency of 'emancipatory' attitudes, values, and beliefs in a society, that is, beliefs and values about whether freedom is important, tolerance of others is to be encouraged, and so on. Let us examine each of these views in turn.

The Legitimacy Theory of Political Change

In its simplest form, the legitimacy theory of political culture claims that political regimes *directly reflect* mass beliefs about their legitimacy, at least over the long term (Beetham, 2013; Gilley, 2009). Thus, political institutions that are not seen to be legitimate by the majority of the population for any reason (perhaps they are seen as foreign, or as violating some deeply held norm about fairness or the uses of authority) will be unlikely to emerge or last, and regimes will change when they experience severe legitimate deficits. With respect to democracy in particular, the theory claims that there must be a certain amount of 'congruence' between popular demands for democracy and the emergence and stability of actual democratic institutions (Inglehart and Welzel, 2005, ch. 7).

Anecdotal evidence for these claims is not hard to find. For example, it is widely agreed among historians that many of the interwar democracies of Continental Europe suffered a catastrophic crisis of legitimacy during the 1920s and 1930s that led in many cases to their breakdown and replacement by authoritarian regimes (Linz, 1978). Similarly, the Russian Revolution (which led to the establishment of the Soviet Communist regime) and the 1989 revolutions in Eastern Europe (which led to the downfall of most Eastern European regimes) have been linked to breakdowns in the legitimacy of these regimes (Goldstone, 2001). These legitimacy crises were brought about by many economic and social factors, including defeat in war, the Great Depression, and economic stagnation, but the *proximate* cause of regime breakdowns was the fact that many people ceased to believe that their institutional structures were useful mechanisms for adjudicating conflicts and distributing power in the face of intractable problems.

In these cases, citizens did not just hold individual leaders responsible for failing to solve their economic and social woes, but blamed the entire structure of the regime, which as a result could no longer count on their 'diffuse support' (Easton, 1975) and acquiescence, much less their active support against organized hostility. When push came to shove, most citizens thus did little to preserve the Weimar Republic's democratic institutions against sustained attacks by Nazis, Conservatives, and Communists; and they refused to rally in support of the Russian autocracy in 1917 or the Eastern European Communist regimes in 1989, instead massing in large numbers to support the opposition.

But though there is a sense in which all regimes that break down in spectacular mass uprisings must have lost popular support almost by definition, the more specific 'political culture' thesis linking explicit support for particular regimes (such as democracy) with their emergence and consolidation is less well supported. Consider 'support for democracy'. Ever since the advent of modern survey research, scholars have found that explicit measures of support for democracy (that is, measures based on questions that ask for people's opinion of whether 'having a democratic political system' is a good thing) are poorly correlated with actual levels of democracy, at least as political scientists measure the latter (Inglehart, 2003).

Partly this is because so many people claim to like democracy, in both democratic and non-democratic countries. In almost every society where the question has been asked recently, huge majorities (over 75 per cent of the population in most countries) say that democracy is the best form of government, regardless of their actual regime. This pattern of approval is today nearly a cross-cultural universal: high levels of support for democracy *in the abstract* can be found in the Middle East (Tessler, Jamal, and Robbins, 2012; Norris and Inglehart, 2002; Robbins, 2015), East Asia, including China (Carlson and Turner, 2009; Wang, 2007), and Africa (Bratton and Mattes, 2001), all of them regions not commonly associated, at least in the popular mind, with long traditions of representative government. Moreover, it does *not* depend on economic conditions, at least outside of East Asia; explicit support for the abstract idea of democracy around the world is high in good times and in bad (Chu et al., 2008).

But if huge majorities of people almost everywhere in the world claim to support democracy, why are more countries not democratic? There is, in fact, a mild correlation between the expression of a preference for democracy and some measures of democracy – smaller majorities tend to express support for democracy in less democratic societies, though such majorities are still quite substantial. But we need to be careful here. Much survey research is simply impossible in the most closed autocracies (such as North Korea), which likely biases these figures in unknown ways. (Perhaps people in North Korea would support democracy even more, given their experience of oppression; or perhaps they would support it less, given their exposure to anti-Western ideologies.) And there is little reason to think that even the mild correlation we observe between 'support for democracy' and the measured level of democracy in a country should be seen as the result of public opinion *causing* democracy.

The reasons are multiple. Given the ways in which democracy is held up as an ideal by the most disparate politicians in the most varied societies (as documented in Chapter 2), it is hardly surprising that most people say they like democracy (Inglehart, 2003; Yun-han and Min-hua, 2010). By the same token, it is also unsurprising that, when scholars probe deeper, they find that high levels of explicit support for democracy can coexist with very undemocratic attitudes, or are based on radically different views of the concept than those of political scientists (Zuern, 2009; Cho, 2012; Carnaghan, 2011; Shin and Cho, 2010). For example, according to the sixth wave of the World Values Survey (World Values Survey Association, 2015), many people in Pakistan, a Muslim-majority country with a long history of both parliamentary government and military rule, see no contradiction between expressing high levels of support for democracy and thinking that 'having the army rule' is also a good thing, and large Pakistani majorities also believe that democracy is perfectly compatible with religious authorities having a role in interpreting the law. In India, a Hindu-majority country which prides itself on being the world's largest democracy, with an uninterrupted tradition of free elections going back to 1949, large majorities of people think that democracy, army rule, strong leader government, and technocracy are all 'very good' or 'good' forms of government, despite their apparent incompatibility to the political scientist (World Values Survey Association, 2015).

To be sure, in many societies most people agree, when pressed, that democracy involves at least free elections and some civil liberties. And many people who cannot articulate a coherent understanding of 'democracy' nevertheless implicitly appreciate basic democratic principles of popular accountability; they do not yearn for arbitrary government (Carnaghan, 2011). But they differ enormously in the importance they give to political liberties relative to socioeconomic equality and religious authority in their conception of democracy (Norris and Inglehart, 2002; Shin and Cho, 2010). Not everyone is a liberal democrat.

Even if most people actually *were* liberal democrats it is not clear how explicit support for democracy (or any other pattern of authority) should translate into regime change or stability in authoritarian contexts. For one thing, supporting 'democracy' in the abstract (or even more specific institutional arrangements, like multiparty government) is perfectly compatible with a preference for stability and a desire not to rock the boat too much (Benstead, 2015; Harmel and Tan, 2012). It is not unreasonable to prefer the devil one knows to the devil one does not know in the concrete circumstances in which one finds oneself, especially if there is a risk that any political transition will be accompanied by violence or socioeconomic turmoil (as the current civil war in Syria illustrates), or if the performance of the current non-democratic system of government is otherwise satis-factory. More generally, actual support for any regime (democratic or non-democratic) may be shaped by a wide variety of factors, from the performance of the economy to the popularity of its leadership, not all of which have much to do with support for the abstract ideal of the regime. Thus, for example, much explicit 'support for democracy', especially in new and imperfect electoral regimes, appears to have an instrumental character (Inglehart and Welzel, 2005; Bratton and Mattes, 2001), that is, support is underpinned by the hope that 'democracy' (the new thing) will improve one's material circumstances, though some of it is also based on the 'social desirability' of the term democracy.

We might be tempted to say that 'support for democracy' is not a good measure of the legitimacy of particular political arrangements. The reason is that what it means to 'support' a regime is not easily captured in what people say about abstract ideas such as 'democracy' or 'military rule'. But more complex survey-based measures of legitimacy, broadly conceived (for example Gilley, 2006; Booth and Seligson, 2009), do not show much correlation with regime change or stability, despite the many efforts of scholars to find a connection. For example, the measured legitimacy of political institutions in the Western democracies has long been declining, with few apparent effects on their stability (Booth and Seligson, 2009; Inglehart and Welzel, 2005). This is not to say that what people think of their regimes does not matter; it may be the case that regimes that have the trust of the population (like the current Chinese regime) have more free-dom of action than regimes that do not. But while it may be tautologically true that a regime without (some) support from (some) important groups in society cannot last or function effectively, the sources of political sup-port, especially in non-democratic regimes, are too various to fit under the rubric of 'legitimacy' (Márquez, 2016b). Put bluntly, whether a society is ruled by a particular sort of regime is never a simple and direct function of whether 'the people' *want* to have that regime, since what 'the people' want always needs to be translated into collective action before it can have any effect on government institutions.

The Civic Capital Theory of Political Change

Possibilities for collective action may nevertheless be constrained in important ways by other beliefs and attitudes. Here the 'civic capital' the-ory of political culture suggests that interpersonal trust, attitudes towards collective action and the like can shape the forms of associational life common in society, and hence the willingness and ability of people to support specific political regimes. In particular, some people in this tradition have seized on Alexis de Tocqueville's (1835) thesis that an active associational life, sustained by trust in institutions, was crucial to the emergence and stability of democracy in America.

But while it is definitionally true that more open political regimes will boast a richer associational life (since in more open regimes there will be fewer restrictions on organizing such groups), this can support *both* democratic *and* non-democratic movements and regimes. Weimar Germany, was not, contrary to mid-twentieth-century portrayals (Arendt, 1973), an atomized mass society, but a society of joiners (Berman, 1997), with a rich and diverse associational life that nevertheless led to the breakdown of the republic. Moreover, trust itself is only ambiguously related to democracy; while societies where generalized trust in other people is high (for example, the Scandinavian countries) tend to have well-functioning states and high levels of democracy, it is striking that trust in government is *negatively* correlated with democracy in many surveys (Inglehart and Welzel, 2005). Perhaps this is because democracy requires 'critical citizens' (Norris, 2011) rather than satisfied and conformist subjects.

This is not to say that democracy does not require particular forms of 'civic capital'. A long tradition of political thought, going back at least to Machiavelli and Montesquieu in the West, has argued convincingly that republican political regimes always require certain 'civic virtues' from citizens to survive, conceived as dispositions to sacrifice one's private interests for the public good. And some scholars have found that in societies where people's circle of concern is very narrowly drawn – where, for example, they trust and care for only for members of their family rather than for fellow citizens – the state (and democracy) tends to work less well (Putnam, Leonardi, and Nanetti, 1993), an observation already made in the nineteenth century in John Stuart Mill's *Considerations on Representative Government* (Mill, 1859). But the fact that narrow circles of trust make the state work 'less well' is sometimes conflated with a more general and more controversial thesis about the incompatibility of 'collectivist' cultures with democracy, which is supposed to be suitable only for more 'individualistic' cultures.

As noted above, this is a view that achieved some political resonance during the 'Asian Values' debate, when it was endorsed by prominent political leaders such as Lee Kuan Yew (Zakaria and Lee, 1994). In collectivist cultures, this view suggests, people are more likely to accept restrictions on liberty because they are more willing to conform to group pressures, regardless of the size of their 'circles of trust'. Hence they are less likely to fight for individual rights, and associational life in such societies may dampen, rather than enhance, pressures for democratization.

As stated, this thesis needs refinement; as an institutional system democracy has emerged in relatively 'collectivist' cultures (such as Japan or India), and it has not always been very successful in some 'individualistic' cultures. Moreover, the degree to which a culture is 'collectivist' or 'individualistic' can change over time; cultures are not static. But there is an important insight here, which is at the core of the (much maligned) 'modernization theory' (Inglehart and Welzel, 2005; Lipset, 1959, 1960).

Modernization, Cultural Change, and Democracy

The basic thesis of 'modernization theory' is that economic development leads to democracy. Political scientists have long noted that, by conventional measures, rich countries tend to be more democratic than poor countries. To be sure, the mere fact that there is a correlation between wealth and democracy does not mean that economic development produces democracy. For one thing, the correlation is by no means perfect (witness the examples of rich non-democratic Saudi Arabia and poor democratic India), and some states have become relatively wealthier (such as China) without showing signs of democratizing yet. Indeed, some research suggests that states have no particular tendency to *become* more democratic as they become wealthier (Przeworski and Limongi, 1997), indicating that perhaps wealth merely helps stabilize all regimes, rather than having any kind of democratizing tendency. But the overall consensus of political scientists and economists after decades of research on this question (Boix and Stokes, 2003; Boix, 2011; Murtin and Wacziarg, 2014) does tend to support the basic thesis that economic development is strongly correlated with democratization (Figure 10.1).

To be sure, as we can see in Figure 10.1, Middle Eastern oil-rich monarchies (which are often very rich by conventional measures) as well as Singapore (a city-state that became rich while remaining less democratic than expected), appear to buck the trend. Moreover, the correlation between democracy and wealth was stronger in the first half of the twentieth century than afterwards, partly because many more countries are rich and democratic today than in the past (Figure 10.2). Already 'developed' countries do not become steadily more democratic when they grow richer, while in the post-Cold War era many poorer countries are more subject to democratization pressures than in the past (Boix, 2011). Nevertheless, in general, most countries tend to remain as democratic as their income level allows – including China, a country that, despite its recent economic progress, is about as democratic today as its income per capita would predict.

Modernization theorists argue that this correlation can be explained by the fact that certain kinds of economic development produce predictable forms of value change which in turn lead, over time, to pressures for

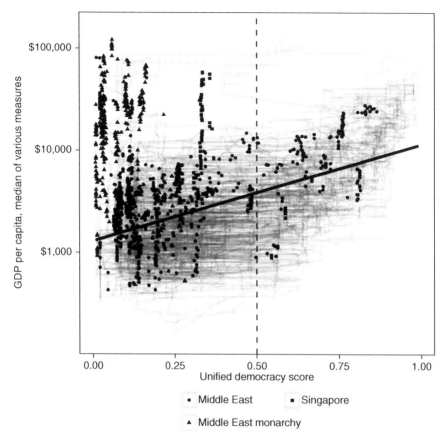

Figure 10.1 *Economic development and democracy, 1800–2014. GDP data from Maddison, (2013), Penn World Tables, and World Bank; democracy data from Pemstein, Meserve and Melton, (2010), extended by the author (Márquez, 2016a). Each point represents a country-year; each line represents a country trajectory over those years where income and democracy data exists. Highlighted points are regimes classified as monarchies by Magaloni, Chu, and Min (2013) for the 1950–2012 period, as well as other regimes in the Middle East (including some regimes for the period before 1950).*

democracy. This is not merely because economic development is typically associated with increases in literacy and education or with the increasing availability of information, as early theorists argued (Lipset, 1959, 1960). The deeper logic of modernization theory stresses the changes in the forms of social connection that 'modernization' brings. Inglehart and Welzel, for example, (Inglehart and Welzel 2005; Welzel 2013) argue that transformative forms of economic development that diminish 'existential insecurity' (the feeling that day-to-day survival is not assured), and reduce people's dependence on 'primary groups' such as the family, enhance the salience and value of individual freedoms.

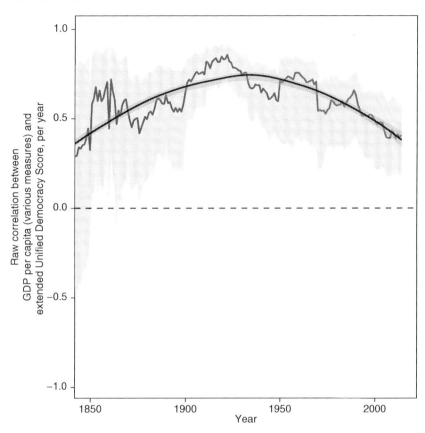

Figure 10.2   *Raw (uncontrolled) correlation between economic development and democracy, per year. Shaded areas represent 95 per cent confidence intervals. GDP data from Maddison, (2013), Penn World Tables, and World Bank; democracy data from Pemstein, Meserve and Melton, (2010), extended by the author (Márquez, 2016a).*

People who are not worried about where their next meal will come from and are not utterly dependent on their extended family for security are more likely to care about their choices and less likely to find value in conformity to the groups to which they belong. And certain forms of capitalist economic development make this possible, by providing an environment of relative abundance (especially when combined with the emergence of a welfare state) and enhancing the value of 'bridging' social capital (that is, connections to relative strangers rather than to members of one's family or other primary groups). In short, when economic change makes people more secure and independent, they come to value individual freedom more, and thus become more willing to push for it in the long run.

The restrictive clauses are crucial; not all forms of capitalist economic development diminish existential insecurity, or make people more independent of important groups, and value change does not immediately result in democracy. For example, in rentier states such as Saudi Arabia, where most of the population is directly or indirectly dependent on the state's oil largesse, value change should be slower and less likely to lead to democracy, since the great wealth of the country does not immediately translate into greater individual independence. And when economic development is associated with increasing precariousness (if, for example, unemployment is high and job security is low) it is also unlikely to bring out people's 'liberty aspirations', as the popularity of 'extremist' parties in today's Europe attests. Moreover, value change happens mostly one funeral at a time, since most people's deepest values are set early in their lives, and in any case cannot translate into collective action pushing for democratic change if external circumstances are not sufficiently propitious.

Nevertheless, Inglehart and Welzel do find that there is a strong correlation between economic development and the spread of what they call 'self-expression values' and 'liberty aspirations', and that these 'emancipatory' values are in turn strongly correlated with the emergence and stability of democracy. And though political change by definition depends on organized collective action (O'Donnell and Schmitter, 1986), Inglehart and Welzel convincingly argue that the existence of a larger pool of people who value freedom makes pro-democratic political movements more likely to succeed in the right circumstances (Welzel and Inglehart, 2008).

The theory is thus at its core a 'culturalist', not a simply economic, account of regime change. It is only when economic development leads to cultural change that it also leads to democracy; mere wealth (as in oil-dependent states) cannot bring stable, high-quality democratic government by itself, unless it also produces changes in people's emancipative values. Moreover, unlike the 'legitimacy' account of political culture, modernization theory claims that the emergence and stability of democracy depends on commitments to tolerance and liberty that are much deeper than merely expressed wishes for democratic government. Ambiguous desires for 'democracy' are compatible with authoritarianism when they are not accompanied by other pro-freedom attitudes. At the same time, modernization theory is not a 'strong' culturalist position (Przeworski, 1998), insofar as it does not claim that cultural change is independent of economic development or other structural, 'objective' factors. Like Marxism, modernization theory argues that 'in the last instance' cultural change depends on economic change, though unlike Marxism it does not argue that economic change should lead to the overcoming of capitalism. Democracy is a 'universal value' not because everyone always wants democracy, but because when existential pressures recede, the desire for liberty emerges naturally everywhere (Welzel, 2013).

Contrast this position with a 'strong' culturalist account of value and regime change. In such accounts, the key mechanism of value change is *intentional persuasion*. Values change less because economic development makes them *dispensable*, and more because particular groups of people intentionally and successfully spread certain ideas (for example, 'Western' individualist values). Education, proselytism, and propaganda thus play crucial roles in the spread of values that ultimately lead to democracy (or indeed to other regimes). In some historical accounts of the spread of democracy, for example, the key role is played not by structural changes in the economy but by the diffusion of Western enlightenment ideas among elites, as well as their slower acceptance by the masses, sometimes through the influence of Protestant missionaries (Woodberry, 2012) or Western education. Similarly, some scholars have argued that the 'democratic deficit' in the Middle East can be attributed primarily to attitudes towards gender roles (Fish, 2002) that lead people to authoritarian attitudes more generally, and, more importantly, that these attitudes are the result of cultural transmission processes that are relatively independent of changes in the economic structure (contrary to, for example, the findings of Inglehart and Welzel (2005) that attitudes towards women become more egalitarian with economic development). From such perspectives, democracy appears indeed to be a 'Western' import rather than a universal aspiration that emerges naturally with structural changes in the economic structure.

But these accounts are not wholly convincing. Too much weight is attributed in them to mere persuasion; but as we have stressed in this book, people are not, in the long term, the dupes of ideas that do not make sense in the conditions of their life. Values spread not (or not primarily) because some people are very good at persuading others even against their interests, but because they fit within a particular mode of life, with all its structural constraints. And to the extent that the 'strong culturalist' thesis can be tested by means of statistical methods, the results have been meagre; little evidence has emerged linking, for example, religion with the emergence and stability of democracy once one controls for economic development, contrary to what one would expect from this position (Norris and Inglehart, 2002; Przeworski, 1998). The real alternative to the 'weak culturalist' position of modernization theory on regime change and stability is thus not the strong culturalist idea that the evolution and spread of political ideas happen through processes that are highly autonomous from structural economic and social changes, but what we may call the 'conflict account' of regime change. This view claims that regime change and stability is less the result of relative mass value consensus than of the sharpness of organized conflicts of interests in a society.

Economic Conflict and Regime Change

In contrast to theories of cultural change that emphasize the importance of mass values (what we might call the consensus of society, its 'culture'), some theorists argue that regime change is primarily driven by conflict among people with very different views of how society should operate. Here it is not the majority of the people who matter, but the balance of forces among two or more contending, organized forces; and we focus less on which values are held by the majority of people than on those matters that are the objects of relative disagreement. Politics, on this view, is primarily about 'who gets what, when, and how' (Lasswell, 1936); and regime change happens because different regimes affect the distribution of gains from social cooperation – in particular, material gains (Acemoglu and Robinson, 2006; Boix, 2003).

Conflict theories of regime change go back at least to Aristotle, who centrally emphasized the role of class conflict in the process of regime change (Márquez, 2011a). Their logic is fairly simple. Imagine a society divided into a (wealthy) elite and a (poor) majority. It is clear that the majority in this society would benefit from (at least some) redistribution; they would prefer to tax or even expropriate the wealthy and distribute the proceeds among themselves. And the elite would prefer not to be taxed. (It is of course possible to complicate this very simple model with all kinds of real-world considerations about the benefits of broad-based economic growth, the deadweight losses of taxation, and so on, but for our purposes right now all we need to assume is that the majority benefits from some redistribution of the elite's wealth.) And the more unequal the distribution of resources between the 'elite' (the included group) and the 'masses' (the group excluded from power), the more the masses gain from redistributive taxation or even expropriation of the elites. By the same token, however, the greater the inequality, the greater the incentive of the elite to resist this redistribution. Inequality, in other words, sharpens redistributive conflicts; and insofar as the state determines 'who gets what, when, and how', it increases the importance of controlling it for different groups in society.

We need not think of 'inequality' too narrowly here. There can be redistributive conflict over status, for example, not just material wealth, though conflict theorists typically focus on conflict over material goods. And these conflicts can be quite sharp. Aristotle quotes an oath supposedly sworn in some oligarchic regimes (controlled by the rich) in ancient Greece: 'And I will be hostile to the people [the poor] and plan whatever evil I can against them' (*Politics* V.1310a 9–11). In the twentieth century the redistributive efforts of the Allende government played an important role in polarizing society into two hostile camps, eventually convincing Chile's economic elites to support Pinochet's coup against his government; some scholars have spoken of the Chile of the period as a 'nation of enemies' (Constable and Valenzuela, 1993).

Regimes as Commitment Devices

Yet in modern states the majority does not typically have the *institutionalized* power (what Acemoglu and Robinson call *de jure* power) to ensure that the elite gives up some of its wealth for redistribution, at least not if the elite controls the machinery of the state. Whenever the majority is excluded from institutionalized power (control over the state), it can at best acquire what Acemoglu and Robinson call *de facto* power. De facto power, unlike institutionalized power, is temporary and fleeting, the product of unusual circumstances that allow excluded groups to suddenly organize, engage in collective action (in street protests, marches, strikes, and so on), and in general pose a threat to the elite's control of the state.

Moreover, concessions extracted from the elite at gunpoint, but not transformed into *de jure* institutional change, have a way of vanishing. For example, during the 'Arab Spring' of 2011 in the Middle East, most of the Gulf monarchies quickly offered large salary increases and other monetary 'gifts' to citizens (Yom and Gause, 2012). But as the threat receded, elites in these countries felt much less compulsion to mollify the masses. The great revolutions of the twentieth century – the Chinese and the Russian in particular – were accompanied by large-scale 'spontaneous' redistributions of land from rich landlords to poor peasants (Tumarkin, 1983; Walder, 2015). But once the victorious communist parties had secured their power in Russia and China, they quickly moved to 'collectivize' agriculture, in effect expropriating the peasants. Once the latter could not present an organized threat to the Communist elite, their interests could be disregarded in both cases, to the point of inducing two of the greatest man-made famines in world history (Walder, 2015; Conquest 1986).

From this point of view, democracy appears as what economists call a 'commitment device': a way of transforming power today into power tomorrow (Acemoglu and Robinson, 2006). The poor should normally prefer democracy to dictatorship, not just because of the redistribution it offers 'today' but because it ensures that any economic concessions granted under the fleeting compulsion of the threat of revolution will continue in the future. Conversely, the rich should normally prefer an authoritarian regime in which they control the state to democracy, and this preference will be stronger the higher the level of inequality.

Factors that Sharpen Redistributive Conflict

To be sure, this simple theory does not account for many other factors that may affect a group's preference for a particular political regime, much less its ability to impose their will on other groups. Much 'pro-democracy' protest, for example, appears to be motivated less by the promise of redistribution than by the humiliations of arbitrary power, as we shall see in Chapter 11 below. Actual societies are not divided into just two separate classes, which means that processes of regime change depend on complex and shifting class alliances. And democracies vary greatly in the degree to which they are actually redistributive, as we will see below in more detail, depending on their ethnic and religious diversity, the effectiveness of their state, and so on. But the theory is not a terrible starting point for thinking about the incentives of key actors in processes of regime change, or the incentives leading to regime stability.

Nevertheless, two complications are necessary (Boix, 2003). First, any theory of regime change must account for the ability of various groups to surmount collective action problems. Since inequality increases *both* the degree to which democracy may be useful to the masses *and* the incentives of the rich to control the state, sufficiently high levels of social conflict may lead to diverse outcomes, including long-term instability, depending on the degree to which the different parties can organize collective action in an open fight and on their calculations about the costs of such fights. In particular, if the rich are 'stronger' – more organized, better able to use military force, and so on – high inequality may lead to repressive, elite-led authoritarian regimes (as it did in Chile in 1973). If the poor are stronger, the result may not be democracy but the revolutionary overthrow of the existing state, under the direction of a party with roots in the working class or the peasantry (as in China or Russia). And sometimes no force can achieve final victory, as in Argentina during the Perón era (1945–80s), which oscillated between military rule and electoral democracy (see also Chapter 6). Moreover, the level of inequality can interact with the ability to organize; low levels of inequality may lead to democracy even with little social conflict, since in such circumstances elites have less to lose from regime change and much to fear from escalating social conflict, so that even if pro-democracy forces are small they may still be able to force democratic concessions.

Second, whether resource inequalities lead to social conflict may depend on whether resources are visible and easily redistributable. It is not surprising that in agrarian societies, where most wealth takes the form of land (which is visible, easily redistributable, and impossible to take to a foreign country), even relatively low levels of inequality can lead to great uprisings, whereas capitalist societies with highly complex and opaque economies can be quite unequal and yet have fairly stable regimes. Thus, while we should expect that, all other things being equal, increases in inequality should lead to more social conflict and eventually to regime change, other things are not always equal. At best we can say that conflict theories predict that regimes where resource inequality is low will tend to be reasonably stable, while regimes where resource inequality is high and visible will tend to be at best brittle. And democracy would thus seem to be most stable where it is *least* needed for redistributive purposes.

Empirical Evidence for Conflict Theories

Conflict theories of regime change are highly intuitive. During the Arab Spring the mass media and some scholarly accounts typically mentioned, among the causes of the uprising in Tunisia and Egypt, the 'rising inequality' in these societies (Gelvin, 2012). This inequality was highly visible in the large fortunes accumulated by both the Ben Ali and the Mubarak clans and other influential insiders (including senior government figures in both countries) and in the lack of opportunity for relatively well-educated people, who struggled to get jobs even with university educations. Moreover, many people – including many citizens of these countries – believed inequality had been rising in these societies for reasons that are common to a lot of other countries – the liberalization of the economy and the concomitant enrichment of well-connected insiders at the expense of most people (Hibbard and Layton, 2010).

Yet it is surprisingly difficult to show a link between 'objective' measures of inequality and regime change. This is partly because numerical measures of inequality, like the Gini index, are often of poor quality and collected on irregular schedules – or not collected at all in many poor dictatorships. Nevertheless it is worth noting that according to these measures neither Egypt nor Tunisia was a particularly unequal society, nor was inequality increasing in them (Hlasny and Verme, 2013; Verme et al., 2014), as Figures 10.3 and 10.4 indicate. (It is hard to say for sure,

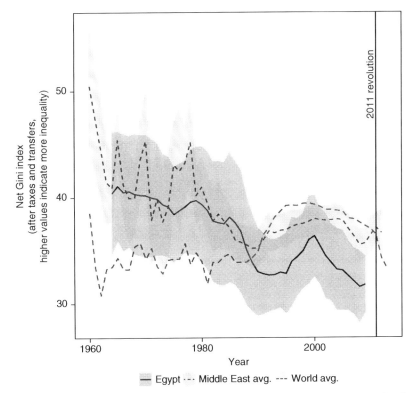

Figure 10.3   *Inequality in Egypt, 1964–2009. Data from Solt's standardized worldwide inequality database (Solt, 2009). Shaded areas represent 95 per cent confidence intervals.*

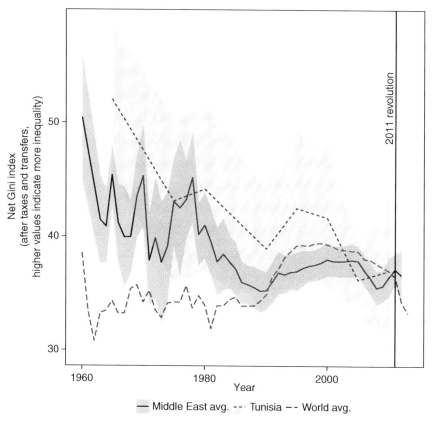

Figure 10.4   *Inequality in Tunisia, 1965–2010. Data from Solt's standardized worldwide inequality database (Solt, 2009). Shaded areas represent 95 per cent confidence intervals.*

given the measurement uncertainties involved, but Egypt seems to have had below average and decreasing inequality, while Tunisia seems to have had average and decreasing inequality.) And Venezuela, where the rise of Chávez was attributed to increasing inequality, already had some of the lowest levels of measured inequality in Latin America when he took over (though it had been rising at the time; see Figure 10.5.)

Moreover, while non-democratic regimes do seem to be, on average, slightly more unequal than democracies (as the theory above would predict), they are not, on average, more unequal than their level of economic development would predict (Przeworski, 2010, p. 86). Sophisticated statistical studies find little connection between the measured level of inequality and the level of democracy or the probability of democratization (Gradstein and Milanovic, 2004; Knutsen 2015a; Houle, 2009), though the connection between high inequality (including high inequality between distinct ethnic groups) and the breakdown of democracy is more

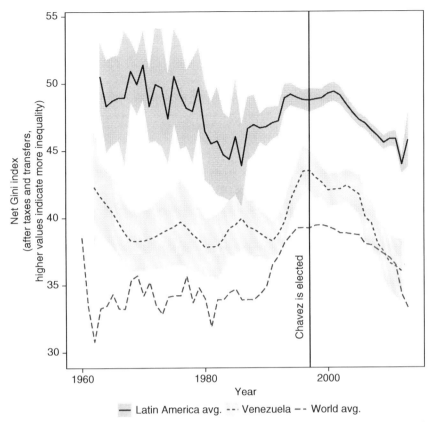

Figure 10.5   *Inequality in Venezuela, 1962–2012. Data from Solt's standardized worldwide inequality database (Solt, 2009). Shaded areas represent 95 per cent confidence intervals.*

robustly supported (Houle 2009, 2015). Careful examinations of specific democratic transitions show a role for redistributive motivations in less than half of all cases (Haggard and Kaufman, 2012). Democracies do not appear to be particularly effective at reducing inequality (Bermeo, 2009; Timmons, 2010), nor is democracy robustly associated in most people's minds with economic redistribution, at least not according to existing survey evidence (Welzel, 2013; Knutsen and Wegmann, 2016). Finally, poorer individuals are less likely to protest in highly unequal societies, and they are more likely to be deferential to those in power (Solt, 2011, 2015). None of these facts seems particularly consistent with the conflict theory of regime change.

But there may still be some connection between inequality, democracy, and democratization. For one thing, even though there is little overall relationship between the measured level of democracy and the measured level of inequality in most societies, distinct regimes do cluster in ways consistent with conflict theories of regime change (see Figure 10.6). Thus, most

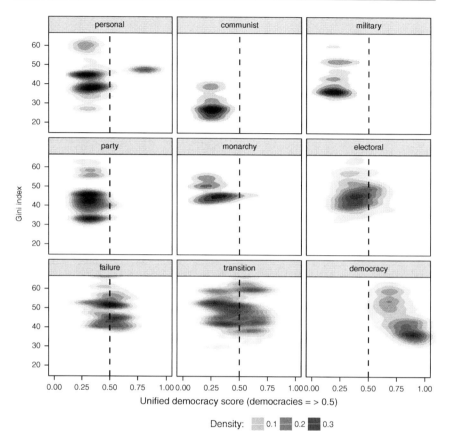

Figure 10.6 *Inequality and political regimes. The inequality measure is the net Gini index of income inequality (net means after taxes and transfers); it goes from 0 to 100, where higher numbers mean more inequality. Data on regimes is from Kailitz, 2013. Inequality data from Solt, (2009), updated to 2013. The democracy data is from Pemstein, Meserve, and Melton, (2010), extended by the author (Márquez, 2016a).*

long-standing, rich democracies have relatively low levels of inequality (much of it achieved through redistribution), while the lowest levels of measured inequality among non-democracies have been found in Communist regimes, which were ideologically committed to redistribution and achieved it mostly through revolutionary means, as the theory would predict.

By contrast, many new and less democratic democracies in places that have been plagued with coups – and thus show signs of redistributive conflict (Svolik, 2012, ch. 5) – have higher levels of inequality, suggesting a process of learning; where class conflict is severe, democracy is only possible when the contending parties agree to settle for less redistribution than the poor want, but this typically happens only after political actors have learned from experience that too much redistribution, too soon, is likely to lead to violence (O'Donnell and Schmitter, 1986). One could argue that this is precisely what happened in Chile; the violence of the Pinochet regime tempered demands for redistribution in the democratic period. It certainly was in the minds of the architects of the 'Pacto de Punto Fijo' in Venezuela in 1958 after the overthrow of the military dictator Marcos Pérez Jiménez. (Pérez Jiménez was widely thought to have overthrown Venezuela's earlier experiment with democracy in 1950 partly because the social democratic party Acción Democrática, which came to power in elections in 1948, had become increasingly radical in its redistributive activities.) Finally, the highest levels of inequality are typically found in very personalistic dictatorships, where (as we saw in Chapter 4) a tiny elite tends to monopolize most resources.

Historical evidence also suggests that class conflict played a hugely important role in the expansion of the suffrage (Przeworski, 2009). The vote was usually 'conquered' through the threat of revolution, often in the teeth of enormous resistance – and not granted by elites out of the goodness of their hearts (or a misplaced desire to imitate Western countries). Moreover, to the extent that scholars can tell, the evidence suggests that the expansion of the suffrage did decrease material inequality through redistribution, just as nineteenth-century elites feared – but also that further democratization was much less effective in reducing inequality (Gradstein and Milanovic, 2004). And though democratization has happened in highly unequal societies (such as late-nineteenth-century Britain), it tended to happen precisely where there was a highly developed capitalist sector, *not* in unequal agrarian or resource-rich economies, just as conflict theories would predict (Houle, 2009; Freeman and Quinn, 2012). By the same token, resource-rich economies tend to have difficulties democratizing because control of economic resources is very highly concentrated. Few oil-dependent economies have ever become fully democratic after the 1970s, when control over oil was nationalized in many developing countries, which has led some scholars to speak of an 'oil curse' (Ross, 2012; Andersen and Ross, 2014; but see Haber and Menaldo, 2011 for a more sceptical look).

Regime Change and Beliefs about Fairness

Nevertheless, the conflicts that led to democratization in many of these cases had often more to do with the desire by more elite groups to protect themselves from the depredations of the state than with the desire of the poor to redistribute wealth (Ansell and Samuels, 2010). Thus, in Egypt the main protests against the Mubarak regime seem to have been led by young professionals who would have suffered quite a bit from its predation. In actual episodes of democratization, the demands for an end to arbitrary treatment by the state – for 'dignity', an end to corruption or police harassment, for free expression, and so on – are very prevalent, even though we can also find demands for redistribution and economic equality driven by more economic interests. In any case, it seems reasonably clear that most people do not react to some objective and generally unobservable measure of inequality; indeed, they are unlikely to be able to estimate the 'actual' level of inequality in their society correctly, sometimes grossly underestimating it (Norton and Ariely, 2011), and sometimes greatly overestimating it (Chambers, Swan, and Heesacker, 2014). Egyptians, for example, consistently *overestimated* how materially unequal their society was in the years before the 2011 revolution (Hlasny and Verme, 2013).

But people strongly object to perceived *unfairness*. One of the most robust findings of social movement theory is that people are more motivated to participate in collective action when they want to correct a perceived injustice to their group, *not* when they expect to gain some individual material benefit (Stekelenburg and Klandermans, 2013). Inequality has to become a moral and political issue before people are willing to take the risk of participating in anti-regime protest. In Egypt, for example, though objectively speaking material inequality was low, people's sensitivity to overt inequality had been increasing: it was felt as more obnoxious and unfair (Hlasny and Verme, 2013). Moreover, increases in the price of bread (always a socially sensitive price in poor societies) were experienced as particularly burdensome and unfair, especially among the poor. In Thailand, another society with relatively low levels of measured inequality (by global standards) and little history of recent class conflict, former prime minister Thaksin Shinawatra succeeded in politicizing and moralizing the issue, riding it to electoral victory several times and polarizing Thai society enough to precipitate a couple of military coups since 2006 (Hewison, 2014).

More generally, the effects of inequality on political change seem to be mediated by beliefs about justice or fairness, which differ quite a bit among societies (Alesina and George-Marios, 2005). In some societies, many people believe that effort brings rewards, and that material gains are justified in this way; in others, most people believe material gain is primarily due to luck, and are strongly suspicious of inequality. Political socialization plays a role; for example, people in Communist regimes were more intolerant of inequality than people in capitalist societies (Alesina and Fuchs-Schündeln, 2007). Sharp departures from these culturally specific norms about inequality promote anti-regime mobilization, less to gain the benefits of redistribution than to redress the perceived unfairness. These departures might be produced by increases in the visibility of elite wealth ('ostentation') or by increases in the incidence of wealth due to unfair processes of distribution ('corruption').

Hence the importance, for revolutionary mobilization, of (objectively speaking) minor incidents like the Shah's grandiose party on the anniversary of the Persian monarchy in 1973 (Axworthy, 2013), which was seen as an obscene display of wealth to little purpose by most Iranians, or the publicity surrounding the comparatively luxurious living conditions of the leaders of the GDR early during the 1989 fall of the Communist regime there. In Eastern Europe, where people had been socialized for decades into an ethos of equality, even the relatively small privileges of the *nomenklatura* – the GDR leaders lived a bit better than most GDR citizens, but did not live *that* luxuriously – were seen as galling. It is thus not the level of inequality that matters for mobilization, but sharp changes in inequality, relative to the culturally specific fairness baseline. Yet at high levels of inequality, even small departures from the fairness baseline will be easily perceived as forms of injustice, so that high inequality societies should be, on this view, more prone both to mobilization leading to democratization (Houle, 2009; Haggard and Kaufman, 2012) and to the breakdown of democracy (because of its threat to the interests of the wealthy).

Conclusion

Conflict and cultural theories of regime change complement one another. Regime change is a conflictive process, and sometimes conflicts are about material resources. Moreover, different regimes do seem to affect the distribution of resources. In particular, consolidated democracies appear to share both power and wealth with wider groups than personalistic dictatorships, while Communist dictatorships shared wealth but not power. But all conflicts are mediated by many culturally specific beliefs about the value of liberty and about the unfairness of current regimes, even as the structure of a society's economy – including, for example, whether it is poor or rich, highly unequal, or dependent on oil resources – shapes both the values and the incentives of major political actors.

Finally, it seems to be the case that democracy is most likely to be stable in more developed societies that are not riven by sharp value conflicts triggered by deep inequalities in resources. But this does not mean that democracy is a merely 'Western' value; as societies develop economically, it becomes increasingly likely that democracy is accepted as a method for peacefully resolving these conflicts.

Chapter 11

How do Regimes Change? Contentious Politics and Its Diffusion

Regime change doesn't just 'happen' when structural conditions are right. Though the long-term 'macropolitical' processes of structural change described in the previous chapter prepare the soil, transitions to and from various political systems are produced by specific people doing particular things, from signing petitions to engaging in protest to taking up arms. To be sure, sometimes regimes change without anybody intending them to change. New institutions evolve that change the meaning of existing institutions; before anyone knows the absolute monarch has turned into a constitutional monarch, hedged everywhere by the weight of custom and law. But even in such cases changes are usually the outcomes of what the Trinidadian writer V. S. Naipaul once evocatively termed 'a million mutinies': small, local conflicts, individually insignificant but together enormously consequential. And sometimes political change – even very significant change – happens in places where structural conditions are very unfavourable.

In this chapter, we thus switch from the 'macropolitical' perspective on regime change of the previous chapter to focus on the 'micropolitical' perspective, exploring the many forms of 'contentious politics' (Tilly and Tarrow, 2006; Tilly, 2006) that people use to push for political change, from solitary dissidence to armed conflict and civil war. A plurality of regime changes in non-democratic political systems (about a third of those in the dataset assembled by Geddes, Wright, and Frantz (2014) for the period 1945–2010) have occurred through coups, and most of these led to another non-democratic regime (as discussed in Chapter 6). But about a quarter of all non-democratic regimes in the post-Second World War era have ended through popular uprisings or civil wars, and another quarter through electoral processes requiring significant popular mobilization (Figure 11.1). Not all of these transitions have resulted in democratization, but all of them have required the participation of many people beyond the elite (unlike the coups we studied earlier); and these are the focus of this chapter.

Regime change requires suitable opportunities. But in most non-democratic regimes, most of the time, there is little opportunity for protest and popular mobilization to induce political change; in some non-democratic regimes it may not be possible to protest at all without running enormous risks. Nevertheless, as we shall see in the first section of this

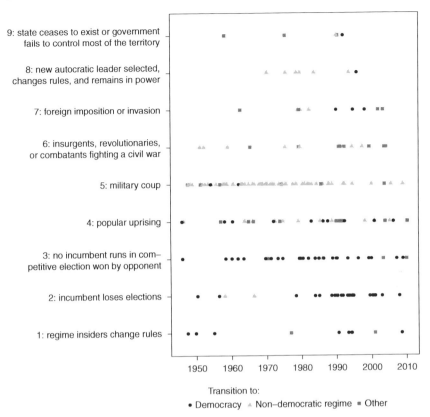

Figure 11.1   *Transition events in non-democratic regimes, 1945–2010. This figure counts only transitions in non-democratic regimes. There are 223 such events in this period: 79 of them towards democracy, 105 towards other forms of non-democracy, and the rest to state breakdown, foreign occupation, or other conditions without clear state authority. Regime data comes from Geddes, Wright, and Frantz, (2014).*

chapter, opportunities for regime-threatening revolt can emerge in even the most repressive regimes. In particular, such opportunities arise when certain events lower the material and emotional costs of contention. These events can be very diverse, ranging from shifts in great power politics, to slowdowns in economic growth, to the example of successful revolt elsewhere, but they all tend to intensify divisions within a regime and to embolden oppositional forces. Using examples from the recent Arab Uprisings, the Revolutions of 1989, and the Colour Revolutions of the first decade of the twenty-first century, we note specifically how such changes mean that contentious politics can 'diffuse' across borders and within countries in unexpected ways.

Regime change has its rituals and tactics. Its great iconic events – the 'ten days that shook the world' of the Russian Revolution, the great protests of Tahrir Square in Egypt in 2011 that led to the fall of Mubarak, the self-immolation of Mohammed Bouazizi in Tunisia that sparked the 'Arab Spring' – are built up from what sociologists call 'interaction rituals' (Collins, 2004): collective gatherings with a focus on particular symbols that mobilize emotion, strengthen identities, and generate anti-regime solidarity. If regimes, as we saw in Chapter 8, use their own rituals of power to instil fear and loyalty, oppositional forces use what we might call 'rituals of contention' to help people get over the 'barrier of fear' and break their pro-regime loyalties.

In the next few sections of this chapter, we thus explore how people come to participate in these often risky practices, how they grow, and how they have changed over the last two centuries, using examples from a variety of countries. In particular, we note how developments in the international system have pulled the 'repertoire of contention' – the set of tactics typically used by protesters – away from violent tactics, and review evidence that non-violent tactics work much more often than most people might think even in the most repressive settings. Yet we also note that this is an evolutionary process, in which ineffective tactics and rituals of solidarity are replaced over time in unpromising environments. Thus, just as some groups of people have learned to deploy new non-violent protest tactics against repressive regimes, so non-democratic regimes have begun to learn how to counter them.

Regime change also has its rhythms. These are often frustrating: ten days of excitement are followed by years of inconclusive negotiation, coalition building, and compromise; or a month of non-violent protest is followed by years of inconclusive civil war. Since regime change means replacing one set of institutions with another, the process of change, especially in transitions to democracy, typically depends not just on the mobilization of large numbers of people, but on the institution-building skills of elites. In the last section of this chapter, we briefly survey the conditions that allow elites to create a new regime out of the ashes of the old, as well as the many pitfalls they face in this process.

Political Opportunity

In most regimes, people who wish to influence policy or change the political system face a definite 'political opportunity structure' (Tilly, 2006). Some actions they might wish to take – voting, protesting in the streets, and so on – may be easy or difficult, politically meaningless or politically powerful, depending on whether the state requires, tolerates, or represses them. Indeed, a regime can be characterized by the 'repertoire' of political activity that it allows, represses, or requires. For example, while totalitarian regimes require certain forms of political activity (participating in regime-glorifying parades, voting on election day) and repress all others severely (participating in unsanctioned protests, forming political parties, printing unofficial newspapers), most democracies neither require nor unduly repress most forms of political activity, leaving a wide area of 'tolerated' practices from which people can choose in their attempts to influence policy or change political structures. Most authoritarian regimes are in the middle of this spectrum, varying in the extent to which particular political activities are repressed or tolerated.

The set of required, tolerated, and repressed activities structures political opportunities, and thus the tactics of resistance that individuals and groups are likely to use against regimes. Where the range of repressed political activities is very large, opportunities for influence by people outside the regime, let alone revolt, are very small, and oppositional activity tends to go underground. Small groups of committed individuals may conspire to seize power (and occasionally succeed, as the long history of successful military coups we explored in Chapter 6 shows), or they may attempt to move popular opinion against the regime with underground newspapers, sabotage, or terrorism, but they will typically be unable to mobilize large numbers openly unless the political opportunity structure changes significantly. By contrast, in authoritarian systems that are unwilling or unable to repress many significant forms of political activity, oppositional forces may be able to use very different tactics, including the occasional mass protest.

We should not think of the political opportunity structure as a static, unchangeable set of conditions. The language of 'structure' merely indicates that at any given time in a society particular forms of collective contention against the state are riskier or safer, or more or less effective, than others, due to the state's 'monopoly on legitimate force', to use the classic Weberian formulation, and that opposition forces are more or less aware of these relative differences and try to use forms of contention that take advantage of them. But opposition forces can, to some greater or lesser extent, *make* their own opportunities through the creative exploitation of weaknesses in the state's repressive and normative apparatuses (Sharp, 2012; Kurzman, 2004). And in any case, though modern states are powerful agents, the entirety of the factors that affect whether particular forms of collective contention become easier or harder for opposition forces to use is never under their full control. Four kinds of factors are especially important: factors that affect the state's capacity to enforce its will, crises that divide the regime's elite, shifts in the international environment that affect people's perceptions of their political opportunities, and periodic but unavoidable events that enable challengers to mobilize opposition.

Weakened State Capacity and Political Opportunity

Geography and history can impose severe constraints on the capacity of a regime to impose its will in particular areas of a country. The importance of these constraints is most obvious in the case of armed insurgency. Under normal circumstances, armed revolt against a modern, effective state in control of its security forces is very difficult if not impossible (O'Donnell and Schmitter, 1986). The state controls far more armed might, and has far more resources, than most insurgent groups. But in many countries, there are some spaces that, due to history or geography, are not under the full control of the central state. Mountainous and remote areas, for example, have often served as bases from which committed groups can mount insurgencies; when Fidel Castro and his companions began his armed struggle against the Cuban military dictatorship of Batista in the 1950s, they went to the most remote areas of the Sierra Maestra, where they were, if not exactly safe, at least better protected from Batista's security forces. Effectively enforcing the state's will throughout a territory is an enormously difficult, multigenerational undertaking, and some states still have not managed it fully (Scott, 2009). More generally, as we noted in our discussion of totalitarianism in Chapter 3, regime leaders may wish to suppress a wide range of groups and repress their political activity, but find that they simply cannot rely on the loyalty of their security forces to do so reliably, and are thus forced to tolerate them, a situation that creates political opportunities for challengers.

Sometimes external events – especially large-scale interstate warfare – can also significantly degrade the capacity of the state to repress oppositions and manage challenges to the regime in power. For example, the Russian state, which was in general quite able to resist opposition challenges, broke down in 1917 under the pressure of losses in the First World War (Kotkin, 2014). By summer of that year, the state could not reliably obtain the resources it needed to prosecute the war, soldiers no longer reliably obeyed orders to shoot, and elites were utterly divided about the Tsar, conditions that threw the political opportunity structure wide open. Indeed, the combination of severe fiscal crisis, deadlocked elites, and generalized breakdown of the state's military and police hierarchies represents the sort of 'perfect storm' that has typically made great social revolutions (the French, the Russian, the Chinese) possible, enabling motivated outsiders (like the Bolshevik Party, with Lenin at its head) to seize state power and force otherwise unthinkable social transformations (Goldstone, 2001).

Economic Crises and Elite Divisions

States are often at the mercy of economic forces they cannot fully control. Sudden slowdowns in growth, capital outflows, and other economic crises can be enormously destabilizing to any regime, but a wide range of research suggests that economic crisis is especially damaging to regimes whose main claim to legitimacy is the promotion of economic growth, like military regimes (O'Donnell and Schmitter, 1986; Gill, 2000); the majority of such regime breakdowns have happened because of economic and fiscal crisis. Economic crisis changes the political opportunity structure not only by encouraging popular mobilization against worsening economic conditions, as in the Middle East before the Arab Spring, but more importantly by dividing authoritarian elites and hindering their ability to act in concert. In particular, under the pressure of economic crisis elites have tended to split into two camps: those who think that surviving the crisis requires 'opening up' the system (whether to 'let off steam' or to 'get new blood'), and those who think that surviving the crisis requires 'toughening up', the 'softliners' and the 'hardliners' in O'Donnell and Schmitter's (1986) influential terminology. Should softliners gain the upper hand, political opportunities for oppositional forces will tend to expand; should hardliners gain the upper hand, they will tend to narrow and be channelled towards different options (including violence).

The 'softliners' vs. 'hardliners' divide is usually due not to fundamental ideological differences within the regime elite, but to the *uncertainty* inherent in a situation of crisis. It is thus in general a *tactical*, not a *substantive* split concerning the best means of dealing with the problem (Gill, 2000). In particular, 'softliners' are not committed democrats; at best, they want to 'change everything so that everything can stay the same'. In the face of a regime-threatening economic crisis, they may seek electoral legitimation to implement unpopular measures, or a wider range of voices in the press and a relaxation of ideological controls to debate possible solutions and cut through the web of falsifications around them (see Chapter 8).

For example, as we briefly noted in Chapter 8, in the mid 1980s Soviet Communist Party General Secretary Mikhail Gorbachev called for 'glasnost' ('transparency') and 'perestroika' ('restructuring'), decreasing or eliminating pre-publication censorship and allowing for a range of groups independent of the Communist Party to form. This relaxation of political control was not meant to eliminate the Communist Party's monopoly on power – Gorbachev really believed in the CPSU's ideological project, and desperately wanted to save socialism in the Soviet Union (Kotkin, 2008) – but to increase the reliability of information available to the party, to help the central apparatus fight corruption, and to reinvigorate its popular support. It is precisely because Gorbachev was an 'idealist', bent on reforming the socialist system, that he was willing to gamble on an opening up of the political opportunity structure. Yet he ultimately lost that gamble, as the opening up allowed new forces to quickly grow and organize, and popular mobilization against the regime to escalate.

This is not to say that the 'hardliner' option is any safer for authoritarian regimes; such regimes simply collapse in different ways, since their political opportunity structure does not allow for the gradual build-up of opposition forces or even for organized protest. For example, the Romanian and East German Communist regimes opted for the 'hardline' option in the face of the economic crisis of the 1980s. They were so repressive that anti-regime activists could be counted on the fingers of one hand, and had no organizations of any kind capable of calling on people to protest in large numbers. In East Germany, moreover, the regime had long sent inconvenient critics to the West, where they could do little harm (Sebestyen, 2010). Yet at the end of the day they were still at the mercy of unpredictable events; and when opportunities for protest opened up – for example, the eviction and attempted arrest of pastor László Tőkés in Romania, or the increasing exodus West of young people in East Germany – the resulting 'unorganized' popular mobilization quickly overwhelmed the regime's security forces, for reasons we shall explore in more detail below. In sum, in the face of a sufficiently severe economic crisis, there may be no 'safe' option for an authoritarian regime; and the resulting tactical uncertainty – is it better to gamble on a limited opening or to increase controls? – will tend to divide authoritarian elites and eventually force open the political opportunity structure.

International Influences and Perceptions of Opportunity

Changes in the international system can also profoundly alter the political opportunity structure in a regime. This is especially clear in those regimes that are directly 'propped up' by a great power, such as the Eastern European Communist regimes during the Cold War. These regimes sometimes had more and sometimes less popular support, but the Soviet army was the ultimate guarantor of their permanence regardless of popular feeling. And this was very much a credible guarantee; the Soviet army had invaded Hungary in 1956 and Czechoslovakia in 1968 to prevent the overthrow of the Communist Party in popular uprisings. But in the mid 1980s this security guarantee started to look wobblier, until it was famously replaced, in 1989, by the so-called 'Sinatra Doctrine'. The phrase, coined by Soviet foreign ministry spokesman Gennadi Gerasimov, referred to a popular Frank Sinatra song ('My Way') to indicate that the Soviet Union would refrain from intervention in the internal affairs of the Eastern European Communist regimes. But as soon as the Soviet Union began to claim that Warsaw Pact members could do things 'their way', even to the extent of rejecting the socialist system, without fear of Soviet invasion (Sebestyen, 2010, p. 198), and was actually believed, efforts to mobilize against the Eastern European Communist parties, seen as 'foreign' implants by much of the population, no longer had to contend with the high probability that success would be crowned with Soviet intervention.

Shifts in great power policies are not the only international changes that affect perceptions of the political opportunity structure. Uprisings in neighbouring countries can change individual perceptions of the possible success of revolt, thus changing the effective political opportunity structure. When Mohammed Bouazizi set himself on fire in Tunisia on

17 December 2010, he triggered a chain of protests that led to the eventual overthrow of long-time leader Zine El Abidine Ben Ali. And *these* events in turn provided a spark for the protests in Egypt in January 2011 by changing Egyptians' perceptions of what was possible in their own society. Similarly, when the Polish union 'Solidarity' won an unprecedented victory in semi-free elections in 1989, anti-communist movements elsewhere in Eastern Europe received a huge boost. The joke was that 'in Poland it took ten years, in Hungary ten months, in East Germany ten weeks, and in Czechoslovakia ten days'; each movement provided further impetus to the next (see Garton Ash, 1999, p. 78, slightly rewritten). These events were made possible by the *diffusion* of information about events and tactics across borders, which in turn changed people's *perceptions* of what opportunities for collective action were actually available to them.

Diffusion of information that changes a society's political opportunity structure may operate via pure 'demonstration' effects or through more explicit 'mediation' efforts (Hale, 2013). Demonstration effects do not require any direct contact between activists from different countries; they trigger contentious activity across borders simply by updating the information available to other people about the probabilities of successful revolt. Mediation, by contrast, involves direct contact between people in different countries.

One of the better studied cases of mediation comes from the so-called 'Colour Revolutions' of the first decade of the twenty-first century (Beissinger, 2007; Bunce and Wolchik, 2006, 2010). These were revolts in a number of hybrid post-Communist regimes: first in Serbia against the regime of Slobodan Milošević (the 'Bulldozer Revolution', in 2000); in Georgia in 2003 (the 'Rose Revolution'), which overthrew Eduard Shevardnadze; in Ukraine in 2005 (the 'Orange Revolution'), which led to the overturning of the 2005 election results; and in Kyrgyzstan in 2005 (the 'Tulip Revolution'), which ended with the overthrow of the government of Askar Akayev. (The term 'Colour Revolution' has since been applied to many other events, from the 'Carnation Revolution' in Portugal in 1973 to the 'Jasmine Revolution' in Tunisia in 2010–11; but these four were the original 'Colour Revolutions'). Though the reasons and outcomes of these revolts varied, the Rose, Orange, and Tulip Revolution activists all benefited from direct contact with Serbian activists, particularly the youth group 'Otpor!' ('resistance'), which was active in the Bulldozer Revolution, and later the Centre for Applied Non-Violent Strategies (CANVAS) founded in 2004 by former members of Otpor!

These Serbian activists have played a mediating role in diffusing new forms of contentious activity, not just during the original Colour Revolutions (Beissinger, 2007), but in many later (successful and unsuccessful) protests, including the Egyptian protests in 2011 that led to the overthrow of Hosni Mubarak and the student mobilization against Chávez's con-stitutional revision referendum in Venezuela in 2007 (Dobson, 2012). And though the role of groups such as Otpor! can be overstated – not every youth group in an authoritarian regime has been advised by former Otpor! members – their success is evident in the number of anti-regime groups that consciously imitate its tactics and even its symbols; their raised fist emblem has been endlessly reused throughout the post-Communist world and beyond, from Belarus to Russia to Egypt.

NGOs such as CANVAS are not the only actors that can alter the political opportunity structure by helping information or other resources cross borders. States can of course play this game as well through democ-racy promotion efforts that may fund opposition groups, or conversely through resource and information sharing to prop up friendly regimes against opposition forces, as the gulf monarchies did in the Arab Spring. Similarly, the media can also shape narratives of revolt, and hence the sorts of opportunities people elsewhere perceive for collective action. For example, research on the Arab uprisings has shown that the television station Al-Jazeera deeply shaped people's understandings of both what was happening in the region as well as of the forms of contentious politics that were being used by activists (Lynch, 2012). But contrary to popular belief, the rapid diffusion of contention across borders is not a new phe-nomenon, dependent on the existence of mass or social media platforms. Contentious politics uses whatever technologies are available at the time as the media of diffusion; protest spread like wildfire in Europe in the 1848 'Springtime of Nations', when media markets were highly frag-mented and local newspapers were the closest thing to a 'mass' medium (Weyland, 2010, 2012).

Periodic Opportunities

Finally, the political opportunity structure of a regime can be affected by periodic events produced by the operation of its *own* institutions. The most important of these are regular multiparty elections, which often change the political opportunity structure of a regime at regular and predictable intervals even if they are fraudulent (Tucker, 2007; Beissinger, 2007). The key point here is that elections can work as a *focal point* (Schelling, 1960) for public mobilization against a regime, temporarily reducing the costs of coordinating anti-regime action. For one thing, so long as elec-tions demand some competition, opposition forces typically have a bit more freedom to organize, while the attention of international observers is more focused on the country, increasing the costs of abuse by the state. And more importantly, if the government is believed to have stolen the election, individual citizens have reason to expect that the costs of pro-testing will be lower (less risk of being thrown in jail or worse), and the potential benefits larger (higher likelihood of 'throwing the bums out' if enough people join in), than at most other times.

The Colour Revolutions in Serbia, Georgia, Ukraine, and Kyrgyzstan again provide a good example of these dynamics (Tucker, 2007). These competitive authoritarian regimes were widely perceived by citizens to be highly corrupt; there was a great deal of 'latent dissatisfaction' with their governments. Yet ordinary citizens had little hope of acting on their grievances most of the time; not paying a bribe, or protesting a single corrupt act by oneself, would not make much difference and might even get one in trouble. Nevertheless, for a variety of reasons the ruling elites in these regimes could not do without periodic electoral competition in which opposition parties genuinely attempted to compete, and they could not easily manufacture the results of these elections. We could say that these were not 'fully consolidated' authoritarian regimes (Way, 2008), but all this means is that elections in these regimes *were* genuine periods of vulnerability, when the costs of repression were higher for the state, and the costs of mobilization were lower for the opposition, precisely because the state could not ensure either that repression of any popular mobilization would be successful or that the elite would remain unified.

And so when these governments appeared to be trying to steal elections, opposition organizations were able to quickly mobilize vast numbers of people against them. Ordinary citizens rightly sensed that *many other people* would also share their feeling of having suffered an injustice (having their votes stolen), and thus would be likely to come out in protest; they had a clear sense of when to protest; and they had a good idea of what the protests could eventually achieve. In other words, elections, and the subsequent electoral fraud, had altered the regime's political opportunity structures in ways that favoured opposition forces.

This is not to say that electoral 'revolutions' always follow electoral fraud, much less that they result in democracy even if they are successful. Electoral fraud can at best heighten the likelihood of revolt by providing an opportunity for mobilization, and even then only in regimes that are not fully in control of the public space, such as the hybrid regimes of much of the post-Communist world. Decades of meaningless elections in the Soviet Union and the Communist regimes of Eastern Europe did not lead to popular mobilization; it was only when the fragility of these regimes became increasingly apparent that protest could even begin to be contemplated, as happened in 1989 in East Germany, when small groups of activists protested the fraudulent results of the 7 May municipal elections (Sebestyen, 2010, ch. 35). But even in hybrid regimes with somewhat meaningful electoral competition most 'electoral revolutions' in the wake of fraudulent elections fail, and even where they succeed in removing a country's leadership they rarely lead to sustained improvements in the quality of democracy (Kalandadze and Orenstein, 2009). Ironically,

Ukraine, which had the most famous of these revolts, the Orange Revolution, in which crowds of as many as 500,000 people in Kiev's 'Maidan' (central square) helped overturn the election of Viktor Yanukovich in 2005, eventually saw Yanukovich's return to power in a free election, and a more violent and more disastrous revolt in 2014 that saw Yanukovich flee in turn. A successful 'colour revolution' is no guarantee of genuine democratization.

False Opportunities

Part of the problem is that the diffusion of information sometimes leads to sudden surges in protest in places where deeper structural opportunities for significant regime change or even successful protest are missing. When activists in Armenia, Belarus, Kazakhstan, or Russia attempted to emulate earlier 'colour revolutions' in the face of electoral fraud, they faced far more entrenched regimes, endowed with the resources and popular support necessary to survive and effectively repress any wave of popular protest (Beissinger, 2007). And elites in many regimes, instead of being discouraged by the fall of neighbouring authoritarian regimes (as had happened in many of the 1989 revolutions against Eastern European Communist regimes), *learned* from these failures to take 'preemptive action' to deter protest (Koesel and Bunce, 2013), which made the job of later activists harder.

Thus Syrian and Libyan leaders, having seen the collapse of the Tunisian and Egyptian leadership, did not passively wait to be overthrown when protests started in their own countries, but took active and indeed brutal measures to suppress them as soon as they began. More importantly, they *could* take these measures because they were able to rely on the loyalty of their security forces to a degree that neither the Egyptian nor the Tunisian leadership could; the structural situation (the *real* political opportunity structure) facing protesters in Libya and Syria was quite different from that facing protesters in Tunisia and Egypt, despite superficial similarities. (And protesters were not entirely unaware of these differences, as interviews with participants reveal; see Pearlman, 2013.)

The problem is more general, however. One important reason why activists and ordinary people may protest in unpromising circumstances is that we all suffer from various cognitive biases – in particular, the 'availability heuristic' and the 'representativeness heuristic' – that lead us to overestimate the significance of striking events in culturally similar contexts and thus to overestimate our chances of success while protesting (Weyland, 2010, 2012). People do get 'carried away' in the excitement of revolution, which accounts in part for the surprising 'clustering' of revolution in the last two centuries, from the European 'Springtime of Nations' in 1848 to the Colour Revolutions. When people went to the streets in

Libya or Syria after witnessing the events in Tunisia and Egypt, they did not rationally weigh the costs and benefits of protesting, or fully account for their chances of success; they instead acted 'in hope', believing that it was time to do something, even if the odds were against them (Pearlman, 2013).

These sudden waves of protest can indeed force change even in unpromising circumstances, as regime elites, caught by surprise, may offer hasty concessions to remain in power. Regime elites also suffer from cognitive biases! But when structural opportunities for fundamental regime change are missing, quick democratic gains can be easily dismantled once protest calms down, as happened in many of the short-lived successes of the 1848 Springtime of Nations, or indeed in Egypt in 2013 (Weyland, 2010, 2012), when the military was able to exploit divisions within the opposition to stage a coup against the elected government of Mohammed Morsi, who represented the Muslim Brotherhood.

The Rebel's Dilemma

Protest nevertheless matters for regime change; without popular pressure, regime change is at best a form of elite circulation (as with many coups). But, as should be clear by now, one basic difference between democratic and non-democratic regimes is that protest is typically *riskier* in the latter than in the former. As we saw in Chapter 8, authoritarian rulers try to *deter* challengers by imposing barriers to coordinated political action by outsiders; and many of these barriers can be quite forbidding, especially as regimes move closer to the totalitarian side of the spectrum of social control. Protest organizers may be harassed, mocked on national TV, sued, fined, imprisoned, and even killed; opposition groups may be denied access to meeting spaces, starved of funds, prevented from publishing their views, and pushed underground; and mass demonstrations or protests may be quickly broken up by riot police, and live ammunition used against unarmed civilians.

To be sure, the difference in risks between democratic and non-democratic contexts is not always marked (democratic governments can respond to protest with repression, as happened in the 1989 'Caracazo' in Venezuela, and non-democratic governments may sometimes prefer to use non-repressive methods to deal with dissent), but it is often quite large, especially in regimes closer to the totalitarian end of the spectrum. As we saw in Chapter 9, authoritarian regimes have tended, empirically, to be more repressive than democracies, especially when it comes to preventing people from meeting together in ways that may challenge the government (Møller and Skaaning, 2013). The people who went out to protest against Qaddafi in Libya, or against al-Assad in Syria in 2011 were soon met with live gunfire; protesting in highly authoritarian contexts is not for the faint of heart.

People in such regimes are typically well aware of the risk of open contention against the regime. This awareness manifests itself in an atmosphere of pervasive fear, discouragement, and cynicism (Pearlman, 2013). And given these risks, the decision to protest does not typically make much sense in purely rational terms. This is because collective action against a powerful regime suffers from the problem of free-riding; from the point of view of an aggrieved individual, it is always better for others to protest and bear the risks of collective action than for me to do so, since my own individual contribution to collective action is likely to be negligible and the benefits of success will accrue to all dissatisfied individuals, whether they protest or not (Olson, 1965). An aggrieved individual will thus rarely have sufficient 'selfish' reason to protest, which can account for the rarity of revolt under regimes of the most dubious legitimacy (Márquez, 2016b). Yet contention, large-scale protest, and even revolution, does break out in authoritarian contexts; the 'rebel's dilemma' (Lichbach, 1994b) faced by opponents of a regime is in fact solved from time to time. There are three basic ways in which this dilemma is dissolved or bypassed: covert resistance, emotional work, and selective incentives.

Covert Resistance and Safe Spaces

In repressive contexts, people may simply avoid open protest and instead make their dissatisfaction known through less open and more ambiguous forms of resistance that minimize individual risks – the sorts of practices that the political scientist James Scott has called the 'weapons of the weak' (Scott, 1985). For example, academic papers in Eastern European Communist regimes made ritual references to Marxist–Leninist ideology in their introductions and then went on to ignore it completely in the body of the text. Playwrights and writers used veiled language to get past the censors; in at least one case in Estonia writers exploited the fact that the censors were Russian and had only imperfect knowledge of the Estonian language to slip controversial messages into their works (Johnston and Mueller, 2001). Today in China people often discuss sensitive topics on Weibo (the Twitter-like microblogging service) in figurative language that can be difficult to filter or censor, using terms like 'heavenly dynasty' to refer to the government, or punning about the 'Grass Mud Horse', a phrase that with only a slight tonal change can mean a 'provocative vulgarity' (Link and Qiang, 2013). To be sure, such more or less covert 'grumbling' rarely has a direct effect on an authoritarian regime, given its limited ability to coordinate collective contention. Indeed, allowing a certain amount of anti-regime talk in private can even serve as a 'safety valve' and information source for the regime, as we have noted. But by pushing almost all anti-regime talk into very private 'niches' (Pfaff, 2001) ruling elites slowly became cut off from knowledge of their own societies, leading to a tendency to underestimate the risks of popular revolt.

Dissatisfied citizens can sometimes also congregate in relatively 'safe' spaces – locations where, for historical reasons, the grip of the state's official ideology has been more relaxed. The tavern and the pub have often been sites where 'unsafe' speech could sometimes be uttered under the cover of alcohol; and in many regimes churches – the Catholic Church in Poland under the Communists and the Philippines under Marcos, the Lutheran Church in East Germany – have been key places where anti-regime citizens could congregate with some semblance of safety (Johnston and Mueller, 2001). Church leaders (for example, Cardinal Sin in the Philippines, Pastor Eppelmann in East Germany) often went on to play important roles in the popular uprisings that led to the breakdown of these regimes, simply because of the limited immunity they possessed as members of transnational organizations with deep local legitimacy. Sometimes labour unions have possessed enough independence from, and legitimacy with, the state to enable a certain amount of contentious activity. For example, the labour union Solidarity was difficult for the Polish Workers' Party to fully repress given its self-conception as a *workers'* party, and unions played a big role in the events of 2011 in Egypt, whose regime had been born in a self-proclaimed *socialist* revolution (Gelvin, 2012). But sometimes even ostensibly non-political associations, such as theatre groups in Czechoslovakia in the late 1970s and 1980s, could also become 'duplicitous organizations' in which some anti-regime sentiments could be expressed in relative safety and where dissatisfied individuals tended to congregate (Johnston and Mueller, 2001). It is not an accident that the 'Magic Lantern' theatre was a hot spot of activity during the Czechoslovak Velvet Revolution in 1989, and that one of its leaders, Vaclav Havel, was a playwright (Garton Ash, 1999).

This observation can be generalized. In many societies where political discussion is dangerous, there are often 'subcultures' that attract the young and dissatisfied and screen out the conformist and satisfied, and thus become eventual *loci* of dissent (Slee, 2012). In 1980s Eastern Europe, theatre and progressive rock (a symbol of Westernization and youthful rebellion) played this role; Havel was not only a playwright, but also a fan of the experimental rock band *Plastic People of the Universe*. Towards the end of the first decade of the twenty-first century in Egypt, Facebook and the new social media played this role instead, becoming a haven for young Egyptians with little stake in the regime. The point is not that choral groups in 1980s Hungary (in which people gathered to sing 'national' songs that implicitly contradicted the official narratives of pan-Soviet solidarity) or Facebook in Egypt around 2010–2011 were highly political environments, but that they tended to be places where people out of step with the establishment could spend time together away from the suffocating orthodoxy of the 'official' public sphere. And since the vast majority of the activities of people in these subcultures were resolutely non-political, they could hardly be shut down altogether without risking much backlash or preventing genuinely useful activity. As we noted in Chapter 8, Facebook could serve as a platform for political expression precisely because most of its content consisted of cute cats, which made it difficult to shut down entirely (Zuckerman, 2015). Thus, though these subcultures do not, by themselves, solve the 'rebel's dilemma', they typically provide the pool of activists from which dissent can eventually grow into more threatening forms.

Emotional Work

The second way in which the rebel's dilemma can be dissolved is through what we may call 'emotional work'. The importance of emotions like indignation for mobilization has been widely noted (Stekelenburg and Klandermans, 2013; Pearlman, 2013). And the power of emotionally resonant symbols of nationhood, religion, or other important aspects of group identity helps to explain why 'communal' leaders who can credibly deploy them against an authoritarian regime – clerics in Iran, nationalist heroes in Burma and the Philippines, Catholic priests in Latin America and in Poland – can be exceedingly dangerous to it when they decide that the time has come to take an oppositional attitude, so long as they are relatively autonomous from the state (Slater, 2009).

Accordingly, the art of the activist is in part to stoke the sorts of emotions that help people overcome the 'barrier of fear' created by a non-democratic regime, thus enabling people to engage in coordinated collective action even in unpropitious circumstances. For example, some Egyptian activists skilfully used a Facebook page, 'We are all Khaled Said', to publicize information about police brutality and generally fuel people's outrage against the regime. Said was a young man who had been beaten up and killed by the police, apparently because he had posted a video on the web showing two policemen taking money and drugs they had seized from busting a drug deal (Gelvin, 2012, pp. 49–50). Though his case was not especially distinctive – the Egyptian police was often brutal, and police corruption is not unknown elsewhere – activists were able to use him as a symbol for the corruption of the regime, and the Facebook page created by Wael Ghonim and other Egyptian anti-regime activists was useful in generating solidarity among a large number of people. The point is not that Facebook was used here to coordinate protest (a role for which it was not well suited, given police surveillance of activist pages (see Rosenberg, 2011)) but that it functioned to generate 'emboldening' emotions – indignation and anger – that helped people overcome the fear of challenging the Mubarak regime in the streets.

The face-to-face rituals of protest are themselves important means by which emboldening emotions are sustained and group solidarity is produced (Pearlman, 2013; Harris, 2012). A good street demonstration is a successful interaction ritual, producing *more* of the emboldening emotions that led people to join them in the first place (Collins, 2004). Sometimes these protests are described as having a 'carnival' atmosphere, as the EDSA protests in the Philippines that led to the ouster of Ferdinand Marcos (Chenoweth and Stephan, 2011), while sometimes their atmosphere is sombre, as in the huge and silent protests of the 2009 'Green Movement' in Iran (Harris, 2012), but whatever the case a successful protest tends to cement people's commitments to the movement. At its best, a huge mass demonstration can be literally electrifying, a cathartic experience that seems to completely change one's life, as many people felt during the Iranian protests in 2009 (Harris, 2012). And skilled activists are very good at using creative tactics to produce these emboldening emotions and to help people overcome their fear of the regime. For example, youth activists in Serbia and Ukraine pioneered the use of 'dilemma actions' designed to put the regime in a bind: either look ridiculous by (say) arresting a barrel or look weak by doing nothing. Such actions emboldened people to join the opposition camp, and made opposition seem 'heroic and cool', especially to young people (Rosenberg, 2011; Nikolayenko, 2007). Similarly, before the Syrian uprising degenerated into a multisided civil war, activists staged many 'emboldening' actions, including dance-a-thons, street theatre and graffiti (MacFarquhar, 2011).

These tactics are not only used by pro-democracy activists; people also need to be emboldened to kill or expropriate others in more violent revolutionary processes. During the Chinese Revolution in the 1940s, for example, Communist Party activists used 'struggle sessions' to embolden villagers to first criticize and then beat up, expropriate, and even kill landlords and other rich peasants (Walder, 2015, pp. 46–7). The typical struggle session was called by party cadres (activists) after the Red Army (later renamed the People's Liberation Army) had moved into a village following the retreat of Japanese forces. Authority figures – the village head or a local landlord accused of collaboration with the Japanese – would be led to a stage, where cadres 'yelled accusations at them, slapped and punched them' in front of the assembled villagers (Walder, 2015, p. 46). Attendance was not optional. The cadres would also call for participation from the villagers in the accusatory ritual.

If participation was not forthcoming, the entire village would be broken up into small groups where the misdeeds of the accused would be reviewed with the assistance of the cadres, and assurances given to the villagers that they did not need to fear retribution for participating in the struggle sessions. (The Red Army was not going to be leaving.) These meetings also served to identify villagers who would be asked to lead the struggle session the next day. The process would then be repeated once or twice, heightening the emotional atmosphere, until most villagers were participating. Eventually the targets of these sessions would be shot or beaten to death, and their property would be redistributed to the villagers (Walder, 2015, pp. 46–7). Though the Red Army could presumably have shot the village's authority figures and redistributed their land to the peasants without so much fuss, the struggle sessions both emboldened the villagers to overcome the normal taboos of social interaction (including simple human decency) and cemented their commitment to the Communists; having participated in the struggle sessions, they had 'burned their bridges' from the previous village society.

Selective Incentives

The previous example also identifies a third mechanism through which collective action problems can be dissolved: selective incentives (Lichbach, 1994a, 1994b). People can be brought to participate in collective action when opposition organizations can credibly offer certain goods to participants while excluding non-participants. Chinese peasants benefited from the land redistribution only insofar as they showed sufficient commitment to the CCP; though the land would later be collectivized, and they would suffer terribly during the Great Leap Forward famine, they were directly rewarded by the Communists at the time. The possibility of materially benefiting from loot may induce some people to participate in riots, as happened during the Caracazo in 1989 in Venezuela; peasants in rural areas may aid guerrilla armies from the calculation that non-cooperation can be credibly punished by them, as in Colombia in the 1980s and Vietnam in the 1970s; and people may go to peaceful opposition demonstrations in part because they want to enjoy the party atmosphere and the free live music, as happened in the Colour Revolutions in the first decade of the twenty-first century. Though scholarly controversy exists about the effectiveness of selective incentives, and they clearly are not the whole story about why people engage in contentious politics (for one thing, opposition organizations do not always have the ability to provide such incentives), it is also the case that people can be brought to participate in relatively risky collective action for purely 'selfish' reasons, or at least before they care much about the cause itself.

The Power of Numbers

It is not enough for a few people to protest if regime change is to happen; many – sometimes millions – must do so, often repeatedly and for long periods of time. Most of the great revolts of the twentieth and twenty-first centuries massed enormous numbers of people on the streets or in great revolutionary armies, day after day, before succeeding; perhaps 10 per cent of the entire country's population actively participated at some point in the Iranian Revolution that toppled the Shah of Iran in 1979, and a good 1 per cent to 2 per cent participated in the 1989 overthrow of the Communist regimes of Eastern Europe (Kurzman, 2004, p. 10). The protests in Tahrir Square in 2011, while small relative to the Egyptian population, were still huge by Egyptian standards, with perhaps 400,000 people massed in the square at peak times. And though it is possible for small bands of armed men to seize control of a state (this is called a military coup, and usually requires the armed men in question to be part of the state they are seizing, as we saw in Chapter 6), statistical studies suggest that the probability of 'success' for an outsider challenge to the state, whether violent or non-violent, increases with the number of participants, to the point in which campaigns where more than 4 per cent of the population participates have almost always succeeded (Chenoweth and Stephan, 2011). 'People power' is not just an empty slogan, and for good reason; without credible numbers of people disrupting the social order on their side, opposition forces cannot hope to put enough pressure on regime elites to yield control of the state.

The key problem opposition forces face is, of course, that authoritarian regimes will use repression to deter protest participation, credibly threatening to punish participants in collective action. And most of the time, the threat of repression 'works'; citizens stay home and perhaps grumble a bit, but they do not go out of their way to oppose the regime, even if they feel that things could be better. Most people are not heroes, and prefer not to participate in contentious politics if the risk is high enough. Nevertheless, protest does sometimes escalate, emerging as if out of nowhere to overwhelm security forces and sweep away seemingly invincible regimes: the Shah of Iran, who fell after 100 days of protest in 1978–79; the hardline communist regimes of Eastern Europe (a case discussed in more detail in the online appendix), including the brutal dictatorship of Nicolae Ceauşescu, who was overthrown after just four days of protests; and many others. When do ordinary people join in protest, swelling the numbers of people involved in anti-regime activities?

The answer is deceptively simple: 'protest movements attract participants through increased participation' (Kurzman, 2004, p. 10). Start with the idea that people differ in how much risk they are willing to bear when opposing the government. In particular, people have different 'thresholds' for protest (Kuran, 1991; Karklins and Petersen, 1993). Some people are willing to engage in risky contentious politics even when few others are likely to join them (and are thus highly likely to be arrested or worse); most others are only willing to do so when many others have already joined and protest is safer. But the risks of protest diminish with numbers; it is much harder to repress hundreds of thousands of people than just a few people. When Erich Mielke, the last chief of the Stasi, was asked by Erich

Honecker, the leader of the Socialist Unity Party in late 1989, to repress the protesters then massing in Leipzig and other East German cities, he supposedly answered 'Erich, we can't beat up hundreds of thousands of people' – not (presumably) because he thought Honecker's request had been immoral, but because he thought it was technically impossible (Przeworski, 1991, p. 64, citing the *New York Times*, 19 November 1989, p. 15).

Risk at the site of a demonstration is not the only thing that matters; penalties for anti-government activity at work or school can also deter people from participating in contentious politics. The so-called 'Tascón list' or 'Maisanta database' in Venezuela (a list of people who had signed the petition for a recall referendum of Hugo Chávez in Venezuela in 2003 and 2004) was used to deny people employment and promotions (Hsieh et al., 2011); individual workers who participated in demonstrations in Eastern Europe in 1989 could be fired from their jobs. But it is harder to punish all the workers in a factory, or all the students in a University; 'when 100,000 out of 136,000 students participated in the general strike in Prague on November 27, 1989, the university administration could impose no sanctions against this percentage of their student body' (Karklins and Petersen, 1993, p. 594). As more people join in protesting (including more people in one's immediate workplace or school), people with higher thresholds for participation feel more secure (and less like they are doing something weird), and so join in as well, feeding an 'avalanche' of protest.

Yet the process of escalation has to get going before participation can feed on itself. After all, most of the time the only people who participate in protest in a repressive context are a few stubborn and idealistic dissidents, or the few members of whatever small and harassed opposition organizations may exist in a regime. Even if lots of people are dissatisfied with the government, they expect (correctly) that few others will be willing to join in, and hence stay home and grumble. *Many* people need to expect other people will join in contentious action before they themselves will join, which seems like a chicken and egg problem. And even when unrest has begun, predicting turnout at demonstrations is often very difficult for individuals, which may deter them from continuing to participate. Iranians found it very hard to predict when demonstrations would increase in size during the Iranian Revolution in 1978, and even seasoned Egyptian activists were surprised at the numbers in the first Tahrir Square demonstrations in 2011 (Pearlman, 2013; Kurzman, 2004). A number of mechanisms can nevertheless help people dissolve this uncertainty and trigger a sudden avalanche of protest, which we may call 'moral awakenings', 'informational updating', and 'reference group updating'. All of these work in a similar way: some event increases the salience of protest motivations and simultaneously produces information about other people's willingness to join in protest.

Moral Awakenings

Particular events may make a deep impression on enough people to suddenly shift their personal thresholds for protest, creating a 'critical mass' (Oliver, Marwell, and Texeira, 1985) of protesters that can then grow rapidly as more and more people find it safe to join in. The self-immolation of Mohammed Bouazizi in Tunisia in December 2010; the violence against demonstrators in Prague and Timişoara in 1989, or in Tehran in 1978; the killing of Benigno Aquino at the Manila International Airport in 1983 – these events can be experienced as moments of personal transformation, when people who had borne all the indignities of oppressive and unaccountable rule suddenly decide that they have had enough (Pearlman, 2013). These personal 'awakenings' increase the relevance of what social scientists sometimes call 'public good motivations' (Karklins and Petersen, 1993) – or, in the phrase common during the 1989 Eastern European revolutions, 'if not me, then who?'

The fact that particular events can 'shift' the thresholds for protest of substantial numbers of people accounts for the fact that repression of small protests does not always deter further protest but sometimes backfires, inducing even more protest (Chenoweth and Stephan, 2011; Karklins and Petersen, 1993). People who have psychologically crossed the barrier of fear may become angrier, not more scared, by regime repression, which appears to them disproportionate and unjust, while sympathetic bystanders who may not have been willing to protest before may turn into active participants insofar as indignation at the injustice of repression increases more than their fear of being personally targeted. Indeed, some research suggests that once mass protest begins in highly repressive regimes, it is *more* likely to lead to regime collapse than in less repressive contexts (Kricheli, Livne, and Magaloni, 2010), precisely because it signals a much greater depth of dissatisfaction, and because the greater repression of large-scale protest may lead to greater 'backfire' effects (Francisco, 1995).

This effect can even be magnified by the lack of reliable information in such regimes. For example, though only about 60 people died when Ceauşescu ordered police to fire on demonstrators in Timişoara on 17 December 1989, the official media did not make any mention of these events, while rumour and broadcasts from the Voice of America put the number of people killed at between 4,000–20,000 people (Sebestyen, 2010, p. 386). These exaggerated numbers, far from deterring protest, enraged many Romanians, who suddenly found the courage to act against Ceauşescu's hated regime. This is not to say that sufficient repression never discourages people from participating in protest – consider the way in which the Tiananmen Square killings by the Chinese authorities effectively ended the Chinese pro-democracy movement – but much research suggests that the repression-protest curve broadly follows an inverted u-shape, as people first begin to protest, are repressed but then become incensed by repression that crosses their normative standards and protest even more, but eventually decide that the risk is too much for them to bear if repression continues to increase.

Informational Updating

Particular events can also provide updated information to people about the *depth of dissatisfaction* in a regime, and hence increase their expectation that *others* will also protest (Lohmann, 1994; Kuran, 1991). For example, as we have noted, one important characteristic of the Eastern European Leninist regimes was that people could usually only express dissatisfaction with the regime within small 'niches' of trustworthy friends or family (Pfaff, 2001). In public settings, however, they had to use the regime's language: clap at boring speeches, express commitment at party meetings, and otherwise act like the famous 'greengrocer' in Vaclav Havel's prison parable, who puts up posters with Communist slogans not because he really believes in them but because 'otherwise there could be trouble' (Havel, 1992). This meant that even though most people were in fact dissatisfied with the regime, they had little idea about how widely shared their feelings were beyond their small niches. Even if they were aware of what dissidents were doing or saying, these were always 'unusual' people, and their activities could not provide evidence that dissatisfaction was widespread among ordinary people (Lohmann, 1994). 'Preference falsification' in public thus led many people, including regime elites, to *overstate* the degree and solidity of popular support the government could count on.

But when the Hungarian government decided not to police its border with Austria (cutting the famous 'iron curtain'), and thousands of people suddenly started to leave East Germany for West Germany via Hungary, or when a rally called in support of Ceauşescu on 21 December 1989 suddenly broke into heckling, people could see that these regimes had far less support than their public 'face' had indicated. And the revelation proved electrifying; the 'Monday demonstrations' in Leipzig, for example, grew from a few dozen people to more than a hundred thousand in a matter of weeks after the exodus of East Germans to the West had begun. The event triggered an 'informational cascade' that increased people's expectation that *others* would participate in contentious politics, thus increasing their *own* incentives to join in (Lohmann, 1994). Indeed, the revelation often came as a surprise to the rulers of these regimes; despite extensive networks of surveillance, Ceauşescu was apparently surprised at the hatred expressed by the supposedly handpicked 100,000-person crowd assembled on Palace Square in Bucharest. And his panicked reaction to the sudden heckling (he freezes, then attempts to make some quick concessions), immortalized on live television (one can easily find clips of the event on YouTube), became the 'moment of weakness' that doomed his regime. As Adrian Donea, a taxi driver who had been recruited that morning to cheer Ceaușescu, and who was probably one of the first people to have booed him on that morning, said: 'We could see that he was scared. At that moment we realised our force, that we had strength' (Sebestyen, 2010, p. 367). Once the majority of Romanians watching the event on live TV realized this as well, Ceaușescu was finished; the critical mass had been reached.

We should nevertheless not overemphasize the importance of preference falsification and information cascades in many revolutions. There is little evidence that Egyptians in 2011, for example, were unaware of how much other Egyptians disliked the Mubarak regime. Indeed, the Egyptian regime, for all its authoritarianism, permitted a surprising amount of open criticism in the press, including criticism aimed directly at Mubarak (Pearlman, 2013). Similarly, people in Syria had long been aware that few other Syrians believed the hyperbolic praise bestowed on the al-Assad clan, or the official propaganda of the regime (Wedeen, 1998). What triggered the avalanche of protest in both Egypt and Syria was not the sudden realization that these regimes were weak, or that they lacked real support (most people were well aware of their coercive capacities), but the emboldening jolt of the Tunisian Revolution and tactical innovations that enabled protesters to overcome the barrier of fear created by the regime's coercive apparatus (Austin Holmes, 2012).

Reference Group Updating

People can also get their cues about what others in their group might do from observing what certain *reference groups* do. Sociologically, the heterogeneity of people's 'thresholds' for protest means that different groups of people tend to join in protest at different times (Karklins and Petersen, 1993). The first (and often the only) people to protest in repressive regimes are typically those whose identity demands that they speak truth to power, or engage in anti-regime contention. These are genuine dissidents – people such as Vaclav Havel, Nelson Mandela, Aung San Suu Kyi, László Tőkés, as well as many more obscure but equally courageous individuals – and they usually pay a heavy price for their attempts to 'live in truth' – repeatedly incarcerated, tried, exiled, sometimes killed. But though most people are not dissidents, what dissidents do may serve as a reference point for larger groups, such as students. Students, young and with fewer dependants than most people in society, are more likely to join in protest than other groups if they feel the time is right; and they may look at what is happening to dissidents, or to committed members of opposition organizations, to decide whether to join in or not. In turn, students can serve as a reference group for people with more dependants and higher demand for safety in numbers, like most workers. And once workers have been mobilized, people within the regime – for example, media people or low-level bureaucrats – may then feel that the tide is turning and 'bandwagon' against the regime. Few people fight to the bitter end once enough others start turning against a regime, but they may decide to 'defect' only when groups sociologically close to them have also defected.

This is of course an idealized story; actual revolutions do not consist of a tidy sequence of groups waiting to join in protest, one after the other. But there is much evidence that in 1989 workers in Eastern Europe, for example, looked up to what was happening to students before deciding to join, in a fairly deliberate way, in mass protests against Communist rule (Karklins and Petersen, 1993). Karklins and Petersen even suggest that one reason the Tiananmen democracy movement in China may have failed was that at crucial points the students at the square refused the help of workers, even going to the extent of linking arms to physically 'prevent workers from joining directly in their ranks' (Karklins and Petersen, 1993, p. 610, citing Perry, 1991 and Dittmer, 1989). The workers had attempted to join in the protests when they saw that students had remained in the square; by discouraging workers from joining in, students lost the opportunity to increase the numbers of participants, and hence to put additional pressure on the government.

Informal Assembly Mechanisms

People also need accurate information about why, how, when, and where to protest not only to effectively estimate whether other people will protest, but before they can participate themselves. When such information does not exist, or is unclear or confusing, the costs of protest can rise significantly. In less repressive contexts, this information is typically disseminated by opposition organizations calling for protests for specific reasons at particular places and times, but in more repressive contexts such organizations may have little access to mass media, or may not even exist. The number of opposition groups in East Germany and Romania in the late 1980s could be counted on the fingers of one hand, or perhaps no hands; the same could be said of Libya or Syria before the uprisings of 2011.

Yet protest in highly repressive contexts can still grow explosively due to the existence of what sociologists call 'informal assembly mechanisms' (Karklins and Petersen, 1993). These are salient features of the environment – 'focal points' (Schelling, 1960) – that allow people to coordinate about where and when to assemble even in the absence of explicit communication. For example, central squares with symbolic value (Tahrir, Tiananmen, Wenceslas square) are a natural target of rebellion, while dates with symbolic significance (anniversaries of a revolution or a death of a nationally revered figure) represent the calendrical equivalent of such squares. Thus people who want to protest often decide to concentrate at a central square on an important anniversary without much central coordination.

In 1989 in Eastern Europe anniversary dates – for example, the founding of the German Democratic Republic on 7 October or of Czechoslovakia on 28 October – determined the timing of the earliest demonstrations (Karklins and Petersen, 1993, p. 600). But demonstrators also had other ways of coordinating their protest. In Leipzig, an informal norm developed of meeting every Monday, reinforced by the slogan 'meet every Monday' shouted at the protests themselves (Karklins and Petersen, 1993, p. 600). Sometimes regimes inadvertently helped to coordinate protest, as when Ceauşescu called the hasty rally where he had his 'moment of weakness' on his return from Iran on 20 December 1989, or when East German and Czechoslovak television warned people against protesting on specific days. Religious tradition has also been co-opted as an informal assembly mechanism. During the Iranian Revolution, both traditional religious processions and traditional mourning meetings 40 days after the death of a person often turned into impromptu rallies. The unexpected death of Khomeini's son in 1977, for instance (Khomeini was the main leader of the opposition, then in exile in Iraq), led to the first calls of 'death to the Shah' (Kurzman, 2004, p. 29), and as repression intensified these ritual occasions increased the ability of the clerical opposition to generate a 'backlash' effect every time the Shah's security forces killed anyone.

The New Social Media

It is tempting to think that the problem of assembling people to protest is now much easier to solve thanks to the emergence of new social media technologies, which can be difficult to censor by states and which seem to power many youth movements around the world (Dobson, 2012). But while doubtless such technologies can be used to incite and coordinate protest activity (Tufekci, 2014; Lynch, 2011), the emergence and coordination of contentious politics has never depended exclusively on any particular technology; in successful revolutions opposition forces have proved very creative in using social connections, word of mouth, and many other means to spur people to protest. For example, during the Iranian Revolution in 1978, opposition supporters got around the Shah's strictly controlled press by smuggling cassette tapes with speeches from the exiled Khomeini and played them at mosques, where they spurred further revolt (Kurzman, 2004, pp. 14, 31). By contrast, Egyptian activists learned early in 2008 (after botched protests at Mahala, the '6 April' strike) that too much reliance on social media exposed them to state surveillance and did not help them to coordinate real-life protests (Rosenberg, 2011). As noted in Chapter 8, research on the effects of new forms of media tends to conclude that their influence on protest coordination is overstated (Lynch, 2011; Tufekci, 2014), since they can be used by both regime proponents and opponents, and there is no clear advantage for opponents in this cat and mouse game (Gunitsky, 2015).

To be sure, as scholars have noted, the new social media is very effective at redirecting global attention to contentious events and mobilizing emotion – sometimes for, sometimes against, protesters (Tufekci, 2014; Lynch, 2011). Nevertheless the reach of these technologies varies enormously within countries; even in Egypt, where Western media was talking about a 'Facebook revolution' even before the overthrow of Mubarak, only about 5.5 per cent of the population had Facebook accounts in 2011, while a measly 0.15 per cent of the population had Twitter accounts (Austin Holmes, 2012). Indeed, perhaps only 35 per cent of the population had any Internet access at all, however spotty (Tufekci, 2014). Egypt, moreover, was exceptional; in a place like Yemen, where revolt also managed to oust a long-serving president for life (Saneh) the numbers were much lower. And the new social media can also become an ineffective substitute for the face-to-face interaction rituals that actually do embolden people to confront repressive states (see Box 11.1 for an example).

BOX 11.1   The failure of the Green Movement in Iran

Perhaps the most spectacular recent example of the failure of the new social media for mobilization was the 'Green Movement' in Iran in 2009, where at one point more than a million people were in the streets protesting what they thought had been a fraudulent election (Harris, 2012; see also Chapter 3 above). This mobilization peaked a few days after the elections in June, without much organizational effort by the opposition, and thereafter died down more or less gradually over the next month. As Harris argues, 'internet activism', far from helping to coordinate and sustain these protests, tended to confuse and demobilize potential participants, leading to the gradual dampening of the 'emotional energy' generated by the face-to-face pre-election meetings and post-election protests that had initially emboldened people to confront the government.

For example, multiple locations and times for a single rally would be announced on social media, and people would not have any means of determining which one was the 'right' one. Moreover, once state repression began in earnest, social media's excessive focus on images of people who had been killed or beaten up tended to have a demobilizing, rather than a mobilizing effect; while such images can help people become indignant and thus to participate in contentious politics, as we have noted, in this case they seem to have led people to *overestimate* the risks of protest. Indeed, compared to the protests in Egypt in 2011, the Iranian protests in 2009 were both larger and less actively repressed – about 100 people were killed by state security and parastatal forces in Iran, while more than 800 people were killed in Egypt in two weeks of revolt (see Harris, 2012, p. 442). This in turn led many people to substitute online for offline contention; but without high-intensity face-to-face protest rituals such as marches, the movement could not sustain its initial emotional charge, and a mood of dejection soon spread.

Repertoires of Contention

People do not just protest abstractly; they stage sit-ins, go on marches or on strike, sign petitions, bang on pots and pans, pick up rifles and go to the hills, write clandestine literature or posts on social media, and occasionally blow themselves up or set themselves on fire. Sociologists call the set of practices through which people in a particular society express their grievances against a state and attempt to change it or at least influence its decisions their *repertoire of contention* (Tilly, 2006; Tilly and Tarrow, 2006). The musical metaphor is appropriate; as in jazz, a society's repertoire of contention allows people to improvise on certain basic 'scripts' (for example, the march, the petition, and so on) and combines old standards with occasional innovations. Consider the classic march to the seat of power: a group of people sharing a family of related grievances assembles at a pre-determined spot and walk to a symbolic location, perhaps the parliament or a central square, while chanting slogans to express their grievances. Yet this simple practice, used the world over, has not always existed; it is the fruit of nineteenth-century developments (Tilly, 2006). And it displays enormous variation in detail across time and place: sometimes speeches are given, sometimes not; sometimes people try to coordinate their clothing, sometimes not; sometimes the atmosphere is festive; sometimes it is sombre; and so on.

Variation in repertoires of contention is partly culturally and historically inflected. In some parts of the world (primarily but not exclusively in Latin America), the 'cacerolazo' (beating pots and pans in a coordinated fashion) is a common protest practice, while in others it is unheard of. Self-immolation in protest is found mostly among Buddhist groups in South and East Asia, though it has also been used to great effect elsewhere, as in the self-immolation of Mohammed Bouazizi that sparked the 2011 uprising in Tunisia. The practice of suicide bombing was used extensively by the Tamil Tigers in their struggle against the Sri Lankan government in the 1980s, but is now mainly associated with 'Islamist' groups. These differences in the repertoire of contention do not always reflect rational assessments of the effectiveness of particular tactics, but are instead tied to particular cultural understandings of what is honourable, what is an appropriate sacrifice for one's cause, and the like.

Nevertheless, within the limits of their repertoire (and sometimes beyond), activists do try to choose tactics that will not be too easily countered by the state, borrow freely from other activists, and create new protest practices. Syrian activists in 2011 dyed fountains red to symbolize blood, and used loudspeakers with pre-recorded protest sounds to mislead police (MacFarquhar, 2011). When the Belarus government banned almost all forms of anti-regime speech, Belarusian activists protested by clapping, and sometimes by gathering together and doing 'nothing at all'

(Barry, 2011; Mouzykantskii, 2011). The creativity of courageous protesters can be impressive, though regimes can also adapt.

Violence vs. Non-Violence

One key choice faced by people who wish to engage in contentious politics is whether to opt for a primarily violent or a primarily non-violent repertoire of contention. Should opponents of an oppressive regime, capable of heinous actions, including killing and torturing political opponents, take to the proverbial hills to fight the government? Or should they engage with the state via primarily non-violent means, such as marches, strikes, sit-ins, and similar tactics, as Syrians did early in 2011 before many opponents of the regime turned to violent methods of contention?

Often, this choice is not well considered. As we have noted, people can be subject to cognitive biases that make them susceptible to fads and fashions, in this as in many other matters (Weyland, 2008). For example, in the 1950s and 1960s the success of the Chinese and Cuban revolutions and their tactics of 'people's war' led to a large crop of leftist insurgencies throughout Latin America, most of which failed. But in fact, the success of the Chinese Revolution was hardly attributable to the tactics of guerrilla warfare pioneered by Mao, as historians are beginning to understand; the enthusiasm for these tactics in Latin America was badly misplaced, despite the apparent anomaly of the Cuban Revolution (Walder, 2015, pp. 16–21). Today the primarily non-violent tactics used in the Colour Revolutions of the early twenty-first century and propagated by CANVAS and other groups are enjoying a great deal of popularity, even though they are not always effective, as shown by the failure of 'colour revolutions' in many states, from Kazakhstan to Russia to Syria.

Yet there is some evidence that this time activists are not wrong about the effectiveness of these tactics. A number of researchers have found growing support for the idea that, since the beginning of the twentieth century, campaigns for significant political change (including regime change) using primarily nonviolent repertoires succeed more often *in their own terms* than campaigns using primarily violent repertoires, even in very highly repressive contexts (Chenoweth and Stephan, 2011; Stephan and Chenoweth, 2008; Schock 2004, 2013). As we can see in Figure 11.2, of the 71 primarily non-violent regime change campaigns launched around the world in the period 1945–2006 and counted in Chenoweth and Lewis (2013), more than half were eventually successful, most within a ten-year period. By contrast, of the 80 violent regime change campaigns launched in the same period, only slightly over a third were eventually successful, many only after decades of struggle.

The success of non-violent campaigns may sound counter-intuitive; it is, after all, easy to point to cases of non-violent campaigns for change

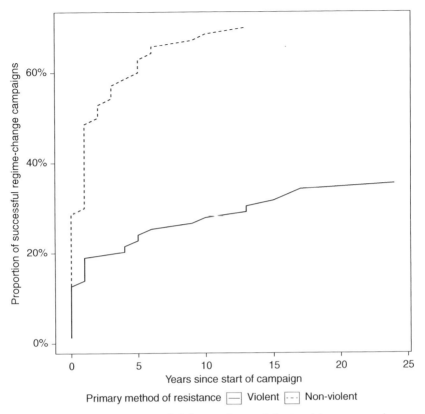

Figure 11.2 *Success rates of violent and non-violent resistance campaigns, 1945–2006. The data on regime change campaigns is from the Nonviolent and Violent Campaigns and Outcomes (NAVCO) data project, version 2.0, described in Chenoweth and Lewis, 2013. The primary method of resistance is an ideal type; campaigns sometimes used both violent and non-violent methods over their lifetime, and some changed their goals as well.*

crushed by highly repressive states (for example, the Saffron Revolution in Burma in 2009, or the Tiananmen Square protests in China), as well as to successful violent revolutions, including some of the greatest of them all, such as the Russian, Chinese, and Cuban revolutions in the twentieth century, all of which included substantial amounts of violence. And one may think that, once a state has decided to engage in serious repression, only violent resistance can help a movement survive. This sort of thinking often informs the reasoning used by proponents of violent methods of resistance in places as diverse as Palestine and Peru, the Philippines and Burma: that violence is a legitimate response to regime repression. Yet though non-violent campaigns do seem more likely to start, and to succeed, in slightly less repressive contexts (see Figure 11.3), they *can* succeed in highly repressive contexts.

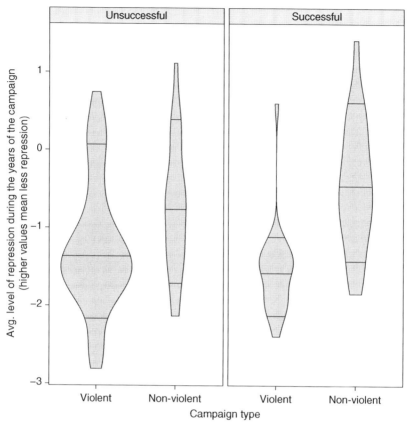

Figure 11.3   *Success of violent and non-violent resistance campaigns by level of repression, 1945–2006. The data on regime change campaigns is from the Non-violent and Violent Campaigns and Outcomes (NAVCO) data project, version 2.0, described in Chenoweth and Lewis (2013). The primary method of resistance is an ideal type; campaigns sometimes used both violent and non-violent methods over their lifetime, and some changed their goals as well. The indicator of repression is a latent variable measure from Fariss (2014), averaged over the years in which the campaign took place; lower values mean more repression, with 0 being the average level of repression in the 1949–2013 period. The area of each violin is proportional to the number of campaigns in each category.*

Non-Violence and the Power of Numbers

The main reason that non-violent campaigns seem to be so successful (when they are tried; they appear to be tried less often than violent campaigns, as we noted) is that they have a 'participation advantage' (Chenoweth and Stephan, 2011), and so they induce more of the 'power of numbers' discussed earlier. Non-violent tactics of contention are generally speaking less risky than violent tactics, even in repressive contexts. This is especially the case when campaigns use a diversity of tactics, switching creatively as needed between 'tactics of concentration', such as protest marches or sit-ins, and 'tactics of dispersion', such as stay-aways, boycotts, and strikes in response to regime repression (Schock, 2013). They thus tend to attract a much wider diversity of participants than violent insurgencies. While violent insurgencies have typically mostly recruited from among young men in rural areas, non-violent campaigns, by contrast, can recruit from a variety of groups in primarily urban areas, from students to workers to pensioners, whose members have lower tolerances for risk (Celestino and Gleditsch, 2013; Chenoweth and Stephan, 2011).

Greater numbers, in turn, mean both more safety (greater crowds are more difficult to repress, as we saw above) and a greater likelihood of linkages between opposition members and regime members. When such links exist – when sons and fathers, for example, are on opposite camps in a polarized society, or when there are class and ethnic linkages between security forces and protesters – they tend to discourage excessive violence, produce backfire effects when violence does happen, and to encourage defections from security forces. Indeed, successful non-violent campaigns typically encourage fraternization between protest participants and security forces; the 'Revolution of the Carnations' in Portugal was so named because participants often brought carnations to security forces, a tactic that was later replicated in many other successful non-violent campaigns, including the Iranian Revolution of 1978 and the similarly floral 'Rose Revolution' in Georgia. By contrast, security forces are much less likely to fraternize with insurgents who directly threaten them, especially when insurgents are from a minority group with few social links to regime personnel, and repression of armed insurgents is less likely to produce 'backfire' effects or to attract unambiguous international condemnation.

We can thus think of the choice between violent and non-violent means of contention as a trade-off between numbers and force, 'power' properly speaking and 'violence', in Hannah Arendt's (1970) classic formulation (see also Márquez, 2011b). Violent insurgency gambles on committed individuals and technical means of coercion to achieve its ends, while non-violent campaigns depend on the mobilization of larger numbers of people to disrupt the social order and induce defections from a regime's 'pillars of support', such as the military or the party hierarchy (Sharp, 2012; Chenoweth and Stephan, 2011). The distinction is not always very sharp, to be sure; successful violent campaigns (the Chinese Revolution, the Vietnam War) have tended to be precisely those campaigns that have *not* been limited in numbers, but have instead managed to mobilize the support of millions of ordinary people, just like successful non-violent campaigns (Chenoweth and Stephan, 2011). But it implies that violent campaigns, when they succeed, tend to be far more unified ideologically, since they do not depend as much on assembling very large and diverse coalitions of supporters. Non-violent campaigns, by contrast, tend to be unified only on broad points – the removal of the dictator, for example – and to split more openly and quickly the moment they win (O'Donnell and Schmitter, 1986).

The Outcomes of Violent and Non-Violent Campaigns

At the same time, even if non-violent revolution is not as effective at *overthrowing* regimes as its proponents claim it is (see Lehoucq, 2016) for some scepticism), it still appears to be associated statistically with a greater chance of more open, more democratic regimes *after* it succeeds. As we can see in Figure 11.4, the level of democracy after a successful

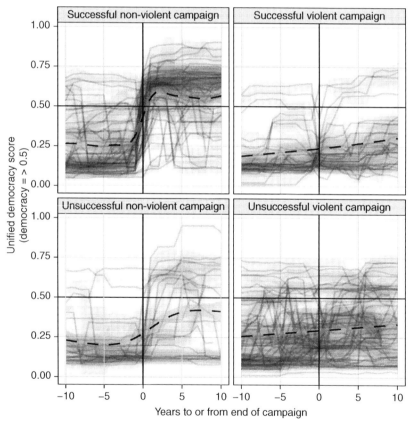

Figure 11.4   *Post-campaign outcomes for successful and unsuccessful regime-change campaigns. The data on regime-change campaigns is from the Nonviolent and Violent Campaigns and Outcomes (NAVCO) data project, version 2.0, described in Chenoweth and Lewis (2013). The primary method of resistance is an ideal type; campaigns sometimes used both violent and non-violent methods over their lifetime, and some changed their goals as well. Democracy data from Pemstein, Meserve, and Melton (2010), extended by the author (Márquez, 2016a).*

regime-change non-violent campaign tends to be significantly higher than the level of democracy before the campaign, while it tends not to change after a successful violent campaign. The few cases in the data such as the Iranian Revolution, where primarily non-violent protests succeeded in overthrowing the Shah but did not lead to a democratic outcome (at least by the standards used in this book), nevertheless tend to result in *more* democratic (even if not fully democratic) political systems; the Islamic Republic of Iran, for all its faults, represents a more democratic regime than the autocratic monarchy it replaced. And even non-violent campaigns identified as *unsuccessful* by Chenoweth and Lewis (2013) tend to be followed by increases in the level of democracy shortly afterward, indicating that the sorts of civil society mobilization that power non-violent campaigns tend to result in more open political systems over time, as some political scientists have hypothesized (Gill, 2000).

The reasons for this outcome are not too hard to imagine (Chenoweth and Stephan, 2011, ch. 8). First, if democracy depends on the active participation of citizens, then campaigns that promote such participation – as do almost all successful non-violent campaigns for regime change – will tend to produce more politically engaged citizens. Second, successful non-violent campaigns tend to produce political cultures where norms of non-violent conflict resolution are more entrenched, part of the 'collective memory' of a society, as Chenoweth and Stephan put it. Thus the elite 'winners' of non-violent campaigns, though they may disagree among themselves, will tend not to engage in internecine violence. By contrast, violent campaigns tend to succeed in ways that entrench military-style hierarchies intolerant of dissent, and to normalize violent means of dispute resolution within the elite. Though there exist a few cases where violent revolt has led to reasonably democratic outcomes in the post-Second World War period – for example, Costa Rica in 1948 – these are few in number, and typically combined violent tactics with a great deal of non-violent popular mobilization (for example, the successful anti-apartheid campaign led by the ANC, which combined both violent and non-violent tactics).

It is worth stressing that non-violent contention is not the only thing that matters for regime change. For one thing, even successful non-violent campaigns of protest can only result in the breakdown of an authoritarian regime, but they do not fully determine the nature of the successor regime. Moreover, the aftermath of revolt is more often than not disappointing to participants. After the excitement of participating in huge protests, the construction of institutions, and the necessary negotiations among elites required to produce a stable and just political order can seem tawdry, even a betrayal. And the artificial unity of large-scale coalitions forged against a dictator tends to break down once the movement 'wins'. Studies of democratic transitions suggest that this is an almost universal phenomenon

(O'Donnell and Schmitter, 1986). So in Egypt the overthrow of Mubarak was followed by the polarization of the Morsi era, brought abruptly to an end with a coup by the armed forces. And in Poland the elation of Solidarity's triumph in the elections of 1989 was followed by acrimonious debates and sometimes dirty tricks that are still – more than 25 years after the transition from Communism – playing out.

The construction of open and democratic regimes is thus a bit like war: endless boredom punctuated by moments of extraordinary excitement. While a detailed examination of the politics of democracy-building is beyond the scope of this book, we can note that success in this endeavour seems to depend in great part on the ability of reasonably 'liberal' elites within the outgoing regime to come to agreements and compromises that prevent repressive reactions and produce new and durable institutions for the regulation of political competition (O'Donnell and Schmitter, 1986). Sometimes these agreements take the form of explicit 'pacts' about the forms that political competition can take, like the 'Pacto de Punto Fijo' in Venezuela in 1958, which was designed to try to avoid a new military regime by excluding the Communist Party from political life, but sometimes the agreements are a bit more implicit. They also often include morally suspect compromises, such as the agreements to grant immunity for potential crimes to outgoing military leaders negotiated in Argentina. Even so, most new democracies fail within 15 years of their founding (Ulfelder, 2010), usually through the actions of chief executives intent on consolidating their power, and as we noted earlier successful democratizing revolts rarely produce significant immediate improvement in society.

Yet if the apparent inability of non-violent revolutions to produce much positive structural change is disappointing, the large-scale, world-historical violent revolutions that *have* produced such change have more often than not been tragic. Indeed, compared to the disasters produced by most of the twentieth-century great revolutions, the installation of open and democratic regimes seems like a genuine and fragile achievement, even if it is not one that seems exciting in today's era of democratic 'fatigue' (Przeworski, 2010). And from this point of view, non-violent revolt has been a much better bet, at least in the post-Second World War era.

Conclusion

Large-scale contention is rare. Most regimes, even very oppressive ones, do not experience large-scale revolt, because revolt is risky, and uprisings in unpromising circumstances rarely lead to durable regime change. But revolt does happen occasionally, mobilizing sometimes millions of individuals in dramatic ways for extended periods of time. As people from Egypt to Iran to Russia have continually rediscovered, these are 'the moments when decades happen'.

Large-scale mobilization is also opportunistic. Many kinds of events can trigger it, from miscarriages of justice to changes in the international situation to other revolutions to elite divisions, by affecting the degree to which non-democratic regimes can impede collective action by outsiders. And sometimes people, in the heat of the moment, *make* their own opportunities even in unpromising environments. Effective mobilization also depends on the emotional work required to help enough people overcome the 'barriers of fear' imposed by non-democratic regimes, and grows as people update their estimates of how many others will protest. Finally, large-scale mobilization can take many forms, from terrorism to peaceful mass marches, but non-violent forms of contention have shown themselves more capable, in recent times, of overthrowing authoritarian regimes and pushing for democratization.

Chapter 12

Conclusion: The Uncertainty of Democratization

Non-democratic politics has changed much over the past two centuries. As documented in Chapter 2, the world has in many ways become much more democratic since the 1800s. Political life used to be structured around monarchical ideas and norms of hereditary selection; it is now structured around the sovereignty of 'the people' and norms of electoral selection almost everywhere.

These changes have not been linear, however, and great crises of democracy have contributed to the three eras of non-democratic innovation we have examined in detail in this book. The crisis of the interwar European regimes gave rise to the 'totalitarian moment', with its highly ideological regimes claiming to speak more authentically in the name of the people than mere 'representative' democracies, and accompanied by unprecedented levels of social control and repression. The optimism of the decolonization process after the traumas of the Second World War gave way to an 'authoritarian' and 'dictatorial' moment, when rulers dispensed with constraints in the name of development, anti-communism, or national unity. And today, we have perhaps entered a 'competitive authoritarian' moment, in which non-democratic rulers have figured out new ways to tame democratic institutions for non-democratic ends, and many democracies have become less democratic.

Like layers of sediment, none of these non-democratic moments has ever completely gone away, and their seeds were usually planted in earlier times. Dictatorial regimes existed long before the Second World War; personal rule continues to exist in many countries in Africa and Central Asia, and has sometimes re-emerged even in competitive contexts such as Venezuela. Competitive authoritarianism is in some ways coeval with the development of representative institutions in the nineteenth century, though their current incarnations (unlike their nineteenth-century ancestors) typically guarantee universal suffrage and proclaim their democratic credentials more loudly. One of the world's great powers, China, though no longer a totalitarian dictatorship, remains fully authoritarian, and shows no signs of becoming less so; indeed, the appeal of the so-called 'Chinese model' seems to have grown in recent years. The globe's most important oil economy, Saudi Arabia, is a stable dynastic monarchy that firmly rejects the most basic democratic norms. And a few remnants of totalitarian domination still drag on in North Korea and Eritrea.

242

While all of these kinds of non-democratic regimes ensure that people not currently in control of the state are excluded, if need be forcibly, from power to a greater or lesser extent, the ones that have prospered in the last century – the most successful forms – have not always been the most repressive or the most personalized. Instead, such regimes have tended to exercise power through institutions – primarily, but not exclusively, political parties – that ensure the unity of ruling elites, providing them with incentives to hang together rather than separately; help them mobilize groups beyond the elite in support of the regime; and allow them to process information intelligently, sifting through the inevitable lies that concentrated power produces while giving more credibility to their own pronouncements. Successful non-democratic regimes have thus borrowed much from the institutional repertoire of representative democracies, using parties and elections to their advantage, ditching obvious and ineffective propaganda, and learning to live with more open public spheres. Some of these regimes can boast genuine achievements in human development, even if, as documented in Chapter 9, democracies still remain the better bet.

Yet non-democratic regimes remain trapped in the contradictions produced by concentrated power and intensified by the great normative shifts of the modern era. The commitment and informational dilemmas that plague non-democratic politics (discussed most fully in Chapter 8), though ameliorated by many institutional innovations, have never fully gone away. And in a context where democratic legitimating norms are the only ones widely accepted around the world, authoritarian claims to be 'really' democratic will always tend to ring hollow – especially if, as we saw in Chapter 10, worldwide economic development and value change does tend to make it increasingly likely that populations will demand liberty and economic conflict shows the hollowness of non-democratic commitments to share resources and power. Finally, the emerging global repertoire of non-violent contention has proven surprisingly successful in pushing non-democratic regimes to democratize; even the most repressive regimes have shown themselves vulnerable to 'people power' under many circumstances.

Non-democratic regimes are thus down but not out. While we have seen that there is some reason to think that the world will become increasingly democratic over time we can have no scientific confidence that the 'arc of history' always 'bends towards justice', as Martin Luther King Jr. once put it. Political leaders and elites constantly come up with new ways to concentrate power and dampen political competition for the control of states, so that struggles for open political competition must always be renewed. But politics is the 'slow, strong drilling through hard boards, with a combination of passion and a sense of judgment' that enables us to continually do so (Weber, 1994 [1919], p. 369).

References

Acemoglu, Daron, and James Robinson. 2006. *Economic Origins of Dictatorship and Democracy*. Cambridge: Cambridge University Press.

Acemoglu, Daron, Suresh Naidu, Pascual Restrepo, and James A. Robinson. 2014. 'Democracy Does Cause Growth'. National Bureau of Economic Research Working Paper No. 20004.

Aguilar, Paloma. 2009. 'Whatever Happened to Francoist Socialization? Spaniards' Values and Patterns of Cultural Consumption in the Post-Dictatorial Period'. *Democratization* 16 (3): 455–84.

Aidt, Toke S. 2009. 'Corruption, Institutions, and Economic Development'. *Oxford Review of Economic Policy* 25 (2): 271–91.

Albertus, Michael. 2015. *Autocracy and Redistribution: The Politics of Land Reform*. New York: Cambridge University Press.

Alesina, Alberto, and Angeletos George-Marios. 2005. 'Fairness and Redistribution'. *American Economic Review* 95 (4): 960–80.

Alesina, Alberto, and Nicola Fuchs-Schündeln. 2007. 'Goodbye Lenin (or Not?): The Effect of Communism on People'. *American Economic Review* 97 (4): 1507–28.

Almeida, Heitor, and Daniel Ferreira. 2002. 'Democracy and the Variability of Economic Performance'. *Economics & Politics* 14 (3): 225–57.

Andersen, Jørgen J., and Michael L. Ross. 2014. 'The Big Oil Change: A Closer Look at the Haber–Menaldo Analysis'. *Comparative Political Studies* 47 (7): 993–1021.

Anderson, Christopher J., Andre Blais, Shaun Bowler, Todd Donovan, and Ola Listhaug. 2005. *Losers' Consent: Elections and Democratic Legitimacy*. Oxford: Oxford University Press.

Anderson, Lisa. 1991. 'Absolutism and the Resilience of Monarchy in the Middle East'. *Political Science Quarterly* 106 (1): 1–15.

Ansell, Ben, and David Samuels. 2010. 'Inequality and Democratization: A Contractarian Approach'. *Comparative Political Studies* 43 (12): 1543–74.

Arendt, Hannah. 1970. *On Violence*. New York: Harcourt, Brace, World.

———. 1973. *The Origins of Totalitarianism*. New York: Harcourt, Brace, Jovanovich.

Aristotle. 1944 [3rd century BC]. Politics. Translated by H. Rackham. (Loeb Classical Library 1998 reprint edition). Cambridge, MA: Harvard University Press.

Austin Holmes, Amy. 2012. 'There Are Weeks When Decades Happen: Structure and Strategy in the Egyptian Revolution'. *Mobilization* 17 (4): 319–410.

Axworthy, Michael. 2013. *Revolutionary Iran: A History of the Islamic Republic*. New York: Oxford University Press.

Banfield, Edward C. 1958. *The Moral Basis of a Backward Society*. Glencoe: Free Press.

Barker, Rodney. 2001. *Legitimating Identities: the Self-presentations of Rulers and Subjects*. Cambridge: Cambridge University Press.

Barro, Robert. 1996. 'Democracy and Growth'. *Journal of Economic Growth* 1 (1): 1–27.

Barry, Ellen. 2011. 'Sound of Post-Soviet Protest: Claps and Beeps'. *New York Times*. http://www.nytimes.com/2011/07/15/world/europe/15belarus.html.

Bartels, Larry M. 2005. 'Homer Gets a Tax Cut: Inequality and Public Policy in the American Mind'. *Perspectives on Politics* 3 (1): 15–31.

Baum, Matthew A., and David A. Lake. 2003. 'The Political Economy of Growth: Democracy and Human Capital'. *American Journal of Political Science* 47 (2): 333–47.

Beetham, David. 2009. 'The Contradictions of Democratization by Force: The Case of Iraq'. *Democratization* 16 (3): 443–54.

———. 2013. *The Legitimation of Power*. 2nd edn. Basingstoke: Palgrave Macmillan.

Beissinger, Mark. 2007. 'Structure and Example in Modular Political Phenomena: The Diffusion of Bulldozer/Rose/Orange/Tulip Revolutions'. *Perspectives on Politics* 5 (2): 259–76.

Belkin, Aaron, and Evan Schofer. 2003. 'Toward a Structural Understanding of Coup Risk'. *Journal of Conflict Resolution* 47 (5): 594–620.

Bell, Daniel. 2015. *The China Model: Political Meritocracy and the Limits of Democracy*. Princeton: Princeton University Press.

Belova, Eugenia, and Valery Lazarev. 2007. 'Why Party and How Much? The Soviet State and the Party Finance'. *Public Choice* 130 (3–4): 437–56.

———. 2008. 'Secret Public Finance: Revenues and Expenditures of the Soviet Communist Party, 1938–1965'. *Europe-Asia Studies* 60 (3): 455–82.

Bennett, Philip, and Moises Naim. 2015. '21st-Century Censorship: Governments Around the World Are Using Stealthy Strategies to Manipulate the Media'. *Columbia Journalism Review*, January/February.

Benstead, Lindsay J. 2015. 'Why Do Some Arab Citizens See Democracy as Unsuitable for Their Country?' *Democratization*, 22 (7): 1183–1208.

Berman, Sheri. 1997. 'Civil Society and the Collapse of the Weimar Republic'. *World Politics* 49 (3): 401–29.

Bermeo, Nancy. 2009. 'Does Electoral Democracy Boost Economic Equality?' *Journal of Democracy* 20 (4): 21–35.

Besley, Timothy J., and Masayuki Kudamatsu. 2007. 'Making Autocracy Work'. CEPR Discussion Paper 6371. Available at http://eprints.lse.ac.uk/3764/1/Making_Autocracy_Work.pdf.

Besley, Timothy, and Stephen Coate. 1998. 'Sources of Inefficiency in a Representative Democracy: A Dynamic Analysis'. *American Economic Review* 88 (1): 139–56.

Bhavnani, Ravi, and Michael Ross. 2003. 'Announcement, Credibility, and Turnout in Popular Rebellions'. *Journal of Conflict Resolution* 47 (3): 340–66.

Bian, Yanjie, Xiaoling Shu, and John R. Logan. 2001. 'Communist Party Membership and Regime Dynamics in China'. *Social Forces* 79 (3): 805–41.

Bicchieri, Cristina, and Yoshitaka Fukui. 1999. 'The Great Illusion: Ignorance, Informational Cascades and the Persistence of Unpopular Norms'. *Business Ethics Quarterly* 9 (1): 127–55.

Blaydes, Lisa. 2010. *Elections and Distributive Politics in Mubarak's Egypt*. Cambridge: Cambridge University Press.

Blaydes, Lisa, and Mark Kayser. 2011. 'Counting Calories: Democracy and Distribution in the Developing World'. *International Studies Quarterly* 55 (4): 887–908.

Boix, Carles. 2003. *Democracy and Redistribution*. Cambridge: Cambridge University Press.

———. 2011. 'Democracy, Development, and the International System'. *American Political Science Review* 105 (4): 809–28.

Boix, Carles, and Susan Stokes. 2003. 'Endogenous Democratization'. *World Politics* 55 (4): 517–49.

Boix, Carles, Michael Miller, and Sebastian Rosato. 2012. 'A Complete Data Set of Political Regimes, 1800–2007'. *Comparative Political Studies* 46 (12): 1523–54.

Booth, John, and Mitchell Seligson. 2009. *The Legitimacy Puzzle in Latin America: Political Support and Democracy in Eight Nations*. Cambridge: Cambridge University Press.

Brady, Anne-Marie. 2008. *Marketing Dictatorship: Propaganda and Thought Work in Contemporary China*. Lanham, MD: Rowman & Littlefield.

———. 2009. 'Mass Persuasion as a Means of Legitimation and China's Popular Authoritarianism'. *American Behavioral Scientist* 53 (3): 434–57.

Brahimi, Alia. 2011. 'Libya's Revolution'. *The Journal of North African Studies* 16 (4): 605–24.

Brancati, Dawn. 2014. 'Democratic Authoritarianism: Origins and Effects'. *Annual Review of Political Science* 17 (1): 313–26.

Bratton, Michael, and Robert Mattes. 2001. 'Support for Democracy in Africa: Intrinsic or Instrumental?' *British Journal of Political Science* 31 (3): 447–74.

Bratton, Michael, and Nicolas van de Walle. 1994. 'Neopatrimonial Regimes and Political Transitions in Africa'. *World Politics* 46 (4): 453–89.

Breuer, Anita, Todd Landman, and Dorothea Farquhar. 2014. 'Social Media and Protest Mobilization: Evidence from the Tunisian Revolution'. *Democratization* 22 (4): 764–792.

Brooker, Paul. 2014. *Non-Democratic Regimes*. 3rd edn. Houndmills: Palgrave Macmillan.

Brownlee, Jason. 2002. '…And Yet They Persist: Explaining Survival and Transition in Neopatrimonial Regimes'. *Studies in Comparative International Development* 37 (3): 35–63.

———. 2007a. *Authoritarianism in an Age of Democratization*. Cambridge: Cambridge University Press.

———. 2007b. 'Hereditary Succession in Modern Autocracies'. *World Politics* 59 (4): 595–628.

Bueno de Mesquita, Bruce, James D. Morrow, Randolph M. Siverson, and Alastair Smith. 2001. 'Political Competition and Economic Growth'. *Journal of Democracy* 12 (1): 58–72.

Bueno de Mesquita, Bruce, Alastair Smith, Randolph M. Siverson, and James D. Morrow. 2003. *The Logic of Political Survival*. Cambridge, MA: The MIT Press.

Bunce, Valerie J., and Sharon L. Wolchik. 2006. 'International Diffusion and Postcommunist Electoral Revolutions'. *Communist and Post-Communist Studies* 39 (3): 283–304.

———. 2010. 'Defeating Dictators: Electoral Change and Stability in Competitive Authoritarian Regimes'. *World Politics* 62 (1): 43–86.

Bush, George W. 2003. 'Speech to the American Enterprise Institute on the Future of Iraq, 26 February 2003'. http://www.presidentialrhetoric.com/speeches/02.26.03.html.

Butkiewicz, James L., and Halit Yanikkaya. 2006. 'Institutional Quality and Economic Growth: Maintenance of the Rule of Law or Democratic Institutions, or Both?' *Economic Modelling* 23 (4): 648–61.

Campbell, Neil, and Shrabani Saha. 2013. 'Corruption, Democracy and Asia-Pacific Countries'. *Journal of the Asia Pacific Economy* 18 (2): 290–303.

Carbone, Giovanni. 2015. 'Democratisation as a State-Building Mechanism: A Preliminary Discussion of an Understudied Relationship'. *Political Studies Review* 13 (1): 11–21.

Carbone, Giovanni, and Vincenzo Memoli. 2015. 'Does Democratization Foster State Consolidation? Democratic Rule, Political Order, and Administrative Capacity'. *Governance* 28 (1): 5–24.

Carlson, Matthew, and Mark Turner. 2009. 'Popular Perceptions of Political Regimes in East and Southeast Asia'. *Democratization* 16 (2): 377–98.

Carnaghan, Ellen. 2011. 'The Difficulty of Measuring Support for Democracy in a Changing Society: Evidence from Russia'. *Democratization* 18 (3): 682–706.

Cederman, Lars-Erik. 2001. 'Back to Kant: Reinterpreting the Democratic Peace as a Macrohistorical Learning Process'. *American Political Science Review* 95 (1): 15–31.

Cederman, Lars-Erik, Kristian Skrede Gleditsch, and Simon Hug. 2013. 'Elections and Ethnic Civil War'. *Comparative Political Studies* 46 (3): 387–417.

Cederman, Lars-Erik, Simon Hug, and Lutz F. Krebs. 2010. 'Democratization and Civil War: Empirical Evidence'. *Journal of Peace Research* 47 (4): 377–94.

Cederman, Lars-Erik, Simon Hug, and Andreas Wenger. 2008. 'Democratization and War in Political Science'. *Democratization* 15 (3): 509–24.

Celestino, Mauricio Rivera, and Kristian Skrede Gleditsch. 2013. 'Fresh Carnations or All Thorn, No Rose? Nonviolent Campaigns and Transitions in Autocracies'. *Journal of Peace Research* 50 (3): 385–400.

Centola, Damon, Robb Willer, and Michael Macy. 2005. 'The Emperor's Dilemma: A Computational Model of Self-Enforcing Norms'. *American Journal of Sociology* 110 (4): 1009–40.

Chambers, John R., Lawton K. Swan, and Martin Heesacker. 2014. 'Better Off Than We Know: Distorted Perceptions of Incomes and Income Inequality in America'. *Psychological Science* 25 (2): 613–18.

Chandra, Siddharth, and Nita Rudra. 2015. 'Reassessing the Links Between Regime Type and Economic Performance: Why Some Authoritarian Regimes Show Stable Growth and Others Do Not'. *British Journal of Political Science* 45 (2): 253–85.

Charron, Nicholas, and Victor Lapuente. 2010. 'Does Democracy Produce Quality of Government?' *European Journal of Political Research* 49 (4): 443–70.

———. 2011. 'Which Dictators Produce Quality of Government?' *Studies in Comparative International Development* 46 (4): 397–423.

Chau, Adam Yuet. 2010. 'Mao's Travelling Mangoes: Food as Relic in Revolutionary China'. *Past & Present* 206 (suppl 5): 256–75.

Chehabi, Houchang E., and Juan J. Linz, eds. 1998. *Sultanistic Regimes*. Baltimore: Johns Hopkins University Press.

Cheibub, José, Jennifer Gandhi, and James Vreeland. 2010. 'Democracy and Dictatorship Revisited'. *Public Choice* 143 (1): 67–101.

Chen, Xueyi, and Tianjian Shi. 2001. 'Media Effects on Political Confidence and Trust in the People's Republic of China in the Post-Tiananmen Period'. *East Asia* 19 (3): 84–118.

Chenoweth, Erica, and Orion A. Lewis. 2013. 'Unpacking Nonviolent Campaigns: Introducing the NAVCO 2.0 Dataset'. *Journal of Peace Research* 50 (3): 415–23.

Chenoweth, Erica, and Maria J. Stephan. 2011. *Why Civil Resistance Works : The Strategic Logic of Nonviolent Conflict*. New York: Columbia University Press.

Cho, Youngho. 2012. 'How Well Ordinary Citizens Understand Democracy: The Case of the South Korean Electorate'. *Democratization* 21 (2): 195–219.

Chorin, Ethan Daniel. 2012. *Exit Gaddafi: The Hidden History of the Libyan Revolution*. London: Saqi Books.

Chŏn, Hyŏn-jun, Moon-Young Huh, Philo Kim, and Chin-soo Bae. 2007. *An Assessment of the North Korean System's Durability*. Seoul: Korea Institute for National Unification.

Chu, Yun-han, Michael Bratton, Marta Lagos, Sandeep Shastri, and Mark Tessler. 2008. 'Public Opinion and Democratic Legitimacy'. *Journal of Democracy* 19 (2): 74–87.

Clague, Christopher, Philip Keefer, Stephen Knack, and Mancur Olson. 1996. 'Property and Contract Rights in Autocracies and Democracies'. *Journal of Economic Growth* 1 (2): 243–76.

Collier, Paul. 2009. *Wars, Guns, and Votes: Democracy in Dangerous Places*. New York: Harper.

Collins, Randall. 2004. *Interaction Ritual Chains*. Princeton, NJ: Princeton University Press.

Conquest, Robert. 1986. *The Harvest of Sorrow: Soviet Collectivization and the Terror-Famine*. London: Hutchinson.

Conquest, Robert. 2008. *The Great Terror: A Reassessment*. New York: Random House.

Constable, Pamela, and Arturo Valenzuela. 1993. *A Nation of Enemies: Chile Under Pinochet*. New York: WW Norton & Company.

Coppedge, Michael, John Gerring, David Altman, Michael Bernhard, Steven Fish, Allen Hicken, Matthew Kroenig, et al. 2011. 'Conceptualizing and Measuring Democracy: A New Approach'. *Perspectives on Politics* 9 (2): 247–67.

Coppedge, Michael, John Gerring, Staffan I. Lindberg, Svend-Erik Skaaning, Jan Teorell with David Altman, Michael Bernhard, M. Steven Fish, et al. 2015. 'V-Dem Codebook V5'. Varieties of Democracy (V-Dem) Project.

Corrales, Javier. 2015. 'The Authoritarian Resurgence: Autocratic Legalism in Venezuela'. *Journal of Democracy* 26 (2): 37–51.

Corrales, Javier, and Michael Penfold. 2010. *Dragon in the Tropics: Hugo Chavez and the Political Economy of Revolution in Venezuela*. Washington, DC: Brookings Institution Press.

Cotton, James. 1989. 'From Authoritarianism to Democracy in South Korea'. *Political Studies* 37 (2): 244–59.

Dahl, Robert. 1989. *Democracy and Its Critics*. New Haven, CT: Yale University Press.

Davenport, Christian. 1997. 'From Ballots to Bullets: An Empirical Assessment of How National Elections Influence State Uses of Political Repression'. *Electoral Studies* 16 (4): 517–40.

————. 2007a. 'State Repression and Political Order'. *Annual Review of Political Science* 10 (1): 1–23.

————. 2007b. 'State Repression and the Tyrannical Peace'. *Journal of Peace Research* 44 (4): 485–504.

————. 2012. 'When Democracies Kill: Reflections from the US, India, and Northern Ireland'. *International Area Studies Review* 15 (1): 3–20.

Davenport, Christian, and David A. Armstrong. 2004. 'Democracy and the Violation of Human Rights: A Statistical Analysis from 1976 to 1996'. *American Journal of Political Science* 48 (3): 538–54.

Davies, Sarah. 2004. 'Stalin and the Making of the Leader Cult in the 1930s'. In *The Leader Cult in Communist Dictatorship: Stalin and the Eastern Bloc*, edited by Balázs Apor, Jan Behrends, Polly Jones, and E. A. Rees, 29–46. London: Palgrave Macmillan.

Decalo, Samuel. 1985. 'African Personal Dictatorships'. *The Journal of Modern African Studies* 23 (2): 209–37.

Demick, Barbara. 2009. *Nothing to Envy: Ordinary Lives in North Korea*. New York: Spiegel & Grau.

Diederich, Bernard, and Al Burt. 1973. *Papa Doc: Haiti and Its Dictator*. London: Penguin.

Dikötter, Frank. 2010. *Mao's Great Famine: The History of China's Most Devastating Catastrophe, 1958–1962*. New York: Walker & Co.

Dittmer, Lowell. 1977. 'Political Culture and Political Symbolism: Toward a Theoretical Synthesis'. *World Politics* 29 (4): 552–83.

————. 1989. 'The Tiananmen Massacre'. *Problems of Communism* 38 (5): 2–15.

Dobson, William. 2012. *The Dictator's Learning Curve: Inside the Global Battle for Democracy*. New York: Doubleday.

Doucouliagos, Hristos, and Mehmet Ali Ulubaşoğlu. 2008. 'Democracy and Economic Growth: A Meta-Analysis'. *American Journal of Political Science* 52 (1): 61–83.

Downes, Alexander, and Jonathan Monten. 2013. 'Forced to Be Free?: Why Foreign-Imposed Regime Change Rarely Leads to Democratization'. *International Security* 37 (4): 90–131.

Doyle, Michael W. 1983a. 'Kant, Liberal Legacies, and Foreign Affairs'. *Philosophy & Public Affairs* 12 (3): 205–35.

————. 1983b. 'Kant, Liberal Legacies, and Foreign Affairs, Part 2'. *Philosophy & Public Affairs* 12 (4): 323–53.

Dunn, John. 2005. *Setting the People Free: The Story of Democracy*. London: Atlantic.

Easterly, William. 2011. 'Benevolent Autocrats'. Working Paper.

Easton, David. 1975. 'A Re-Assessment of the Concept of Political Support'. *British Journal of Political Science* 5 (4): 435–57.

Egorov, Georgy, and Konstantin Sonin. 2011. 'Dictators and their Viziers: Endogeneizing the Loyalty-Competence Trade-off'. *Journal of the European Economic Association* 9 (5): 903–30.

Egorov, Georgy, Sergei Guriev, and Konstantin Sonin. 2009. 'Why Resource-Poor Dictators Allow Freer Media: A Theory and Evidence from Panel Data'. *American Political Science Review* 103 (4): 645–68.

El-Kikhia, Mansour O. 1997. *Libya's Qaddafi: The Politics of Contradiction*. Gainesville: University Press of Florida.

Ellner, Steve. 2010. 'Hugo Chavez's First Decade in Office'. *Latin American Perspectives* 37 (1): 77–96.

Epstein, Catherine. 2004. 'The Stasi: New Research on the East German Ministry of State Security'. *Kritika: Explorations in Russian and Eurasian History* 5 (2): 321–48.

Evans, Peter. 1995. *Embedded Autonomy*. Princeton, NJ: Princeton University Press.

Evans, Richard J. 2004. *The Coming of the Third Reich*. New York: The Penguin Press.

———. 2006. *The Third Reich in Power*. New York: Penguin Books.

Fariss, Christopher J. 2014. 'Respect for Human Rights Has Improved over Time: Modeling the Changing Standard of Accountability'. *American Political Science Review* 108 (02): 297–318.

Feaver, Peter D. 1999. 'Civil-Military Relations'. *Annual Review of Political Science* 2 (1): 211–41.

Feenstra, Robert Inklaar, Robert C., and Marcel P. Timmer. 2013. 'The Next Generation of the Penn World Table'. Dataset. www.ggdc.net/pwt.

Fernández, Carlos. 1983. *El general Franco*. 2nd edn, revised. Barcelona: Argos Vergara.

Finer, Samuel. 1962. *The Man on Horseback: The Role of the Military in Politics*. London: Pall Mall Press.

Fish, M. Steven. 2002. 'Islam and Authoritarianism'. *World Politics* 55 (1): 4–37.

Fjelde, Hanne, and Håvard Hegre. 2014. 'Political Corruption and Institutional Stability'. *Studies in Comparative International Development* 49 (3): 267–99.

Formisano, Ronald P. 2000. 'The Concept of Political Culture'. *Journal of Interdisciplinary History* 31 (3): 393–426.

Foucault, Michel. 2007. *Security, Territory, Population: Lectures at the Collège de France, 1977–1978*. New York: Palgrave Macmillan.

———. 2008. *The Birth of Biopolitics: Lectures at the Collège de France, 1978–79*. New York: Palgrave Macmillan.

———. 1995 [1975]. *Discipline and Punish*. 2nd edn. New York: Vintage Books.

Francisco, Ronald A. 1995. 'The Relationship Between Coercion and Protest: An Empirical Evaluation in Three Coercive States'. *The Journal of Conflict Resolution* 39 (2): 263–82.

Freeman, John, and Dennis Quinn. 2012. 'The Economic Origins of Democracy Reconsidered'. *American Political Science Review* 106 (1): 58–80.

Friedrich, Carl J., and Zbigniew Brzezinski. 1965. *Totalitarian Dictatorship and Autocracy*. 2nd edn. Cambridge, MA: Harvard University Press.

Fukuyama, Francis. 2013. 'Democracy and the Quality of the State'. *Journal of Democracy* 24 (4): 5–16.

Fulbrook, Mary. 1995. *Anatomy of a Dictatorship: Inside the GDR, 1949-89*. Oxford: Oxford University Press.

Galíndez, Jesús de. 1956. *La era de Trujillo*. Santiago de Chile: Editorial del Pacífico.

Gallagher, Mary E., and Jonathan K. Hanson. 2015. 'Power Tool or Dull Blade? Selectorate Theory for Autocracies'. *Annual Review of Political Science* 18 (1): 367–85.

Gandhi, Jennifer. 2008. *Political Institutions under Dictatorship*. Cambridge: Cambridge University Press.

Gandhi, Jennifer, and Ellen Okar. 2009. 'Elections Under Authoritarianism'. *Annual Review of Political Science* 12 (1): 403–22.

Gandhi, Jennifer, and Adam Przeworski. 2006. 'Cooperation, Cooptation, and Rebellion Under Dictatorships'. *Economics & Politics* 18 (1): 1–26.

Garton Ash, Timothy. 1999. *The Magic Lantern: The Revolution of '89 Witnessed in Warsaw, Budapest, Berlin, and Prague.* New York: Vintage.

Gartzke, Erik. 2007. 'The Capitalist Peace'. *American Journal of Political Science* 51 (1): 166–91.

Gartzke, Erik, and Alex Weisiger. 2014. 'Under Construction: Development, Democracy, and Difference as Determinants of Systemic Liberal Peace'. *International Studies Quarterly* 58 (1): 130–45.

Geddes, Barbara. 1999. 'What do we know about Democratization after 20 years?' *Annual Review of Political Science* 2 (1): 115–44.

Geddes, Barbara, Erica Frantz, and Joseph G. Wright. 2014. 'Military Rule'. *Annual Review of Political Science* 17 (1): 147–62.

Geddes, Barbara, Joseph Wright, and Erica Frantz. 2014. 'Autocratic Breakdown and Regime Transitions: A New Data Set'. *Perspectives on Politics* 12 (1): 313–31.

Gelvin, James L. 2012. *The Arab Uprisings: What Everyone Needs to Know.* New York: Oxford University Press.

Gerring, John, Phillip J. Bond, William T. Barndt, and Carola Moreno. 2006. 'Democracy and Economic Growth: A Historical Perspective'. *World Politics* 57 (3): 323–64.

Gerring, John, Svend-Erik Skaaning, Matthew Maguire, and Eitan Tzelgov. 2013. 'Democracy and Growth: A Lexical Approach'. *Boston University and Aarhus University: Working Paper.*

Getty, J. Arch. 2002. '"Excesses Are Not Permitted": Mass Terror and Stalinist Governance in the Late 1930s'. *The Russian Review* 61 (1): 113–38.

Gibler, D. M., and J. Tir. 2010. 'Settled Borders and Regime Type: Democratic Transitions as Consequences of Peaceful Territorial Transfers'. *American Journal of Political Science* 54 (4): 951–68.

Gilens, Martin, and Benjamin I. Page. 2014. 'Testing Theories of American Politics: Elites, Interest Groups, and Average Citizens'. *Perspectives on Politics* 12 (3): 564–81.

Gill, Graeme. 1980. 'The Soviet Leader Cult: Reflections on the Structure of Leadership in the Soviet Union'. *British Journal of Political Science* 10 (2): 167–86.

———. 2000. *The Dynamics of Democratization: Elites, Civil Society, and the Transition Process.* New York: St. Martin's Press.

———. 2006. 'A New Turn to Authoritarian Rule in Russia?' *Democratization* 13 (1): 58–77.

———. 2011. *Symbols and Legitimacy in Soviet Politics: The Life and Death of the USSR.* Cambridge University Press.

Gilley, Bruce. 2006. 'The Meaning and Measure of State Legitimacy: Results for 72 Countries'. *European Journal of Political Research* 45 (3): 499–525.

———. 2009. *The Right to Rule: How States Win and Lose Legitimacy.* New York: Columbia University Press.

Gilson, Ronald J., and Curtis J. Milhaupt. 2011. 'Economically Benevolent Dictators: Lessons for Developing Democracies'. *The American Journal of Comparative Law* 59 (1): 227–88.

Ginsburg, Tom, and Alberto Simpser, eds. 2013. *Constitutions in Authoritarian Regimes*. Cambridge: Cambridge University Press.

Gleditsch, Kristian. 2004. 'A Revised List of Wars Between and Within Independent States, 1816–2002'. *International Interactions* 30 (3): 231–62.

———. 2010. 'Expanded Population Data'. Dataset. http://privatewww.essex. ac.uk/~ksg/exppop.html.

Goemans, Henk, Kristian Gleditsch, and Giacomo Chiozza. 2014. 'Introducing Archigos: A Dataset of Political Leaders'. *Journal of Peace Research* 46 (2): 269–83. Available at: http://www.rochester.edu/college/faculty/hgoemans/ data.htm, accessed 31 December 2015.

Goldstone, Jack. 2001. 'Toward a Fourth Generation of Revolutionary Theory'. *Annual Review of Political Science* 4 (1): 139–87.

Goodin, Robert E. 1978. 'Rites of Rulers'. *British Journal of Sociology* 29 (3): 281–99.

Gradstein, Mark, and Branko Milanovic. 2004. 'Does Liberté = Egalité? A Survey of the Empirical Links between Democracy and Inequality with Some Evidence on the Transition Economies'. *Journal of Economic Surveys* 18 (4): 515–37.

Grzymała-Busse, Anna. 2001. 'The Organizational Strategies of Communist Parties in East Central Europe, 1945–1989'. *East European Politics & Societies* 15 (2): 421–53.

Guerrero, Alexander A. 2014. 'Against Elections: The Lottocratic Alternative'. *Philosophy & Public Affairs* 42 (2): 135–78.

Guliyev, Farid. 2011. 'Personal Rule, Neopatrimonialism, and Regime Typologies: Integrating Dahlian and Weberian Approaches to Regime Studies'. *Democratization* 18 (3): 575–601.

Gunitsky, Seva. 2015. 'Corrupting the Cyber-Commons: Social Media as a Tool of Autocratic Stability'. *Perspectives on Politics* 13 (1): 42–54.

Haber, Stephen. 2006. 'Authoritarian Government'. In *The Oxford Handbook of Political Economy*, edited by Barry Weingast and Donald Wittman, 693–707. Oxford: Oxford University Press.

Haber, Stephen, and Victor Menaldo. 2011. 'Do Natural Resources Fuel Authoritarianism? A Reappraisal of the Resource Curse'. *American Political Science Review* 105 (1): 1–26.

Haggard, Stephan, and Robert Kaufman. 2012. 'Inequality and Regime Change: Democratic Transitions and the Stability of Democratic Rule'. *American Political Science Review* 106 (3): 495–516.

Haggard, Stephan, and Marcus Noland. 2012. 'Economic Crime and Punishment in North Korea'. *Political Science Quarterly* 127 (4): 659–83.

Hale, Henry. 2013. 'Regime Change Cascades: What We Have Learned from the 1848 Revolutions to the 2011 Arab Uprisings'. *Annual Review of Political Science* 16 (1): 331–53.

Hanley, Eric. 2003. 'A Party of Workers or a Party of Intellectuals? Recruitment into Eastern European Communist Parties, 1945–1988'. *Social Forces* 81 (4): 1073–1105.

Harmel, Robert, and Alexander Tan. 2012. 'One-Party Rule or Multiparty Competition? Chinese Attitudes to Party System Alternatives'. *Party Politics* 18 (3): 337–47.

Harris, James R. 2005. 'Stalin as General Secretary: The Appointments Process and the Nature of Stalin's Power'. In *Stalin: A New History*, edited by Sarah Davies and James R. Harris, 63–82. Cambridge: Cambridge University Press.

Harris, Kevan. 2012. 'The Brokered Exuberance of the Middle Class: An Ethnographic Analysis of Iran's 2009 Green Movement'. *Mobilization: An International Journal* 17 (4): 435–55.

Hassig, Ralph, and Kongdan Oh. 2009. *The Hidden People of North Korea: Everyday Life in the Hermit Kingdom*. Lanham, MD: Rowman & Littlefield Publishers.

Havel, Vaclav. 1992. 'The Power of the Powerless'. In *Open Letters: Selected Writings, 1965–1990*, edited by Paul Wilson, 125–214. New York: Vintage Books.

Hawkins, Kirk A. 2016. 'Chavismo, Liberal Democracy, and Radical Democracy'. *Annual Review of Political Science* 19 (1): 311–29.

Hegre, Håvard. 2014. 'Democracy and Armed Conflict'. *Journal of Peace Research* 51 (2): 159–72.

Hegre, Håvard, Tanja Ellingsen, Scott Gates, and Nils Petter Gledtisch. 2001. 'Toward a Democratic Civil Peace? Democracy, Political Change, and Civil War, 1816–1992'. *American Political Science Review* 95 (1): 33–48.

Herb, Michael. 1999. *All in the Family: Absolutism, Revolution, and Democracy in the Middle Eastern Monarchies*. Albany: State University of New York Press.

Hewison, Kevin. 2014. 'Considerations on Inequality and Politics in Thailand'. *Democratization* 21 (5): 846–66.

Hibbard, Scott, and Azza Salama Layton. 2010. 'The Origins and Future of Egypt's Revolt'. *Journal of Islamic Law and Culture* 12 (3): 197–214.

Hlasny, Vladimir, and Paolo Verme. 2013. 'Top Incomes and the Measurement of Inequality in Egypt'. The World Bank.

Hosking, Geoffrey. 2000. 'Patronage and the Russian State'. *The Slavonic and East European Review* 78 (2): 301–20.

Houle, Christian. 2009. 'Inequality and Democracy: Why Inequality Harms Consolidation but Does Not Affect Democratization'. *World Politics* 61 (4): 589–622.

———. 2015. 'Ethnic Inequality and the Dismantling of Democracy: A Global Analysis'. *World Politics* 67 (3): 469–505.

Hsieh, Chang-Tai, Edward Miguel, Daniel Ortega, and Francisco Rodríguez. 2011. 'The Price of Political Opposition: Evidence from Venezuela's Maisanta'. *American Economic Journal: Applied Economics* 3 (2): 196–214.

Huang, Haifeng. 2015a. 'A War of (Mis)Information: The Political Effects of Rumors and Rumor Rebuttals in an Authoritarian Country'. *British Journal of Political Science* FirstView: 1–29.

———. 2015b. 'Propaganda as Signaling'. *Comparative Politics* 47 (4): 419–44.

Huang, Yasheng. 2008. *Capitalism with Chinese Characteristics: Entrepreneurship and the State*. Cambridge: Cambridge University Press.

Huntington, Samuel P. 1968. *Political Order in Changing Societies*. New Haven, CT: Yale University Press.

———. 1993. *The Third Wave: Democratization in the Late Twentieth Century*. Norman: University of Oklahoma Press.

Hyde, Susan D., and Nikolay Marinov. 2012. 'Which Elections Can Be Lost?' *Political Analysis* 20 (2): 191–210.

Inglehart, Ronald. 2003. 'How Solid Is Mass Support for Democracy: And How Can We Measure It?' *PS: Political Science and Politics* 36 (1): 51–7.

Inglehart, Ronald, and Christian Welzel. 2005. *Modernization, Cultural Change, and Democracy: The Human Development Sequence*. Cambridge: Cambridge University Press.

Jackson, Robert H., and Carl G. Rosberg. 1982. *Personal Rule in Black Africa: Prince, Autocrat, Prophet, Tyrant*. Berkeley: University of California Press.

Jang, Jin-sung. 2014. *Dear Leader*. Translated by Shirley Lee. London: Rider Books.

Jenco, Leigh. 2013. 'Revisiting Asian Values'. *Journal of the History of Ideas* 74 (2): 237–58.

Jiang, Jiehong. 2010. *Red: China's Cultural Revolution*. London: Jonathan Cape.

Johnston, Hank, and Carol Mueller. 2001. 'Unobtrusive Practices of Contention in Leninist Regimes'. *Sociological Perspectives* 44 (3): 351–75.

Joshi, Devin K., J. S. Maloy, and Timothy M. Peterson. 2015. 'Popular vs. Elite Democratic Structures and International Peace'. *Journal of Peace Research* 52 (4): 463–77.

Kailitz, Steffen. 2013. 'Classifying Political Regimes Revisited: Legitimation and Durability'. *Democratization* 20 (1): 39–60.

Kalandadze, Katya, and Mitchell A. Orenstein. 2009. 'Electoral Protests and Democratization Beyond the Color Revolutions'. *Comparative Political Studies* 42 (11): 1403–25.

Kalenborn, Christine, and Christian Lessmann. 2013. 'The Impact of Democracy and Press Freedom on Corruption: Conditionality Matters'. *Journal of Policy Modeling* 35 (6): 857–86.

Kamrava, Mehran. 2010. 'The 2009 Elections and Iran's Changing Political Landscape'. *Orbis* 54 (3): 400–12.

Kant, Immanuel. 1983 [1795]. 'To Perpetual Peace: A Philosophical Sketch'. In *Perpetual Peace and Other Essays*, 107–43. Indianapolis: Hackett.

Karklins, Rasma. 1986. 'Soviet Elections Revisited: Voter Abstention in Noncompetitive Voting'. *The American Political Science Review* 80 (2): 449–70.

Karklins, Rasma, and Roger Petersen. 1993. 'Decision Calculus of Protesters and Regimes: Eastern Europe 1989'. *The Journal of Politics* 55 (3): 588–614.

Karsh, Efraim, and Inari Rautsi. 1991. *Saddam Hussein: A Political Biography*. London: Futura.

Katouzian, Homa. 1998. 'The Pahlavi Regime in Iran'. In *Sultanistic Regimes*, edited by Houchang E. Chehabi and Juan J. Linz, 182–205. Baltimore: JHU Press.

Keane, John. 2009. *The Life and Death of Democracy*. New York: W.W. Norton & Co.

Kendall-Taylor, Andrea, and Erica Frantz. 2015. 'Mimicking Democracy to Prolong Autocracies'. *The Washington Quarterly* 37 (4): 71–84.

Kern, Holger, and Jens Hainmueller. 2009. 'Opium for the Masses: How Foreign Media Can Stabilize Authoritarian Regimes'. *Political Analysis* 17 (4): 377–99.

Kershaw, Ian. 1987. *The 'Hitler Myth': Image and Reality in the Third Reich*. Oxford; New York: Clarendon Press.

———. 1993. '"Working Towards the Führer." Reflections on the Nature of the Hitler Dictatorship'. *Contemporary European History* 2 (2): 103–18.

Kertzer, David I. 1988. *Ritual, Politics, and Power*. New Haven, CT: Yale University Press.

Khrushchev, Nikita Sergeevich. 1956. 'Speech to 20th Congress of the C.P.S.U'. Web Page. http://www.marxists.org/archive/khrushchev/1956/02/24.htm.

King, Gary, Jennifer Pan, and Margaret Roberts. 2013. 'How Censorship in China Allows Government Criticism but Silences Collective Expression'. *American Political Science Review* 107 (2): 326–43.

Knutsen, Carl. 2010. 'Investigating the Lee Thesis: How Bad is Democracy for Asian Economies?' *European Political Science Review* 2 (3): 451–73.

———. 2012. 'Democracy and Economic Growth: A Survey of Arguments and Results'. *International Area Studies Review* 15 (4): 393–415.

———. 2015a. 'Reinvestigating the Reciprocal Relationship Between Democracy and Income Inequality'. *Review of Economics & Institutions/Economia, Societa E Istituzioni* 6 (2): 1–37.

———. 2015b. 'Why Democracies Outgrow Autocracies in the Long Run: Civil Liberties, Information Flows and Technological Change'. *Kyklos* 68 (3): 357–84.

Knutsen, Carl Henrik, and Hanne Fjelde. 2013. 'Property Rights in Dictatorships: Kings Protect Property Better Than Generals or Party Bosses'. *Contemporary Politics* 19 (1): 94–114.

Knutsen, Carl Henrik, and Simone Wegmann. 2016. 'Is Democracy About Redistribution?' *Democratization* 23 (1): 164–92.

Koesel, Karrie J., and Valerie J. Bunce. 2013. 'Diffusion-Proofing: Russian and Chinese Responses to Waves of Popular Mobilizations Against Authoritarian Rulers'. *Perspectives on Politics* 11 (03): 753–68.

Kohli, Atul. 2004. *State-Directed Development: Political Power and Industrialization in the Global Periphery*. Cambridge: Cambridge University Press.

Kotkin, Stephen. 2008. *Armageddon Averted: The Soviet Collapse, 1970–2000*. Oxford: Oxford University Press.

———. 2014. *Stalin*. New York: Penguin Press.

Krasner, Stephen D. 1999. *Sovereignty: Organized Hypocrisy*. Princeton, NJ: Princeton University Press.

Krastev, Ivan, and Stephen Holmes. 2012. 'An Autopsy of Managed Democracy'. *Journal of Democracy* 23 (3): 33–45.

Kricheli, Ruth, Yair Livne, and Beatriz Magaloni. 2010. 'Taking to the Streets: Theory and Evidence on Protests Under Authoritarianism'. *Social Science Research Network Working Paper Series*. http://ssrn.com/abstract=1642040.

Kung, James Kai Sing, and Shuo Chen. 2011. 'The Tragedy of the Nomenklatura: Career Incentives and Political Radicalism during China's Great Leap Famine'. *American Political Science Review* 105 (1): 27–45.

Kuran, Timur. 1991. 'Now Out of Never: The Element of Surprise in the East European Revolution of 1989'. *World Politics* 44 (1): 7–48.

———. 1997. *Private Truths, Public Lies: the Social Consequences of Preference Falsification*. Cambridge, MA: Harvard University Press.

Kurzman, Charles. 2004. *The Unthinkable Revolution in Iran*. Cambridge, MA: Harvard University Press.

Landemore, Hélène. 2013. *Democratic Reason: Politics, Collective Intelligence, and the Rule of the Many*. Princeton, NJ: Princeton University Press.

Landsberger, Stefan R. 2002. 'The Deification of Mao'. In *China's Great Proletarian Cultural Revolution: Master Narratives and post-Mao Counternarratives*, edited by Woei Lien Chong, 139–84. Lanham, MD: Rowman & Littlefield Publishers.

Lane, Christel. 1981. *The Rites of Rulers: Ritual in Industrial Society*. Cambridge: Cambridge University Press.

———. 1984. 'Legitimacy and Power in the Soviet Union Through Socialist Ritual'. *British Journal of Political Science* 14 (2): 207–17.

Lane, Ruth. 1992. 'Political Culture: Residual Category or General Theory?' *Comparative Political Studies* 25 (3): 362–87.

Lasswell, Harold D. 1936. *Politics: Who Gets What, When, How*. New York: McGraw-Hill.

Layne, Christopher. 1994. 'Kant or Cant: The Myth of the Democratic Peace'. *International Security* 19 (2): 5–49.

Lee, Kuan Yew. 1992. 'Speech by Mr Lee Kuan Yew, Senior Minister of Singapore, at the Create 21 Asahi Forum on 20 Nov 92, Tokyo'. National Archives of Singapore.

Leese, Daniel. 2007. 'The Mao Cult as Communicative Space'. *Totalitarian Movements and Political Religions* 8 (3–4): 623–39.

———. 2011. *Mao Cult: Rhetoric and Ritual in China's Cultural Revolution*. Cambridge: Cambridge University Press.

Lehoucq, Fabrice. 2016. 'Does Nonviolence Work?' *Comparative Politics* 48 (2): 269–87.

Lehoucq, Fabrice, and Aníbal Pérez-Liñán. 2014. 'Breaking Out of the Coup Trap: Political Competition and Military Coups in Latin America'. *Comparative Political Studies* 47 (8): 1105–29.

Lenin, Vladimir Illich. 1965 [1920]. 'A Contribution to the History of the Question of the Dictatorship: A Note'. In *Collected Works*, 4th English ed., 31:340–61. Moscow: Progress Publishers. https://www.marxists.org/archive/lenin/works/1920/oct/20.htm.

Leogrande, William M. 1980. 'The Communist Party of Cuba Since the First Congress'. *Journal of Latin American Studies* 12 (2): 397–419.

Levitsky, Steven, and Lucan Way. 2010. *Competitive Authoritarianism: Hybrid Regimes after the Cold War*. New York: Cambridge University Press.

———. 2012. 'Beyond Patronage: Violent Struggle, Ruling Party Cohesion, and Authoritarian Durability'. *Perspectives on Politics* 10 (4): 869–89.

Lichbach, Mark I. 1994a. 'Rethinking Rationality and Rebellion: Theories of Collective Action and Problems of Collective Dissent'. *Rationality and Society* 6 (1): 8–39.

———. 1994b. 'What Makes Rational Peasants Revolutionary? Dilemma, Paradox, and Irony in Peasant Collective Action'. *World Politics* 46 (3): 383–418.

Link, Perry, and Xiao Qiang. 2013. 'From 'Fart People' to Citizens'. *Journal of Democracy* 24 (1): 79–85.

Linz, Juan. 1976 [1964]. 'An Authoritarian Regime: Spain'. In *Politics and Society in Twentieth-Century Spain*, edited by Stanley Payne, 160–207. New York and London: Franklin Watts.

————. 1978. *The Breakdown of Democratic Regimes: Crisis, Breakdown, and Reequilibration*. Baltimore, MD: Johns Hopkins University Press.

————. 2000 [1975]. *Totalitarian and Authoritarian Regimes*. Boulder, CO: Lynne Rienner Publishers.

Lipset, Seymour Martin. 1959. 'Some Social Requisites of Democracy: Economic Development and Political Legitimacy'. *The American Political Science Review* 53 (1): 69–105.

Lipset, Symour Martin. 1960. *Political Man: The Social Bases of Politics*. New York: Anchor Books.

Lohmann, Susanne. 1994. 'The Dynamics of Informational Cascades: The Monday Demonstrations in Leipzig, East Germany, 1989–91'. *World Politics* 47 (1)· 42–101.

Londregan, John B., and Keith T. Poole. 1990. 'Poverty, the Coup Trap, and the Seizure of Executive Power'. *World Politics* 42 (2): 151–83.

Lucas, Russell E. 2004. 'Monarchical Authoritarianism: Survival and Political Liberalization in a Middle Eastern Regime Type'. *International Journal of Middle East Studies* 36 (1): 103–19.

Lukes, Steven. 1975. 'Political Ritual and Social Integration'. *Sociology* 9 (2): 289–308.

Luttwak, Edward. 1969. *Coup d'État: A Practical Handbook*. New York: Alfred A. Knopf.

Lynch, Marc. 2011. 'After Egypt: The Limits and Promise of Online Challenges to the Authoritarian Arab State'. *Perspectives on Politics* 9 (02): 301–10.

————. 2012. *The Arab Uprising: The Unfinished Revolutions of the New Middle East*. New York: PublicAffairs.

MacFarquhar, Neil. 2011. 'In Protests, Syrians Find the Spark of Creativity'. *New York Times*. http://www.nytimes.com/2011/12/20/world/middleeast/in-uprising-syrians-find-spark-of-creativity.html.

MacMillan, John. 2003. 'Beyond the Separate Democratic Peace'. *Journal of Peace Research* 40 (2): 233–43.

MacRory, Robbie. 2013. 'Dilemmas of Democratisation: Media Regulation and Reform in Argentina'. *Bulletin of Latin American Research* 32 (2): 178–93.

Magaloni, Beatriz. 2006. *Voting for Autocracy: Hegemonic Party Survival and its Demise in Mexico*. Cambridge: Cambridge University Press.

Magaloni, Beatriz, and Ruth Kricheli. 2010. 'Political Order and One-Party Rule'. *Annual Review of Political Science* 13 (1): 123–43.

Magaloni, Beatriz, Jonathan Chu, and Eric Min. 2013. 'Autocracies of the World, 1950–2012 (Version 1.0)'. Dataset.

Magee, Christopher S. P., and John A. Doces. 2015. 'Reconsidering Regime Type and Growth: Lies, Dictatorships, and Statistics'. *International Studies Quarterly* 59 (2): 223–37.

Mainwaring, Scott. 1995. 'Weak Parties, Feckless Democracy'. In *Building Democratic Institutions: Party Systems in Latin America*, edited by Scott Mainwaring and Timothy R. Scully, 354–98. Stanford: Stanford University Press.

Mann, Michael. 1984. 'The Autonomous Power of the State'. *Archives Europeénnes de Sociologie* 25 (2): 185–213.

Mansfield, Edward D., and Jack Snyder. 1995. 'Democratization and the Danger of War'. *International Security* 20 (1): 5–38.

Maoz, Zeev, and Bruce Russett. 1993. 'Normative and Structural Causes of Democratic Peace, 1946–1986'. *American Political Science Review* 87 (3): 624–38.

Marinov, Nikolay, and Hein Goemans. 2014. 'Coups and Democracy'. *British Journal of Political Science* 44 (4): 799–825.

Marshall, Monty G., Ted Robert Gurr, and Keith Jaggers. 2010. 'Polity IV Project: Political Regime Characteristics and Transitions, 1800–2009'. Online Database. Center for Systemic Peace. http://www.systemicpeace.org/inscrdata.html

Martel García, Fernando. 2014. 'Democracy Is Good for the Poor: A Procedural Replication of Ross (2006)'. *Research and Politics* 1 (3): 1–10.

Martin, John Levi. 2009. *Social Structures*. Princeton, NJ: Princeton University Press.

Mauzy, Diane K., and R. S. Milne. 2002. *Singapore Politics under the People's Action Party*. London: Routledge.

Márquez, Xavier. 2011a. 'Cicero and the Stability of States'. *History of Political Thought* 32 (3): 397–423.

———. 2011b. 'Spaces of Appearance and Spaces of Surveillance'. *Polity* 44 (1): 6–31.

———. 2013. 'A Model of Cults of Personality'. *APSA 2013 Annual Meeting Paper*. http://ssrn.com/abstract=2301392.

———. 2014. 'Authoritarianism'. In *The Encyclopedia of Political Thought*. John Wiley & Sons, Ltd.

———. 2016a. 'A Quick Method for Extending the Unified Democracy Scores'. *Available at SSRN 2753830*. doi:10.2139/ssrn.2753830.

———. 2016b. 'The Irrelevance of Legitimacy'. *Political Studies* 64 (1, suppl): 19–34.

Mbembe, Achille. 1992. 'Provisional Notes on the Postcolony'. *Africa: Journal of the International African Institute* 62 (1): 3–37.

McCargo, Duncan. 2005. 'Network Monarchy and Legitimacy Crises in Thailand'. *The Pacific Review* 18 (4): 499–519.

McGregor, Richard. 2010. *The Party: The Secret World of China's Communist Rulers*. London: Harper.

Mcmillan, John, and Pablo Zoido. 2004. 'How to Subvert Democracy: Montesinos in Peru'. *Journal of Economic Perspectives* 18 (4): 69–92.

McNulty, Mel. 1999. 'The Collapse of Zaïre: Implosion, Revolution or External Sabotage?' *The Journal of Modern African Studies* 37 (1).

Menaldo, Victor. 2012. 'The Middle East and North Africa's Resilient Monarchs'. *The Journal of Politics* 74 (3): 707–22.

Merolla, Jennifer, and Elizabeth Zechmeister. 2011. 'The Nature, Determinants, and Consequences of Chávez's Charisma: Evidence From a Study of Venezuelan Public Opinion'. *Comparative Political Studies* 44 (1): 28–54.

Mill, John Stuart. 1859. *Considerations on Representative Government*. Vol. XIX. The Collected Works of John Stuart Mill. Toronto: University of Toronto Press.

Mittler, Barbara. 2008. 'Popular Propaganda? Art and Culture in Revolutionary China'. *Proceedings of the American Philosophical Society* 152 (4): 466–89.

———. 2012. *A Continuous Revolution: Making Sense of Cultural Revolution Culture*. Cambridge, MA: Harvard University Asia Center.

Mobarak, Ahmed Mushfiq. 2005. 'Democracy, Volatility, and Economic Development'. *Review of Economics and Statistics* 87 (2): 348–61.

Mousseau, Michael. 2009. 'The Social Market Roots of Democratic Peace'. *International Security* 33 (4): 52–86.

Mouzykantskii, Ilya. 2011. 'In Belarus, Just Being Can Prompt an Arrest'. *New York Times*. http://www.nytimes.com/2011/07/30/world/europe/30belarus.html.

Mulligan, Casey, and Kevin Tsui. 2006. 'Political Competitiveness'. Working Paper 12653. National Bureau of Economic Research Working Paper Series.

Mulligan, Casey, Ricard Gil, and Xavier Sala-i-Martin. 2004. 'Do Democracies Have Different Public Policies than Nondemocracies?' *Journal of Economic Perspectives* 18 (1): 51–74.

Murtin, Fabrice, and Romain Wacziarg. 2014. 'The Democratic Transition'. *Journal of Economic Growth* 19 (2): 141–81.

Myers, B. R. 2010. *The Cleanest Race: How North Koreans See Themselves and Why It Matters*. New York: Melville House.

Møller, Jørgen, and Svend-Erik Skaaning. 2013. 'Autocracies, Democracies, and the Violation of Civil Liberties'. *Democratization* 20 (1): 82–106.

Narayan, Paresh Kumar, Seema Narayan, and Russell Smyth. 2011. 'Does Democracy Facilitate Economic Growth or Does Economic Growth Facilitate Democracy? An Empirical Study of Sub-Saharan Africa'. *Economic Modelling* 28 (3): 900–10.

New Focus International. 2014. 'Why does autocratic North Korea hold elections? It's not merely a political ruse'. http://newfocusintl.com/autocratic-north-korea-hold-elections-merely-political-ruse/

Nikolayenko, Olena. 2007. 'The Revolt of the Post-Soviet Generation: Youth Movements in Serbia, Georgia, and Ukraine'. *Comparative Politics* 39 (2): 169–88.

Norris, Pippa. 2011. *Democratic Deficit: Critical Citizens Revisited*. Cambridge: Cambridge University Press.

Norris, Pippa, and Ronald Inglehart. 2002. 'Islamic Culture and Democracy: Testing the 'Clash of Civilizations' Thesis'. *Comparative Sociology* 1 (3–4): 3–4.

Norton, Michael I., and Dan Ariely. 2011. 'Building a Better America—One Wealth Quintile at a Time'. *Perspectives on Psychological Science* 6 (1): 9–12.

Nur-tegin, Kanybek, and Hans J. Czap. 2012. 'Corruption: Democracy, Autocracy, and Political Stability'. *Economic Analysis and Policy* 42 (1): 51–66.

Ofer, Gur. 1987. 'Soviet Economic Growth: 1928–1985'. *Journal of Economic Literature* 25 (4): 1767–1833.

Oliver, Pamela, Gerald Marwell, and Ruy Texeira. 1985. 'A Theory of the Critical Mass. I. Interdependence, Group Heterogeneity, and the Production of Collective Action'. *American Journal of Sociology* 91 (3): 522–56.

Olson, Mancur. 1965. *The Logic of Collective Action: Public Goods and the Theory of Groups*. Cambridge, MA: Harvard University Press.

———. 1993. 'Dictatorship, Democracy, and Development'. *American Political Science Review* 87 (3): 567–76.

Overholt, William H. 1986. 'The Rise and Fall of Ferdinand Marcos'. *Asian Survey* 26 (11): 1137–63.

Overland, Jody, Kenneth Simons, and Michael Spagat. 2005. 'Political Instability and Growth in Dictatorships'. *Public Choice* 125 (3): 445–70.

O'Donnell, G. 1992. 'Delegative Democracy?' *Journal of Democracy* 5 (1): 55–69.

O'Donnell, Guillermo A. 1973. *Modernization and Bureaucratic-Authoritarianism.* Berkeley: Institute of International Studies, University of California Berkeley.

O'Donnell, Guillermo, and Philippe Schmitter. 1986. *Transitions from Authoritarian Rule: Tentative Conclusions About Uncertain Democracies.* Baltimore: The Johns Hopkins University Press.

O'Kane, Rosemary H. T. 1981. 'A Probabilistic Approach to the Causes of Coups d'Etat'. *British Journal of Political Science* 11 (3): 287–308.

Padgett, John F. and Christopher K. Ansell. 1993. 'Robust Action and the Rise of the Medici, 1400–1434'. *American Journal of Sociology* 98 (6): 1259–1319.

Page, Benjamin I., Larry M. Bartels, and Jason Seawright. 2013. 'Democracy and the Policy Preferences of Wealthy Americans'. *Perspectives on Politics* 11 (1): 51–73.

Papaioannou, Elias, and Gregorios Siourounis. 2008. 'Democratisation and Growth'. *The Economic Journal* 118 (532): 1520–51.

Pargeter, Alison. 2012. *Libya: The Rise and Fall of Qaddafi.* New Haven, CT: Yale University Press.

Paxton, Robert. 2006. *The Anatomy of Fascism.* London: Harper.

Payne, Stanley G. 1987. *The Franco Regime, 1936–1975.* Madison: University of Wisconsin Press.

Pearlman, Wendy. 2013. 'Emotions and the Microfoundations of the Arab Uprisings'. *Perspectives on Politics* 11 (2): 387–409.

Peceny, Mark, Caroline Beer, and Shannon Sanchez-Terry. 2002. 'Dictatorial Peace?' *American Political Science Review* 96 (01): 15–26.

Pemstein, Daniel, Stephen Meserve, and James Melton. 2010. 'Democratic Compromise: A Latent Variable Analysis of Ten Measures of Regime Type'. *Political Analysis* 18 (4): 426–49.

Perlmutter, Amos. 1981. *Modern Authoritarianism: A Comparative Institutional Analysis.* New Haven, CT: Yale University Press.

Perry, Elizabeth J. 1991. 'Intellectuals and Tiananmen: Historical Perspective on an Aborted Revolution'. In *The Crisis of Leninism and the Decline of the Left: The Revolutions of 1989*, edited by Daniel Chirot, 129–46. Seattle: University of Washington Press.

Pfaff, Steven. 2001. 'The Limits of Coercive Surveillance: Social and Penal Control in the German Democratic Republic'. *Punishment Society* 3 (3): 381–407.

Pinto, Pablo M., and Jeffrey F. Timmons. 2005. 'The Political Determinants of Economic Performance: Political Competition and the Sources of Growth'. *Comparative Political Studies* 38 (1): 26–50.

Plamper, Jan. 2012. *The Stalin Cult: a Study in the Alchemy of Power.* New Haven, CT: Yale University Press.

Policzer, Pablo. 2009. *The Rise and Fall of Repression in Chile.* Notre Dame: University of Notre Dame Press.

Pomerantsev, Peter. 2014. *Nothing Is True and Everything Is Possible: The Surreal Heart of the New Russia.* New York: PublicAffairs.

Popplewell, Richard. 1992. 'The Stasi and the East German Revolution of 1989'. *Contemporary European History* 1 (1): 37–63.

Powell, Jonathan M., and Clayton L. Thyne. 2011. 'Global Instances of Coups from 1950 to 2010: A New Dataset'. *Journal of Peace Research* 48 (2): 249–59.

Preston, Paul. 1995. *Franco: A Biography*. New York: Basic Books.

Pritchett, Lant, Michael Woolcock, and Matt Andrews. 2012. 'Looking Like a State: Techniques of Persistent Failure in State Capability for Implementation'. *The Journal of Development Studies* 49 (1): 1–18.

Przeworski, Adam. 1991. *Democracy and the Market: Political and Economic Reforms in Eastern Europe and Latin America*. Cambridge University Press.

———. 1998. 'Culture and Democracy'. In *World Culture Report: Culture, Creativity, and Markets*, 125–46. UNESCO.

———. 2009. 'Conquered or Granted? A History of Suffrage Extensions'. *British Journal of Political Science* 39 (2): 291–321.

———. 2010. *Democracy and the Limits of Self-Government*. New York: Cambridge University Press.

———. 2013. 'Political Institutions and Plitical Events (PIPE) Data Set'. Dataset. Department of Politics, New York University.

Przeworski, Adam, Michael Alvarez, Jose Cheibub, and Fernando Limongi. 2000. *Democracy and Development: Political Institutions and Well-Being in the World, 1950–1990*. Cambridge: Cambridge University Press.

Przeworski, Adam, and Fernando Limongi. 1993. 'Political Regimes and Economic Growth'. *The Journal of Economic Perspectives* 7 (3): 51–69.

———. 1997. 'Modernization: Theories and Facts'. *World Politics* 49 (2): 155–83.

Puddington, Arch, and Tyler Roylance. 2016. 'Anxious Dictators, Wavering Democrats'. *Journal of Democracy* 27 (2): 86–100.

Purcell, Susan Kaufman. 1975. *The Mexican Profit-Sharing Decision : Politics in an Authoritarian Regime*. Berkeley: University of California Press.

Putnam, Robert D., Robert Leonardi, and Raffaella Nanetti. 1993. *Making Democracy Work : Civic Traditions in Modern Italy*. Princeton, NJ: Princeton University Press.

Quackenbush, Stephen L., and Michael Rudy. 2009. 'Evaluating the Monadic Democratic Peace'. *Conflict Management and Peace Science* 26 (3): 268–85.

Quinlivan, James T. 1999. 'Coup-Proofing: Its Practice and Consequences in the Middle East'. *International Security* 24 (2): 131–65.

Regan, Patrick M., and Errol A. Henderson. 2002. 'Democracy, Threats and Political Repression in Developing Countries: Are Democracies Internally Less Violent?' *Third World Quarterly* 23 (1): 119–36.

Rigby, T. H. 1988. 'Staffing USSR Incorporated: The Origins of the Nomenklatura System'. *Soviet Studies* 40 (4): 523–37.

Robbins, Michael. 2015. 'People Still Want Democracy'. *Journal of Democracy* 26 (4): 80–89.

Rock, David. 1985. *Argentina, 1516-1982: From Spanish Colonization to the Falklands War*. Berkeley: University of California Press.

Rock, Michael T. 2008. 'Corruption and Democracy'. *The Journal of Development Studies* 45 (1): 55–75.

———. 2009. 'Has Democracy Slowed Growth in Asia?' *World Development* 37 (5): 941–52.

Rodrik, Dani. 1999. 'Democracies Pay Higher Wages'. *The Quarterly Journal of Economics* 114 (3): 707–38.

———. 2000. 'Institutions for High-Quality Growth: What They Are and How to Acquire Them'. *Studies in Comparative International Development* 35 (3): 3–31.

Romer, Paul M. 1990. 'Endogenous Technological Change'. *Journal of Political Economy* 98 (5): S71–S102.

Rosato, Sebastian. 2003. 'The Flawed Logic of Democratic Peace Theory'. *American Political Science Review* 97 (4): 585–602.

Rosenberg, Tina. 2011. 'Revolution U'. *Foreign Policy*, 16 February 2011.

Ross, Michael. 2006. 'Is Democracy Good for the Poor?' *American Journal of Political Science* 50 (4): 860–74.

———. 2012. *The Oil Curse: How Petroleum Wealth Shapes the Development of Nations*. Princeton, NJ: Princeton University Press.

Rothstein, Bo. 2015. 'The Chinese Paradox of High Growth and Low Quality of Government: The Cadre Organization Meets Max Weber'. *Governance* 28 (4): 533–48.

Rummel, Rudolph J. 1994. 'Power, Genocide and Mass Murder'. *Journal of Peace Research* 31 (1): 1–10.

———. 1995a. 'Democracies Are Less Warlike Than Other Regimes'. *European Journal of International Relations* 1 (4): 457–79.

———. 1995b. 'Democracy, Power, Genocide, and Mass Murder'. *The Journal of Conflict Resolution* 39 (1): 3–26.

Rød, Espen Geelmuyden, and Nils B. Weidmann. 2015. 'Empowering Activists or Autocrats? The Internet in Authoritarian Regimes'. *Journal of Peace Research* 52 (3): 338–51.

Sahliyeh, Emile. 2010. 'The Presidential Election in Iran, June 2009'. *Electoral Studies* 29 (1): 182–5.

Salah, Ahmed, and Alex Mayyasi. 2013. 'The Spark: Starting the Revolution'. Web Page. http://brooklynquarterly.org/the-spark-starting-the-revolution/.

Sartori, Giovanni. 1987. *The Theory of Democracy Revisited*. Chatham: Chatham House.

Schedler, Andreas, and Bert Hoffmann. 2016. 'Communicating Authoritarian Elite Cohesion'. *Democratization* 23 (1): 93–117.

Schelling, Thomas C. 1960. *The Strategy of Conflict*. Cambridge, MA: Harvard University Press.

Schmitt, Carl. 2014 [1921]. *Dictatorship: From the Origin of the Modern Concept of Sovereignty to Proletarian Class Struggle*. Oxford: Wiley.

Schmitter, Philippe C., and Terry Lynn Karl. 1991. 'What Democracy Is … and Is Not'. *Journal of Democracy* 2 (3): 75–88.

Schock, Kurt. 2004. *Unarmed Insurrections: People Power Movements in Non-democracies*. Minneapolis: University of Minnesota Press.

———. 2013. 'The Practice and Study of Civil Resistance'. *Journal of Peace Research* 50 (3): 277–90.

Schumpeter, Joseph A. 1950. *Capitalism, Socialism, and Democracy*. 3rd edn. New York: Harper.

Scott, James C. 1985. 'Weapons of the Weak: Everyday Forms of Peasant Resistance'. Yale University Press.

———. 1998. *Seeing Like a State: How Certain Schemes to Improve the Human Condition Have Failed*. New Haven, CT: Yale University Press.

————. 2009. *The Art of Not Being Governed: An Anarchist History of Upland Southeast Asia*. New Haven, CT: Yale University Press.

Sebestyen, Victor. 2010. *Revolution 1989: The Fall of the Soviet Empire*. New York: Knopf Doubleday.

Sen, Amartya. 1983. *Poverty and Famines: An Essay on Entitlement and Deprivation*. Oxford: Oxford University Press.

————. 1999a. 'Democracy as a Universal Value'. *Journal of Democracy* 10 (3): 3–17.

————. 1999b. *Development as Freedom*. New York: Anchor Books.

Sevillano Calero, F. 2000. *Ecos de Papel: La Opinión de Los Españoles en la época de Franco*. Madrid: Biblioteca Nueva.

Sharp, Gene. 2012. *From Dictatorship to Democracy: A Conceptual Framework for Liberation*. New York: New Press.

Shih, Victor, Christopher Adolph, and Mingxing Liu. 2012. 'Getting Ahead in the Communist Party: Explaining the Advancement of Central Committee Members in China'. *American Political Science Review* 106 (1): 166–87.

Shin, Doh Chull, and Youngho Cho. 2010. 'How East Asians Understand Democracy: From a Comparative Perspective'. *Asien* 116: 21–40.

Singh, Naunihal. 2014. *Seizing Power: The Strategic Logic of Military Coups*. Baltimore: John Hopkins University Press.

Skaaning, Svend-Erik, John Gerring, and Henrikas Bartusevičius. 2015. 'A Lexical Index of Electoral Democracy'. *Comparative Political Studies* 48 (12): 1491–1525.

Skidmore, T. E. 1988. *The Politics of Military Rule in Brazil, 1964–85*. Oxford: Oxford University Press.

Skrede Gleditsch, Kristian, and Andrea Ruggeri. 2010. 'Political Opportunity Structures, Democracy, and Civil War'. *Journal of Peace Research* 47 (3): 299–310.

Slater, Dan. 2009. 'Revolutions, Crackdowns, and Quiescence: Communal Elites and Democratic Mobilization in Southeast Asia'. *American Journal of Sociology* 115 (1): 203–54.

Slee, Tom. 2012. 'Identity, Institutions, and Uprisings'. *Social Science Research Network Working Paper Series*. http://ssrn.com/abstract=2116471.

Snyder, Richard. 1992. 'Explaining Transitions from Neopatrimonial Dictatorships'. *Comparative Politics* 24 (4): 379–99.

Solt, Frederick. 2009. 'Standardizing the World Income Inequality Database'. *Social Science Quarterly* 90 (2): 231–42.

————. 2011. 'The Social Origins of Authoritarianism'. *Political Research Quarterly* 65 (4): 703–13.

————. 2015. 'Economic Inequality and Nonviolent Protest'. *Social Science Quarterly* 96 (5): 1314–27.

Sondrol, Paul C. 1991. 'Totalitarian and Authoritarian Dictators: A Comparison of Fidel Castro and Alfredo Stroessner'. *Journal of Latin American Studies* 23 (3): 599–620.

Steinmüller, Hans. 2010. 'How Popular Confucianism became Embarrassing: On the Spatial and Moral Center of the House in Rural China'. *Focaal* 2010 (58): 81–96.

Stekelenburg, Jacquelien van, and Bert Klandermans. 2013. 'The Social Psychology of Protest'. *Current Sociology* 61 (5–6): 886–905.

Stephan, Maria, and Erica Chenoweth. 2008. 'Why Civil Resistance Works: The Strategic Logic of Nonviolent Conflict'. *International Security* 33 (1): 7–44.

Sung, H. E. 2004. 'Democracy and Political Corruption: A Cross-National Comparison'. *Crime, Law and Social Change* 41 (2): 179–93.

Svolik, Milan. 2012. *The Politics of Authoritarian Rule.* Cambridge and New York: Cambridge University Press.

Talmadge, Eric. 2014. 'Inside North Korea's elections, where the winner is already decided and loyalty is monitored at every turn'. Web Page. The Associated Press. http://news.nationalpost.com/2014/03/07/inside-north-koreas-elections-where-the-winner-is-already-decided-and-loyalty-is-monitored-at-every-turn/.

Tavares, José, and Romain Wacziarg. 2001. 'How Democracy Affects Growth'. *European Economic Review* 45 (8): 1341–78.

Teiwes, Frederick C. 2001. 'Normal Politics with Chinese Characteristics'. *The China Journal*, no. 45: 69–82.

Teiwes, Frederick C., and Warren Sun. 1999. *China's Road to Disaster : Mao, Central Politicians, and Provincial Leaders in the Unfolding of the Great Leap Forward, 1955–1959.* Contemporary China Papers. Armonk, NY: M.E. Sharpe.

Tessler, M., A. Jamal, and M. Robbins. 2012. 'New Findings on Arabs and Democracy'. *Journal of Democracy* 23 (4): 89–103.

The Maddison Project. 2013. 'The Maddison Project'. http://www.ggdc.net/maddison/maddison-project/home.htm.

Thompson, Mark. 2001. 'Whatever Happened to 'Asian Values'?' *Journal of Democracy* 12 (4): 154–65.

Tikhomirov, Alexey. 2012. 'Symbols of Power in Rituals of Violence: The Personality Cult and Iconoclasm on the Soviet Empire's Periphery (East Germany, 1945–61)'. *Kritika* 13 (1): 47–88.

Tilly, Charles. 2006. *Regimes and Repertoires.* Chicago: University of Chicago Press.

———. 2007. *Democracy.* Cambridge: Cambridge University Press.

Tilly, Charles, and Sidney Tarrow. 2006. *Contentious Politics.* London: Paradigm Publishers.

Timmons, Jeffrey. 2010. 'Does Democracy Reduce Economic Inequality?' *British Journal of Political Science* 40 (4): 741–57.

Tismaneanu, Vladimir. 1989. 'The Tragicomedy of Romanian Communism'. *East European Politics & Societies* 3 (2): 329–76.

———. 1993. 'The Quasi-revolution and its Discontents: Emerging Political Pluralism in Post-Ceauçescu Romania'. *East European Politics & Societies* 7 (2): 309–48.

Tocqueville, Alexis. 2000 [1835]. Democracy in America. Translated, edited, and with an introduction by Harvey C. Mansfield and Delba Winthrop. Chicago: University of Chicago Press.

Tucker, Joshua. 2007. 'Enough! Electoral Fraud, Collective Action Problems, and Post-Communist Colored Revolutions'. *Perspectives on Politics* 5 (3): 535–51.

Tufekci, Zeynep. 2014. 'Social Movements and Governments in the Digital Age: Evaluating a Complex Landscape'. *Journal of International Affairs* 68 (1). http://jia.sipa.columbia.edu/social-movements-governments-digital-age-evaluating-complex-landscape/.

Tumarkin, Nina. 1983. *Lenin Lives! The Lenin Cult in Soviet Russia*. Cambridge, MA: Harvard University Press.

Turner, Thomas. 1988. 'Decline or Recovery in Zaire?' *Current History* 87 (529): 213.

Ulfelder, Jay. 2010. *Dilemmas of Democratic Consolidation: A Game-Theory Approach*. Boulder, CO: FirstForum Press.

Verme, Paolo, Branko Milanovic, Sherine Al-Shawarby, Sahar El Tawila, May Gadallah, and Enas Ali A. El-Majeed. 2014. 'Inside Inequality in the Arab Republic of Egypt: Facts and Perceptions Across People, Time, and Space'. The World Bank.

Verweij, Marco, and Riccardo Pelizzo. 2009. 'Singapore: Does Authoritarianism Pay?' *Journal of Democracy* 20 (2): 18–32.

Veyne, Paul. 1988. 'Conduct Without Belief and Works of Art Without Viewers'. *Diogenes* 36 (143): 1–22.

Vreeland, James Raymond. 2008. 'The Effect of Political Regime on Civil War: Unpacking Anocracy'. *Journal of Conflict Resolution* 52 (3): 401–25.

Wahman, Michael, Jan Teorell, and Axel Hadenius. 2013. 'Authoritarian Regime Types Revisited: Updated Data in Comparative Perspective'. *Contemporary Politics* 19 (1): 19–34.

Walder, Andrew G.. 1995. 'Career Mobility and the Communist Political Order'. *American Sociological Review* 60 (3): 309–28.

———. 2015. *China Under Mao: A Revolution Derailed*. Cambridge, MA: Harvard University Press.

Wallace, Jeremy L.. 2016. 'Juking the Stats? Authoritarian Information Problems in China'. *British Journal of Political Science* 46 (1): 11–29.

Wang, Zhengxu. 2007. 'Public Support for Democracy in China'. *Journal of Contemporary China* 16 (53): 561–79.

Way, Lucan. 2008. 'The Real Causes of the Color Revolutions'. *Journal of Democracy* 19 (3): 55–69.

Weber, Max. 1978. *Economy and Society*. Berkeley: University of California Press.

———.1994 [1919]. 'The Profession and Vocation of Politics'. In *Political Writings*, 309–69. Cambridge: Cambridge University Press.

Wedeen, Lisa. 1998. 'Acting 'as if': Symbolic Politics and Social Control in Syria'. *Comparative Studies in Society and History* 40 (3): 503–23.

———. 1999. *Ambiguities of Domination: Politics, Rhetoric, and Symbols in Contemporary Syria*. Chicago: University Of Chicago Press.

Weeks, Jessica. 2012. 'Strongmen and Straw Men: Authoritarian Regimes and the Initiation of International Conflict'. *American Political Science Review* 106 (2): 326–47.

Welzel, Christian. 2013. *Freedom Rising: Human Empowerment and the Quest for Emancipation*. Cambridge: Cambridge University Press.

Welzel, Christian, and Ronald Inglehart. 2008. 'The Role of Ordinary People in Democratization'. *Journal of Democracy* 19 (1): 126–40.

Weyland, Kurt. 2008. 'Toward a New Theory of Institutional Change'. *World Politics* 60 (2): 281–314.

———. 2010. 'The Diffusion of Regime Contention in European Democratization, 1830-1940'. *Comparative Political Studies* 43 (8–9): 1148–76.

————. 2012. 'The Arab Spring: Why the Surprising Similarities with the Revolutionary Wave of 1848?' *Perspectives on Politics* 10: 917–34.

Wiarda, Howard J.. 1968. *Dictatorship and Development: The Methods of Control in Trujillo's Dominican Republic*. Gainesville: University of Florida Press.

Wilson, Matthew C. 2014. 'A Discreet Critique of Discrete Regime Type Data'. *Comparative Political Studies* 47 (5): 689–714.

Winterling, Aloys. 2011. *Caligula: a Biography*. Berkeley: University of California Press.

Wintrobe, Ronald. 1990. 'The Tinpot and the Totalitarian: An Economic Theory of Dictatorship'. *The American Political Science Review* 84 (3).

————. 2000. *The Political Economy of Dictatorship*. Cambridge: Cambridge University Press.

————. 2008. 'Dictatorship'. In *Readings in Public Choice and Constitutional Political Economy*, edited by Charles Rowley and Friedrich Schneider, 345–67. Springer US.

Wood, Geoffrey. 2004. 'Business and Politics in a Criminal State: The Case of Equatorial Guinea'. *African Affairs* 103 (413): 547–67.

Woodberry, Robert. 2012. 'The Missionary Roots of Liberal Democracy'. *American Political Science Review* 106 (2): 244–74.

Woodward, Peter. 1992. *Nasser*. London: Longman.

World Values Survey Association. 2015. 'World Values Survey Wave 6 2010–2014 Official Aggregate'. Spain. www.worldvaluessurvey.org.

Wright, Joseph. 2008. 'To Invest or Insure?: How Authoritarian Time Horizons Impact Foreign Aid Effectiveness'. *Comparative Political Studies* 41 (7): 971–1000.

Wrong, Michela. 2000. 'The Emperor Mobutu'. *Transition* 9 (1): 92–112.

Yamani, May. 2009. 'From Fragility to Stability: A Survival Strategy for the Saudi Monarchy'. *Contemporary Arab Affairs* 2 (1): 90–105.

Yom, Sean, and Gregory Gause. 2012. 'Resilient Royals: How Arab Monarchies Hang on'. *Journal of Democracy* 23 (4): 74–88.

Young, Crawford. 1994. 'Zaïre: The Shattered Illusion of the Integral State'. *The Journal of Modern African Studies* 32 (2): 247–63.

Youngs, Richard. 2015. 'Exploring "Non-Western Democracy"'. *Journal of Democracy* 26 (4): 140–54.

Yun-han, Chu, and Huang Min-hua. 2010. 'Solving an Asian Puzzle'. *Journal of Democracy* 21 (4): 114–22.

Zakaria, Fareed, and Kuan Yew Lee. 1994. 'Culture Is Destiny: A Conversation with Lee Kuan Yew'. *Foreign Affairs* 73 (2): 109–26.

Zuckerman, Ethan. 2015. 'Cute Cats to the Rescue? Participatory Media and Political Expression'. In *Youth, New Media, and Political Participation*, edited by D. Allen and J. Light, 131–154. Cambridge: MIT Press.

Zuern, Elke. 2009. 'Democratization as Liberation: Competing African Perspectives on Democracy'. *Democratization* 16 (3): 585–603.

Index

267

41683523R00163

Printed in Poland
by Amazon Fulfillment
Poland Sp. z o.o., Wrocław